Unequal Justice

Blacks in the Diaspora
Darlene Clark Hine, John McCluskey, Jr., and David Barry Gaspar
General Editors

Unequal Justice

A QUESTION OF COLOR

Coramae Richey Mann

Indiana University Press

BLOOMINGTON AND INDIANAPOLIS

Quotations from the following works are reprinted here by permission
of the publishers:
Langston Hughes, *Black Misery* (New York: Paul S. Eriksson, Inc., 1969).
ricardo sánchez, *Milhaus Blues and Gritos Norteños* (Milwaukee: University of
Wisconsin College of Letters and Science, 1978).

The paper used in this publication meets the minimum requirements of American
National Standard for Information Sciences—Permanence of Paper for Printed
Library Materials, ANSI Z39.48-1984.

Manufactured in the United States of America

Library of Congress Cataloging-in-Publication Data

Mann, Coramae Richey, date.
   Unequal justice : a question of color / Coramae Richey Mann.
     p.   cm. — (Blacks in the diaspora)
   Includes bibliographical references and index.
   ISBN 0-253-33676-7 (alk. paper). — ISBN 0-253-20783-5 (pbk.)
   1. Discrimination in criminal justice administration—United
States. 2. United States—Race relations. 3. Minorities—United
States. I. Title. II. Series.
HV9950.M26 1993
364'.089'96073—dc20   92-25110

2   3   4   5   97 96 95 94

Contents

Preface

An abundance of studies have been undertaken and numerous books, chapters, and articles have been written about African Americans and crime, but the nexus between African Americans and other racial minorities in the United States criminal justice system has been consistently overlooked. As a woman of color, I have always been cognizant of a correlation between the condition of women and the condition of racial minorities in this nation, but I had somewhat simplistically attributed the subordinate statuses of these groups to their historically oppressed economic situation. It seemed clear that economics was the underlying element in both gender and racial subjugation in the United States. Under that premise I began the original manuscript for this book. Over the next few years of research and writing, I gradually came to believe that although the economic factor was certainly a valid theoretical basis for the white male dominance of women and peoples of color in the context of the larger society, the circumscribed world of the criminal justice system reflects disparate treatment of racial minorities that is not experienced by women.[1] While not rejecting the economic aspect, since it is inescapably threaded throughout the fabric of the American racial minority experience,[2] I came to what will undoubtedly be considered a controversial deduction, because it is based on a taboo topic: racial injustice has its origins in color.

In private social circles as well as on street corners, whenever violent crime is discussed or when a serious crime of a violent nature—for example, a mugging, an assault, or a rape—is the subject of the nightly television news or captures the local newspaper headline, the perpetrator who comes immediately to the public mind is a person of color. The race/ethnicity of the stereotyped offender usually varies depending upon the specific concentration of African Americans, Asian Americans, Hispanic Americans, or Native Americans in an area, but the notion persists that members of these American subpopulations are more criminal or dangerous than the Euro-American[3] majority group. White Americans typically stereotype (and often caricature) other Americans who happen to be of a different skin color by, for example, viewing the classic rapist as a "black man," the representative opium user as a "yellow man," the archetypal knife wielder as a "brown man," the "red man" as a drunken Indian, and each of these peoples of color, individually and collectively, as constituting the "crime problem."

Criminologists and other social scientists, law enforcement agencies, and criminal justice policy makers appear to agree that racial minority groups in the United States are disproportionately involved in crime. For example, the 1990 United States Census is expected to estimate that African Americans constitute 12.4 percent of the population ("1990 Census," 1990: 229), yet according to the latest available official crime statistics, in 1988 this group accounted for 35.7

percent of persons arrested for Index, or serious, crimes. Included in this figure are arrests of African Americans for 46.8 percent of the violent crimes and 32.6 percent of the property crimes (FBI, 1989: 186). Further, African Americans were arrested for 53.5 percent of all murders and nonnegligent manslaughters in 1988 (ibid.). Although the proportions are not as dramatic, similar disproportionate arrest statistics are reported for Hispanic Americans, Native Americans, and, to a lesser extent, Asian Americans relative to their distributions in the population.

Statistics such as these can be analyzed from more than one perspective and accordingly provide a different picture of the alleged "minority crime problem."[4] Nonetheless, these "facts" are typically explained by varying claims that (1) there is a high prevalence and intensity of various criminogenic factors within minority group cultures (e.g., high unemployment, criminal subculture, relative deprivation); (2) crime is a reaction to the frustration of such groups; (3) typical behaviors of minorities are criminalized; or (4) there is inherent structural bias in the criminal justice system which leads to the overrepresentation of peoples of color in arrest and prison statistics.

In sum, it is generally assumed that race plays a role in the determination of criminality, but extant research on this topic has not clearly demonstrated how or why this happens. The available studies focus primarily on African Americans and neglect other racial minorities who historically have had similar life experiences in the United States. According to the National Minority Advisory Council on Criminal Justice (NMAC) (1980: 7), one reason that traditional research approaches have failed to produce adequate theories on race and crime is that nonminority social scientists "have carefully avoided genuinely challenging new intellectual thrusts from minority scholars which would force them into a real confrontation with their own contradictions and myopia." It is hoped that *Unequal Justice: A Question of Color* will stimulate other scholars to meet the challenge presented by the National Minority Advisory Council on Criminal Justice.

Although it is impossible to comprehensively address each of the subject minority groups in a single volume (e.g., the anthology of the African American experience alone includes over 700 references), this book nonetheless provides a brief overview of the historical and social contexts of each of the racial minorities, the similar results of their collective life experiences, and the possible influence of their unequal positions in American society on their recorded criminal activity.

Another major objective of the book is to investigate the experiences shared by historically disadvantaged racial minorities—African Americans, Asian Americans, Hispanic Americans, and Native Americans—at each level of the criminal justice system. Greater attention is necessarily devoted to African Americans, since this subgroup has been the subject of more extensive research in the criminology/criminal justice discipline and other social sciences. As previously noted, the primary focus of the book is the adult male racial minority offender, but where feasible, research and data on minority female offenders and juveniles are introduced.

A Minority View

Woven throughout the description of the history, lives, and criminal justice experiences of the four primary American racial minorities is the belief that since racial discrimination is endemic to the United States, it permeates the criminal justice system—as well as every other American institution—and results in the unjust treatment of these minorities. Evidence is also presented which suggests that economic motives underlie this oppression and maltreatment. The exploitation of African Americans, Asian Americans, and Hispanic Americans as sources of slave or cheap labor in the history and ongoing development of this country and the original seizure of the country from the indigenous Native Americans clearly indicate the manifest politico-economic underpinnings of a once patent, but now more subtle pattern of racial discrimination. In order to maintain their hegemony, Euro-Americans, who at first simply enslaved, misemployed, or through cunning and duplicity seized the property of these racial groups, later turned to more meticulous manipulations of the law itself to accomplish the original plan. Such maneuvers are not unusual in the world scheme; one can readily point to appropriate exemplars of economic exploitation and differential treatment because of skin color in, for example, Australia, China, India, Africa, or, closer to our own shores, Central America and the Caribbean. However, there are two unique features of this scenario taking place in the United States today: first, racial minorities are still predominantly unequal in this country, and second, the legal structure, primarily the criminal law, by design and implementation is maintained to keep them in that status.[5]

Over the years it became increasingly obvious that university students, both minority and, especially, nonminority, knew little about the history, current status, or criminal justice experiences of African Americans, Asian Americans, Hispanic Americans, or Native Americans in this country. Even more shocking was the observation that the majority of these students were more knowledgeable about stereotypes and innuendos concerning these racial subgroups. To them, the myths were realities.

Many courses in criminology, criminal justice, law, sociology, social work, political science, history, psychology, and minority studies include discussion of the "race problem" or the "race-crime problem," but no single book has heretofore encompassed all of the major racial minorities (and some of their subgroups, e.g., Vietnamese, Puerto Ricans, West Indians) in a comparative treatment of their historic and current life experiences and the relationship between these experiences and their disproportionate and unequal criminal justice processing. As a result of this informational famine, scholars and teachers were forced to piece together material from an ever-growing number of studies, articles, and books that individually address the topic of racial minorities and crime on compartmentalized, uncomprehensive levels.

There can never be a solution to the problem of minority crime in the United States, or a reduction in such crime, until we recognize the flaws in previous crime-control models as applied to these subgroups, acknowledge the misfeasance of American law, and take a long, intense look at the basic structure of our nation. With a deeper understanding of the fundamental institutions, particularly a criminal justice system that perpetuates the criminalization process, there is hope that specific public policies may be planned, recommended, and implemented to result in equality and justice under the law.

Organization of the Book

The three chapters contained in Part One, "Minorities and Crime," address the questions raised earlier of how and why unequal justice is applied to peoples of color in the United States. Chapter 1, "Defining Race through the Minority Experience," begins with a discussion of definitions and the meaning and significance of race in the United States by briefly examining the relevant nomenclature which is frequently, and often inappropriately, used in the research and literature on minorities and crime. For example, terms such as "minority," "race," and "ethnic" are differentiated when the definitional perspectives followed throughout the book are established. The life experiences of African Americans, Native Americans, Asian Americans, and Hispanic Americans are traced through their early interactions with the majority group (Euro-American), and the results of those encounters are described in terms of past and current effects on the minority subpopulations. The chapter concludes with a contemporary picture of U.S. racial minorities conveyed through demographic information and employment and economic status data. This background material places the racial minority condition in perspective and is requisite to understanding the thrust of the remaining chapters.

Chapter 2, "The Minority 'Crime Problem,'" cites official statistics on race and crime and describes the problems associated with such statistics, particularly as they concern racial minorities. One of the first questions broached is whether crime is actually more prevalent among peoples of color in the United States, as is popularly believed, or whether the official accounting of minority crime is a reflection of racial bias in the country generally, and in the criminal justice system specifically. The unreliability of "official" statistics and other crime data-collection methods is outlined, with particular attention devoted to the special problems associated with official statistics and unofficial data which purportedly describe the incidence of crime among racial minorities. A major task of Chapter 2 is the analysis of crime statistics for each of the subject groups to identify those specific crimes for which each group is predominantly arrested and thereby provide a measurement of minority involvement in crime. For clarity, the crimes are categorized as personal (violent), property, and public-order (vice) offenses.

A significant work by John Helmer, *Drugs and Minority Oppression* (1975), is detailed in Chapter 2 because it clearly demonstrates how public policy (and opinion) toward drugs has been systematically linked to minorities in the United States—i.e., the Chinese with opium, African Americans with cocaine and heroin, and Mexican Americans with marijuana. These linkages have led to national campaigns and legislation that negatively affected the specific groups toward which such laws were directed. It appears that each time a minority group posed an economic threat to the majority (white) group, it was labeled by association with a drug, narcotic laws were then passed, and the minority members were removed from society through deportation or incarceration.

Theoretical and conceptual perspectives of race and violent crime are the substantive foci of Chapter 3, "Explanations of Minority Crime." Of vital concern to the criminal justice system and to the population at large is the occurrence of violent personal crimes, since these are the offenses that arouse fear within the populace. Despite the fact that such crimes are less than one-fourth as frequent as property and other nonviolent crimes—for example, in 1988 there were 16,090 arrests for murder and nonnegligent manslaughter in the United States, yet there were 1,279,121 arrests for driving under the influence, situations in which each driver was a potential killer (Flanagan and Maguire, 1990: 430)—it is violent personal crimes such as rape and murder that instill anxiety into the public psyche. Racial minority members are believed to be dangerous and violent and thus are those most feared. Chapter 3 explores theories of violent crime in relation to racial minorities and includes a more detailed history of American violence than that introduced previously in Chapter 1: the frontier tradition, with its emphasis on gun ownership and machismo; blood feuds; organized crime; the local, state, and federal governments' use of deadly force; and labor violence. An integral component of the minority experience in America is racism based on color and the associated violence directed toward those who are different. The exposure of each minority group to such violence is explored, and the effects of these early events on subsequent minority behavior and life conditions are suggested (e.g., the colonial model). Special attention is devoted to how this ingrained violent way of life has been directed toward racial minorities in the form of lynchings, racial conflicts, and genocide. The long-range effects on minorities of such a violent history are hypothesized.

Several traditional sociological theories of deviant behavior have been applied to individual minority subgroups. The *subculture of violence* and contraculture theories, for example, have frequently been associated with African Americans, and more recently with Hispanic Americans. Recent counter responses to such perspectives developed by minority researchers offer such models as Staples's (1975) "colonial" theory, the psychological conception of Fanon (1967), and Darnell Hawkins's (1983) emphasis on historical-structural, situational, and economic factors which contribute to the devaluation of African American life. The *control theory* position on bonding and family strength has been applied to

Asian Americans to explain their low official criminality,[6] while the crime and delinquency of Native and Hispanic Americans have been attributed by some theorists to problems with acculturation, social organization, and social disorganization.[7] All four racial minorities are viewed by some as simply "criminal groups," and these subgroups share the problems of racial prejudice and over-surveillance in their communities, factors that often result in arrests.

Part Two, "The Response to Minority Crime," addresses the legal reactions of society to its perception of racial minority crime, the subsequent responses of the criminal justice system, and the repercussions experienced by peoples of color on their arduous journeys through the system.

The first chapter in this section, Chapter 4, "Law and Its Enforcement against Minorities," demonstrates the parallels and connections between racial minorities, public policies, laws, and oppression that have historically been an integral part of the American social and legal fabric, particularly with respect to criminal laws. An important focus of Chapter 4 is how the laws of the United States have been tailored to oppress peoples of color, beginning in colonial times and continuing throughout our nation's history to the omnibus, net-widening criminal laws of today. There are substantial differences among the states in their laws and sentencing practices, with more recent tendencies toward legislation enabling mandatory sentencing.

Enforcement of the law is almost exclusively under the purview of police agencies where racial minorities are concerned,[8] particularly urban-based police officers. In discussing the application of the law to racial minorities by law enforcement agencies and their members, Chapter 4 includes an overview of police personnel and practices by introducing the reader to police recruitment and socialization, the police personality, discretion, and racial prejudice. Also emphasized is a perspective of how these customs and subsequent behaviors ultimately affect the minority population caught in the criminal justice web. The interaction between the four racial minority groups under examination and law enforcement personnel, particularly in minority communities, is continued, with more detailed attention devoted to police brutality and deadly use of force against minority populations. The chapter also includes a description of the racial prejudice and mistreatment accorded minority officers by their Euro-American peers and the implications of such divisiveness for effective law enforcement.

The substantive issues of Chapter 5, "Unequal Justice: A Question of Color," are those events taking place after an arrest and through sentencing that intimately affect minorities in their trek through the criminal justice system. The chapter begins with the assignment of bail and preventive detention, which demonstrate that either minorities are denied the opportunity to make bond and thereby secure release from jail, or bond is frequently set at such an exorbitant level that the minority defendant is unable to make bond. In either event the accused is stigmatized, deprived of his/her freedom, and denied the right to assist in the adequate preparation of the case.

One of the most fundamental due process rights guaranteed to an individual in a court proceeding is the right to counsel. The major Supreme Court cases and their provisions, the types of indigent defense systems, and the quality of attorneys available to minority defendants in criminal cases (the private counsel versus public defender controversy) are described. An added perspective—minority defendants' opinions of defense attorneys—is included. Poor and minority defendants are more likely to waive their constitutional right to a trial and thus tend to plea bargain in hopes of obtaining a reduced number of charges or more lenient sentences. The ramifications of this process for minorities are elaborated.

The exclusion of peoples of color from grand juries and trial juries has been, and continues to be, a central problem in the administration of justice. In an examination of juries, jury selection, and jury composition, types of juries are defined, and methods of selection of their members are described; recent scholarly debate on this issue and the latest Supreme Court ruling on the topic are also themes of Chapter 5. Other significant members of the court workgroup—prosecutors, judges, and probation officers—who have immense discretion in determining the fate of accused persons play significant roles in the processing of minority defendants and are therefore carefully scrutinized in terms of their backgrounds, beliefs, motives, and actions as they impact sentencing.

The implications of the various sentencing practices, in the past as well as those identified in recent evidence, suggest racial discrimination in sentencing. Research on this subject documents perspectives supporting racial disparity in sentencing, and also a contrary position that there is no discrimination in sentencing based on racial status. Both sides of this controversial question are minutely examined in Chapter 5, with particular attention directed to the empirical findings of minority researchers. It is suggested that criminal activity, as defined by those in power, is one of the adaptive responses of racial minorities to institutional racism. While not specifically adopting a Marxist position, the chapter is critically concerned with the problems of capitalistic (white-collar) crime, as contrasted to the crimes for which minorities become enmeshed in the criminal justice system, and the differential treatments afforded the two groups under that system, particularly noting the power (class) relationships that make such circumstances possible.

Finally, many of the studies on sentencing focus on whether the ultimate sentence, death, is disproportionately applied to racial minorities, especially African Americans. Recent evidence is reported which indicates clearly that racial status significantly affects capital punishment decisions. The discussion of the death penalty and its ramifications for racial minorities begins with a historical overview of the inconsistent use of capital punishment based upon race and concludes with the implications of the reinstatement of capital punishment for minorities.

Who is punished is the basic theme of Chapter 6, "Warehousing Minorities: Corrections." According to the latest statistics, a record number of persons are being held in jails in the United States, and prisons are bulging with so many inmates that some states are being forced by federal court order to release them before their time is served. The overwhelming majority of those incarcerated are persons of color. Chapter 6 provides statistical information on minorities in jails and federal and state prisons, as it details the major problems faced by those imprisoned—overcrowding, AIDS, racial discrimination, and brutality from guards and white inmates—and the effects of these conditions on minority prisoners.

Many minority inmates view themselves as political prisoners, and there seems to be some validity to such a charge. In 1979, a report by a group of international jurists who investigated complaints filed by incarcerated minority Americans concluded that there was a persistent pattern of brutalization and denial of the due process rights of prisoners in clear violation of human rights (Hinds, 1979). Prisoners' rights issues have long been protested by minority inmates and include, in addition to complaints about poor food, inadequate facilities, and programs, the denial of religious freedom and practices (e.g., to Muslims and Native Americans). Racism and prison brutality on the part of both correctional officers and other inmates are frequent allegations made by incarcerated minorities in the United States. Racial discrimination in parole decisions and length of time served are additional political issues raised over the years by minority inmates and are examined in this chapter.

The roles played by racial minorities in major prison riots (e.g., at Attica in 1971 and Santa Fe in 1980) and their motives for participating are analyzed. Finally, descriptions of the prison social climate, prison sexual violence, violent participants, the possible reasons underlying prison violence, and the contribution of such violence to racial polarity in correctional settings close the chapter.

Every effort was made to provide an objective and balanced presentation of the literature and available research on each specific topic. However, there is another informed perspective frequently overlooked in the mainstream literature when questions of racial minorities and crime are addressed. To remedy that neglect, at the end of each of the chapters, "A Minority View" summarizes the problems delineated in the chapter and offers alternative analyses and interpretations of the topics examined from a minority perspective.

Acknowledgments

I gratefully acknowledge the hundreds of students in my classes at the Florida State University and Indiana University whose eagerness to learn and to acquire enlightened knowledge about other racial/ethnic groups in the United States gave me the inspiration and impetus to produce this book.

I owe a special debt of thanks to the three secretaries who worked side by side with me for their outstanding word processing of the manuscript. Edwina Ivory (Florida State), Gina Lake Doglione, and Jacquelyn Moore (Indiana University) will always be counted among the "special" people in my life, since each of them became a part of my life.

I am indebted to John McCluskey for encouraging me to submit the manuscript to Indiana University Press and for reading and commenting on the first, very rough, draft. There are not enough accolades for Jane Lyle, my manuscript editor, for her careful and meticulous review, her guidance and patience, and her thoughtfulness.

Finally, and most important, I thank my father, Edward Grant Richey, for his patience in giving up a large portion of his "quality time" with me over the past five years so that I could research and write *Unequal Justice: A Question of Color*.

Part One

Minorities and Crime

1

Defining Race through the Minority Experience

Misery is when you heard
on the radio that the neighborhood
you live in is a slum but
you always thought it was home.

—Langston Hughes

Definitions can be problematic, especially when the topic is race or ethnicity. As Daniel Georges-Abeyie (1984a: 11) insightfully points out, "there is no single universally accepted definition of race." Definitions of "race" vary from those in *Webster's New Collegiate Dictionary* (1976: 950),[1] "a family, tribe, people, or nation belonging to the same stock," or "a division of mankind possessing traits that are transmissible by descent and sufficient to characterize it as a distinct human type," to sociological definitions: "a subgroup of the human species characterized by physical differences which result from inherited biological characteristics" (Popenoe, 1974: Glossary), or "a human group that defines itself and/or is defined by other groups as different by virtue of innate and immutable physical characteristics" (Smith and Preston, 1977: 547-548).

"Ethnicity" further complicates the definitional quandary, since according to *Webster's,* an ethnic is "a member of a minority group who retains the customs, language, or social views of his group" (1976: 393). Sociologists view an ethnic group variously as "any group which is socially distinguished from other groups, has developed its own subculture, and has a shared feeling of peoplehood" (Popenoe, 1974: Glossary), or more specifically, "a human group, such as Mexican Americans or the Jewish people, that defines itself and/or is defined by other groups as different by virtue of certain cultural characteristics" (Smith and Preston, 1977: 542). In definitions concerning race and ethnicity, the signal concept might well be "defined by other groups."

Further, these "accepted" definitions must be examined with care, since in his investigation of African Americans, Johari Amini (1972: 1, 2) finds that "Western civilization has attempted to define, and has largely succeeded in defining, existence for Africans in the Americas and elsewhere," and adds that since "our entire existence is made up of definitions, not only in WHAT is defined, but HOW it is defined, and very importantly, WHO is defining it," the crucial point involves the legitimacy or credibility of the definer. Amini thus suggests that if definitions were made by a member of one's own reference group, they would have more credibility and legitimacy; while on the other hand, a definition by someone with different needs, values, interests, goals, and backgrounds would be more discredited.

The plight of Asians of Japanese descent in the U.S. during World War II is one example of Amini's position. Despite the fact that there were large numbers of people of German and Italian descent living in the United States in 1942, only the Japanese were confined to concentration camps until the end of the war in 1945. Germany and Italy were defeated through conventional warfare, yet Japan was defeated by the destruction of cities with nuclear weapons, a form of genocide. The legitimization for such bombings evolved from the European definition of "Japanese" as "Yellow Jap," "slant-eyed, snake like, vicious in characterization" (ibid.: 1972: 3). Naming, name calling, and labeling play integral roles both in race relations and in minority group interaction with agents of the criminal justice system in this country. Thus, it is essential to establish a clear perspective of racial/ethnic naming or labeling before the remainder of the book's theme is presented.

Lampe (1982: 542) finds that name calling, a propaganda device, is one form of naming, involving "the use of a particular word or phrase to place an object referred to into a category which elicits a desired attitude or behavior." Further, "name calling indicates the speaker's feelings toward or evaluation of the object referred to" (ibid.). In testing his hypotheses, Lampe found that a sample of Mexican Americans and Anglos in San Antonio, Texas indicated more positive responses to the term "Negro" than to "black," since the latter term elicited a more negative and threatening image. The African Americans in the sample had the opposite reaction, viewing "Negro," a term invented by Euro-American people and applied to African American people in the United States, as more negative, and "black," a self-selected term, as indicative of pride in their heritage. All three respondent groups (African American, Mexican American, and Anglo) found the term "Chicano" negative and suggestive of gang membership, dangerousness, laziness, and untrustworthiness. Lampe (ibid.: 547) concludes that "people referred to are, in the eyes of others, transformed into different people by the changing of identificational ethnic labels. . . . Thus ethnic labels can be naming for some but can be name calling for others."

Although the terms "race," "ethnic," and "ethnic group" are used throughout this book, because of reader familiarity with them and because of their frequent usage in pertinent literature, the preferred term for the subgroups described is "minority" or "minority group." Not only is there apparent consensus in the definition of this term, but also "minority" more accurately reflects the political/economic status of the African Americans, Hispanic Americans, Asian

Americans, and Native Americans in this country. *Webster's,* for instance, defines minority as "a group having less than the number of votes necessary for control; a part of a population differing from others in some characteristics and often subjected to differential treatment" (1976: 733). Such treatment is further delineated by Popenoe (1974: Glossary) when he depicts a minority group as "any recognizable ethnic, racial, or religious group in a society which suffers from disadvantage due to prejudice or discrimination." Smith and Preston (1977: 545) hammer the final nail in the definitional coffin by defining minority as "a small social group that possesses little economic, political, and social power." The following historical reviews of the minority subgroups with whom this text is concerned demonstrate the reality of these definitions.

Defining U.S. Minority Groups

African Americans

Defining "race" for African Americans is particularly enigmatic since, in an anthropological sense, we categorize persons as "white," "black," "brown," "red," or "yellow" somewhat arbitrarily. Biologists and anthropologists have used the term "race" in reference to three groups—Caucasoid, Mongoloid, and Negroid—depending upon certain physical characteristics such as skin color, hair texture, type of eyelids, and other traits that have been transmitted by genes through heredity (Hodges, 1974; Popenoe, 1974). Yet, if we think about it, over 80 percent of alleged African American crimes in the United States are committed by people who are part Euro-American. Since all people on earth are thought to have some mixed ancestry, and Euro-Americans are a blend of many ethnic and tribal groups that originated in Africa and Europe, even Euro-Americans are not racially pure. In addition to the millions of African Americans who have "passed for white" in this society, many millions of Africans were absorbed into the populations of Mediterranean countries such as Spain, Portugal, Italy, and Greece (Haskell and Yablonsky, 1974: 211). Furthermore, when we consider the rapes of African female slaves in the early years of this country and the resultant millions of mulattoes who were the offspring of these forced alliances, and those children born as a result of legalized miscegenation and other forms of interracial mixing in the U.S., the notion of a "black" race becomes somewhat ambiguous (Mann and Selva, 1979).

The first African slaves arrived in Virginia in 1619 (Bennett, 1975), a fact that illustrates two salient points: (1) African Americans were the only racial or ethnic group brought here against their will, and (2) African Americans are among the oldest Americans with a history and cultural heritage largely formed in this country (Sowell, 1981).

Many thousands (some estimates indicate 500,000) of former African American slaves, or "free persons of color," were not enslaved before the Emancipation Proclamation of 1863. Nonetheless, they were as stigmatized as slaves were by a Constitution that "sanctioned human slavery based upon race and color, and decreed that persons of color who were held in bondage should be counted as three-fifths of a man" (National Minority Advisory Council [NMAC], 1980). This notion that "white" men are by nature superior to other men, specifically black slaves, "encouraged physical and psychological brutality that was dehumanizing, life-threatening, and detrimental to the development of a sense of well being among Blacks" (Delaney, 1979: 3).

The political and economic factors which are suggested throughout this book as the real bases for racism against African Americans in this country are clearly seen in two historical facts. First, in the forging of the new Constitution, northerners were trying to limit the southern representation in the new government; therefore the slaves could not be counted as people, but only as property, or "three-fifths of a man" (Loye, 1971). Second, despite President Lincoln's denial that the war had anything to do with his issuance of the Emancipation Proclamation during the midst of the Civil War, the South was fighting desperately "to defend its way of life, which depended significantly on the slave system" (Rose, 1974: 31).

After the war between the North and South, additional "Black Codes" were proposed in the South to augment the earlier codes and laws that had regulated the lives of "free blacks" and slaves (Sowell, 1981). Although the new laws granted African Americans the rights to bear witness in court and to marry, they were also highly restrictive and prohibited blacks to own land or work in particular occupations. Fortunately, these new codes were never effective, and during the Reconstruction era, African Americans gained equal status in law through enfranchisement (1868) and through the Sumner Act of 1875, which allocated equal rights in public accommodations until its repeal by the Supreme Court in 1883 (Rose, 1974: 32).

Over the years, the gradual erosion of African American rights culminated in the "Jim Crow" segregationist and discriminatory statutes of the 1890s, which "divided southern society into a two-caste system, with whites occupying positions of power and Negroes reduced to second-class citizenship" (ibid.: 32). Although the Thirteenth Amendment to the Constitution gave equality to African Americans, the Fourteenth gave citizenship, and the Fifteenth accorded African Americans the right to vote, the U.S. Supreme Court again dealt a blow to African American people when in *Plessy v. Ferguson* (1896) it was proclaimed that "separate but equal" facilities were constitutional. This action of the land's highest court "confirmed the permanent inferior status of black people in the United States" (Moss, 1971: xv).

As African Americans slowly emerged from the status of slavery, they continued in the same occupations they had held during their enslavement—agricultural labor and domestic work. Since only one out of ten African Americans lived outside the South, most of them, including the tenant farmers, were dependent on Euro-Americans, or those who had never wanted them free in the first place. Such a status resulted in an almost complete usurpation of economic freedom and opportunity, a condition of being kept in a virtual state of poverty.

This economic condition, combined with the vicious attacks, lynchings, and terrorism of the vigilante Ku Klux Klan, led to the black exodus from the South to the North. Although there had always been a slow migration of rural African Americans and "free persons of color" away from the oppressive South, at least 90 percent of blacks, 80 percent of whom were in rural areas, lived in the South until the turn of the century (Sowell, 1981: 208; Rose, 1974: 33). This mass movement, which was primarily to the Northeast and the Midwest, served to introduce new problems for the African American migrants, who "experienced residential, social, and economic discrimination wherever they went" (Rose, 1974: 33-34).

Some idea of the extent of this vast, continuous historic movement is seen in the fact that more than three-quarters of a million African Americans left the South in the 1920s after World War II. After a hiatus during the Great Depression of the 1930s, the movement began once more, with over a million African Americans leaving the South in the 1940s, and another million in the 1950s; between 1940 and 1970, more than four million more made the northward trek—"a number comparable to the great international migrations in all of history" (Sowell, 1981: 244). Thus, poor, rural African Americans, who were largely uneducated and had few work skills, escaped the Klan and other forms of discrimination in the South, only to be faced with the insidious racism of the North.

If one looks retrospectively at the virtual ease with which millions of European immigrants have been assimilated into the American mainstream, while African Americans and other peoples of color have yet to be assimilated, a picture emerges of entrenched racism based upon color. The beginning of the twentieth century found the Ku Klux Klan moving into northern cities; however, the resistance and violence African Americans faced in the North came from already present Euro-Americans, who felt threatened by the new arrivals in terms of jobs, education, housing, and social interrelations.

Between 1915 and 1949, thirty-three major race riots occurred in the United States, the two worst and bloodiest in Illinois—in East St. Louis and Chicago (Rose, 1974: 34). The urban burnings in the civil rights era of the 1960s followed. In most of these uprisings, it is the African American who suffers, largely at the hands of the police. The National Minority Advisory Council on Criminal Justice reports that most of the riots between 1965 and 1980 were direct responses to police violence; it cites the fact that in the Newark, N.J. riot of 1967, more than twenty blacks were killed by police who "seized on the initial disorder as an opportunity and pretext to perpetuate the most horrendous and widespread killing, violence, torture, and intimidation, not in response to any crime of civilian disorder, but to satisfy their own desire for violence" (NMAC, 1980: 25).

A NOTE ON WEST INDIANS

Although black West Indians had been trickling into the United States since the eighteenth century, by the twentieth century significant numbers began to arrive, mostly to New York City. Recent Haitian refugees, however, have settled largely in South Florida, primarily Miami. In terms of occupations and income, with the exception of the boat Haitians, West Indians have fared better in this country than native African Americans (Sowell, 1981). Nationally, West Indian incomes are 52 percent higher than those of African Americans, and second-generation West Indians have higher incomes than Euro-Americans. This differential is largely due to the higher average proportion of West Indians who are professionals and the fact that while African Americans have an unemployment rate far above the national rate, the West Indian unemployment rate is far below the national average.

Hispanic Americans

Mexican Americans have the distinction of being among the oldest and the newest Americans, since many settlements of people in the Southwest came from Mexico and were here long before the Anglo-Americans[2] arrived. However, most Mexican Americans came to this country in the twentieth century, particularly during the Second World War and afterwards. The explorers, missionaries, and adventurers from Spain who established settlements in what is now California, Texas, and New Mexico attempted to conquer the Indians and bring them into a virtual state of bondage, just as they had conquered and similarly treated the Aztecs in Mexico. After the fall of the Spanish monarchy, Mexican independence was secured in 1821, and the new Mexican government allowed the Anglo-American immigrants to settle on Mexican terrain. Ultimately, these territories led to the war over Texas and the annexation of Texas to the United States in 1845. The war against Mexico resulted in the acquisition of vast areas that are now California, Nevada, Arizona, Utah, New Mexico, and parts of Colorado, Kansas, Oklahoma, and Wyoming (Sowell, 1981). Suddenly the Mexicans, who originally had a country larger than the United States, became the minority in the new states.

These early conflicts between Mexico and the United States are believed to have initiated and perpetuated the hostility and racial discrimination faced by Mexican Americans today. In addition to the hostilities ensuing from the Mexican American War, the way of life imposed upon the Mexican Americans kept them isolated from other Americans in their own Spanish-speaking, separate world. Some movie houses were not designated for Mexican Americans until 1958; and one national study, reported in 1981, revealed that darker-skinned Mexican Americans were still experiencing housing discrimination to a greater extent than African Americans or light-skinned Mexican Americans (Fitzpatrick and Parker, 1981: 113). This segregated way of life was economically based: most of the Mexicans who came to the United States in the early twentieth century worked as lower-level employees or laborers on the railroad, or in agriculture or mining—occupations that kept them in remote enclaves away from others, living in boxcars or shacks near their places of work (Sowell, 1981: 249).

There was obviously little opportunity for education, health services, or upward mobility.

The two-thousand-mile border between Mexico and the United States has varying levels of security to prevent illegal immigration, but it is generally quite accessible, and millions of Mexicans came, and continue to come. Often they were invited; more often they were uninvited, or deported. When their labor in the fields was needed, laws were magically altered or new ones introduced, but when the labor was no longer needed, Mexican Americans were (and still are) rounded up and shipped back to Mexico. No other minority has ever been deported from this country as massively as the Mexicans (Moore, 1976).

Mexicans were permitted to enter and work as virtual slaves in the early 1900s. A first wave of immigration between 1910 and 1920 defined the Mexican immigrants as "temporaries" who were to return to Mexico after the railroads were built, the mines were worked, or the crops were picked. But two things happened: the Mexican migrants did not return to Mexico, and thousands more continued to come. The Great Depression of the 1930s led to a radical drop in legal immigration and massive deportations of Mexican workers, who were no longer needed because other sources of cheap labor were available among the growing number of unemployed throughout the country (ibid.: 40). The U.S. Immigration Service was expanded and its activities were accelerated, particularly when it was discovered that it was cheaper to send the Mexicans back to Mexico than it was for the state to support them on welfare. Many of those massively and forcefully deported were American citizens, but such legal statuses could not be discovered, since formal hearings were rarely held (Sowell, 1981: 254).

The Great Depression led to two distinct migratory patterns among southwestern Mexican Americans—those who went from the urban barrios back to their original rural home villages, and those who went the other way, from the poverty-ridden villages to the urban centers. The Mexicans in the cities had lost the meager jobs they once had, while those on the farms had lost their lands through mortgage foreclosures or lack of money to pay taxes. There was no work, especially for Mexicans, not even "low-pay, back-breaking agricultural work"; and typically, a California law banned the employment of aliens on any public works projects (Meier and Rivera, 1972: 153). Some help came with the Roosevelt New Deal programs of the thirties, but the economic situation of the Mexican Americans during this period was so drastic, the repercussions are still felt today.

The Bracero program, started in 1942, was a contract labor program to bring in Mexican farm workers during World War II, when millions of Americans were in the military and a wartime "emergency" existed. This war also provided Mexican Americans new economic opportunities through military service and war industries, and they were "abruptly uprooted and obliged to become part of the labor force of a massive war machine" (ibid.: 184), after having been isolated in the city barrios and rural villages.

According to their numbers in the country, Mexican Americans tended to be disproportionately represented in the armed services and in combat divisions during World War II, partly because of "machismo," and partly because of patriotism (ibid.: 186). After the war, job training opportunities, education through the GI Bill, and newly available home loans offered Mexican Americans new hope. Even though they had fought for their new country, upon their return they found that basically nothing had changed—discrimination against Mexican Americans was still the order of the day. Deportations became more frequent, and the number expelled "reached new heights in the postwar world," with expulsions in 1947 at ten times the previous record-breaking deportations of eighteen thousand in 1930. The deportations of a half-million Mexicans in 1951 and more than a million in 1954 indicate that during the postwar years, almost four million people were sent back to Mexico.

In what is called the "third wave of immigration," illegal emigrants from Mexico began to come back in the 1960s; by 1970 they had passed the old peak in numbers (Sowell, 1981: 255). There was a reversal of public opinion and a hardening against Mexican immigrants and contract laborers in 1960, the Bracero program was eliminated in 1964, and in 1965 Congress limited the number of immigrants from the entire Western Hemisphere to 120,000. Thus, "the 'close and friendly' border had disappeared, perhaps forever" (Moore, 1976: 44). Yet, Mexicans still come, and most stay, where they remain isolated in their barrios, and now find themselves labeled as the "Mexican Problem."

MEXICAN AMERICANS
The terms "Mexican American" and "Chicano" are used interchangeably to define persons of Mexican descent, while "Hispanic" is commonly used to include people of Mexican, Puerto Rican, Cuban, and other Latin American descent (Pachon and Moore, 1981: 112). Mexican Americans are a product of Mexican, Spanish, and Aztec heritage who have experienced an Anglo-Saxon or American influence (Aguirre, 1975: 2). The term "Chicano" used to be a derogatory name, largely applied by Mexican Americans to themselves, similar to the term "black," which used to be an insult until the advent of black pride in the 1960s (Aguirre, 1975; Stoddard, 1973).[3] Today very few Mexicans are either pure Caucasian (of Spanish ancestry) or pure Indian (Sowell, 1981: 246).

Although each of the Hispanic American minority groups has been met with varying intensities of racism and hostility in the United States, the irony of the plight of the Mexican Americans is that they have been in this country almost as long as the Native Americans, yet they have experienced economic and educational deprivations more intensely than Cubans, Puerto Ricans, Santo Dominicans, or Central and South American new arrivals. Clearly one difference is language. Puerto Ricans, for example, know some English when they come to the mainland; also they are U.S. citizens who generally come from urban areas and have some work skills (Rose, 1974: 58). Since many Cubans and other Hispanic "political refugees" who came to these shores are from the upper and middle classes, they "fit" economically, whereas people who come from the bottom of the economic ladder, such as laborers, or Braceros, particularly those of darker color, are apparently viewed as "misfits," at least according to the American ideal.

Several groups make up the large and expanding Hispanic minority, a group that it is believed will constitute the largest minority in the United States by the turn of the century. In 1988, Hispanic Americans totaled almost 20 million, or 8.1 percent, of the population (U.S. Department of Commerce, 1990: 17). Hispanic Americans live in every state but are largely concentrated in nine states (Valdivieso and Davis, 1988: 15).[4] Puerto Ricans (13 percent of Hispanic Americans) reside predominantly in the eastern United States, mainly New York City; Cubans (5 percent of Hispanic Americans) are located primarily in Florida, and large numbers of them also live in New York and New Jersey; newcomers from Santo Domingo and Central and South America (12 percent of Hispanic Americans) tend to settle in California, but there are large numbers of them in New York City and other large eastern cities as well; and Mexican Americans (62 percent of Hispanic Americans) are distributed in the western and southwestern United States (U.S. Census, 1980: Table 1-134; Valdivieso and Davis, 1988: 4).

Hispanic Americans have generally been examined as an entity, with a resultant loss of the cultural nuances of each group. The diversity of these groups and the scant data available on each subgroup clearly limit any in-depth discussion of each one; thus, only a brief examination of the major subgroups is possible.

PUERTO RICANS, CUBANS, AND OTHER HISPANIC AMERICANS

Puerto Ricans are a racial mixture of Spanish, African, and Indian strains, a group that ranges from pure Caucasian to pure African American. Dominicans, like Puerto Ricans, range in color from completely Caucasoid to completely Negroid. Cubans, with the exception of many of the Negroid refugees, are predominantly Caucasoid. Other Hispanic Americans from Central and South America may be Caucasoid, Indio, or a mixture (Fitzpatrick and Parker, 1981: 101).

Whereas color differences are not socially significant in Puerto Rico, on the "mainland," or in the continental United States, such differences pose a serious problem: "The social and economic opportunities open to white Puerto Ricans provide an incentive for some of them to assimilate with the larger American society, while a desire to avoid being mistaken for American Negroes has provided incentives for darker Puerto Ricans to cling to the Spanish language and culture" (Sowell, 1981: 235). One of the most difficult and painful experiences of Puerto Ricans and other new arrivals from the Caribbean is adjustment to the color problem in the United States (Fitzpatrick and Parker, 1981: 110). Puerto Ricans on the mainland are defined as minority group members, but in Puerto Rico they are the majority group (Mizio, 1979: 9).

A final definition concerns the group variously referred to as "Ricans," "Nuyoricans," or "Neo-Ricans," those second-generation New York City, and other urban, Puerto Ricans who have "adopted the language of the streets and are much more aggressive and sophisticated than their Puerto Rican born parents about the means of survival in the inner city" (Fitzpatrick and Parker, 1981: 108). Discrimination, the economic situation in New York, the low educational level of Puerto Ricans, and the large number of female-headed families (44 percent among Puerto Rican families) all contribute to the "continuing poverty of the Puerto Rican community on the mainland" (ibid.: 107). Studies in New York City reveal higher rates of mental illness for Puerto Ricans than for both the total population and other ethnic groups. "Black" Puerto Ricans experience greater stress because of their color, which, added to other social problems in a racist society, is indicated in their higher rates of admission to mental hospitals compared to "white" Puerto Ricans (Mizio, 1979: 6, 10).

Cubans, on the other hand, have fared much better than other Hispanic groups in this country. They have become very influential in Miami, for instance, both politically and economically. Cubans have "transformed it, created in it a new and active Spanish-speaking center of international commerce, and are developing into a local but important political force" (Fitzpatrick and Parker, 1981: 109). The strong political power of Miami and other Floridian Cubans contributed significantly to the election of the Spanish-surname governor in 1986. However, a study recently reported by Portes and Stepick (1985) indicates that the 124,779 Mariel (boat) Cuban refugees who arrived on these shores in 1980 are in distinct contrast to the Cubans who came in the sixties. Labeled by the Cuban government as "scum" (although only 5 percent of this population was subsequently determined as deviant), predominantly "black," having little education or English-speaking skills, and coming in the midst of an economic recession, these Cuban immigrants faced a different reception from that which greeted the earlier, more affluent, professional Cuban refugees. According to Portes and Stepick (1985), in 1983, 39 percent of these Cubans were involuntarily unemployed, and those who were employed typically held minimally paid jobs.

A recent comparative study of 1980 Cuban and Haitian boat immigrants indicates that in 1984, the unemployment rates of these groups were three to four times greater than the 1980 figures for the state of Florida, where these groups are concentrated (ibid.: 497). Whereas 39 percent of the Cuban respondents in the study were out of work, 63 percent of the Haitians were, statuses which were found to be mostly involuntary. The difference between the employment of the two groups was due to the fact that Cuban immigrants had a readily available enclave labor market in Cuban-owned firms, a resource sorely lacking in the Miami African American community (ibid.: 499).

Asian Americans

The term "Asian American" includes over twenty nationality groups whose members vary widely in identity, language, and culture and are America's fastest-growing minority group (O'Hare and Felt, 1991). Their differences have often been reduced to stereotypes that reflect negative images largely rooted in the physiological notion that since "they all look alike," they must all think and act alike. "World War II portrayed the fanatical Japanese; the Korean War pictured the Communist hordes from Korea and China, while the Vietnamese fiasco projected a ruthless, cunning enemy; . . . the little 'brown brothers' of the Philippines, the dope fiends and white slavers of Hong Kong, and the sinister Fu Manchu," while "the most visible Asian today is the ubiquitous tourist from Japan" (Kitano, 1981: 125-127).

Emphasis will be placed on the two major Asian American groups, the Chinese and the Japanese, since what data are available primarily concern them. Other immigrants, such as those from small, isolated Pacific islands (Guam and Samoa), Indonesia, Malaysia, Korea, the Philippines, and the new arrivals from Vietnam, Cambodia, and Laos, can be discussed only on the basis of the limited information available.

CHINESE AMERICANS

China's culture goes back thousands of years before Christ; the economic development in place in China by the eleventh century would not be paralleled in Europe until the eighteenth century. The Chinese were the first Asians to come to this country in substantial numbers. They came largely to the West Coast in the Gold Rush days of the 1840s, arriving, and remaining, primarily in California. Many were contract laborers, or "coolies," hired to work as miners or as the railroad workers who, performing the "hardest, dirtiest, most menial jobs," laid the Central Pacific Railroad tracks from California through the Sierra Mountains to Utah (Kitano, 1981: 128). Others, on borrowed money, came from southeast China, where economic conditions and political unrest had forced them to leave home (Rose, 1974: 49).

Most of the initial Chinese immigrants were men who planned either to return to China or to bring their wives into the United States later. Some did go back to China, but most stayed and ultimately faced harsh and vicious attacks. At first the Chinese arrivals were treated favorably and viewed as "quaint curiosities," but "as the concrete conditions in the economy, combined with the growing nativist feelings, resulted in strong anti-Chinese sentiments," this image was soon replaced (NMAC, 1980: 117-118). Although physically smaller than Americans, the Chinese worked harder and more cheaply, lived frugally, and saved money out of the pittance they were paid, virtues that together with their "differentness" made them hated and feared as competitors by Anglo workers (Sowell, 1981: 136).

By 1854 a great deal of the surface gold had been "panned out." Anglo miners whose claims became less productive felt threatened by the Chinese and Mexican miners, so they turned in anger against the Chinese by violently taking over the more desirable claims (NMAC, 1980: 118). Chinese who attempted to be independent gold miners were forcibly driven from the mining camps by Anglo miners, who took the Chinese claims. Casual forms of harassment such as cutting off their long pigtails, viewed as "pranks," escalated into cruel, serious violence. For example, twenty-nine Chinese were massacred at a Rock Spring, Wyoming coal mine in 1885; an entire population in one California Chinese community had to leave because of mob violence; and Seattle and Tacoma, Washington expelled their entire Chinese populations (Rose, 1974; Sowell, 1981). Chinatowns throughout the West were sporadically attacked by mobs of Anglos, who sacked, burned, and killed the Chinese indiscriminately.

The legal apparatus was equally brutal for the Chinese. Congress passed the Chinese Exclusion Act in 1882, which prohibited immigration for ten years. It was renewed in 1892, made permanent in 1902, and not repealed until 1943 (Kitano, 1981: 128). Other laws affected the Chinese punitively, including one in 1854 that prohibited Chinese from testifying against a "white" person and left them no recourse when Anglos robbed, vandalized, or assaulted them; laws that prevented Chinese already in the country from becoming citizens; laws that made citizenship necessary for owning land or entering certain occupations; local ordinances excluding Chinese children from public schools; and rigid tax laws that discouraged the Chinese from certain businesses or drove them out of the businesses they were in (NMAC, 1980; Sowell, 1981).

The devastating effects of these laws were probably most vividly seen in the impact on Chinese families. As previously indicated, most of the early Chinese immigrants were males seeking work. Many had left wives and families behind in China—loved ones they were unable to see for decades, or ever again. Restrictions on employment and business opportunities prevented these men from earning money to return to their families and left most of the American Chinese population without hope of a normal social or family life. As a result, the smuggling of Chinese, particularly women, became a major activity. Many of these women were voluntary prostitutes; some were forced here against their will. When, after forty-eight years, the immigration laws were modified in 1930, small numbers of wives were permitted to come from China and join their husbands (Sowell, 1981). Without a family life, Chinese males in the United States turned to gambling as a means of coping with the loneliness, and perhaps to win enough to return home; they embraced prostitutes as substitutes for their wives; and they sought escape from the harsh realities of their miserable existence through opium use (NMAC, 1980: 120).

It was not until 1965 that immigration restrictions against the Chinese were lifted. But when China adopted a communist form of government, the "Red Scare" instigated by the federal government in 1949 effectively turned the American people against the Chinese and once again inflamed anti-Chinese sentiment and hostility (ibid.: 140). The Communist take-over in China forced thousands of Chinese to flee to Hong Kong, where they quickly became westernized, thus losing their traditional values and constraints in the process. Thereafter thousands of "Hong Kong" Chinese made their way to American shores, and ultimately into its Chinatowns (Sowell, 1981).

JAPANESE AMERICANS
Since "all Asians look alike," the Japanese were not far behind the Chinese in their early travails in this country. The first Japanese came in 1869, twenty-one years after the first Chinese had entered. They were initially welcomed to Ha-

waii for plantation work, and to the mainland to work the agricultural fields and for other strenuous work on the railroads, in the mines, and in the lumber mills. After all, passage of the Chinese Exclusion Act (1882) did not exclude the need for cheap, hard-working laborers. But the virtues of working hard, living frugally, and saving for a better time had a countereffect that produced a backlash of fear and hatred against the Japanese from American workers and labor unions who saw them as rivals. Even those thrifty and ambitious Japanese who had managed to buy small farms or businesses were met with intense hostility from the same farmers and businessmen who had welcomed them as employees, but later resented them as rivals (Sowell, 1981). As they had for the Chinese earlier, laws became a legal nightmare for the American Japanese. Anti-Japanese legislation was passed for dozens of years in California, the state where most Japanese lived. In 1906, for example, the city of San Francisco attempted to assign Japanese children to segregated Chinese schools, but when the issue reached international proportions involving the Japanese and U.S. governments, the city backed away. As a result of the trade-off, known as the "Gentleman's Agreement with the Japanese Government" (1907), Japan limited its emigration of farm labor workers, and the U.S. allowed Japanese wives and children to join their male family members already here. Not to be bested, in 1913 California passed the Alien Land Law, which made it illegal for alien Japanese to own land, but since there was no restriction against purchasing land, the Japanese caught in this legal "crunch" simply transferred title of their lands to their American-born children (NMAC, 1980: 121). Other legislation totally excluded Japanese immigration in 1924. And, in the "ultimate demonstration of racism," in 1942 110,000 men, women, and children, citizens and aliens alike, almost the entire Japanese American population, were rounded up on the West Coast and placed in concentration camps in the desert, the Rocky Mountains, and Arkansas (Rose, 1974: 53).

The Executive Order by President Roosevelt that led to this massive internment in isolated, barren regions of the country—"places where nobody had lived before and no one has lived since"—did not specifically mention Japanese Americans, yet they were the only group gathered en masse and confined for the duration of the war. Our other enemies, the Italians and Germans, were not processed under this order because only the Japanese were "deemed a criminal threat to America, solely on the basis of their race" (NMAC, 1980: 121). Such drastic measures were enforced despite the fact that not a single Japanese American was convicted of sabotage during World War II. As wartime manpower needs grew, however, there was a lifting of the barbed wire, and some Japanese Americans were released to bring in the crops as seasonal agricultural workers; others were furloughed to work on the railroads; and some students were permitted to continue college programs in the East and Midwest. In 1943 the army began to recruit Nisei,[5] who had previously been regarded as "enemy aliens" and denied military service. As a result, over three hundred thousand Japanese Americans fought in World War II in some of the bloodiest battles, and one of their combat units emerged as "the most decorated combat unit in American History" (Sowell, 1981: 174).

According to estimates, the forced evacuation resulted in a loss of over $400 million to Japanese Americans. This massive financial disaster meant that few were ever able to recoup their losses, and most had to begin anew in different occupations from those they had had before internment (Sowell, 1981; Rose, 1974). The unrecoverable thousands of businesses and farms were a financial disaster, but the traumatic emotional devastation caused by the forced uprooting was a human disaster. The internment camps changed the traditional Japanese family structure and way of life considerably. All who worked in the camps were paid equal pittances, thereby undermining the male father/husband provider role. Additionally, those Japanese who were accorded administrative roles had to be citizens, which meant that the younger generations were placed above their elders, thus threatening the latter's previous leadership roles. Finally, the primitive, tiny quarters the internees were packed into effectively destroyed the privacy of the family (Sowell, 1981).

By 1969, however, the average Japanese American family income was 32 percent above the national average, and the personal income of Japanese Americans was 11 percent above the national average. In large part this was due to the change from previous farming and other occupations to professional occupations, the tendency to have smaller families, and interracial marriages, and the Japanese American's intense emphasis on education.

Japanese Americans differentiate generations within their society. The Issei were first-generation immigrants who came to the U.S. between 1890 and 1924, retained their native language and heritage, and were minimally acculturated. Nisei, or the second generation, also known by the general term "Nikkei," or Japanese born in the United States (about 88 percent of Japanese Americans), are the children of the Issei, were born between 1910 and 1940, and are now middle-aged parents and grandparents who grasped educational opportunities and used them for upward mobility. The third generation, the Sansei, children of the Nisei, have no identification with Japan and identify more with their friends and neighbors; while the Yonsei, or fourth generation, are even more heterogeneous and may be the last of the specific generationally identified groups (Kitano, 1981: 131).

KOREANS AND OTHER ASIAN AMERICAN GROUPS

The first Korean immigrants, who came to Hawaii largely between 1902 and 1905, were small in number, particularly compared to the high numbers who entered after the 1965 Immigration Act. This Act, which took effect in 1968, gave priority to those with advanced education, training, and skills (Kitano, 1981). From that initial immigration of less than 10,000, the number of U.S. Koreans has swelled to 357,000 (U.S. Department of Commerce, 1990: 39), who are primarily located in urban centers such as Los Angeles, San Francisco, Chicago, New York, Baltimore, Houston, Honolulu, and Seattle (Kim, 1977: 15).

Despite the fact that the new Korean arrivals had advanced educational and occupational backgrounds, and more Ph.D.s than the other Asian groups combined, language problems at first led to their employment in lower-status occupations (NMAC, 1980: 129). In fact, language seems to be the most glaring problem hindering assimilation, especially since Korean Americans continue to speak the Korean language in their homes, and their children are encouraged to continue the study of the Korean language and culture. The language problem is compounded by the fact that there is little correspondence between the English and Korean languages, which makes the acquisition of English extremely difficult. Although there are bilingual classes, many Korean youngsters are placed in lower-level classes because of their difficulty with English, and some feel that they are being discriminated against because of this practice. Since in Korean families both parents work, they cannot devote the attention needed to help their offspring, particularly if they, too, are having difficulty with the language (Kim, 1977; Pitler, 1977). The resilience and perseverance of these new Americans is seen in the fact that in 1980, 78.1 percent of Koreans had attained four or more years of high school, and 33.7 percent had completed four or more years of college (U.S. Department of Commerce, 1990: 39).

Filipinos. Filipinos differ from the other Asian groups described by their racial strain, which is Malaysian, or a mixture based upon prior colonial rule of Spanish, American, Japanese, Chinese, and German peoples. Their United States migration, mostly to Hawaii, consisted of young men who were desired for their labor but not desired as citizens.

Four distinct categories of Filipinos can be identified based upon their immigration history: the first generation of males, who came in the 1920s, retained their native dialect, and went into agricultural (plantation) work; the second generation, who were American-born; a third group of World War II veterans and war refugees; and the newest, who came for better economic opportunities under the Immigration Act of 1965 as engineers, doctors, nurses, lawyers, and teachers. Despite their educational and professional backgrounds, these newcomers are frequently found in lower-status jobs; for example, Hawaii Filipinos are in the lowest strata of economic and social life (Kitano, 1981).

Southeast Asians. After the American withdrawal from Vietnam in 1975, refugees from that conflict—Vietnamese, Cambodians, and Laotians—became America's newest refugee group, together totaling about 346,000 by April 1980 (Kitano, 1981: 136). Most were Vietnamese (245,000) who settled in California, Texas, Virginia, the state of Washington, and Oregon (U.S. Department of Commerce, 1990: 39) and now constitute the largest Asian American subgroup at almost one million, or about one-fourth of the Asian American population (O'Hare and Felt, 1991: 2). Some of the early arriving Southeast Asian immigrants had outstanding educational backgrounds, while other late arrivals were illiterate; most are resented by Americans, who have opposed their immigration, particularly that of the Vietnamese, out of prejudice as well as a fear of job competition (Kitano, 1981: 137).

According to the National Minority Advisory Council on Criminal Justice, 60 percent of the Vietnamese were white-collar workers in Vietnam, but even when downgraded to craftsmen, operatives, laborers, and other blue-collar workers in the United States, they reduced their unemployment rate of 32 percent during the first three months after arrival, to 14 percent after fifteen months in this country (NMAC, 1980), and further to 8.2 percent in 1980 (U.S. Department of Commerce, 1990: 39). However, in that same year, 35.1 percent of the Vietnamese population in America was below the poverty level.

Native Americans

Today's American Indian population are descendants of Mongolians from Asia who came to this country and Canada twenty thousand years ago. Thus, although Native Americans are the oldest inhabitants, they, too, are not truly indigenous. At one time, before the arrival of the Europeans, an estimated thirty to forty million Indians lived in the Western Hemisphere as members of hundreds of different tribes with different dialects, customs, and culture patterns (Rose, 1974: 20). Native Americans include American Indians, Aleuts, and Eskimos—the people of Arctic America who refer to themselves as Inuits, which in their language means "people" (Galey, 1973). Most available information concerns American Indians, since empirical data are lacking on Aleuts and Inuits, who, compared to native American Indians, are few in numbers.

It is also difficult to define Indians, since the definitions often change. For example, in 1950 the census defined people of mixed Indian and "white" or "black" ancestry as "others," and later, in the 1960 and 1970 censuses, individuals were asked to identify themselves (Deloria, 1981: 140). The fact that there are over 482 federally recognized tribes contributes heavily to the definition problem (Baker, 1977: 7).

Movies and history books, some honest, others dishonest, have depicted both sides of the Native American/"white" conflict throughout the years, and cultural historians are still coping with the problem. It is generally believed that the European occupation of the American continent contributed to the decline of the American Indian:

> Whether the settler out of sheer viciousness or unconquerable greed drove the native population from its ancestral home, decimating tribe after tribe until the pathetic survivors were herded onto reservations in the late nineteenth century, or merely brought to the new land the trappings of a foreign environment, liquor and disease, hostile to the Indian's continued existence, the result was still the same. (Sheehan, 1972: 7-8)

Beginning with the Spanish invaders, who were after both their riches and their religious fealty, and ending with the northern Europeans, who wanted their lands, practically every European group that came into contact with American Indians maltreated and abused them. In 1754 the British monarchy established a policy recognizing the tribes as independent nations who, along with their lands, were under the protection of the Crown. The American settlers, however, had different views, and as they moved farther and farther westward, the new American government "vacillated between attempts at bilateral negotiations with the members of the so called sovereign Indian nations and outright massacre and removal" (Rose, 1974: 21-22).

There are indications that some government policy makers in the first half of the eighteenth century had good intentions toward the Native Americans. Since attempts at civilizing the Indians had failed and the white man was having a deleterious effect on the Indian, it was thought that "the native could be saved only by removing him from harm's way. . . . Beyond the Mississippi, out of reach of the corrosive elements in the white man's way of life, he could be preserved and possibly civilized before the next advance of American society rolled over him" (Sheehan, 1972: 17). The forced, often brutal movement of thousands of Indians from eastern states to the Western Territories followed a route known as the "Trail of Tears." The Cherokees of Georgia and North Carolina who were uprooted from their tribal lands and driven along this trail in 1838 are reported to have lost one-third of their population in the trek to exile in the west (Rose, 1974: 22). One historian poignantly described the Indians struggling on this journey as "with bitter sorrow in their hearts, weakened by hardship and privation, decimated by disease, oppressed by penury, despondent and disheartened" (Sheehan, 1972: 9).

After the Civil War, government reservations were established to deal with the "Indian Problem," and soon after, Indians were made wards of the federal government when Congress, in 1871, passed legislation that no longer recognized Indian tribes as independent powers (Rose, 1974: 22). However, it was not until 1924 that Indians obtained United States citizenship; thus, "American Indians as a group are the nation's only minority group specially mentioned in the Constitution, the only minority once affirmed to have the sovereign right of self-government, the only minority whose sovereign government was denied the sovereignty of its territory—all profound and unique distinctions" (NMAC, 1980: 11).

During the first half of this century, located deep in their pastoral lands and rarely seeing non-Indians, Native Americans continued attempts to adjust to life on the reservations. Then World War II involved many Indians in the military and as war workers, thus linking the people of the reservations to the outside world. Since that time, Native Americans have fought numerous battles with the federal government, at least partially winning many of them over time. Congress tried, for example, to terminate federal responsibility for Indians in 1953, and Indians lost some federal rights in the process, but the policy was officially declared a failure by 1958. This era is also a part of the previously mentioned period when Indian families were forced from the reservations to urban areas. The 1960s civil rights epoch brought the plight of the American Indian to public attention as the "model racial minority," and through successful lobbying, tribes secured many benefits. But the Indians still feared termination. The 1970s did not clarify federal policy toward Native Americans any more than previous decades had, a situation that left "relations with state, federal, and local authorities in such areas as taxation, zoning and land use, civil and criminal jurisdiction, political representation, hunting and fishing, and access to social services" difficult or unresolved (Deloria, 1981: 141). The 1980s were not impressive in terms of settling many Native American concerns, but one thing seems certain: "The pervasive fear of Indians is that they will in the years ahead move from their plateau of small nationhood to the status of another ethnic group in the American melting pot. While such a development would be eagerly applauded by liberal policymakers in the federal government, for Indians it would mean the final spiritual surrender to dark forces" (ibid.: 149).

More than half of all Indians (719,047) live in urban-suburban areas, having migrated to such areas after World War II and in the middle 1950s, when federal policy initiated the movement of Indian families to the cities. Yet a large percentage of these families have relatives still living on reservations with whom they maintain close clan and kinship ties. The urban Indians tend to be older and to have smaller families, higher incomes, and better educations than the reservation Indians (ibid.: 148-149).

Some authors believe that the extensive Indian poverty is a result of government policy, and that Indians have had a harder time in this country than other minorities (Cummings and Harrison, 1972). There is clearly evidence to support this belief. For example, in 1980 the median Indian income was only $13,678, and 23.7 percent of Indians were living at or below the U.S. poverty level (U.S. Department of Commerce, 1990: 39).

The death risk today for Native Americans under age forty-five is almost twice that of Euro-Americans. Whereas 87 percent of excess deaths occur before the age of forty-five among American Indians, the comparative figure for African Americans is 39 percent. The majority of these deaths are due to six causes: unintentional injuries, cirrhosis, homicide, suicide, pneumonia, and diabetes (Heckler, 1985: 79).

Alcoholism, cirrhosis of the liver, and tuberculosis have long been major health problems among Indians. Average alcoholism mortality rates for the Indian population are five to six times the U.S. rate for all races (U.S. Department of Health, Education, and Welfare, 1978). The Secretary's Report on Minority Health states that "alcohol abuse is one of the most serious contributors to premature deaths among young adult American Indians" (Heckler, 1985: 79). The secretary's finding that motor vehicles are involved in almost half of all Native American accidental injuries is probably also alcohol-related, and such accidents are higher for Indians than for any other group.

In addition to health problems related to alcoholism, estimates of alcohol-related crimes range from 65 to 85 percent among American Indians, and their violent death rate is five times the Euro-American rate (Westermeyer and Brantner, 1972). Alcoholism has been described as reaching "epidemic proportions" among the Cheyenne-Arapaho Indians of western Oklahoma, where it is estimated that 75 percent of the remaining tribal members have some type of alcohol problem (Fairbanks, 1973: 55). Despite the fact that Indians seem to kill each other, and perhaps themselves, because of alcohol abuse, at least one study has shown that Indians have a lower suicide rate than other American groups (Westermeyer and Brantner, 1972). Although the use of drugs other than alcohol may be on the rise among Indian youth, in contrast to drug abuse among non-Indians in the United States, Indian narcotic abuse is rather uncommon. There is no historical evidence of drug abuse among Native Americans, but some drugs such as peyote have traditionally been an integral part of Native American culture through their use for religious and medicinal purposes (Baker, 1977).

Although exploited in the past, some tribes on reservations are now earning royalties for the rich minerals, oil, and other natural resources found on their tribal lands. Ranching, farming, fishing, recreation, and timber production are other traditional sources of income from these lands (Deloria, 1981: 145-146).

A Minority View

Any effort to understand the plight of racial minorities in the American criminal justice system must include the historical and experiential background of each of the groups and the evolutionary circumstances that helped to determine how they are defined and how these definitions have led to their contemporary status in that system. After their intensive national assessment of the impact of the criminal justice system on minorities and the impact of crime on minority communities, the National Minority Advisory Council on Criminal Justice (1980: 1) concluded that "America stands as a distinctive example of ethnic, religious, and linguistic pluralism, but it is also a classic example of heavy-handed use of state and private power to control minorities and suppress their continuing opposition to the hegemony of white racist ideology." According to these distinguished scholars, the root causes of conflict and disorder in the American criminal justice system are racism, political exploitation, and economic exploitation.

Race *prejudice* is rooted in the belief that one's own race warrants a positive attitude and that other races should be viewed negatively. When institutional power is added to prejudice, the result is *racism*. Within such a perspective, if the social, political, economic, religious, and educational structures or the major institutions in a society benefit a particular race—the "white" race in the United States—at the expense of other races, the practice is identified as *institutional racism*. While American minority peoples, similar to Euro-Americans, can be prejudiced, the fact that they lack control of institutional power prevents their subordination of Euro-Americans and negates definitions of them as racists. Therefore, the only accurately defined racists in the United States are those who control the primary institutions which are used to the advantage of one race at the expense of other races. Notions of "black racism" and "reverse racism" as practiced by minority group members are definitionally impossible. Finally, the negative and differential impact of racist practices against the subordinate American minorities by the Euro-American dominant group is *discrimination*.

Anyone who claims that racism and discrimination are not pervasive in the United States today, and that these insidious practices have not existed throughout the history of this country, is out of touch with the reality of the American structure. This chapter has only touched upon the historical racist mistreatment of minorities in the United States: the massacre of Native Americans, the lynchings of blacks and Orientals, the harassment and beatings of Hispanics, and the unjust criminal justice processing and incarceration of each of these groups. It is sufficient to note that the history of violence against minorities in this country and other countries, e.g., Viet Nam, is more typical than atypical, and it is rooted in racism. Further, the United States did not intern Americans of German or Italian descent during World War II, yet more than $1 billion in reparations were recently awarded to Japanese Americans for the shameful treatment they received, although they were also United States citizens, and not the enemy. That is racism.

A recent Media Genral–Associated Press poll found that "a majority of Americans say [our] society remains racist" (*Tallahassee Democrat*, 1988: 3A). That national survey revealed that four in ten believed that racial equality would not occur within their lifetimes, and 55 percent of the respondents said that overall the United States society is racist. Regarding treatment in the justice system, 61 percent of the black respondents said minorities are not treated as being equal to whites, compared to 40 percent of whites who felt that way, while 15 percent of whites surveyed did not know.

Racial prejudice, racism, and violence against African American citizens, for example, at New York's Howard Beach, against Vietnamese American citizens in Boston, against Cuban, Vietnamese, and Haitian American citizens in Florida, against Mexican American citizens in the West and Southwest, against Asian American citizens on the West Coast, and against Native American citizens just about anywhere in the continental United States, are common and are reported more and more frequently by the media. One has only to read the daily newspaper to realize the extent of race prejudice felt toward minorities in this country, as demonstrated by the numerous "incidents" taking place in almost every state in the union. In January 1988 the National Council of Churches stated, "A 'national epidemic' of hate-motivated violence against a growing variety of minority groups has affected every section of the country. . . . Not a day has passed in the last seven years without someone in the United States being victimized by hate violence" (*The Washington Post*, Nov. 14, 1988: A28). The council sought legislation to require the Justice Department to investigate hate crimes by such white-supremacist groups as the Aryan Nations, the Ku Klux Klan, Posse Comitatus, and the Order.

According to *The New York Review* (1988), in a survey by Howard Schuman and his colleagues, reported in their 1986 book, *Racial Attitudes in America,* one-third of the white American respondents supported laws against interracial marriages. This could be considered an improvement, since in 1963, 62 percent of white Americans felt that miscegenation should be a crime. The authors conclude that "while white people talk with considerable tolerance about blacks, this is a 'veneer that conceals continued profound racism on the part of most or all white Americans.' "

In 1989, a study released to the Associated Press by Northeastern University in Boston found that "crimes motivated by bigotry are more violent than previously assumed" (Levinson, 1989). The study examined 452 crimes which the Boston Police Community Disorders Unit identified as motivated by bigotry. Fifty-three percent of these crimes, which were reported from 1983 to 1987, were classified as physical assaults; 63 percent were perpetrated by whites, 33 percent by blacks, and the remaining 4 percent were committed by persons of Hispanic or Asian origin. Among the 65 percent of the victims who were non-white, the largest proportion, 32 percent, were black, followed by 12 percent Vietnamese, 11 percent other Asian, 7 percent Hispanic, and 1 percent Jews. At the time of the attacks, the victims in 30 percent of the cases were told they "did not belong" in the neighborhood. Most of the racial attacks involved four or more people ganging up against a lone victim. In one-third of the cases, the victims were females.

There are other notable facts to consider:

- Almost all of our cities (96.4 percent) are racially segregated.
- A former Ku Klux Klan Grand Dragon was elected a state representative in Louisiana, and later almost became governor.
- The National Council of Churches in 1988 deplored "a national epidemic of hate-motivated violence against a growing variety of minority groups."
- Research funded by the National Institute of Justice currently underway in New York City and Baltimore County concerns such bias-based violence, and Jim Garofalo's preliminary findings suggest what many people of color have known for most of their lives—minorities are targets of hatred and violent acts simply because of their skin color.

These are not isolated incidents but are mentioned to highlight only a small part of the very large problem of racism in this country.

Although minorities attending predominantly white majority colleges and universities have been aware of and experienced race prejudice for years, only recently have the hallowed halls of academe been exposed as racist and discriminatory. Professors and administrators in their ivory towers who appear to be removed from and oblivious to such practices—recently brought to light at Harvard and Brown universities, at Dartmouth and Swarthmore colleges, at the universities of Massachusetts, Rhode Island, Alabama, Maryland, and Texas (Curwood, 1986)—should take a closer look at their own campuses and talk to their minority students and faculty for enlightenment about prejudice, racism, and discrimination on the campuses of America. It is even more amazing that some social science researchers report that there is no discrimination in the criminal justice system.

If our surveyed citizens believe there is racism in this nation, if our media report proliferating racist incidents directed at minorities throughout the country, and if our own institutions of higher education—the universities—recognize that there is a problem, how can any social scientist seriously deny that there is racism in the criminal justice system, a system that has always been oppressive and repressive toward minorities? How could such an institutionalized, inhumane warehousing system, run predominantly by Euro-Americans and disproportionately inhabited by racial minorities, avoid the charge of racism? In answer, we are told to look at "the statistics."

To minority criminologists and criminal justice practitioners, such proclamations are especially disconcerting when these conclusions are based primarily upon routine manipulations of statistics and little or no contact with the "real" world. African American criminologist/geographer Daniel Georges-Abeyie (1990: 26) sums up the error of viewing institutionalized racism in the criminal justice system as a "myth" by finding one such argument (Wilbanks, 1986) "critically flawed because while he purports to examine the reality, mythology, and ideology of alleged systematic racial bias in the formal decision making process of the U.S. criminal justice system, his analysis consists of: the selective presentation of data, the selective utilization of his findings, unfounded ideological statements, and interpretation of 'fact.' "

2

The Minority "Crime Problem"

Stateside when they
say:
crime in the streets or
welfare cheats
they talkin bout us.

—Sam Greenlee

Statistics on Minority Crime

In criminal justice research, *statistics* describe criminal phenomena in terms of alleged actual incidents—generally arrests—and are usually transformed into rates and percentages for standardizations that enable cross-comparisons over time, by geographical area, or according to cultural, gender, or racial statuses (Sheley, 1985: 73). *Official statistics* are data collected by criminal justice agencies such as law enforcement, judicial, or prison systems. These figures concern incidents and offenders coming to the attention of the criminal justice system (Parisi, 1982: 112). The most frequently used official statistics are the United States crime data reported in the FBI Uniform Crime Reports, commonly known as UCRs.

Unofficial statistics are derived from "information that is not hampered by bias in the screening decisions of law enforcement personnel" (ibid.: 113) and include ongoing victimization survey studies such as those reported by the National Opinion Research Center (NORC) and the National Crime Survey (NCS), self-report studies, and information obtained from other research methods, for example, observational studies, case histories, and anecdotal data.

Any examination of race and crime first requires a description and explanation of the measures of crime and the problems associated with each. The types of statistics collected, how they are collected and interpreted, and by whom, are all important contributions to the notion of the "crime problem." It should be kept in mind, however, that elements external to minority communities such as racial discrimination and relative deprivation may also affect minority crime rates:

Therefore, efforts to determine whether there is a connection between race and crime should examine the empirical evidence and the legal/historical material to determine the extent to which crime rates are affected by inequalities in legislation, law enforcement, and data collection. In addition to considering the justice system itself as one source of racial discrimination, other sources that affect minority group crime must be explored. (Sample and Philip, 1984: 27)

Although an individual's criminal history includes all information gathered by criminal justice agencies from arrest through final release from correctional supervision, the linchpin of such a record is the arrest.

The two most common indices of crime currently accepted in the United States are the Uniform Crime Reports (UCR) and victimization surveys. With the exception of a very few studies, self-report data in which offenders are asked the extent of their involvement in crime are primarily concerned with juvenile offenders. Such self-reported crime is often summarily dismissed by social scientists because of the limited population examined (teenagers), despite the potential value of validation through the cross-checking of offenders' reports with "official" records.

The Uniform Crime Reporting Program

In 1927, a subcommittee of the International Association of Chiefs of Police (IACP) was charged with the task of studying uniform crime reporting. This Committee on Uniform Crime Records suggested standards for reporting crime information and initiated a voluntary national data collection effort in 1930. Later that year the United States Congress appointed the Federal Bureau of Investigation (FBI) as the national clearinghouse for statistical information on crime. Crime data were first published monthly, then quarterly, then semi-annually; since 1958, the Uniform Crime Reports (UCR) have been published on an annual basis, drawing upon arrest information obtained from the nation's law enforcement agencies. Today, nearly sixteen thousand law enforcement agencies across the country voluntarily contribute crime statistics based on offenses coming to their attention, providing a periodic assessment of the extent of crime in the nation (Reid, 1979).

Data on the offenses that come to the attention of law enforcement agencies were selected by the IAPC subcommittee since, at that time, these data were more readily available than any other reportable crime information, and further, as complete a picture as possible of crime in the United States was desired. Because of their frequency, seriousness, and odds-on chance of being reported to law enforcement agents, seven serious offenses known as the Crime Index offenses were initially selected to serve as an index for evaluating fluctuations in the volume of crime. Today, with the addition of arson, there are eight Crime Index offenses, also known as Part I offenses, which include four violent Index crimes (murder and nonnegligent manslaughter, forcible rape, robbery, and aggravated assault) and four property Index crimes (burglary, larceny-theft, motor vehicle theft, and arson). Part II, or the less serious, offenses include other assaults, forgery and counterfeiting, fraud, embezzlement, stolen property (buying, receiving, possessing), vandalism, weapons (carrying, possessing), prostitution and commercialized vice, sex offenses (except forcible rape and prostitution), drug abuse violations, gambling, offenses against family and children, driving under the influence, liquor law violations, drunkenness, disorderly conduct, vagrancy, all other offenses (except traffic), suspicion, curfew and loitering violations, and runaways (a juvenile status offense).

Although the Part II crimes are the most prevalent, the FBI Index offenses are the crimes of most concern to the general public and to social scientists. Other crimes, such as organized crime, computer crimes, and other "white-collar" crimes, particularly those committed by corporations (e.g., hazardous wastes, price fixing) and professionals such as medical doctors, lawyers, and accountants (e.g., fee splitting), and many occupational crimes (e.g., false advertising, bogus auto and appliance repairs), are not identified in the UCRs despite the billions of dollars in losses involved and the physical and mental injuries incurred by victims and their families.

LIMITATIONS OF UCR ARREST DATA

As Nettler (1978: 57) points out, "All social statistics are suspect." The dubious validity of official crime measures has handicapped studies of crime and deviance and the scope of the public policies they address (Skogan, 1981). Problems with official crime measurements, such as UCRs, not only render findings on crime questionable, but "the misreporting and underreporting apparently endemic in current official statistics has led to their widespread devaluation" (Skogan, 1975: 19). Gove, Hughes, and Geerken (1985: 455) face the problem squarely when they state: "Unless we have a fair understanding of the characteristics of crimes that become official and those that do not, we are on very tenuous ground when we use official statistics to try to determine if crime is related to such things as income, racial inequality, urban density, city size, governmental structure, or a variety of other variables, for we do not know what the crime rates measure."

In an empirical examination of the validity of official crime statistics, Skogan (1974: 25-26) describes these statistics as a reflection of the interaction between crime, victim reporting, and police discovery and recording. Crime, or what goes on "out there" in the environment (Skogan, 1974), must first be defined before it can be reported. Crime is viewed by some as a matter of perception, a perception frequently "mediated through newspapers and television" (Abadinsky, 1987: 46). Perceived seriousness of crime is apparently universal across all segments of our society and thus largely determines the crimes that warrant reporting, particularly if a weapon is used and serious personal injury or large financial loss occurs. As Gove, Hughes, and Geerken (1985: 467) note, "Detection of a criminal offense involves both observing an event and defining that event as a criminal act." Such an event, they add, may not be viewed as a crime by a citizen if s/he does not agree with the legal definition of the act as criminal and/or does not recognize the illegal nature of the act. Clearly, citizen perceptions and definitions of crime influence the amount of crime officially known, since most crimes become officially known through victims or witnesses. Some crimes are witnessed in progress by the police, but for the most part, the role of modern-day law enforcement is reactive, or a response to citizens' crime complaints. Furthermore, there is the additional problem of discovery: some crimes are simply never uncovered (Hindelang, 1974).

Reporting. Once a crime is discovered, there are two potential sources of reporting error—the victim and the police.

A number of studies reveal several reasons why citizens, particularly victims, do not report Index crimes to the police (e.g., Skogan, 1974, 1975; Booth, Johnson, and Choldin, 1977; Cohen and Land, 1984; Gove, Hughes, and Geerken, 1985). Some property crimes are considered not worth the trouble of going to court and possibly losing time from employment. Victims of robbery, burglary, and larceny may view the crime as trivial if the amount involved is small. Other victims do not want to initiate contact with the police because they do not view law enforcement as very effective and feel that not much would be done, especially if the perpetrator was a stranger. In some instances, the victim may be fearful of coming to the attention of the police because of a past record or some other trouble with the law that might be uncovered. Then there are groups, particularly minorities, who, through negative past experiences, are suspicious of and biased against police officers. Rape victims typically are shamed and humiliated by their experience and would rather not discuss it with police officers. Many rape victims may fear reprisals from their assailants and, if the rapist was a friend or family member, would prefer not to report the crime. Finally, many victims consider the incident, particularly assault, a private matter which they intend to settle themselves by exacting their own forms of "justice."

Policing. The numerous problems found in law enforcement procedures and practices that contribute to the question of valid official crime statistics include indicators concerning discovery, police discretion, recording, classification, technical law enforcement procedures, and organizational and political issues.

Decker and Kohfeld (1985: 437) describe the broad role of the police, who, as "street-level bureaucrats," have vast discretionary powers. They argue that "police activity follows criminal activity," or that increased frequency of crimes leads to a corresponding amount of police activity and increased arrests in the particular crime area (ibid.: 445). Similarly, observational studies of police-citizen encounters find that the decision to write a formal report is greatly influenced by the seriousness of the offense and the preferences of the complainant (Black, 1970). In such instances, it was observed that if the protagonists in the dispute are close, or nonstrangers, there is a small likelihood that the case will result in final court action. Further, police were found to file reports which involved complainants of high social status, especially those who showed deference to the police (Skogan, 1975; Booth, Johnson, and Choldin, 1977). Police discretion in the screening of such cases is of utmost concern when the validity and usefulness of police statistics are considered (Gove, Hughes, and Geerken, 1985: 470).

A study of bureaucratic decision making within police departments in Chicago illustrates a two-stage, discretionary selection process that reduces the validity of official police statistics. Maxfield, Lewis, and Szoc (1980) compared calls for police service with crime reports filed by investigating officers. The first decision point was when a police dispatcher screened citizen calls, 40 percent of which were resolved at that point; the second decision involved the investigating officers, who had the discretion to determine if the incident was a crime to be recorded. Police involvement in a call for service is terminated if the incident was not recorded as a verified crime. In such instances the failure to record incidents functions as a means of regulating police workloads, or "load-shedding," with resultant reduced police time on the crime scene and subsequent reduced paperwork (Maxfield, Lewis, and Szoc, 1980: 228).

Organizational and political factors affect the number of crimes reported to the FBI in a variety of ways. Sutherland and Cressey (1978: 29) note that an accurate index of crime is possible only when honesty, efficiency, and consistency are characteristic of the officers preparing the reports. Police may underreport crime and underarrest criminals for political reasons—for example, at election time to demonstrate a low crime rate. Police departments may also "down-classify" crimes to demonstrate a lower Crime Index (reducing grand larceny to petty larceny), systematically "unfound" complaints to indicate a low crime rate in a jurisdiction (Abadinsky, 1987: 58-60), or use both measures to show the voters the effectiveness of a new administration (Booth, Johnson, and Choldin, 1977: 188). On the other hand, to reflect "good" police work, arrest figures can also be inflated through frequent and increased arrests, and by counting numbers of offenses, not numbers of people arrested. Often more than one crime is involved in an incident: a burglary may include breaking and entering, or a homicide may have involved a rape. Although the UCR counts only the most serious offense in Index crimes—the "hierarchy rule" (Abadinsky, 1987: 53)—statistics may be inflated at the local level by counting each crime committed in a single incident.

The amount of crime reported to the FBI is influenced by more efficient police training, increases in the number of police personnel, the institution of highly specialized police divisions, and organized drives against specific crimes. Law enforcement professionalism and fiscal resources have also been found to be related to more accurate and complete reporting of crime (Gove, Hughes, and Geerken, 1985).

Victimization Surveys

In 1967, members of ten thousand households across the country were asked about their victimization experiences over the twelve months prior to the interview. This first nationwide victimization study was conducted for the President's Commission on Law Enforcement and the Administration of Justice by the National Opinion Research Center (NORC). Since many people do not report crimes to the police, it was no surprise that the rate of Index offenses found in the NORC results was almost twice that found by the UCR (Hinde-lang, 1974). Since July 1972, a series of even more comprehensive victimization surveys have been conducted by the National Crime Survey (NCS) program administered by the Bureau of the Census for the U.S. Justice Department (Brown and Woolley, 1983).[1]

Unlike the UCRs, which are dependent upon a vast number of reporting law enforcement agencies with different classifications of crime, reporting, and cod-ing procedures, the NCS is conducted by a single data-collection agency using a uniform method. The NCS program comprises two sets of surveys: periodic surveys of twenty-six central U.S. cities and a continuing panel design utilizing a representative national sample of 100,000 persons, or about 50,000 American households, whose members twelve years of age and over are interviewed every six months for three years. Whereas early studies randomly selected an adult as an informant about the victimization experiences of the entire household, today total household enumerations are employed to reduce survey error (Skogan, 1975: 23). As a major new source of data about rape, robbery, assault, burglary, larceny, and vehicle theft, the NCS provides previously unavailable detailed in-formation concerning these specific crimes, such as victim losses and reasons for nonreporting of crime (Garofalo and Hindelang, 1977: 33).

A redesigned National Crime Survey of victimizations in the United States was implemented in 1986 to address three major concerns: "the accuracy of data collected by the survey, the methodology used to collect data, and the enhance-ment of options for data analysis provided by the survey" (Taylor, 1989: 3). These new changes and revisions and the training of interviewers for a 100 percent phase-in were scheduled to be completed by July 1991 if no serious problems had been uncovered in earlier stages of the redesign project (Taylor, 1989: 10). Meanwhile, as with official Uniform Crime Reports, a number of limitations remain that need to be overcome in victimization surveys.

LIMITATIONS OF VICTIMIZATION SURVEYS

Various problems concerned with the samples have been emphasized by some critics of the National Crime Survey. Brown and Woolley (1983) are critical of the use of NCS city data to calculate correlation and regression coefficients, and they seriously question the representativeness and results of such applications. According to these critics, sampling theory implications are violated because of the small number of cities included in the sample (N = 26). Questions of sample size were raised regarding the ten thousand households and twenty-five hundred commercial establishments included in the city surveys. A much larger number is needed to locate significant numbers of crimes for each of the eight NCS catego-ries. In Philadelphia, for example, only twenty-nine interviews with rape victims formed the basis for the rape victimization rate; and among about ten thousand households, the survey in Detroit yielded only 150 robbery victims (Gove, Hughes, and Geerken, 1985; Abadinsky, 1987).

Another deficiency is seen in the fact that sampling occurs within a city's geographical boundaries, yet an estimated 13 percent of the daytime population in cities consists of suburban commuters, a figure that does not include tourists, visitors, conventioneers, and transients such as people who move from the area just prior to the survey (Skogan, 1975; Booth, Johnson, and Choldin, 1977). Brown and Woolley (1983) point out that this automatic exclusion of some classes of victims results in their victimizations' being undetected. Even if they report their experiences to the police, these victims are not included in the sampling frame and thus are not interviewed; yet they are a population at risk of crime victimization.

An additional source of error related to the surveyed, or target, population occurs when victimizations of a city resident are counted whether the incident occurs within the resident's city or the resident is outside the city at the time of the victimization (Gove, Hughes, and Geerken, 1985).

In an intensive treatise on the issues involved in the measurement of victimization, Skogan (1981) describes measurement and procedural problems. Victimization surveys collect information about criminal incidents through interviews with respondents; thus, this form of self-reporting of past events raises important measurement issues reflective of fundamental human processes which lead to four kinds of error described by Skogan (1981): ignorance of events, forgetting or failure to tell of incidents, inaccurate or incomplete recall of incidents, and differential productivity of survey respondents.

Victimization surveys rely on the victim's definition of criminal acts. Respondents may not recognize an incident as a crime or may tend to exclude broad ranges of their experience as not contained within criminal law. Record checks demonstrate that police crime classifications differ from those of victims, with the latter tending to be more serious (Gove, Hughes, and Geerken, 1985).

In addition to forgetting events, some respondents lie, or deliberately suppress reports of events about which they have full knowledge. In such instances, they may have been victimized by persons they know, or simply may consider that it is not the interviewer's business. The survey may raise the memory of a painful situation which the victim would like to forget; "traumas may remain vivid as though they 'happened only yesterday' " (Abadinsky, 1987: 69). As in official reports, rapes are highly underreported in victimization studies. In such cases, more accurate information concerning the rape incident is obtained if the offender was a stranger. Finally, victims who are themselves culpable may also be motivated to suppress information about criminal incidents, for example, in "victim precipitated" crimes (Skogan, 1981), or when their own negligence is a factor, such as leaving the key in the front door lock and subsequently being burglarized (Abadinsky, 1987).

Inaccurate or incomplete recall of incidents may result from mistakes by the victim-respondent, but may also reflect a deliberate attempt to misconstrue the victim's role in a crime, the value of a stolen object, or the identity of an offender (Skogan, 1981). Victims are reluctant to report clashes with friends or relatives and, as in official statistics, rapes by family members very often go unreported. An additional problem is fraudulent claims made for reasons of personal vendettas, to hide one's own involvement, or for purposes of filing excessive insurance claims for stolen property (Skogan, 1975).

Differential respondent productivity is indicated when victimization survey respondents differ in their willingness and ability to be productive in the interview. Level of respondent sophistication is also influential—"in general, more highly educated respondents are more cooperative, more at ease in interview situations, and more able to recall the details of events" (ibid.: 22).

Interviewer Skills and Effects. Some interviewers elicit more and varied information from respondents than others (Gove, Hughes, and Geerken, 1985). Not only do the skills of interviewers vary, based on the degree of their training and supervision, but variations in their biases may substantially affect the survey data. Interviewers differ in their understanding of the survey purpose, the interpretation of survey items, and their explanations of them to respondents, the assessment and recording of respondents' answers to questions, and the depth and vigor of probing for more detailed comments, as contrasted to ready acceptance of nonresponses (Skogan, 1981: 27-28). Finally, some critics suggest that interviewers with vested interests in victimization surveys sponsored by the government may lead the respondent during the interview, or at the coding stage demonstrate bias in classifying responses, in an unconscious or intentional effort to exaggerate the crime problem (Brown and Woolley, 1983).

Problems with the Measurement of Minority Crime

Each of the previously outlined problems in the official and unofficial measurement of crime (Uniform Crime Reports and victimization surveys) affects crime rates and statistics involving minorities. In addition, there are factors that uniquely impact the measurement of minority crime. As Nettler (1978: 73) observes: "The major charge against the use of official statistics as data for criminological theory is that they are biased, and biased principally against poor people and visible minorities." The consequences of such errors for visible, and especially poor, minorities in the United States are far-reaching both for the minorities involved and for race relations in the nation. This quandary is intimately related to the reporting, policing, recording, and measurement of crime as it concerns visible minorities.

Reporting. Reporting practices for certain crimes, such as forcible rape, have been found to differ in accordance with racial status. White rape victims tend to report black offenders more often to the police than they do white offenders (Hindelang, 1978). Also, black rape victims are more likely to overreport black perpetrators and underreport white perpetrators (Weiss and Borges, 1973). Rapists and other offenders of Spanish heritage are often reported as black, which leads to false statistics. Other racial characteristics may affect victims' accounts because of popular stereotypes and misconceptions of criminals (Hindelang, 1978).

Wilbanks reanalyzed 1981 victimization survey results and introduced the question of choice or selection of victim. He concluded that "violent crime by black offenders appears to be predominantly interracial with 55.2% of the black offenders choosing white victims" (1985: 120). The implication, and a common belief of Euro-Americans, is that blacks are looking for whites to victimize. Wilbanks, like other social scientists, seems particularly concerned with interracial rape, which according to Robert O'Brien has "received more attention in the literature than . . . research on all other violent crimes combined" (1987: 820). O'Brien points out that a focus on tabular data, by column, from the offender perspective, such as Wilbanks emphasizes, would "dramatically portray the interracial nature of rape and, more specifically, the greater relative frequency of black involvement" (1987: 822), but the more realistic model would take into account the relative sizes of the black and white populations in the United States, their rates of interaction, and the proportions of such crimes expected. Under such an analysis, O'Brien finds that interracial rapes (and other interracial violent crimes, except homicide) of both black offender–white victim and white offender–black victim are less frequent than expected. Conversely, rates of intraracial rape are greater than expected. Instead of blacks' seeking out white victims, as Wilbanks would have it, O'Brien suggests that rates of interaction are relatively greater for minority groups. Put another way, in at least seven Standard Metropolitan Statistical Areas, the probability of a black's interacting with a white is .57, or 19 to 1, while the probability of a white's interacting with a black is .03, or 7.72 to 1 (ibid.: 833). In other words, there are more whites for blacks to interact with, and therefore potentially more black-white crime compared to white-black crime.

Statistics on black-white rape are undoubtedly inflated because of false accusations. The two most common occurrences of such false reporting take place when a white woman has voluntary sexual relations with a black male and upon discovery cries "rape," or when the assailant is white and known by the victim, who attributes the rape to the "proverbial black stranger" (Baughman, 1966). A victim might participate in such deception, according to Mintz (1973: 708), "to conceal promiscuous behavior, to obtain an abortion, to take revenge," or, in the case of lower-class women acquainted with the offenders, to use the police as a weapon to control men. McNeely and Pope (1978: 409) further suggest that whites may characterize behavior differently based upon their perceptions of an antagonist's racial identity: "A belligerent attempt to establish contact with a white female stranger may be interpreted as an attempted rape if the person attempting to make the contact is black; it may be interpreted quite differently if he is not." Another example of the possible influence of racial sterotypes on perception is cited by McNeely and Pope (1981a) in a study in which subjects were shown pictures of a white man holding a razor during an argument with a black man. When the pictures were described to others, the white subjects recalled the black man as wielding the razor!

A forward record check during a Portland, Oregon victimization survey which matched crimes reported to the police by respondents with the retrieved original police reports found only 34 percent agreement on racial characteristics of suspects between the survey and police data (Schneider, 1981: 43). Further, the victims tended to overestimate the number of incidents including black suspects compared with police estimates of the suspects' race. Concern was expressed that "victimization survey data may not be an accurate reflection of racial characteristics of offenders if victims project racial bias or prejudice into their perception of who committed the crime" (Schneider, 1981: 43). Also, it is not uncommon for white offenders to blacken their faces in order to disguise themselves and be mistaken for blacks in the commission of crimes (Baughman, 1966).

Policing. A person's initial contact with the criminal justice system is customarily with law enforcement personnel. There is an abundance of research and literature indicating differential treatment of minorities by police officers, a topic addressed in more detail in Chapter 4. The disproportionate arrest rate for minorities may be the result of police selection bias (Savitz, 1973; McNeely and Pope, 1980). There is more police surveillance in minority communities, and since, for example, the black and Hispanic populations are youthful and more likely to be in the streets, and thus more visible, it is conceivable that they are at higher risk of being arrested. The noted geographer Keith Harries (1984: 41) suggests that black crime may be inflated in the UCR because of this "surveillance effect": since blacks are in the streets for recreation and social contact, they are "more likely to be picked up for acts that might occur in private in a white middle-class neighborhood."

When the initiation of the arrest process involves a complainant—the most frequent method of police response to an offense—the vigor of subsequent police action has been found to relate to police biases. The tendency to arrest minorities more than nonminority offenders is exacerbated when the victim is white (Agopian, Chappell, and Geis, 1974). In such instances, the police may respond differently in the way they investigate and record the case. The arrest situation may also be expedited if a minority suspect does not show deference to the officer. In a number of early studies, extralegal factors such as demeanor and attitude were found to possibly influence the police processing of black youth (Piliavin and Briar, 1964; Thornberry, 1973). Despite the fact that minorities are more militant today, some social scientists continue to believe that such social factors have only a modest influence on police arrest decisions (e.g., Gove, Hughes, and Geerken, 1985).

Recording. A police recording practice that tends to inflate minority arrest statistics is listing only the number of arrests and not the number of people arrested. If, for example, one minority male is arrested several times for several different rapes, each of these arrests appears in the reports as a separate incident. Under such a reporting method, the arrest statistics give the erroneous impression that there are several minority rapists who have perpetrated several rapes, instead of a lone rapist, thus disproportionately inflating the total number of minorities arrested for rape. This problem is further compounded in other personal crimes where each person is considered a victim; that is, if a person assaults five people, the police report includes five acts of assault, again inflating the arrest rate (Savitz, 1973).

Measurement. Crime and arrest rates are computed on the basis of census-enumerated general populations. It has been long established that the U.S. Census undercounts substantial numbers of minorities, particularly young black males and other minorities in the same age group as the offending population. The result is an artificially inflated minority crime rate, since if the population base is smaller, the rate is larger. Harries (1980: 11) notes the problem of expressing crime as a total population-specific rate (per 100,000 persons) instead of crime-specific rates which adjust the denominator in the calculation according to the population "at risk," for example, for rape, the specific target female age group.

The previous discussion of problems with victimization surveys referred to the skill levels and effectiveness of interviewers. Clearly, surveys undertaken in minority communities would provide more accurate results if minority interviewers were involved, but this is usually not the case. Cultural, economic, and language differences are a few of the potential differences between nonminority interviewers and minority survey respondents that could lead to distortions or misinterpretation of events described by respondents. Of course, this assumes that a minority respondent would be truthful and/or cooperative with an interviewer who is not a member of the respondent's minority subgroup. There is a tendency for minorities who are queried by nonminority researchers and surveyers to "tell them what they want to hear." In urban ghettos and barrios, any stranger with a clipboard or briefcase who knocks on your door is immediately suspect, whatever the skin color.

Another measurement issue involving victimization surveyors concerns their possible personal biases. If an interviewer brings racial prejudice, preheld misconceptions, or biases into the interview situation, such prejudgments and attitudes could seriously affect the final reports.

Although each of the reporting, policing, recording, and measurement problems described tends to overinflate minority involvement in crime, there are also indications that there is underreporting of such crime which leads to biased official statistics. It has been noted that blacks and possibly members of the lower class are less likely to report incidents to the police unless they are more serious crimes (Gove, Hughes, and Geerken, 1985: 470). Also, police dispatchers may filter calls from minority areas of a city and not send police to investigate minor incidents in those areas (Maxfield, Lewis, and Szoc, 1980: 234). Lastly, the "under class" hypothesis suggests that "the poor, black, unemployed and otherwise disaffected segments of the urban population receive services that are lower in quality and quantity compared to those received by their middle class counterparts" (ibid.: 227). As applied here, this hypothesis would find police less likely to respond, with resulting lower crime recording, in poor, minority, urban areas.

In sum, official statistics are fraught with a variety of problems, including an array of special problems associated with minority involvement in crime. In noble attempts to find congruence, and perhaps some validity for the Uniform Crime Reports, comparisons of UCR and victim survey data have yielded mixed findings. For example, Gove, Hughes, and Geerken (1985: 491) conclude that "the UCR are at least as valid and probably more valid than the data from victimization surveys." They also add, "When the UCR are used it should perhaps be made clear that one is dealing with the relatively serious crimes which tend to pass through the citizen and police filters and are officially reported" (ibid.). While noting their inability to bring the UCR and NCS rates into correspondence for some Index crimes, Cohen and Land (1984: 523) suggest that "provided sufficient urban structural control variables are utilized," certain officially determined Index crimes may reasonably coincide with their victimization counterparts. Finally, Booth, Johnson, and Choldin (1977: 196) conclude that while not totally inconsistent, neither the UCR nor victimization surveys are satisfactory indexes of crime, since they are measuring different phenomena. Obviously, the question of accurate crime measurement, particularly serious crime involving minorities, remains unanswered.

Types of Minority Crime

The following description of types of minority crime is based primarily on analyses of the 1986 Uniform Crime Reports (UCR). Prior to 1980, it was difficult to extract the extent of Hispanic crime from the UCR, since this subgroup was variously categorized as white, black, or "other."[2] The 1986 UCR define Hispanics as an ethnic group and compare them to non-Hispanics. Clearly, this classification introduced new problems for comparisons between Hispanics and whites, as well as comparisons with other minority groups, since the non-Hispanic group presumably includes all others who are not Hispanic. At any rate, the problem will be of little future consequence, since designation by ethnic origin of persons arrested was discontinued after the 1986 UCR reporting year (FBI, 1987: 5).

Since several problems with official statistics were reviewed earlier, they will not be reiterated here, but the weaknesses in such measurements should be kept in mind during the following discussion of each of the four major minority groups—African Americans, Hispanic Americans, Native Americans, and Asian Americans. The arrests of these minorities are examined and compared with those for the white subgroup in terms of types of crime for which they were arrested in 1986. Two methods were used to examine the arrest statistics: the customary across-race analysis and an approach that may provide a more accurate portrayal of types of crime committed—the proportion of arrests within racial/ethnic groups. The within-group comparisons utilized here are not affected by the UCR Hispanic/non-Hispanic dichotomy, but comparisons across groups, while descriptive, are less reliable.

The rationale for the within-group reporting method is best understood by an example from the UCR arrest tables categorized by gender of the offender. Among other ways of reporting arrest statistics, when addressing female arrests the UCR record two percentage distributions: one that compares males and females and a second that provides the proportion of male and female arrests for each crime. In the latest available statistics, use of this technique shows that females were 68.4 percent of those arrested for prostitution and commercialized vice in 1988, but also reveals that this offense was only 3 percent of all female arrests (FBI, 1989: 185). Thus, if we look at only the female proportion of prostitution arrests, we are easily misled into concluding that prostitution is a major arrest offense of females, when it clearly is not; instead, larceny-theft, at 19.6 percent of all female arrests, is the most frequent crime for which females are apprehended. Unfortunately, the UCR do not provide this information based on race, with the result that we obtain a distorted picture of minority crime (and also white crime) from researchers who rely on this reporting method. In an attempt to adjust for this methodological oversight and thereby more precisely express the types of crime which lead to arrest, recalculations of arrest offenses were made for each of the five racial/ethnic subgroups. Each of the minority groups under scrutiny and the white group are examined and compared by the 1986 UCR record for each of total crime arrests, Crime Index offenses, non-Index offenses, and their ten most frequent arrest offenses.[3] Studies of minority crime, which are also described, demonstrate that the emphasis on certain crimes, while reflective of researcher interest or public concern, is not always indicative of the most frequent crimes committed by minorities.

Another Perspective of Minority Crime

From Table 2-1 we note that, except for Asian Americans, minority groups are overrepresented in UCR arrests compared to their respective proportions in the U.S. population. Minorities constituted an estimated 20.5 percent of the population in 1980 (U.S. Census, 1980) but were 28.7 percent of the total persons arrested in 1986, 35.5 percent of those arrested for Index crimes, and 20.9 percent of non-Index crime arrestees.[4] On the other hand, whites were underrepresented: as 79.5 percent of the U.S. population, their respective arrest proportions were: total arrests, 71.3 percent; Index crimes, 64.5 percent; non-Index crimes, 73.1 percent.

Another interpretation of Table 2-1 is that the serious, or Index, crimes, which range from a low of 18.9 percent of total white arrests to 26.1 percent for both blacks and Asian Americans, do not account for a substantial proportion of any group's arrests. In fact, violent Index crimes are a small part of the crime committed by any group, with the lowest percentage represented by Native Americans (3.2 percent) and the highest by blacks (7.7 percent). Property Index crimes contribute the major portion of total Index crime for every group under consideration—whites are lowest, at 15.6 percent, while Asian Americans are highest, at 22.3 percent. From this analysis, it is apparent that non-Index, or less serious, crimes are the primary cause of American arrests.

TABLE 2-1: **Percentage of Crime Index Arrests by Race, 1986 Compared to U.S. Population Distribution***

Category	White	Minority*	Percent distribution**									
			White	Percent White	Black	Percent Black	Native Amer.	Percent Nat. Amer.	Asian Amer.	Percent Asian Amer.	Hispanic Amer.	Percent Hisp.
U.S. Population***	79.5	20.5	79.5	—	12.0	—	0.6	—	1.4	—	6.5	—
Total Arrests	71.3	28.7	71.3	—	27.0	—	1.0	—	0.7	—	12.7	—
Index Crimes	64.5	35.5	64.5	18.9	33.7	26.1	1.0	19.4	0.8	26.1	13.3	21.3
Violent	52.2	47.8	52.2	3.3	46.5	7.7	0.7	3.2	0.6	3.8	14.7	5.0
Property	67.8	32.3	67.8	15.6	30.2	18.4	1.0	16.2	0.9	22.3	12.9	16.3
Non-Index Crimes	73.1	20.9	73.1	81.1	25.2	73.9	1.1	80.6	0.6	73.9	12.6	78.7

*Source: FBI *Uniform Crime Reports, 1986*: Table 38 (p. 182) and Table 39 (p. 185).
**Excludes Hispanic arrests which in UCR are compared with non-Hispanics.
***U.S. Census *United States Summary*, General Population Characteristics, 1980.

AFRICAN AMERICAN ARRESTS

The usual statistic reported on African American crime is the proportion of Index crimes attributed to blacks. For example, according to the UCR, in 1986 blacks were arrested for 46.5 percent of violent crimes and 30.2 percent of property crimes, for an overall Crime Index proportion of 33.7 percent (FBI, 1987: 182). As seen in Table 2-1, the total percentage of blacks arrested in that year was more than twice (27 percent) the percentage of blacks in the U.S. population (12 percent). Further, the proportion of blacks arrested for violent crime (46.5 percent) is almost four times the black population percentage, while property crime (30.2 percent) and the total Crime Index (33.7 percent) percentages are more than twice that proportion.

An examination of the eight offenses making up the Crime Index[5] reveals that whites are arrested at a rate far below their proportion in the U.S. population (79.5 percent) in every offense category, while the reverse is true for black arrestees. However, not surprisingly, because of their larger population numbers, white Crime Index arrests exceed black arrests for every offense except robbery (37 percent vs. 62 percent).

This is the usual way that UCR arrests are compared across race. Another way of examining these UCR statistics is within the subgroup instead of between subgroups. This method provides a different picture of an offender population by expressing the proportion of each type of crime relative to that specific group's total arrests. Looked at from this internal perspective, we find that only 7.7 percent of black arrests are for violent crimes, and 18.4 percent are for property crimes, yielding a total within-group Crime Index of 26.1 percent. In other words, 73.9 percent of the crimes for which blacks are arrested are less serious, non-Index crimes. It is commonly reported that blacks are 46.5 percent of those arrested for violent Index crimes, but it is seldom reported that such crimes are only 7.7 percent of all black arrests. Of the four violent Index crimes—murder and nonnegligent manslaughter, forcible rape, robbery, and aggravated assault—blacks are arrested primarily for aggravated assault (4.2 percent) and robbery (2.7 percent), which together are 6.9 percent of total black arrests. Two of the crimes most feared by the public, murder and rape, account for an extremely small proportion of black crime (less than 1 percent combined).

Index property crime reveals a different picture, for we now find that although whites make up 67.8 percent and blacks 30.2 percent of those arrested, within-group analysis reveals that these crimes are 18.4 percent of total black arrests, although this proportion is not as high as that for Asian Americans (22.3 percent), a minority which exceeds all of the other subgroups in this category. Larceny-theft is the crime contributing most to the Index property crime statistic and is the most frequent arrest offense of all groups. Larceny-theft, burglary, and aggravated assault constitute the three most frequent Crime Index arrest offenses of all five subgroups.

With regard to non-Index crime, blacks are arrested for "all other offenses" (27.3 percent) more frequently than whites and any other minority group except Asian Americans (28.1 percent). This "catchall" category reflects parochial crime legislation and includes all violations of state or local laws not listed as Crime Index offenses, non-Index offenses, or traffic offenses (FBI, 1987: 332). Drug abuse violations (7.9 percent), other assaults (6.9 percent), disorderly conduct (6.2 percent), and driving under the influence (5.0 percent) are the major non-Index arrest offenses of blacks.

Excluding the category "all other offenses" (27.3 percent), which is the most frequent UCR arrest category for all subgroups of offenders, and juvenile offenses such as curfew and loitering violations and runaways,[6] a within-group rank ordering of the ten most frequent arrest offenses of African Americans in 1986 is as follows: (1) larceny-theft, (2) drug abuse violations, (3) other assaults, (4) disorderly conduct, (5) driving under the influence (DUI), (6) drunkenness, (7) aggravated assault, (8) burglary, (9) fraud, and (10) robbery. As noted in Table 2-2, four out of these ten are Index crimes, which is more than for any other subgroup. An additional four out of the ten most frequent arrests are for "victimless crimes," or crimes against the public order, which together constitute 41.4 percent of the top ten arrest offenses of blacks. These ten offenses made up more than half (57.9 percent) of all black arrests in 1986.

TABLE 2-2: **Within Group Ranking of the Ten Most Frequent 1986 Arrest Offenses, by Race***

Offense	White	Black	Rankings Hispanic	Indian	Asian
D.U.I.**	1	5	1	2	2
Larceny-Theft***	2	1	3	3	1
Drunkenness**	3	6	2	1	9
Drug Abuse Violations**	4	2	4	7	4
Liquor Laws**	5	–	8	4	5
Other Assaults	6	3	5	6	3
Disorderly Conduct**	7	4	6	5	7
Burglary***	8	8	7	8	6
Fraud	9	9	–	–	–
Vandalism	10	–	–	10	10
Aggravated Assault***	–	7	9	9	8
Robbery***	–	10	–	–	–
Weapons	–	–	10	–	–

*Excludes "all other offenses," the most frequent arrest for all groups.
**A "victimless" crime.
***An Index crime.
Source: FBI *Uniform Crime Report, 1986.*

A look at the three most frequent arrest offenses of blacks—larceny-theft, drug abuse violations, and other assaults—gives a clearer portrayal of African American crime. These offenses, an Index crime (larceny-theft), a "victimless crime" (drugs), and a non-Index violent crime (other assaults), portray black crime more realistically than the customary method of UCR reporting. The fourth-, fifth-, and sixth-ranked crimes—disorderly conduct, driving under the influence, and drunkenness—are all "victimless" crimes commonly associated with alcohol. With the exception of fraud (ranked ninth), the remaining lower-ranking arrest offenses of blacks are Index crimes: aggravated assault (seventh), burglary (eighth), and robbery (tenth). These serious crimes are only 11.5 percent of all of the crimes for which black Americans are arrested; and when larceny-theft is added, the total Index crimes in this ranking account for less than one-fourth (24.2 percent) of black arrests.

In sum, although there is obvious disproportionate involvement of African Americans in official arrest statistics compared with Euro-Americans and other minorities, with the exception of larceny-theft, the types of crime in which blacks are involved for the most part tend to reflect vague offenses peculiar to each jurisdiction ("all other offenses"), offenses against the public order (drugs, disorderly conduct, driving under the influence), or violent offenses most commonly committed against other blacks (other assaults, aggravated assault).

HISPANIC AMERICAN ARRESTS

Table 2-1 shows that Hispanic Americans are an estimated 6.5 percent of the U.S. population, but compared to non-Hispanics they were 12.7 percent of all persons arrested in 1986, a proportion almost twice that of their population. For total Crime Index arrests, the Hispanic percentage is 13.3 percent, with violent crimes at 14.7 percent and property crimes at 12.9 percent. Within the Hispanic American subgroup, Index crimes account for 21.3 percent of their total arrests, a percentage that ranks them second to blacks and Asian Americans (both at 26.1 percent). The majority of their arrests are for non-Index offenses (78.7 percent). As with the within-group black proportions, Index property crimes (16.3 percent) also exceed Index violent crimes (5.0 percent) in the Hispanic subgroup. Thus, although both African and Hispanic Americans would be reported as having higher violent than property Index offenses across groups, the within-group analysis reveals an opposite picture in terms of their criminality.

As indicated above, the Index crimes for which Hispanics are arrested most frequently are the same, and in the same order, as those for whites, Native Americans, and Asian Americans: larceny-theft (10.6 percent), burglary (4.1 percent), and aggravated assault (3.3 percent). With the exception of larceny-theft, which is lower for Hispanics than for any subgroup, the proportions of these crimes as a part of total Hispanic arrests do not vary by more than 1 percent from those for any other subgroup.

Nonserious Index arrests of Hispanic Americans yield a slightly different picture. As with whites and other minorities, "all other offenses" (18.7 percent) is the most frequent arrest category of Hispanics. In the total amount of Hispanic American crime, there are some variations in the proportions of non-Index offenses when compared with whites, but generally we find that Hispanics more closely resemble whites in their rates of arrest for non-Index crimes than they do other minorities in such offenses as driving under the influence (15.9 percent), drunkenness (12.1 percent), and drug abuse violations (10.4 percent). The non-Index crimes of whites and Hispanics also suggest similar crime patterns.

The ten most frequent arrest offenses of Hispanic Americans in 1986 were (1) DUI, (2) drunkenness, (3) larceny-theft, (4) drug violations, (5) other assaults, (6) disorderly conduct, (7) burglary, (8) liquor law violations, (9) aggravated assault, and (10) weapons violations. Within-group analysis reveals that these crimes account for over two-thirds (69.8 percent) of all the crimes for which Hispanic Americans were arrested, and an almost equal proportion (65.6 percent), or five out of ten, are victimless crimes. From Table 2-2, we note that four of the five public-order crimes are among the top-six-ranking Hispanic arrest categories—DUI (1), drunkenness (2), drug abuse violations (4), and disorderly conduct (6). Drinking, drug abuse, and the offenses associated with such practices seem to be the primary "crimes" of Hispanic Americans. Further, as in the African American group, the three Crime Index offenses in this ranking—larceny-theft, burglary, and aggravated assault—constitute a relatively small proportion of Hispanic crime, at 18 percent.

ASIAN AMERICAN ARRESTS

Until 1983, UCR statistics for Asian Americans were categorized as Chinese or Japanese, a classification that often revealed different arrest profiles for the two groups. For example, a within-group analysis of Crime Index offenses in 1979 (FBI, 1980) showed that 7 percent of Chinese arrests were for violent crimes, compared to only 3 percent for Japanese. Index property crime arrests that year were also higher for the Chinese (29 percent) than the Japanese (21 percent). The new UCR category, "Asian or Pacific Islander," referred to here as Asian American, leaves much to be desired, since any differences between cultural groups are masked.

As with whites, in 1986 the percentage of Asian American UCR arrests was lower than their representation in the U.S. population. Asian Americans are 1.4 percent of the nation's population, while their arrests make up less than 1 percent (0.7 percent) of total arrests, with Index crimes at .8 percent of all arrests, and violent and property crimes at .6 percent and .9 percent, respectively. Within-group analysis of the Asian American Crime Index arrests reveals some rather striking findings concerning the nature of their crime, normally concealed by the usual method of statistical reporting.

As previously noted, Asian Americans and African Americans have identical percentages of Index crimes (26.1 percent) as a proportion of all crimes for which they are arrested. Second, among all their arrests, violent crime arrests of Asian Americans (3.8 percent) slightly exceed those of whites (3.3 percent). A third, and unexpected, finding is that arrests for Index property crime are higher among Asian Americans (22.3 percent) than in any other within-group examination. It was previously mentioned that within all five subgroups, three Index crimes predominated—larceny-theft, burglary, and aggravated assault—a finding which demonstrates that minorities and whites are highly similar in the commission of crime. Larceny-theft, at 17.2 percent of Asian American Index crimes, is substantially higher than the within-group proportion of whites or any of the other minorities.

In 1986, Asian Americans were more likely to be arrested for "all other offenses" than whites or other minorities (28.1 percent). Only African Americans had a lower within-group DUI arrest proportion (5.0 percent) than Asian Americans, which at 11.8 percent was the second most frequent non-Index arrest offense of the Asian subgroup. Other assaults (5.6 percent) and drug abuse violations (4.7 percent) were the remaining primary offenses for which Asian Americans were arrested in this category.

Reference to Table 2-2 shows the ten most frequent 1986 arrest offenses of Asian Americans to be (1) larceny-theft, (2) DUI, (3) other assaults, (4) drug abuse violations, (5) liquor law violations, (6) burglary, (7) disorderly conduct, (8) aggravated assault, (9) drunkenness, and (10) vandalism. These ten offenses constitute 56.5 percent of all arrests of Asian Americans. Three of the top ten are Crime Index offenses—larceny-theft, burglary, and aggravated assault—which total 23.2 percent of the crimes of this subgroup. The five victimless crimes—DUI, drunkenness, drug violations, liquor laws, and disorderly conduct—are 45.1 percent of total Asian American arrests.

The within-group analysis suggests that Asian Americans, at least in terms of arrests, are more similar to African Americans with regard to crime statistics than to any other minority subgroup, or to Euro-Americans. This observation is indicated by the findings that the ten most frequent arrests of both groups as proportions of their total arrests are almost identical (blacks, 57.9 percent; Asian Americans, 56.5 percent); the percentage of victimless crimes is much lower than for all the other groups (blacks, 41.4 percent; Asian Americans, 45.1 percent); and their within-group total Crime Index proportions are identical (26.1 percent).

NATIVE AMERICAN ARRESTS

Designated in the UCR as "American Indian or Alaskan Native" (classified here as Native Americans), this minority group presents the most dismal picture of all the groups, since the preponderance of their arrests are for victimless crimes. Native Americans are estimated at less than 1 percent of the population (0.6 percent) but constituted 1 percent of those persons arrested in 1986 for total Index crimes and Index property crimes, and 0.7 percent of those arrested for violent Index crimes. The within-group violent crime proportion of all Native American arrests is the lowest of any of the groups examined (3.2 percent).

With the exception of larceny-theft (12.3 percent), Native Americans have the lowest within-group proportions of Index crime arrests of any of the minority groups examined. They are lowest in violent Index crime (3.2 percent), with only whites slightly lower in both Index property crime (15.6 compared to 16.2 percent for Native Americans) and the overall Crime Index (18.9 percent vs. 19.4 percent). Moreover, the three most frequent Crime Index arrests, which, as for all groups, are larceny-theft (12.3 percent), burglary (2.7 percent), and aggravated assault (2.3 percent), together total 17.3 percent (or 89 percent) out of the 19.4 percent of all Native American Index crimes.

It is the non-Index arrest offenses that more accurately portray Native American crime involvement. Whereas "all other offenses" (17.4 percent) is the lowest arrest category compared to the other four groups, the next three most frequent Native American arrest offenses—drunkenness (16.8 percent), driving under the influence (14.2 percent), and liquor law violations (9.1 percent)—clearly distinguish this group from all other subgroups and demonstrate the influence of alcohol use on the arrests of Native Americans.

The ten most frequent arrest offenses of Native Americans in 1986 (Table 2-2) accounted for almost three-fourths (73.2 percent) of all their arrests, the highest proportion of any subgroup. Half of these arrests are for victimless crimes, which totaled 66.4 percent of all Native American arrests, the highest proportion of any of the subgroups. In rank order, the ten are (1) drunkenness, (2) DUI, (3) larceny-theft, (4) liquor law violations, (5) disorderly conduct, (6) other assaults, (7) drug abuse violations, (8) burglary, (9) aggravated assault, and (10) vandalism. As a percentage of their total arrests, the three Index crimes among the top ten crimes—larceny-theft, burglary, and aggravated assault—together reveal the lowest proportion for all subgroups (17.3 percent) except whites (14.4 percent). In fact, the within-group Crime Index picture for Native Americans and Euro-Americans is quite similar.

A Summary Comparison

Comparisons of within-group proportions of UCR arrest offenses of the five subgroups analyzed reveal a dramatically different picture of minority crime than the criminology literature projects and the American public believes. It is obvious that, within their respective groups, there is very little difference in the commission of Index violent crime between Euro-Americans (3.3 percent), Native Americans (3.2 percent), and Asian Americans (3.8 percent). However, the within-group percentages of arrests for such crimes of African Americans (7.7 percent) and Hispanic Americans (5.0 percent) are higher than the proportions for the other three groups. Further examination suggests that arrests for robbery and aggravated assault account for these differences.

Earlier mention was made of the within-group similarities between Asian Americans and African Americans with respect to the extent of crime, with both having identical proportions of Crime Index arrests. An examination of the total Crime Index by race yields the following results: the proportions of such crimes within the African American and Asian American subgroups are 26.1 percent; such arrests are 21.3 percent for Hispanic Americans, 19.4 percent for Native Americans, and 15.6 percent for Euro-Americans. For minorities and whites, the predominant arrest offenses making up the Crime Index are the same—larceny-theft, burglary, and aggravated assault. However, only two Index crimes (larceny-theft and burglary) are among the ten most frequent causes of arrest for whites.

A parallel was also noted between Native American and Euro-American arrest offenses, with both subgroups revealing the lowest within-group Index crime percentages and, concomitantly, the highest proportions of non-Index arrests. In types of non-Index arrest offenses, Euro-Americans and Hispanics are highly alike in crime involvement, since the most frequent offenses for both are driving under the influence, drunkenness, and drug abuse violations. Further resemblances between Euro-Americans, Native Americans, and Hispanic Americans can be found in Table 2-2, which indicates that the three most frequent causes of arrest—DUI, larceny-theft, and drunkenness—are identical for these groups, although there is a slight variation in order.

Alcohol-related offenses predominate for Native Americans and clearly differentiate them from the other subgroups. In contrast, drug abuse violations rank high for all other subgroups, particularly for African Americans. Burglary is evenly ranked for whites, blacks, and Native Americans, but ranks slightly higher for Asian and Hispanic Americans. Among violent crimes, "other assaults" ranks third for both African and Asian Americans, but lower, and at about the same ranked level, for the other subgroups. The more serious crime of aggravated assault, while generally ranked low, is nonetheless numbered among the top ten frequent arrests of minorities, but not of whites. Vandalism is equally characteristic of Asian Americans, Euro-Americans, and Native Americans, yet not a major offense of African and Hispanic Americans. Fraud is one of the top ten arrest categories only for whites and blacks, and weapons charges only for Hispanics, and African Americans are the only subgroup arrested for robbery at that frequency level. With these exceptions, there is little variation between the groups as to ranked types of crime arrests.

Such a comparison reveals that the differences between minority and white crime, and between the crimes of each minority subgroup, are not substantial; in fact, they are quite similar. It is not suggested that minority involvement in crime, as measured by UCR arrests, is not more extensive than that of whites relative to their proportions of the U.S. population. Obviously the *extent* of minority crime is disparate, according to official statistics. And, as we will see in this and later chapters, explanations other than racial/ethnic status have been hypothesized to account for the minority/white crime differential. The point being made here is that minority status notwithstanding, persons are arrested in this country for essentially the same crimes. A look within each subgroup's arrest portfolio has demonstrated that the proportions of each type of crime do not vary substantially between minorities, or between minorities and whites.

Studies of Minority Involvement in Crime

The few available studies of minorities and crime generally focus on African Americans. In this section, these offenses are categorized as personal, property, and public-order crimes. Minority crimes of violence, particularly the violent Index crimes of murder, rape, and robbery, are those most feared by the populace, thus they have been more frequently examined by criminologists and other social scientists. Similarly, among felony property crimes, although larceny-theft, motor vehicle theft, and arson combined account annually for over $10 billion in losses to victims, the most feared property crime, burglary, has received more study. This research interest may be a result of the perceived liability by Euro-Americans of a potential personal encounter with a minority perpetrator during the commission of a residential burglary, particularly at night. Although not as frequently studied as the more personally threatening crimes, public-order offenses, which are primarily "victimless" crimes, are more descriptive of the true extent and nature of minority crime.

Personal Crimes

Homicide among African Americans has been described as a form of black genocide, since the victim of homicide is most often another black person and the incidence of this crime is so pervasive. Homicide is the primary cause of death for African American males age fifteen to twenty-four years (U.S. Department of Health and Human Services, 1983), and black homicide is viewed as a serious public health issue today (O'Carroll and Mercy, 1986). The epidemic proportions of blacks killing blacks led to national studies of African American homicide commissioned by the National Institutes of Health (U.S. Department of Health and Human Services, 1986) and a 1987 national conference, "Black Homicide: A Public Health Crisis," sponsored by the Johns Hopkins University, the Office of Minority Health (Department of Health and Human Services), and the National Institute of Mental Health. A black male has 1 chance in 21 to be murdered, whereas a white male's lifetime chances of being murdered are 1 in 131 (U.S. Department of Justice, 1985). The odds of being a homicide victim are far greater for a black female (1 in 124) than for a white female (1 in 606), which ranks black females second to black males as high-risk homicide victims (Stengel, 1985).

In 1986, the Uniform Crime Reports listed 20,613 murder and nonnegligent manslaughter arrests, an increase of 8.6 percent from the previous year (FBI, 1987: 7). In the 11,474 incidents in which there were a single victim and a single offender, 50.7 percent of the victims were white, 47.1 percent were black, 2 percent were classified as other races, and compared with non-Hispanics, 13 percent were Hispanic. According to adjusted homicide rates, in 1986 the black murder rate was almost six times that for whites, or 31.2 versus 5.4 per 100,000 (Whitaker, 1990: 10). The homicide rates were highest for black males (52.3), followed by black females (12.3), white males (7.9), and white females (2.9) (ibid.).

The disproportionate homicide rates (per 100,000) and patterns of African American homicide have persisted for decades; the high incidence has been recorded in early national studies (Brearley, 1932 cited in Hawkins, 1986a), as well as contemporary national research (Rose, 1981; Riedel, 1984; Wilbanks, 1986; Mann, 1987) and local state and city reports (Wolfgang, 1958; Pokorny, 1965; Block, 1976; Block, 1985; Humphrey and Palmer, 1986). Whereas Pokorny (1965: 486) found that blacks in Houston were six times more likely to die from homicide than whites, there are recent indications that the white homicide rate is rising and the black homicide rate is decreasing; nonetheless, the black rate is still five times the white rate (O'Carroll and Mercy, 1986).

The data are limited, but a few studies reveal that other minorities are also overrepresented as homicide offenders and victims. Levy, Kunitz, and Everett (1969: 129) found the Navajo criminal homicide rate to be stable and, while lower than the black rate, considerably higher than the white rate. A report on high-risk homicide among racial and ethnic groups from 1970 to 1983 revealed that Native Americans are only 12 percent among the nonblack U.S. minority population, yet in 1980 their homicide rate was 70 percent higher than that for whites; in 1982, they accounted for 43 percent of all the homicides in the nonblack minority group (Centers for Disease Control, 1986: 8).

Pokorny's (1965: 480) partial replication of Wolfgang's classic Philadelphia criminal homicide study indicated Latin American victimization rates of 12.1 per 100,000 in Houston from 1958 to 1961; the white rate was only 5.86. The criminal homicide offender rate for the Hispanic subgroup was 13.3, while the white rate was 4.39. A study by Smith, Mercy, and Rosenberg (1984) of Hispanic (Mexican) and Anglo (white) homicide in Arizona, California, Colorado, New Mexico, and Texas from 1976 through 1980 found the Hispanic victim rate to be more than three times the national white rate, and almost three times (21.6 per 100,000) the five-state Anglo rate (7.7 per 100,000). Compared to non-Hispanics, Hispanics in the Southwest, mostly Mexican Americans, are found to be at increasingly higher risk of homicide, particularly males. Hispanic males were more than three times as likely to become victims of homicide as Anglo males (Centers for Disease Control, 1986: 8). In Los Angeles from 1970 to 1979, Loya and Mercy (1985: 40) report a crude Hispanic homicide rate 2.3 times that for Anglos. Over the ten-year period studied, the Hispanic rate increased from 11.1 to 18.2, compared to the Anglo increase from 6.7 in 1970 to only 8.1 in 1979 (ibid.: 87, Table 27). Finally, an in-depth homicide study by Block (1985: 21) over a seventeen-year period in Chicago (1965-1981) found an increase in the Latino victimization rate from 23 per 100,000 in 1970 to 36 per 100,000 in 1980. During the seventeen-year period studied, Latinos were 10 percent of all homicides, either as victims or as offenders, which Block describes as high in relation to Chicago's Latino population.

Every homicide study has found that people are usually killed by someone known to them (Wolfgang, 1958; Pokorny, 1965; Riedel, 1984; O'Carroll and Mercy, 1986). From 1976 to 1984, O'Carroll and Mercy (1986: 31) report that in 60 percent of the 75,000 homicides of black Americans, the assailants were family members (13.2 percent) or acquaintances (44.9 percent). Such proportions are also typical of whites and the other minority groups; those who kill choose someone who is in a close, personal relationship with them. The circumstances surrounding a homicide are the factors that explain choice of victim. For example, Native Americans, specifically Navajos, typically kill a wife or lover, parents, or other relatives (Levy, Kunitz, and Everett, 1969: 147).

An argument between the offender and victim has been the primary motive for the killing in every study of homicide which examines the underlying "causes." In his classification of motives, Wolfgang (1958: 188-192) listed altercations and family quarrels as predominant, with significant differences by race and gender. Black females were victims twice as often as white females, and were five times more likely to be homicide offenders when a general altercation was the motive. The second-largest category, domestic quarrels, included twice as many black males (12 percent) as white male victims (6 percent) and was the most frequent motive for deaths of females (26 percent). Jealousy, the third most frequent motive, also differed significantly by race and gender, as indicated in the following victim proportions: black females (23 percent), white females (14 percent), black males (12 percent), white males (2 percent). Sexual jealousy has also been found to be a dominant homicide motive for Navajo homicides, as have marital strife and domestic quarrels. A very high proportion of Navajos kill themselves after committing homicide (Levy, Kunitz, and Everett, 1969: 147).

A more recent study, which analyzed FBI Supplementary Homicide Reports (SHR) from 1976 to 1984, corroborates Wolfgang's earlier discovery by finding that about two-thirds of all black homicides resulted from arguments or other nonfelony situations (O'Carroll and Mercy, 1986: 36). In his examination of FBI-SHR data for 1980, Wilbanks (1986: 50) also found that arguments were the most common motive for whites' killing blacks. In addition, his findings question the frequently held misconception that blacks are more likely to kill whites.

Wolfgang (1958: 245) notes: "The victim may be one of the major precipitating causes of his own demise." Quarrels, provocative language, and some demonstration of physical force directed at the perpetrator commonly led to victim-precipitated homicides in the Philadelphia slayings. In Chicago, Block (1985: 22-23) reports assault as the most common victim-precipitating crime for every racial/ethnic group of homicide offenders. Assault homicides were more frequent among white offenders (85 percent), followed by the "other races" category (84 percent), Latinos (83 percent), and blacks (76 percent). Homicides precipitated by robbery, however, are more likely to involve black offenders (16 percent) than the other racial/ethnic groups: Latino (9 percent), white (6 percent), "other races" (5 percent). An earlier nine-year study (1965-1973) attributed the increase in homicides over that time period to killings committed during a robbery, noting that such incidents accounted for 19 percent of all homicides in Chicago (Block, 1976: 505). While finding that robbery tended to be largely intraracial, the 1980 national data reported by Wilbanks (1986: 50) reveal that the most common circumstance precipitating black/white homicides was robbery (41 percent). Secondary homicides occur during the commission of another crime and thus are most often stranger homicides, the major type of homicide involving black offenders and white victims (Riedel, 1984: 57).

RAPE

In 1986, there were 90,434 known forcible rapes in the United States, an increase of 3.2 percent over the previous year, or a rate of 37.5 per 100,000 (FBI, 1987: 13). When translated into ratios involving the predominant rape victim group—females—it is estimated that 73 of every 100,000 females in the country were reported rape victims. A little over one-half (52 percent) of these rapes were cleared by arrest or exceptional means. Whites were 52 percent of those arrested, blacks 46.6 percent; Native Americans (.8 percent) and Asian Americans (.5 percent) constituted the remaining proportion; and Hispanics compared with non-Hispanics accounted for 11.5 percent.

The most recent available victimization data provide a clearer picture of the extent of this largely unreported crime. In the 124,600 single offender/single victim rapes reported by respondents in 1985, 57.4 percent of the offenders were perceived as white, 32.9 percent as black, and 1.1 percent as "other"; 8.6 percent were not known or the data were not available (U.S. Department of Justice, 1987: 38). By 1988, the 115,820 reported rapes in the victimization survey revealed a decrease in the percentage of perceived black offenders (29.2 percent), a slight increase in perceived white offenders (58.6 percent), and a substantial increase to 12.2 percent in rape offenders of other races (U.S. Department of Justice, 1990a: 47).

Like homicide and other personal victimizations (e.g., robbery, assault), rape is primarily an intraracial offense. Overall, black males and females are victims of personal crimes at appreciably higher rates than white males or females (Harries, 1984: 43). In 1988, for example, 85.3 percent of the black victims of single-offender rapes perceived their rapists as black, and 14.7 percent as "other." Among white rape victims, 81.5 percent perceived their offenders as also white, 11.3 percent as black, and 7.2 percent as members of other races (U.S. Department of Justice, 1990a: 48). The rape victimization rate for black females age twelve and over was 2.6 per 1,000 population, or nearly three times the comparable white female rate of .9 per 1,000 in 1988 (U.S. Department of Justice, 1990a: 19). However, it is generally believed that "official rapes are only the tip of a statistical iceberg" (Schwendinger and Schwendinger, 1974: 18) because, for a variety of reasons, most rapes go unreported. Despite the fear of this crime and the fact that such fear inhibits the freedom of women, only in the last dozen or so years has attention been devoted to the study of rape, and much of the literature has been theoretical.[7]

Although there is a paucity of empirical studies of forcible rape involving minorities as victims or offenders, it is widely assumed that rape is a lower-class black phenomenon that is primarily interracial (e.g., Amir, 1971; Curtis, 1974; Hindelang, 1978; LaFree, 1982). However, Weiss and Borges (1973) suggest that rape is not infrequent among other socio-economic classes and racial groups when one considers, for example, the rarely reported "date rapes," rapes by men in higher social statuses, and the tendency for middle-class rape victims to avoid the police and report the incident only to their family doctor or psychiatrist. Furthermore, it is rarely noted that there are far fewer minority sexual offenders than white sexual offenders (Cohen and Boucher, 1972); and it is seldom mentioned that sadistic rapists and lust murderers are almost exclusively white.

ROBBERY

The crime of robbery, "the taking or attempting to take anything of value from the care, custody, or control of a person or persons by force or threat of force or violence and/or by putting the victim in fear" (FBI, 1987: 16), is classified as a personal, violent crime and included in the serious Crime Index offenses of the FBI Uniform Crime Reports. Some criminologists (e.g., Carey, 1978: 296) emphasize two characteristics of robbery that could define it as a property crime: (1) the desire for money that cannot be legitimately acquired and thus requires the selection of a target with money, and (2) the rarity of violence in robbery.

In 1986, robbery in the United States increased 9 percent compared to 1985, with 542,775 estimated offenses, yielding a rate of 225.1 per 100,000 and totaling 4 percent of the Crime Index and 36 percent of violent crime (FBI, 1987: 17). Most robberies that year took place on streets and highways (56 percent) through the use of weapons (57 percent), although in 43 percent of the incidents strong-arm tactics were used (ibid.: 18).

About one out of four robberies (123,649) was cleared by arrest, with the following racial breakdown: blacks were 62 percent of the arrestees, whites were 37 percent, and Native Americans and Asian Americans were 0.5 percent each. Compared to non-Hispanics, 13.9 percent of the persons arrested for robbery were Hispanic. Returning to our within-group analysis, in 1986 robbery accounted for 2.7 percent of the arrests of blacks, a figure twice the proportion found for Hispanics (1.3 percent), three times that for Asian Americans (0.9 percent), over four times the percentage within the white group (0.6 percent), and over five times the proportion of Native American arrests (0.5 percent).

The proportion of black arrests for robbery has remained consistent for the last dozen or more years. In 1974, for example, Hindelang (1978: 100) reported the greatest racial disproportion among common-law crimes (forcible rape, robbery, and assault) in robbery, with 62 percent of arrestees black, 34 percent white, and 4 percent of other races.

Robbery is the least violent of the common-law personal crimes, yet studies find it demonstrates the greatest racial differences (Hindelang, 1978: 107). A 1987 U.S. Department of Justice report (Harlow, 1987: 2-3) examined robbery victimizations from 1973 through 1984 and found that male offenders—who were nine out of ten robbers—were more likely to be black (51 percent) than white (36 percent). Where the race of the robber was perceived, other races (4 percent) and mixed races (4 percent) made up the remainder of the offender group. Although the majority of victims were white (75 percent), blacks were robbed at two and a half times the rate of whites (14.2 vs. 5.9 per 1,000 victims); and the robbery rates of victims of other races also exceeded the white rate (7.2 vs. 5.9 per 1,000). The person least victimized by robbery was a white female (4 per 1,000), but a black female (9 per 1,000) was more likely to be the victim of robbery than a white male (8 per 1,000). The most frequent robbery victim was a black male (21 per 1,000).

A National Crime Survey report (NCS) on Hispanic victims (U.S. Department of Justice, 1980) found that over the period 1973-1978, the *overall* violent crime rates of Hispanics and non-Hispanics were not significantly different, but persons of Hispanic heritage had a significantly higher robbery rate (8.7 per 1,000) than non-Hispanics (6.4 per 1,000). Upon closer examination of each year in the time frame, in 1973 the Hispanic robbery rate was 8.5 compared to 6.7 per 1,000 for non-Hispanics; but by 1978, the Hispanic rate had increased to 10.4, while the non-Hispanic rate had dropped to 5.7 per 1,000. In the period from 1976 to 1986, the picture changed drastically for the worse, with the major finding of the NCS that "compared to other groups Hispanics are victimized particularly by robbery" (Bastian, 1990: 1). Hispanics were robbed more often than any other persons. There were 11 robberies for every 1,000 Hispanics, compared to 6 for every 1,000 non-Hispanics. By race and ethnicity, 1990 robbery victimization rates per 1,000 were as follows: Hispanics, 13.9; blacks, 13.0; other races, 8.4; and whites, 4.5 (Bastian and DeBerry, 1991: 6). Both black and Hispanic robbery victims are more likely than whites to face an armed offender—57 percent for both blacks and Hispanics, versus 43 percent for whites (Bastian, 1990).

It is generally believed that the use of weapons reduces the incidence of violence; more victims are injured in unarmed robberies than in armed robberies (Carey, 1978). According to the Uniform Crime Reports, in 1986 strong-arm methods were indicated in 43 percent of robberies, while in the remaining robberies the following weapons were used: firearms, 34 percent; knives or other cutting weapons, 13 percent; and other weapons, 10 percent (FBI, 1987: 18). Skogan (1977) comments on the role of weapons in robberies:

> One important function of weapons in criminal activity is to incapacitate victims, rendering them helpless either to flee the scene, resist demands for their money or goods, or turn on their attackers and pummel them in return. More lethal weapons create a buffer zone between the parties, making it more dangerous for the victim to approach the offender. They present a credible threat of death, reinforcing demands by the assailant and forestalling attempts to escape.

While victims may feel they cannot argue with a gun or a knife, they may not feel as threatened in a one-on-one robbery situation where there is no weapon and therefore may use aggressive self-protective measures that result in injury. According to the latest NCS criminal victimization data, white and black robbery victims were almost equally likely to sustain physical injuries in robberies, with the percentage of injuries slightly higher for blacks (36 percent) than for whites (35.6 percent) (U.S. Department of Justice, 1990a: 67).

Violent crimes most often involve offenders and victims of the same race, but crimes by strangers tend to be interracial. Of the violent crimes measured by the National Crime Survey between 1982 and 1984, Timrots and Rand (1987: 2) found that robbery was more likely to be committed by a total stranger (71 percent) than rape (49 percent), aggravated assault (44 percent), or simple assault (39 percent). Unfortunately, Timrots and Rand (ibid.: 4) did not classify the violent victimizations by crime, but their analysis by race of offender and victim presents some interesting stranger-to-stranger crime findings. Not surprising is the fact that whites are victimized more frequently in violent crimes by white strangers (70 percent); and comparatively, blacks are more often victimized by black strangers (77 percent). Members of other races, however, are victims of strangers of their own races only 13 percent of the time and are more often victimized in violent crime by white (46 percent) and black (36 percent) strangers. Even though in violent crime victimizations by strangers a white is slightly more often the victim of a black offender (24 percent), a black victim is nonetheless victimized by a white stranger in 19 percent of violent crimes. Finally, blacks and whites are almost equally the victims of violence by strangers of other races (3 and 4 percent, respectively). According to a recent NCS report (Bastian, 1990: 6), the percentages were substantially higher in robberies involving strangers for Hispanic victims (65 percent) than for either white (58 percent) or black (54 percent) victims.

BANK ROBBERY

Rhodes (1984: 2) provides a profile of the typical bank robber as a young, black male recidivist who is steadily unemployed and tends to use drugs (42 percent). According to Rhodes, one in three bank robbers is classified as using opiates, 28 percent are considered addicted, and 8 percent were intoxicated from alcohol or narcotics at the time of the bank robbery. Presentence investigation reports indicate that the proceeds of the crime are believed to be needed to support drug use (ibid.). Rhodes found most bank robbers to be unprofessional and unsophisticated: they used no disguises (76 percent), had no prior plan and did not inspect the bank before the crime (86 percent), and had no long-range plan to avoid capture or spend the money unobtrusively (95 percent).

In a California study of forty-nine career criminals serving time for armed robbery, Petersilia, Greenwood, and Lavin (1977) found a progression from juvenile auto thefts and burglaries to adult robberies and forgeries, with little specialization in types of crime. The offenders did not plan or prepare for their crimes, which might have been a consequence of being under the influence of drugs or alcohol at the time of their commission (60 percent). One-third of those studied cited the desire for money to buy drugs or alcohol as the reason for committing crimes, while two-thirds admitted regular use of one or both of those substances.

This limited description of robbers reflects the paucity of research on the topic, particularly the lack of studies of minority robbers. Even though most of the information on this offender group is derived from UCR and victimization data, both of which have their limitations, there is little evidence which contradicts the consistent finding that blacks, especially black males, have the highest robbery offending rates.

Property Crime

The Uniform Crime Report (UCR) and National Crime Survey (NCS) definitions of burglary are slightly different; also, the legal definition may vary depending upon the jurisdiction. Although the UCR, for example, categorizes burglary as forcible entry, unlawful entry without force, and attempted forcible entry, it defines burglary as "the unlawful entry of a structure to commit a felony or a theft" (FBI, 1987: 24). On the other hand, while also including attempted forcible entry, the NCS views burglary as the "unlawful or forcible entry of a residence, usually, but not necessarily, attended by theft" (U.S. Department of Justice, 1987: 111). The breaking into or entering of a garage, shed, or other structure on the premises, a hotel, or a vacation residence where members of a household are staying is also classified as a burglary. The public view of burglary is of a strange intruder entering a home with intent to steal property either by force or by stealth, but actually many burglaries are committed by relatives or persons known by the victims (Rand, 1985: 2).

Among Index property crimes, household burglary is only about one-third as frequent as larceny-theft, and a little over twice as frequent as motor vehicle theft, but the public perception of burglary makes it a highly feared crime, more so than other property crimes. In 13 percent of all burglaries, someone is at home, and on such occasions, 30 percent of the incidents result in a violent crime (U.S. Department of Justice, 1985: 10). Persons whose homes have been burglarized report experiencing a feeling of violation, similar to rape. Often a rape does take place along with a burglary—three-fifths of all rapes in the home, three-fifths of all robberies in the home, and one-third of all household assaults occur with burglaries (Rand, 1985: 1).

The clearance rate of burglary is low; for example, in 1986, only 14 percent of the 3.2 million burglaries known to law enforcement agencies were cleared by arrest (FBI, 1987: 25). The 374,081 arrests included 69.1 percent whites, 29.5 percent blacks, 14.7 percent Hispanics (compared to non-Hispanics), 0.8 percent Native Americans, and 0.6 percent Asian Americans. As a proportion of the total within-group arrests by race, the subgroups varied little. Burglary was highest for Hispanics (4.1 percent), followed closely by blacks (4 percent), whites and Asian Americans (3.5 percent), and lastly Native Americans (2.7 percent), but ranked fairly low for all subgroups among their ten most frequent arrests (see Table 2-2).

Any attempt to determine the extent of minority involvement in burglary is hampered by the surreptitious character of the crime: it occurs at night, usually when no one is home. Historically, most studies of burglary have examined the characteristics of burglary incidents, with much less attention devoted to the criminal offender than is accorded to crime prevention (e.g., Jeffery, 1977; Pope, 1977; Harries, 1980). Since the early work of Sutherland (1937), a burglar has generally been viewed as a professional thief. More recent attempts to establish criminal typologies have categorized burglars as common-law career criminals involved in either "conventional" criminal behavior, which Clinard and Quinney

(1973: 132) rank at the "bottom scale of career crime," or "professional" crime (Letkemann, 1973; Inciardi, 1975).

Blacks are most frequently victimized by burglary. A study of household burglary based on ten years of data from the National Crime Survey (1973-1982) found that forcible-entry burglary rates for minority households were higher than comparable white rates (Rand, 1985: 2, Table 3). The forcible-entry rate for blacks, at 59.7 per 1,000 households, was over twice that for whites (27.9), and was also substantially higher than the rate of 32 for "other races" (excluding Hispanics). Rand's report did not include Hispanics, but in a later NCS study, this group was reported to have a forcible-entry burglary rate of 32.4, compared to a rate of 19.9 per 1,000 households for non-Hispanics (U.S. Department of Justice, 1987: 28, Table 18). Household burglary victimizations for 1990 yield the following rank-ordered rates per 1,000: black (85.4), Hispanic (71.8), other races (67.7), and white (49.1) (Bastian and DeBerry, 1991: 7).

A consistent finding in both studies is that, regardless of race, the poorest families—those with an annual family income under $7,500—have the highest overall burglary victimization rates (Rand, 1991: 5). Moreover, such victims are also more likely to be renters (83.7 percent) than homeowners (49.8 percent) (Johnson and DeBerry, 1989: 7). Thus, in addition to being more frequently murdered, raped, and robbed, the poor, especially poor minorities, are more frequently burglarized and thereby deprived of what few possessions they have.

Public-Order Crimes

Crimes against the public order are often viewed as "victimless" crimes because they are without unwilling victims (Sheley, 1985). Drug addicts, gamblers, or prostitutes usually do not define themselves as "victims," but such crimes do have victims (Abadinsky, 1987: 37). Victimizations may occur in the commission of these offenses: for example, some customers of prostitutes get "mugged" or robbed; many violent and property crimes are engaged in either under the influence of alcohol or drugs or because of the desire for money to obtain these substances; compulsive gambling frequently destroys families; and alcohol-related crimes too often lead to family disintegration, or death. Some public-order crimes are also defined as vice crimes (prostitution, illegal gambling, and illegal substance possession) because they are crimes against the public morals and disturb the community by involving "activities thought by many to be immoral and liable to bring spiritual and even bodily harm to those engaging in them" (Sheley, 1985: 116).

Prostitution and commercialized vice, drug abuse violations, gambling, and those offenses associated with alcohol—driving under the influence, liquor law violations, drunkenness, disorderly conduct, and vagrancy—together account for about 40 percent of all arrests in this country. Public-order crimes are the reason for one-half of all Native American arrests. Hispanics (47.5 percent) also exceed Euro-Americans (44.2 percent) in the proportion of their arrests considered victimless crimes. Compared to the other racial/ethnic subgroups, public-order arrests are much less significant for African (27.8 percent) and Asian Americans (28 percent). As proportions of total public-order arrestees, Asian Americans tend to be underrepresented in comparison to their percentage of the general population (0.5 vs. 1.4 percent), Euro-Americans are arrested for such offenses almost in proportion to their numbers in the general population (79.4 vs. 79.5 percent), while African Americans (18.9 vs. 12 percent), Native Americans (1.3 vs. 0.6 percent), and Hispanic Americans (21.4 vs. 6.5 percent) are overrepresented.

PROSTITUTION

Over time, the most extensive body of research on public-order crimes has been devoted to the study of prostitution (see, e.g., Davis, 1937; Lemert, 1951; Bryan, 1965; Winick and Kinsie, 1971; James, 1976; James and Vitaliano, 1979; Heyl, 1979; Best, 1982; Widom, 1983).[8] Although earlier studies reported the phenomenon (e.g., Butts, 1947; Jersild, 1956; Craft, 1966), it was not until the 1970s that serious attention was given to young male prostitutes, who typically sell their bodies and services on the streets to other males (see Hoffman, 1972; Allen, 1980; Luckenbill, 1986). However, throughout history the majority of arrestees for the act of prostitution have been females, and prostitution was defined as both sex-specific—a crime which by definition excludes one sex— and sex-related—crimes which either sex may commit but are committed more frequently by one sex (Smart, 1976). The FBI Uniform Crime Reports have consistently contained disproportionate arrest statistics for females, as compared to males, in the prostitution and commercialized vice category. With recent arrests in some states of male customers of prostitutes and the arrests of pimps and other males involved in commercialized vice, the proportion of males arrested in 1986 under this classification was 34.6 percent, compared to the female percentage of 65.4 percent (FBI, 1987: 181). Among the subgroups under examination, African Americans (38.8 percent) and Hispanic Americans (10.1 percent) were the only minorities whose arrests for prostitution and commercialized vice exceeded their proportions in the U.S. population (ibid.: 182, 185).

In the late nineteenth and early twentieth centuries, until the Mann Act of 1910, which prohibited interstate and international trafficking of females for sex purposes ("white slavery"), prostitution was the largest illegal industry. The Chinese traditionally had a history of illegal enterprise in China and the United States, typified in their secret criminal tong organizations, that was not found among African Americans. While not sharing a criminal tradition, both minority groups shared low status in the labor force and discriminatory practices because of their skin color (Light, 1977a: 467). Illegal enterprises offered both the Chinese and African Americans an alternative livelihood. The demand for prostitution was high, since not only were recent white male immigrants from Southern and Eastern Europe mostly bachelors, but concomitantly they faced a paucity of women. Light (ibid.: 468) notes that in 1880, the sex ratios were 115.6 men per 100 women for foreign-born whites, and 2,106.8 per 100 for Chinese. By 1920, these figures were 121.7 and 465.7, respectively (ibid.: 469, Table 2). Between

1880 and 1920, the sexual demands of white men doubled the volume of prostitution in Chinatowns and trebled prostitution in black ghettos. Even with these dramatic increases in the vice industry, Light (ibid.: 468) states that these two minority illegal industries never claimed more than one-third of the total white vice traffic during this time period.

The characteristics of the African and Chinese American prostitution industries differed: the African American enterprise was largely made up of streetwalkers and pimps, while the Chinese vice enterprise consisted of brothels. Some African American brothels existed, but they were franchises managed by Euro-Americans who, through a deliberate racial policy, restricted the clientele to whites. Through their political clout, the white syndicates who franchised the black brothels paid police to drive the black streetwalkers and pimps away. Another difference between the two minorities in their vice enterprises involved violence. Although there were high homicide rates in the black ghettos, because of their free-market vice organization, there were no gang wars at that time. Customers of black streetwalkers were frequently robbed and sometimes killed in the robbery attempt, but petty crimes and individualistic killings were more prevalent. Chinatowns, on the other hand, had rampant gang wars, but the secret society (tong) prevented petty street robberies of visiting men (customers) and unregulated conflicts among individuals (Light, 1977a: 471). From the late nineteenth century up to World War II, three kinds of vice crimes predominated in the Chinese community—prostitution, opium smoking, and gambling. After that, Chinese offenses became "Americanized" (Pao-Min, 1981: 363).

Light (1977a) points out that even though the sex ratio began to stabilize, the syndicated brothels disappeared, and there was less public demand for vice, the demand of white customers for black prostitutes never abated until after World War II, when whites began to fear the juvenile muggers in urban black ghettos. Apparently the white appetite for black streetwalkers returned, since the primary market of prostitutes today comprises white, middle-class men between the ages of thirty and sixty, who come in contact with black female prostitutes forced onto the streets by bar owners, hotels, and landlords, because "racism is as prevalent in the business of prostitution as everywhere else in our society" (Haft, 1976: 212). The risk of arrest for a prostitute is highest on the streets, and black women are seven times more likely to experience a prostitution arrest than women of other races (ibid.).

Minorities and Drugs

Arrests of minorities for drug abuse violations in 1986 demonstrate how critical this problem is, particularly for blacks (31.8 percent of such arrests) and Hispanics (19.9 percent of arrests compared to non-Hispanics). The within-group analysis reveals that drug offenses are the second most frequent arrest offense for African Americans. Federal arrests for drug offenses in 1986 were more concentrated among whites (79 percent) than among Hispanics (31 percent vs. 69 percent non-Hispanic), blacks (19 percent), or offenders of other races (2 percent).

This is largely because whites are those most frequently arrested for importation (81 percent), general trafficking (83 percent), and distribution/manufacture (81 percent), whereas minorities are more likely to be arrested for possession (40 percent) (Chaiken and McDonald, 1988: 2).

A report on the percentage of male arrestees who tested positive for any drug during the last quarter of 1988 (October–December) in fourteen major cities revealed that between 54 and 82 percent of the men who had committed serious offenses had positive tests for illicit drugs (*National Institute of Justice Reports*, 1989: 8).[9] In 45 percent of the cases, arrestees charged with violent crimes or income-producing crimes (e.g., burglary) tested positive for one or more drugs. Recent victims of violent crimes reported that in about 36 percent of the incidents, they thought that their attackers were under the influence of drugs or alcohol at the time and perceived their assailants as 42 percent white, 27 percent black, and 39 percent of other races (Dillingham, 1990). The first-quarter results of drug-use forecasting for 1990 (January–March) in twenty-three cities indicated that between 57 and 80 percent of male arrestees had tested positive for a drug (De Witt, 1990: 2).[10] There were startling increases in cocaine use and concomitant reductions in the use of other drugs (Wise and O'Neil, 1989: 2-3).[11]

Gallup Poll respondents have increasingly described drug abuse as the most important problem in the nation today. In 1985, only 2 percent of respondents listed drug abuse as the most serious problem; by May 1989, 27 percent felt that way (U.S. Department of Justice, 1990b: 15). The defining of drug use by minorities as a social problem and the enactment of laws at various levels of government bear a distinct relationship to minority drug abuse and society's reaction to it. Society's perception and reaction to drugs has been based on a drug mythology which, among other factors, includes (1) the medical designation of the use of morphine and opium in the 1880s as "a vice, a habit, an appetite, and a disease"; (2) the early association of opium smoking with the Chinese, who have always been perceived by Americans as "alien . . . odd and mysterious"; (3) through American criminal law, the definition of all addicts as criminal offenders; and (4) the potent influence on public opinion and rule makers held by American moralists who defined drug use as evil (Inciardi, 1974: 206).

In addition to Inciardi's concept of drug mythology, Helmer (1975) points to other myths related to drug use that influenced societal reaction and ultimately biased policy formation concerning the "minority drug problem" in the United States. The first myth concerns the use of drugs. Many people believe that the passage of the Harrison Act (1914) and other Supreme Court rulings that prohibited the unregulated use of drugs caused drugs to become concentrated in the working class; but Helmer argues convincingly that narcotics use has always been a predominantly working-class phenomenon. Second, while it is generally believed that "present public policy toward narcotics is an inheritance of the irrationality, ignorance, or confusion of the past and can now be superseded and reformed by rational and scientific solutions . . . there has always been reasoned support for both prohibitionist and nonprohibitionist positions; as well as for policies with punitive and medical solutions" (Helmer, 1975: 7). The third myth describes the common belief that narcotic addiction is "the inevitable outcome of prolonged narcotics use," or that it is "a chemically induced physiological condition which deprives the addict of his capacity to control consumption, let alone stop it, which impels him to irrational extremes of behavior, including violent crime" (ibid.: 7). In reality, "intermittent, or occasional use, regulated by social norms and self-willed without internal compulsion, physiological symptoms, or irrational behavior during withdrawal from the drug has been observed regularly throughout the twentieth century among several groups, including Indians, American Chinese, and Vietnam War veterans" (ibid.: 8). In other words, contrary to this myth, many consumers are able to exercise control over the size of the dosage, many are not addicted, and there are occasional drug users who do not experience withdrawal symptoms.

It is such myths about drugs and their use that have influenced and consequently determined society's definition of minority drug abuse as a social problem. The definition evolved from Euro-Americans because of their fears of the effects of specific drugs on specific minority people:

> Certain drugs were dreaded because they seemed to undermine essential social restrictions which kept these groups under control: cocaine was supposed to enable blacks to withstand bullets which would kill normal persons and to stimulate sexual assault. Fear that opium smoking facilitated sexual contact between Chinese and white Americans was also a factor in its total prohibition. Chicanos in the Southwest were believed to be incited to violence by smoking marihuana. Heroin was linked in the 1920s with a turbulent age-group: adolescents in reckless and promiscuous urban gangs. (Musto, 1987: 244-245)

In *The Legislation of Morality: Law, Drugs, and Moral Judgment,* Troy Duster (1970: 5) directs critical commentary at how the contemporary drug issue has been historically affected by moral interpretations, moral indignation, and moral directives regardless of the "physiological and physical aspects of addiction." When society was able to impute criminal intent to drug addicts, the "bridge between law and morality was drawn" (ibid.: 16-17), and "moral hostility comes faster and easier when directed toward a young, lower-class Negro male" (ibid.: 21).

CHINESE AMERICANS

The first national campaign against narcotics began in the 1880s when the Chinese were associated with opium. There were no reports of widespread use of opium until the mid-1870s, when anti-Chinese demonstrations and the move to curb Chinese immigration began. This period, 1875-1880, was the first of the great anti-narcotic quests in U.S. history and is notable for the initial attempts to legislate against drug use (Helmer, 1975: 19-20). There are no indications as to what motivated the American Chinese to smoke opium, but by the end of the nineteenth century, it is estimated that 35 percent of the Chinese immigrant population smoked somewhat regularly (ibid.: 27). By 1880, the linking of opium use to the Chinese resulted in laws aimed specifically at the Chinese, possibly because of class conflict and racism (Musto, 1973; Reasons, 1974).

The Chinese were willing to undertake hard labor at long hours and for lower wages than whites would. Some whites even felt that the Chinese competition was responsible for the prevailing conditions of low wages, high unemployment, and economic depression at that time. The white response was frequent attacks on the Chinese because of their supposed association with the dire economic condition, and also for their "differentness." As Helmer puts it:

> The opium issue . . . was part of the general ideological response to labor market failure, reflecting the extent to which the secondary labor market, with its Chinese concentration, offered no "work relief" to the unemployed, insecure, white working class. The ideological role of the anti-opium campaign was to get rid of the Chinese. It had a practical consequence—providing a legal basis for the unrestrained and arbitrary police raids and searches of Chinese premises in San Francisco. Ostensibly to identify opium dens, these raids served the same purpose as that of the vigilantes in the mine fields. (1975: 32)

Racism also contributed to the stigmatization of the Chinese as "opium eaters." As a person of color, the Oriental was categorized the same as blacks, particularly by southerners coming to California at that time (Musto, 1973); and laws were enacted at the local, state, and federal levels to exclude the Chinese from participation in American society.

The second national campaign against narcotics extended from 1905 to 1920, with the passage of three major anti-narcotics laws: the Pure Food and Drug Act (1906), an Act to "Prohibit Importation and Use of Opium" (1909), and the Harrison Act (1914). Whereas the American Medical Association initiated the fight against opium, heroin, morphine, and cocaine that resulted in the 1906 Act, prohibitionists among the medical profession were the driving force behind passage of the 1909 and 1914 legislation. The most fervent anti-narcotic proponent, Hamilton Wright, felt that the smoking of opium and the injection of morphine or heroin were rampant in American society, with cocaine as the most threatening drug because of its potential to spread from the "outlaw" class to the higher social classes (Helmer, 1975: 37).

Although the finger of narcotics abuse was pointed at the Chinese, it has been suggested that Orientals were simply the scapegoat in what was actually a fight for control of the medical industry, where doctors had been steadily losing prestige and popularity. Pharmacists, druggists, and others who offered services or products for the cure of disease and other illnesses had rapidly developed a powerful patent medicine industry that threatened the credibility and legitimacy of doctors. As a result of the anti-narcotics acts, members of the medical profession were exclusively licensed to prescribe drugs and ultimately realized the AMA's long-standing aim of control of drug production and supply (ibid.: 36-38).

A 1966 study of male Chinese narcotic addicts discharged from the Lexington hospital between July 1957 and June 1962 found that 72 percent were born in China (Ball and Lau, 1966). Most were intravenous heroin users. Ball and Lau (ibid.: 72) describe these addicts as "unsuccessful sojourners" who migrated to America in search of riches, only to find themselves alienated from the mainstream of society and restricted to "the segregated, ghetto way of life of the Chinese-Americans." Although Ball and Lau report that opiate use among American Chinese has decreased markedly since the 1960s, it is still ranked fourth among the crimes for which Asian Americans are arrested in the United States.

AFRICAN AMERICANS

Just as the Chinese had been linked with opium use and singled out for tailor-made legislation and subsequent law enforcement, the second campaign against narcotics was directed at blacks and cocaine. New myths about blacks and cocaine use developed, such as the belief that blacks were more susceptible to the drug because of its "euphoric and stimulating properties" (Musto, 1987: 6).

Cocaine was extensively available at the turn of the century and during the early 1900s and was a favorite ingredient in medicine, soda pop, and wine. The Parke Davis Company, a pharmaceutical producer of cocaine, sold coca leaf cigarettes and coca cheroots (cigars) (ibid.: 7). The coca leaf, from which cocaine is extracted, was the Coca in the original Coca Cola and was identified in forty other brands of soft drink by the federal government in 1908 (Helmer, 1975: 51). In the 1880s South, soft drinks and patent medicines were used for headaches and other ailments because they were cheap and readily available, particularly in comparison to liquor and cocaine. Black southerners were especially attracted to these remedies, since liquor or cocaine for them was unaffordable. Also, Helmer suggests that liquor prohibition in the South may have contributed to the widespread use of cocaine in that region.

Despite the use of soft drinks and patent medicines containing cocaine by whites in the South, it was Coca Cola usage by blacks that was feared. Southern whites believed that cocaine use by blacks would cause them to "forget their place" and lead to violence against whites, particularly the dreaded rape of white women. In addition to the myth that cocaine use inclined blacks to rape, there was also the belief by southern whites that cocaine made blacks more efficient criminals. A third myth circulating was that cocaine rendered .32 caliber bullets ineffective against blacks, with the result that southern police departments began to issue the more lethal .38 caliber revolvers (Musto, 1987: 7).

In 1986, the 219,159 black Americans arrested for drug abuse violations accounted for 31.8 percent of all arrestees for that offense. A scant two years later, in 1988, the number of black drug arrests had increased 52.4 percent, to 334,015, and while the proportion of blacks arrested for drug abuse violations now stood at 39.6 percent, white arrests decreased to 59.6 percent, and the percentage distribution of Native Americans and Asian Americans remained the same (FBI, 1989: 186).

MEXICAN AMERICANS

The third minority group affected by a narcotics campaign directed specifically against them by white Americans was Mexican Americans. In this case, the drug evoking the fear was marijuana. Although included originally in the 1914 Harrison Act, in the final act passed, marijuana was not listed as a dangerous drug. Some western states passed anti-marijuana statutes in the 1920s, but the federal government did not take formal action until the Marijuana Tax Act of 1937. The first mention of drug use by Chicanos in the United States was in the 1920s, when some migrant field workers were observed smoking marijuana (Bullington, 1977: 43). Again, myths played an important role in the labeling of Mexican Americans as dangerous drug users, since the common myth in the Southwest was that marijuana use was a major cause of violence, particularly homicide, and other "horrible" crimes committed by Mexican Americans (Musto, 1987: 219). Helmer reports a different underlying reason for these actions against Chicanos:

> Public concern about marijuana grew because Americans wanted to drive the Mexicans back over the border, for reasons which had nothing to do with the nature of the drug or its psychological effects. All the same, a theory about the evils of the drug—linking its use and supply to being Mexican—was invented with the result that hostility toward the Mexicans began to seem more reasonable and public policy to remove them that much more acceptable. . . . The problem of Mexican labor and the unemployed surplus after 1928 is the key factor in determining what became public policy and ultimately the law on marijuana we still live with. (1975: 56)

The enforcement of state marijuana laws in Los Angeles thus reduced the economic threat of a Mexican labor surplus in that city, since the options were "jail on drug or other charges, or repatriation by force or choice" (Helmer, 1975: 74). Later, in the 1930s and 1940s, marijuana use became fairly widespread among Chicano youth gangs, but other drugs now became the targets of white sentiment.

The use of opium was practically unknown at this time, with the successful treatment of the Chinese fifty years earlier. But after World War II, servicemen who had picked up the habit overseas, where opium was cheap and readily available, brought the use of heroin, the most potent form of opium, home with them. Along with the increased use of hard narcotics in the postwar years, an addict subculture developed in the Mexican barrios, since "association with other drug users protected the individual user from detection and subsequent arrest and also provided him with a camaraderie with others who could appreciate the pleasures to be derived from the illicit drugs" (Bullington, 1977: 45). Increasing demands for heroin in the 1950s made the Chicano barrio the drug distribution center for the entire city of Los Angeles, particularly since Chicano users were the logical resource because of their connections with the drug source, Mexico.

The 1960s and 1970s saw a rapid increase in illicit drug use in Chicano communities, as well as throughout the country. Today barrio youth are also sniffing glue and other inhalants as early as eight years of age. The Chicano community of East Los Angeles has an inordinate number of known addicts, and with

Chicanos constituting at least 50 percent of those in institutions and on "release status," it is clear that they "predominate among the ranks of California's identified addicts" (Bullington, 1977: 47).

AGAIN, AFRICAN AMERICANS

The next strenuous campaign against narcotics took place in the 1950s and for the second time publicly linked blacks to a drug, in this case heroin. As with cocaine and the black "Coca Cola fiends," the public was led to believe that blacks were somehow more susceptible to heroin. Rumors and myths circulated about black involvement with this drug, much like the innuendos of previous decades about blacks, Chinese, and Mexican Americans. The implication this time was that there was a connection between black heroin addicts and crime that was responsible for the high crime rate. It was commonly believed that drug use led to delinquent behavior and crime because of the need to support expensive drug habits. Officially, the period from 1949 to 1953 revealed an epidemic of adolescent drug addiction, but in actuality, there had been a gradual rise in addicts during the prewar and war years (Helmer, 1975: 90). Furthermore, research at that time indicated that "the total amount of delinquency was independent of narcotics use, and that the reported rise in other than drug offenses reflected increased activity on the part of the police" (ibid.: 94).

As previously noted, after World War II heroin was popular in minority communities. The number of narcotics prosecutions began to rise, and the rate of increase among blacks was three times faster than that among whites, peaking in 1951, and steadily rising ever since (ibid.: 89-90). The myths concerning the effects of heroin on blacks influenced the passage of the Narcotics Drug Act of 1951, the Boggs Amendment, and other laws which fixed mandatory minimum sentences, increased the prison term to ten years for repeated offenses and to two years for first convictions of narcotics possession, and allowed no provisions for probation on second and subsequent convictions (Musto, 1987: 230).

It must be remembered that these were the times of Senator Kefauver's organized crime investigations and the beginnings of the McCarthy Communist witch-hunting era. The congressional hearings found "virtually no record of the fact that most narcotics users, young or old at the time, were black" (Helmer, 1975: 101), yet the drug stigma was applied to black Americans. Also, the Kefauver Committee reintroduced the Chinese drug connection by claiming that the Chinese tongs were behind narcotics distribution in some parts of the country, a position supported by the Boggs subcommittee, which suggested that the narcotics epidemic was some type of Communist plot (ibid.: 103). By 1956, the hearings conducted by Senator McCarthy included minority groups among those considered to be under the influence of an international Communist conspiracy, since it was believed that drug addiction was used as a means of subversion. Ironically, the societal reaction against black heroin users as any form of threat was misplaced, since there were relatively more white drug offenders than black drug offenders (ibid.: 120).

Today we are witnessing an echo of this earlier history and a return to a "wave of drug intolerance" directed at cocaine and black Americans that "will again translate into a simple fear of the drug user and will be accompanied by draconian sentences and specious links between certain drugs and distrusted groups within society, as was the case with cocaine and Southern blacks in the first decade of this century" (Musto, 1987: 277).

A new form of cocaine, "rock," first popularized in Los Angeles in 1985, involves the crystallization of cocaine into small pebbles (Inciardi, 1986: 82). This smokable form of cocaine, now called "crack," is cheap, easily made, easy to conceal, and rapidly absorbed into the blood stream, and it yields a fast, potent high (Musto, 1987; Kamiya, 1989) that has been described as the "ultimate high," and as "better than sex."[12] In 1985, a jumbo vial of crack sold for $40 in New York City; by 1988, the cost was only $15 ("Hour by Hour," 1988: 65). Since one gram of cocaine can be transformed into six or more crack rocks (Inciardi, 1986), and in the first ten months of 1988 the U.S. Drug Enforcement Administration (DEA) confiscated 40,034 kilos of cocaine ("Hour by Hour": 65), the staggering enormity of the "crack epidemic" is obvious. It is estimated that the amounts seized by the DEA and other law-enforcement agencies— 233,094 pounds of cocaine in fiscal 1990 (Timrots, Byme, and Finne, 1991)— represent only about 10 percent of the cocaine that eludes detection in this multi-billion-dollar-a-year drug industry (Kamiya, 1989).

About 12 percent (29 million people) of the U.S. population is believed to be "at risk," and as of 1985, 22 million Americans admitted they had used cocaine (Morganthau and Miller, 1988: 77). In 1987, one out of eighteen high-school seniors had tried crack, and 14 percent admitted they had used other forms of cocaine; 6.7 percent of young adults have tried crack, and 40 percent have experienced cocaine ("Hour by Hour": 75). When Carlos Lehder Rivas, a Colombian cocaine kingpin who was tried in the United States and is currently serving 135 years in a U.S. penitentiary, said that "cocaine is the Third World's atomic bomb" (Morganthau and Miller, 1988: 76), he was frighteningly accurate. Although the cocaine-crack problem does not differentiate by class or race, ranging from inner-city ghetto streets to Wall Street, it has been particularly devastating to black and Hispanic communities (Kamiya, 1989). Research indicates that "the compulsive use of cocaine may represent a unique and more expensive form of addiction than heroin" and is therefore associated with increasing levels of illegal income (Collins, Hubbard, and Rachal, 1985: 759).

NATIVE AMERICANS

Historically and traditionally, many Indian cultures used substances such as peyote, mushrooms, and coca plants primarily for medicinal and religious purposes—substances which were not ethnically considered drugs (Baker, 1977: 3). With the decline of cultural symbolism and the significance of Indian religion, there have been increases in drug abuse among Native Americans. Although most drug research involving Native Americans has been directed at alcohol abuse (Winfree, Theis, and Griffiths, 1981: 469), it is now known that marijuana, inhalants, barbiturates, amphetamines, hallucinogens, cocaine, and heroin have been found on and off the Indian reservations, particularly among Native Americans under age thirty (Baker, 1977: 12).

Most of the marijuana research in the United States has been focused on students and indicates that approximately 10 to 48 percent of all U.S. youths in grades seven to twelve have used marijuana. Studies of Indian youths in the same grades reveal a range from 22 to 62 percent (May, 1982b: 38). Winfree and his colleagues found, for example, that 35 percent of all sixth- through twelfth-grade students in a Rocky Mountain state rural school district indicated that they had used marijuana (Winfree, Theis, and Griffiths, 1981: 471): 32 percent of the Native American youths were classified as experimenters, 7 percent as occasional users, and 11 percent as regular marijuana users (Winfree and Griffiths, 1983: 57). According to Winfree and Griffiths, Native American youths appeared to begin using marijuana earlier than white youths and became more involved with the drug at increasing grade levels (ibid.: 66). Drugs were more available because as Indian youths grew older, they were more mobile; additionally,

> He or she is a minority group member growing up in a relatively hostile social environment. A growing awareness of the limitations and restrictions that society has placed on him or her—combined with conflicts involving parents, peers, and the law about drugs—may result in lowered perceptions of the risks of smoking marijuana. The end product of these processes conceivably is an isolated, frustrated, disoriented individual who might turn to drugs as an escape from both a disintegrating and depressing aboriginal world, and an uncaring and disinterested outside world. (Ibid.: 65)

National college polls have shown consistently that 50 to 55 percent of students use marijuana. The figures for Indian youths in this age bracket, drawn from studies undertaken in post–high school technical schools, are 70 to 78 percent (May, 1982b: 38).

Whereas the true extent of marijuana abuse among young Indians is not known, in many cases it is believed to be part of a polydrug pattern. Solvent sniffing among Native Americans, which often begins at age ten, commonly involves glue, gasoline, paint, and hair spray because of their availability and low cost (Baker, 1977: 13). The use of inhalants has been reported as quite popular among Indian youths. Studies of Indians ages twelve through nineteen reveal that between 17 and 22 percent reported inhalant use, compared to the 9 to 11 percent of U.S. youths overall in this age group who reported such usage (May, 1982b). In general, almost twice as many Indian youths have used inhalants as have youths nationally.

In most drug categories except alcohol, marijuana, and inhalants, Indians use drugs at about the same rate as the population at large. The oral and intravenous use of amphetamines occurs on a relatively small scale in Indian communities, as does the use of barbiturates and hallucinogens. In fact, Indians in grades seven through twelve were found to be less likely to use barbiturates than other U.S. youths (ibid.).

Peyote, regarded by the Native American Church as a sacrament, is not classified as a drug by Indians or generally used outside of the church (Baker, 1977: 14). Its use is strictly controlled by the church, and it is taken only during highly organized religious functions. Under such conditions, the side effects are minimal, and group functioning and group solidarity are enhanced (May, 1982b: 39). However, the use of hallucinogens, particularly peyote, is reported to be higher among Indian youths than other U.S. youths, and adult Indian use of peyote is probably higher than that of other U.S. adults (May, 1982b).

Because of the poor economic status of Native Americans, cocaine and heroin are of questionable use both on and off the reservation. There are a few known incidents of intravenous heroin use, but cocaine seems to be more widely accessible and used (Baker, 1977: 14). As the national drug problem increases, Indian communities are feeling the impact, and there is a growing concern about drug abuse among the younger Indians. Social conditions such as socioeconomic stress, culture conflict, peer pressure, and family disharmony are strong influences believed to contribute to the problem (ibid.: 16).

Clearly, alcohol is the most significant drug abused by Native Americans. Whereas drug abuse violation arrests in 1986 indicate that Native Americans are underrepresented compared to their population percentage (0.4 vs. 0.6 percent, respectively) and such offenses represent 2.7 percent of their arrests, alcohol and alcohol-related offenses (liquor law violations, DUI, drunkenness, disorderly conduct, vagrancy) together account for 47.8 percent of all Native American arrests. Alcohol and crime have been associated with American Indians since the mid-nineteenth century. One of the first reports to note the phenomenon was undertaken by von Hentig (1945), who studied forty volumes of the *Survey of Conditions of Indians in the United States,* which referred to the offenses of Native Americans in seven states.[13] Although the statistical information was scanty, von Hentig reported a pre–World War II comparison between Indian and white arrests that showed significant disparity. Over this period of time, Indian males had arrest rates that were three times the white male rate, while felony rates were five times those for white males (ibid.: 76).[14] An examination of types of offenses revealed that drunkenness headed the list. Indians were charged with drunkenness in 58 percent of the Indian court cases and in 53.2 percent of regular court cases (ibid.: 79).

A later analysis of 1960 Uniform Crime Reports by Omer Stewart (1964: 61) revealed Indian criminality to be seven times the national average and alcohol-related crimes to account for 76 percent of Indian arrests, 71 percent of which were for drunkenness. Stewart found that the percentages for Indian crimes involving alcohol were twelve times greater than the national average and over five times the average for blacks: alcohol was connected with 33 percent of black arrests and 47 percent of white arrests (ibid.: 62). Stewart suggested that the high Indian arrest rate might also be a result of prejudice and discrimination: "Indians alone have been subjected to selective prohibition against alcohol for over a century and a half. From the passage of the general Indian Intercourse Act of 1832 until 1953, it was illegal nationally for Indians to possess liquor in any form any place" (ibid.: 66).

Those Native Americans who did drink had to do so illegally and at great expense, since they had to pay bootleggers or disreputable bar owners double the price (Riffenburgh, 1964: 42). Riffenburgh (ibid.: 41) notes that the geographic isolation of most Indian reservations leads to negative relationships between Indians from the reservation and non-Indians in the nearest towns and cities, particularly when Indians become intoxicated in these communities. When an Indian drinks in these towns and cities, frequently he cannot make it to his home to sleep it off, so many are arrested in "parked cars, wagons, doorways, parks, and alleys—places to which they retreated and where they were sleeping away the effects of too much alcohol" (ibid.: 41-42).

Ironically, when the federal government passed legislation on August 15, 1953 that permitted Native Americans to purchase and drink liquor, each tribe was to decide whether liquor would be legalized on its reservation. Those tribes that did not take action placed Indians desiring to drink in a peculiar position, since it would be a violation of both tribal and federal law to have liquor on the reservation. Therefore, an Indian caught in this situation could not drink at home on the reservation but could legally drink in a bar off of the reservation. This led to the growth of taverns on the outskirts of reservations that frequently charged higher prices than the bars in town. Because of the remote locations of these taverns, there is less law-enforcement scrutiny, thus making it possible to sell to underage Indians and to those who are already intoxicated (Riffenburgh, 1964).

When alcohol is legalized, Indian arrest rates decrease. May (1982a: 231) examined local arrests on a South Dakota reservation where there was legalized alcohol and discovered that Indian arrests in the towns surrounding the reservation dropped significantly, and there was no increase in reservation arrests. In a comparison of on-reservation arrest rates of tribes with legalized alcohol ("wet" tribes) with those tribes that prohibited alcohol ("dry" tribes), May found that the "arrest rates for all offenses and particularly alcohol-related offenses were found to be consistently and significantly lower on the 'wet' or legalized reservations" (ibid.: 231-232). Further, in towns contiguous to the "wet" reservations, Indian arrests were low compared to those in towns bordering "dry" reservations, where such arrests were a constant problem.

There are some indications that Native American drinking facilitates aggressive acts. Levy and Kunitz (1974: 103) noted that the presence of alcohol among Navajo homicide offenders (73.3 percent) was significantly more frequent than in cases of urban white (39.7 percent) or black killers (60 percent). In the cases of urban blacks and whites, the use of alcohol increased the violence of the homicide; in contrast, among the Navajos, the homicide was less violent when the offender was drunk than when he or she was sober (ibid.: 104). The researchers also found variations in the reasons for drinking and drinking patterns among the Hopi, Navajo, and White Mountain Apache tribes and concluded that Indian drinking behavior was circumscribed by traditional Indian culture (ibid.: 180).

For many years it was believed that Indians may have deficient ability to metabolize or process alcohol. Research in this area, controlling for body weight and drinking experience, shows no difference in alcohol metabolism between Indians and whites. Further, it has been consistently shown that individual Indians have an equal or even greater ability to metabolize ethanol than people of other ethnic groups. Although some questions linger about high acetaldehyde levels of Indians and several brain-based enzymes, at present there is no proof of any metabolic deficit among Indians (May, 1977).[15]

OTHER MINORITY ALCOHOL USE

Alcohol is not the major drug abused by blacks, and further, alcohol-related crime constitutes only 18.1 percent of black arrests. Nonetheless, there is sufficient and strong evidence that alcohol is a major detriment to African Americans. Williams (1982: 31) points out that "the violent consequences of alcohol abuse have been extreme for black Americans (especially black males) in terms of homicides, accidents, criminal assaults, and other conflicts with the law." Alcohol use has been involved in more than 50 percent of black homicides (Williams, 1985: 53). Recent research, however, indicates that the rate of drinking among African Americans is comparable to that for whites when age and socioeconomic levels are controlled for; a study by Williams found that (1) black high-school students were twice as likely to abstain from alcohol as white students; (2) four times as many white students as black students drank heavily; (3) black students who drank were found to consume less alcohol than white students; (4) 19 percent of adult black males were heavy drinkers, compared to 22 percent of their white counterparts; and (5) 38 percent of adult black males did not drink, in comparison to 31 percent adult white male abstainers (ibid.).

Public drinking and drunkenness are among the most frequent arrest offenses of African Americans. In 1986, 137,043 blacks were arrested for drunkenness, an offense that ranks sixth among within-group black arrests. An ethnographic study of blacks in Washington, D.C. accurately describes the men found typically on any ghetto streetcorner:

> The streetcorner men usually return day after day to the same hangout. There they talk and drink, play cards and shoot crap, or just do nothing. Some go home to eat, others get something from the carry-out or the streetcorner grocer—some bread and coldcuts, perhaps, things they can eat while they are standing on the corner. There is continuous drinking—a lot of gin and somewhat less whiskey, while some men drink only cheap wine. If they are not already alcoholics, they are well on their way. Many of them have had attacks of *delirium tremens;* the symptoms of "deetee" are familiar to most ghetto dwellers. Now and then somebody at the corner mentions that yet another friend has cirrhosis of the liver, and everybody knows of friends and acquaintances who have died from ailments caused by their drinking. (Hannerz, 1969: 54)

The black men who drink in the back alleys or on the streetcorner are constantly on guard against police officers and patrol cars, particularly since ghetto residents "find themselves under constant surveillance from slow-moving patrol cars" (ibid.: 165).

Even though Hispanics are the youngest, the fastest-growing, and the second-largest U.S. minority group, their drinking patterns have largely been ignored by researchers. However, there are convincing indications that alcohol use is a major factor in Hispanic life. The drinking habits and other alcohol-related characteristics of Hispanics have been found to vary radically among, for example, Dominicans, Guatemalans, and Puerto Ricans in the same northeastern city (Rogan, 1985: 82). In the Southwest, studies suggest a disproportionate relationship between alcohol and Hispanic deaths: 52 percent of all deaths of Mexican American men in Los Angeles were found to be alcohol-related, compared to 22 percent for black men and 24 percent for white men (ibid.: 81).

Gambling

Bloch (1951: 215) describes gambling as not necessarily an evil, but an important form of institutionalized recreation with an ancient history. The significance of gambling as "an escape from the routine and boredom characteristic of much of modern industrial life" (ibid.: 217) is especially relevant for inner-city minorities who have few outlets from the dreariness of their day-to-day existence. The 11,701 black Americans arrested for gambling in 1986 were 46.1 percent of all arrestees for that public-order offense, but gambling was only .4 percent of their within-group arrest offenses, or less than one-fourth as frequent as the white within-group category (1.7 percent) and almost one-third less than for Asian Americans (1.1 percent). Only the rate of Native American within-group arrests for gambling was lower than the black proportion (.01 percent).

Policy wheels were the primary type of lottery among lower-class, inner-city blacks and urban whites from the late nineteenth century until the 1940s. In 1938, for example, the policy syndicate on the south side of Chicago employed 5,000 persons and grossed $18 million annually (Light, 1977b: 893-894). The Jones brothers, originally from Evanston, Illinois, had one of the largest black operations, but "retired" from policy after paying ransom on the kidnapping of one of the brothers. Small policy wheels, in which the numbers were drawn from a drum or "wheel," were still operating on Chicago's south side at least until the late 1950s, but were soon replaced by the "numbers," which had been in existence since the 1920s. Hannerz (1969: 141) describes a complex business hierarchy within the Washington, D.C. numbers racket, with whites reputedly at the top, as in most cities, and the ghetto resident numbers runners in the bottom echelon of the enterprise. Numbers gambling, once extremely popular in all major American cities, today has largely been replaced by legal state lotteries, which, like policy, also use the drum.

One study of Detroit numbers gambling, described by Light (1977b: 894-895), points to an underlying "culture complex" that included "dream interpretation, folklore and music, social roles, spiritualism, ceremonial festivities, fad and fashion in playing style, and an extensive gambling jargon." Numbers may be selected on the basis of "idiosyncratic attachments" such as one's birthday (January 25 as 1 and 25) or one's street number. There are "dream books" that contain "lucky" numbers, and "readers," "spiritualists," and "psychic advisors" in the ghetto who, in addition to giving advice on love, sickness, and magic, are considered experts on numbers (Hannerz, 1969: 142). However the numbers are selected, there is usually a methodical style of playing them and some regularity to the practice. A New York City study found that 72 percent of the numbers bettors placed a bet two or three times a week, and 42 percent bet daily. Further, while 41 percent had been betting numbers for ten years or more, 59 percent had been playing the numbers for six to ten years (Light, 1977b: 896).

According to Light, Caribbean blacks in this country invented the numbers game, which was popularized and concentrated primarily among minorities. In 1934, 60 percent of the numbers players were black (ibid.: 894). By 1973, blacks and other ethnic-group numbers bettors in older eastern and midwestern cities were wagering an estimated $2.5 billion, or 10 percent of all illegal gambling revenue (ibid.). In New York City, for example, it was estimated that in 1972, $600 million a year was bet on numbers, and $180 million of that sum was wagered by blacks, who were 30 percent of the bettors (ibid.). At a rate of $87 for every black person in New York City, Light offers a conservative estimate of 5 percent of black family income spent on numbers gambling that year (ibid.).

Gambling has been connected to crime in three ways: "gambling is a crime in most states, crooked gambling is criminal, and illegally gotten money is used to finance gambling or to pay gambling debts" (Lesieur and Klein, 1985). In their study of male and female prisoners in two New Jersey state correction institutions, Lesieur and Klein found that 30 percent of the inmates demonstrated clear signs of gambling addiction, as evidenced by lying about gambling wins and losses, and family, job, and financial disruptions due to gambling. However, it seems that these indices of pathological gambling are not applicable to the black numbers gamblers described above, many of whom view the numbers game, for example, as "a rational economic activity" and their number bets as "investments" or savings strategies (Light, 1977b: 896).[16] Light (ibid.: 897-898) lists several functions served by numbers betting: (1) social interaction when the bet is placed; (2) provision of employment in the black community; (3) availability of credit from numbers "banks"; and (4) investment of profits in the black community by numbers racketeers.

In sum, like dope pushing, selling "hot" merchandise, pimping, bootlegging liquor, and other forms of "hustling," gambling in the black urban ghettos of the United States is an escape from demeaning ghetto life, a chance for instant "wealth," and an integral part of the "hidden economy." For Asian Americans, gambling is an important form of entertainment that takes place in the privacy of their homes and their clubs. We know little about the gambling practices of Hispanic Americans, but since they account for almost one-fourth of those arrested for this crime, we should make a serious effort to learn the dynamics of this public-order crime.

A Minority View

Although there are a number of possible approaches that could be used in analyzing the types of crimes for which American racial minorities are arrested, for the minority perspective we return to the earlier discussion of definitional analyses described by Amini (1972), in this instance, a discussion of *what* types of crimes are defined, *how* they are defined, and *who* is defining them (see Chapter 1).

It is clear from the arrest statistics on types of crime that in terms of their proportions in the United States population, African Americans, Hispanic Americans, Native Americans, and, for some offenses, Asian Americans have disproportionately high rates of arrests compared to Euro-Americans. While it is not the intention to disclaim minority overrepresentation in crime commission as reflected by arrests, it is curious, and far from coincidence, that each of these minority groups unequally shares this common experience when compared to the majority (white) group. For many decades, the intense research focus on African American crime has obscured the fact that other racial minorities are also unevenly represented in high percentages of arrests relative to their population proportions.

Both arrest figures and descriptions of research on those selected crimes most frequently studied were examined in this chapter. In the first instance, two methods were used to examine the "official" statistics: the customary method of across- or between-group crime type categories, and a relatively little used within-group description of the arrests of each racial/ethnic subgroup. The latter technique, which revealed the similarity in patterns of crime commission as measured by arrests, demonstrates clearly that despite race or ethnicity, Americans differ little in the types of crimes for which they are arrested. Contrary to a recent vitriolic criticism of my use of this analytical method, no claims are made, or were ever made, that African Americans, or any other racial minority group, *as reflected in arrest figures,* "do not offend at a higher rate than whites" (Wilbanks, 1990: 23); crime rates were not the focus of this analysis. Zatz describes my position most accurately:

> Richey Mann presents 1986 Uniform Crime Report data showing very similar patterns of offending for blacks, Asian Americans, Hispanics, American Indians, and whites. Wilbanks' rejoinder is appalling for its shockingly condescending and paternalistic tone, inexcusable in scholarly debate. Beyond this, his criticism is wrong. While he is certainly correct in noting the difference between rates and patterns, he improperly assumes that between-group variation is the only valid indicator of difference, thereby summarily dismissing the vast literature on comparisons of within-group variance that allow us to determine whether the same model operates for

two or more subgroups. . . . Between-group effects are clearly important; but, so are comparisons of patterns within-groups, and ignoring them is a serious flaw in Wilbanks' work. (1990: 117)

The within-group comparative examination of crime patterns by minority subgroups and whites appears to clearly reflect the involvement of minorities in the criminal justice system because of their commission of offenses that transgress the mores of the majority group. This imposition of moral elitism is particularly seen in the current treatment of Native and Hispanic Americans as a result of alcohol use, and with African Americans' drug abuse. Further, as we have seen, throughout their histories in this nation, all minority subgroups have been criminalistically stigmatized for involvement with drugs. Recent evidence introduced by Christina Johns in her revealing book *Power, Ideology, and the War on Drugs* suggests that the stigmatization continues:

There is no question that the enforcement tactics of the War on Drugs are focused on minority populations. In fact, drug panics have been used historically in this country as part of a larger war against marginalized populations, designed to further marginalize them and legitimate their oppression. . . . Prejudice against the Chinese was a large factor behind widespread legislation prohibiting opium smoking in the latter nineteenth century. Campaigns to prohibit the use of intoxicants in the South and to disenfranchise and repress blacks were frequently led by the same people, and they were part of a wider movement to keep blacks in a subordinate position. (1992: 73-73)

What has been predominantly defined as criminal is the criminalization of the means minorities use to escape the racial oppression, discrimination, and frustration each group shares.

How types of minority crime are defined occurs in at least three major ways. First, as detailed above, is the inordinate and almost exclusive use of across-group (between-group) arrest and victimization rates, with the subsequent neglect of within-group comparative pattern analyses. A second major influence on the definition of minority crime is found in the selection of the types of crimes studied. And finally, the methods used to collect the data are selectively narrow and focused.

Previous studies of minority involvement in crime appear to target those offenses that Euro-Americans most fear at the hands of a person of color (rape, robbery, burglary, homicide), or abhor purportedly for moral reasons (prostitution, drugs, drinking, gambling), even though whites themselves appear to excel at such offenses against the public order. Euro-Americans are the most frequent customers of prostitutes and have always controlled organized prostitution rings. Aside from their personal use and abuse of drugs, Euro-Americans operate, control, and maintain the major importation networks and distribution channels for drugs, including alcohol, in this country. The major casinos, lotteries, and other "legal" means of gambling are under the domain of Euro-

Americans, who in many cases skim and launder proceeds from their illegal gains in order to avoid paying taxes on them.

In addition to the media, criminologists and other social scientists have made accusations and perpetuated myths that minorities, particularly African Americans, "select" or "choose" Euro-Americans as their victims of crime (e.g., Wilbanks, 1985). Even the most casual examination shows that most crimes are intraracial and involve harm inflicted upon a member of the perpetrator's own racial/ethnic subgroup. Such victimization is circumscribed by racial distribution and racial segregation in the United States.

The almost exclusive reliance on quantitative methods of crime data analysis and the neglect of rich qualitative techniques such as observational, anthropological, anecdotal, and ethnographic studies in minority communities indicate the final major weakness of how types of minority crime are defined, and ultimately recorded. In his criticism of the "reliance on a particular explanatory form, the hypothetico-deductive model," in the study of minority crime (1981: 49), Takagi observes that

> the etiology of crime in minority communities cannot be understood by a science that does not take into account thoughts and experiences of the people in the community. . . . A minority perspective does not, however, discount standard empirical analytic procedures. . . . Yet, at the same time, a minority perspective goes beyond the production of objective data; it seeks to penetrate—and emancipate—the consciousness of the persons described by such data. (Ibid.: 50)

The *who* in our attempt to understand minority crime concerns who is undertaking the research on the topic. Minority scholars have been systematically and effectively denied the opportunity to initiate funded research on minority crime, a topic with which most minority researchers are intimately acquainted. Only in the past decade have a few minority researchers been awarded major grants to address any research subject, much less studies of minorities like themselves. In fact, the assignment of minority academicians as peer reviewers for the major criminology/criminal justice journals is also a recent phenomenon. The irony of this exclusion from the "good old boy network" is that most minority scholars are potentially outstanding, competent researchers who had to be exceptional in order to successfully pass the rites of academic passage in the face of the racial discrimination found in most institutions of higher education.

As Takagi (1981: 59) accurately notes, "We need to have good ethnographic descriptions and especially cultural and biographical studies on the phenomenon to be investigated. It is only through fieldwork that we can obtain such information." Who can best accomplish such a charge in minority communities but minority researchers? Obstructions to the inclusion of minority researchers in federally funded studies—the major criminal-justice funding resource—are justified on the assumption that "minorities are too sensitive and subjective in cases related to other minorities," an assumption that "presupposes the existence of value-free, objective research" (NMAC, 1980: 280). The notion of value-free research is undeniably fallacious in light of the "special interest nature of government-sponsored research" (ibid.: 280) and the many ethnocentric biases that for decades have plagued the examination of types of minority crime and the criminal-justice processing of peoples of color.

3

Explanations of Minority Crime

Scholarship
Ever notice that
all the experts on
Black folks is white?
—Sam Greenlee

Most theories of race and crime are concerned with violent crime, specifically the violent crimes of African Americans, and are primarily concentrated on homicide. A majority of the studies of violence and homicide have been limited to the lower classes, while the circumstances of criminal homicides and the characteristics of victims and offenders in the middle and upper classes have been largely ignored. Yet, at least one study found that not one of the 121 upper-class homicide offenders examined was African American (Green and Wakefield, 1979: 175). Further, Green and Wakefield found a complete absence of the victim-precipitated killings that typify lower-class African American homicides. Instead, the white, upper-class murderers studied were found to have calculated their homicides, and the primary motive was financial gain (ibid.: 180).

Another frequently overlooked finding in research on African American homicide is the potential impact of medical resources upon lethality. Doerner (1983) hypothesizes that many homicide victims might have survived if they had received prompter and better medical attention. Police response to emergency calls and other related public services (e.g., ambulance response and transportation, medical emergency and other hospital care) in lower-income, particularly African American, communities have repeatedly been criticized as lacking, slow, or inadequate (Mann, 1990: 192).

Finally, the literature is replete with explanations of African American (and occasionally other minority) homicide and other forms of violence based on *biogenic, psychogenic,* and *sociogenic* factors while neglecting the theories of minority violence submitted by minority researchers.

Homicide Theories

Thio (1978: 106-107) distinguishes three kinds of murder theory, based upon where the cause is found: inside the human body (biogenic), within the human psyche (psychogenic), or in the social milieu (sociogenic). Within the classification of biogenic theories, Thio identifies three major approaches: *racist theory, ethological theory,* and *genetic theory.*

Racist theory equates blackness with criminality because of the high homicide rate among African Americans. There is no empirical evidence to support the idea that African Americans have a more powerful instinct to kill than whites. On the contrary, studies in Africa reveal that African blacks not only have lower homicide rates than African Americans, but also such rates are lower than those for the general American population (ibid.: 107). Moreover, in our examinations of "race," we have already seen that so-called black Americans are not a pure racial type, since the majority have "white" blood.

Ethological theory suggests that humans are far more homicidal than other animals with the instinct to kill, particularly since those dangerous animals rarely kill other animals of the same species. Ethological theorists state that other ferocious animals have an instinct to inhibit their killing instincts, but that this inhibitory instinct did not develop in humans. They attribute this to the fact that weapon development was too sudden for evolution to cope with. Since all of us have the same evolutionary past, the same killer instinct, and the same lack of instinctual inhibition against killing, according to ethological theory, we should all have the same likelihood of killing others. This theory is challenged by statistics which indicate that males, minorities, and the poor are more frequently arrested for homicide than females, whites, and the rich (ibid.: 108).

Genetic theory also has limited validity. The notion here is that the X chromosome from the mother yields gentle and passive characteristics, while the Y chromosome from the father is indicative of toughness and aggression. Males who have extra Y chromosomes are believed to be more violent: XYY males, who are one-seventh of one percent of the male population, are considered genetically abnormal and aggressive (ibid.: 108-109). There are no indications that any racial group predominates among XYY males. Further, since the samples have been limited to criminals in institutions, a possible bias is introduced; perhaps more XYYs are not in prisons. Some murderers have the XYY configuration, but most do not.

A review of the research on heredity and crime reveals a fairly consistent relationship between genes and criminal behavior, but generally concludes:

> Genetic factors are undoubtedly correlated with measures of criminality, but the large number of methodological flaws and limitations in the research should make one cautious in drawing any causal inferences at this point in time. Our review leads us to the inevitable conclusion that current genetic research on crime has been poorly designed, ambiguously reported, and exceedingly inadequate in addressing relevant issues. This criticism applies to studies that are generally supportive of the

crime-heredity hypothesis as well as to studies that fail to substantiate the basic tenets of the genetic argument. Perhaps even more significant, however, these studies have muddied the already turbid waters of genetic research on crime. (Walters and White, 1989: 478)

Recent efforts of Jeffery (1979; 1990) and his followers (e.g., Fishbein, 1990) introduce a "new" approach to biosocial criminology, which Balkan, Berger, and Schmidt find is not "new" at all, but is "a continuation of the tradition of looking for individual biological bases of criminal behavior" (1980: 18-19). Jeffery's perspective draws upon genetics in conjunction with the environment, or "nature and nurture in interaction," when he states that "genes influence behavior through pathway mechanisms such as the brain, brain chemistry, and hormonal systems, all in interaction with one another and with the environment" (1990: 184). Accordingly, violence and aggression are products of "genetic, neurological, and environmental factors," with certain (chemical) neurotransmitters (especially acetylcholine, dopamine, and norepinephrine) increasing different types of aggression (ibid.: 368). As yet, Jeffery and his colleagues have not attempted to apply these notions to African Americans or other minorities. In fact, in her review of biological perspectives in criminology, Fishbein (1990: 55) notes that the "weaknesses in design, sampling techniques, and statistical procedures delineated above preclude drawing definitive conclusions, and results are frequently contested and unreliable"; thus, she cautions against "the premature application of biological findings."

Within the psychogenic theories, Thio includes psychoanalytical and psychological perspectives. Psychoanalytical theory assumes problems with the Freudian-defined id, ego, superego triad such that if a person is deprived of love or subjected to brutal attacks in childhood, the aggressive (id) drive would become too irrational for the ego to cope with and too powerful for the superego ("conscience") to subdue; the result is a condition that could lead to extremely violent and bizarre murders. On the other hand, if parents severely punish a child for expressing even the mildest form of aggression, the superego becomes so powerful that it completely suppresses aggressive drives. Without a normal release for this aggressive energy, it builds up and overwhelms the superego. This explanation is offered to explain how a very nice, "normal" person suddenly commits murder and shocks family, friends, and neighbors (Thio, 1978: 109-111).

Alvin Poussaint, an African American professor of psychiatry at Harvard University, applies the psychology of the African American experience when he suggests that African Americans kill African Americans[1] because of low self-esteem and rage which is turned against those around them. Poussaint states: "Many of the problems in the Black community are related to institutional racism, which fosters a chronic lack of Black self-respect, predisposing many poor Blacks to behave self-destructively and with uncontrollable rage" (1983: 163). He is also careful to add that the vast majority of urban, inner-city African Americans are strongly opposed to violence and crime.

Psychological theory is the most popular of the psychogenic explanations, and concomitantly, the *frustration-aggression theory* is the most accepted as well as the most pertinent to homicide (Thio, 1978: 111-112). Under this perspective, aggression is always a consequence of frustration. Frustration is defined as the blockage of one's attempt to achieve a goal. It has been observed that a source of frustration for African Americans is the experiences associated with discrimination and caste status, which "incessantly irritate the black man's psyche" (Guterman, 1972: 231). According to this perspective, the anger resulting from their daily frustrations takes the form of arguments, verbal abuse, and fights that are directed by African Americans toward other African Americans, especially toward family members. In his assessment of black-on-black homicide, Poussaint (1972; 1983: 163) also refers to the influence of one's level of frustration on any violent act. The frustrations of ghetto African Americans accordingly lead to "estrangement, cynicism, expectations of double-dealing in others," characteristics that make it difficult to establish and maintain self-control systems (Heilbrun and Heilbrun, 1977: 370).

A Georgia study of 126 male felons designed to test the influence of deficient self-control on African American violent crime used three measures of self-control: the impulsiveness of the crime, a psychometric index of impulsivity (the Minnesota Multiphasic Personality Inventory, or MMPI), and two cognitive control tasks believed to be behavioral assessments of impulse control. On every measure, the Heilbruns found violent African American criminals to show less self-control than violent Euro-American criminals. However, no differences in self-control were found between African American and Euro-American nonviolent offenders on the measures of impulsivity employed. Even though the violent African American inmates studied demonstrated poorer self-control on the defining measures, Heilbrun and Heilbrun state that violent criminals represent better parole risks than nonviolent criminals. Further, despite having engaged in more impulsive crimes, African Americans were the most successful parolees, although the reason why was unclear to the researchers (1977: 376).

In a recent discussion, Bernard (1990) offers a refinement of the frustration-aggression theory. The new structural theory predicts high levels of angry aggression among the "truly disadvantaged," even if the group "does not possess any abnormal biological or psychological characteristics," because of the additive effect of three key social factors—urban environment, low social position, and racial and ethnic discrimination (ibid.: 74). Bernard defines his theory as a subcultural theory that overcomes the criticisms previously directed at such theories.[2]

Two sociogenic theories have been conceived by sociologists to explain homicide: *external restraint theory* and the *subculture of violence theory,* both of which locate the cause of murder in the social environment, or outside both the body and the psyche (Thio, 1978: 113-116). The strength of external restraint reflects the amount of social control circumscribing a person's freedom and behavior. Strong external restraint and its concomitant frustrations would lead to homicide or other-directed, not self-directed, aggression. On the other hand, weak external restraint leads to suicide (self-directed aggression). Essentially, external restraint theory views suicide and homicide as basically the same phenomenon. Both are acts of aggression resulting from frustration—suicide is aggression directed inward against oneself; homicide is aggression directed outward against another person. The theory tries to explain why an individual who is intensely frustrated would choose one type of aggression over another.

According to the external restraint theory, people who suffer a great amount of social control are more inclined toward homicide, because they can legitimately blame others for their frustration. Higher African American and lower-class homicide rates are therefore thought to be associated with the experience of stronger external restraint due to parental socialization practices which relied on physical, as opposed to psychological, punishment. During the socialization process, physical punishment leads to outward aggression against another, while psychological punishment leads to inward aggression against the self. Thus, support for external restraint theory is based upon the assumption that the significantly higher homicide rates of African Americans and the lower classes are a result of their parents' having used more physical punishment during their childhood than the parents of white or middle-class children. However, Thio points out that "from the scientific point of view, the validity of the theory has to depend on more than the assumption. It has to depend on empirical data directly supporting the relationship between strong external restraint itself and homicide. Such data, however, do not exist" (1978: 114). Furthermore, Thio is critical of the theory because it assumes that African Americans and lower-class people experience more physical punishment as children, when research has demonstrated that there are no race or class differences in parental use of physical punishment.

In an earlier version of the subculture of violence theory, Wolfgang (1958) described the basic cause of high homicide rates in poor neighborhoods and African American urban ghettos as a result of association and identification with a model of violence inherent in the community. Violence becomes a part of the lifestyle and a way of solving interpersonal problems. Wolfgang and Ferracuti (1967) discuss a subculture that differs from the dominant culture, or larger value system, through having a social value of its own which conflicts with the wider, central, cultural order.

These alleged values, which Amir (1971) applied to rape, include (1) an emphasis on the importance of seeking thrills through aggressive actions and sexual exploits; (2) a male obsession with masculinity and the need to display it; (3) the idealization of personal violence and prowess; and (4) a milieu that encourages sexual permissiveness, early sexual experience, the use of sex by boys for achieving status in peer groups, and promiscuous behavior by girls. Under this perspective, the use of violence is not seen as immoral, nor is there guilt about such aggression. Since homicide is considered the most extreme form of violence, Wolfgang and Ferracuti (1967: 158) found that its expression is indicative of "a subcultural normative system, and that this system is reflected in the psychological traits of the subcultural participants."

In addition to personality variables which determine whether or not subcultural values will be transmitted, Wolfgang and Ferracuti (ibid.: 140) suggest that such values, which include "a potent theme of violence," are learned in the subculture and "make up the lifestyle, the socialization process, the interpersonal relationships of individuals living in similar conditions." Furthermore, they assume that by examining the highest homicide rates (for Amir these would be rape rates), the subculture of violence is identified.

In sum, following the subculture of violence perspective, certain subgroups in the United States are said to live in a cultural and social milieu that encourages physical aggression, or at least does not actively discourage it (Hawkins, 1983: 412). The subculture of violence theory tends to identify the value system of a given subculture as the locus of the crime causation. Despite a paucity of research on African American culture and its characteristics, and the fact that Wolfgang and Ferracuti state that they are not prepared to assert how a subculture of violence arises, their conceptualization appears to be the "most influential contemporary explanation among criminologists interested in the determinants of violence" (Hawkins, 1983).

A recent cultural model of violence is proposed by Luckenbill and Doyle (1989), who introduce the term "disputatiousness" to account for the impact of structural position on criminal violence. The position one occupies along certain structural dimensions—race, income, age, gender, area of residence—affects one's disputatiousness and aggressiveness. Luckenbill and Doyle hypothesize that "young adults, males, blacks, lower-income persons, and urban and southern residents are more likely than their respective counterparts to name a negative outcome, to claim reparation, and to persevere and use force in resolving a dispute" (1989: 425). They suggest the use of artificial scenarios to measure such dispositions at the individual level of data.

Darnell Hawkins (1983: 414-415) offers a number of criticisms of the subculture of violence perspective that could apply equally to other "cultural" theories:

1. There is an overemphasis on individual value orientations which, when aggregated, are said to generate a subculture.
2. The theory is not empirically grounded and is challenged by some research findings.
3. A great deal of the theory underemphasizes a number of structural, situational, and institutional factors that affect interpersonal violence; for example, for African Americans such factors extend from historical patterns evolving from slavery, to the ramifications of an individual homicide, to the manner in which the criminal justice system operates.
4. The theory downplays the effects of the law on criminal homicide patterns.
5. In addition to the implanting of values, there are other possible ways that the social, economic, and political disadvantages faced by African Americans may lead to high homicide rates.

Hawkins later adds:

The belief that a high rate of violence among blacks is inevitable and normal is partly grounded in racial stereotype. It is also a product of observations made by social scientists who have sought to explain disproportionate levels of violence within the black community. These social scientific conceptions, as well as racial bias, often are used to support conclusions that the prevention of violence among blacks will be largely unsuccessful absent major changes in the political economy or black subcultural values. (1987: 199)

In their discussion of the myth of the African American rapist, Mann and Selva (1979) criticize the subculture of violence theory on the basis of ignorance of the African American subculture. They point out that the findings of both African American and Euro-American social scientists who have explored the African American community as a subculture have been overlooked. Cole (1970), for example, describes such a subculture as consisting of three subdivisions: shared values with the dominant culture, components shared with other oppressed peoples, and a subculture that is unique to African Americans. In her anthropological study, Cole identifies four African American lifestyles: (1) the "down home" lifestyle, rooted in the rural, traditional folkways of the South, yet located in both northern and southern African American communities; (2) the "militant" lifestyle, which is reflective of the African American struggle against oppression today seen in revolutionary ideas and demonstrations of college and other youth; (3) the "upward bound" lifestyle, exemplified by the African American middle class, whom African American sociologist E. Franklin Frazier (1965) called the "black bourgeoisie"; and (4) the "street" lifestyle, basically an urban phenomenon and the lifestyle most frequently, and inaccurately, associated with and erroneously assigned to all African Americans.

Mann and Selva (1979) note that data concerning the African American "subculture" are consistently and overwhelmingly concentrated on one lifestyle—the street lifestyle, "to the neglect of the diversity and variation of life styles in the black communities of this country."

An even more fundamental argument against the subculture of violence theory is offered by Haft-Picker (1980: 181), who begins by stating, "Despite an obvious preoccupation with the concept, criminologists no longer agree on what the subculture of violence actually is or whether it exists at all." Haft-Picker buttresses her thesis by drawing upon information from the natural sciences, linguistics, history, and anthropology and concludes that criminologists have no right to try to explain "sub" when they do not even understand "the greater entity 'culture.'" In questioning Wolfgang and Ferracuti's geographical detachment as a major criterion for selecting their case studies, Haft-Picker finds it "illogical to generalize their propositions to a poly-cultural society where subcultures cannot easily be isolated. Thus, it would be ridiculous to even suggest that poor, young black males form a subculture of violence" (1980: 182).

Turning to theories of human nature, Haft-Picker defines violence as "an instinctive reaction to violent threats," but insists that what is perceived as a survival threat varies among cultures—what is viewed as a nonthreatening hindrance in one culture may be seen as a survival threat in another (ibid.: 189-190).

Social Structural Explanations of African American Crime

Attempts to explain African American crime have generated a great deal of ecologically oriented research on both microlevels and macrolevels of analysis. Explanatory models have evolved that are variously centered on the interrelationships between the social structure and urbanism. Some of these perspectives focus on economic indices and other factors endemic to urban metropolitan areas such as socioeconomic status or social class, unemployment, economic inequality, and poverty. Most frequently these components are associated in research and theory formulation with African American homicide and other personal crimes, or with African American "street crime."

URBANISM AND AFRICAN AMERICAN CRIME
Beginning with the seminal urban ecology work of the Chicago School (e.g., Burgess, 1926; Park, 1936; Wirth, 1938; Shaw and McKay, 1942), urbanism has been generally considered one of the most consequential correlates of criminal behavior (Laub, 1983). In an early test of the relationship between ecological structure and African American homicide, Pettigrew and Spier (1962) tested hypotheses concerning African American homicide rates and their relationship to (1) general traditions of states' violence, (2) African American in-migration to states, (3) African Americans' socioeconomic levels in states, and (4) African American family disorganization in states. They found that the "homicidal culture index," a measure based theoretically upon the violent tradition of the frontier culture (particularly the South), "combined with the out-of-state birth measure of non-white male migration offer the best two-variable prediction of the Negro state homicide rates," especially in the Midwest and other northern states which had constant incoming southern African American migrants (1962: 625). Admitting that the migration findings were confounded by socioeconomic variables, for example, that African American migrants are "at the bottom rungs of urban society," Pettigrew and Spier suggested that African American violent crime rates are more than simply a function of socioeconomic status alone: "It might well be that the Negro turns to homicide because he is often a product of a region with a violent tradition, and because he is often a migrant in a new and threatening environment that makes it difficult for him to throw off this cultural predilection for homicide" (ibid.: 628-629). As we will see later, recent studies of urban African American unemployment, poverty, and economic inequality lend support to this early argument.

In his test of *compositional theory,* which "questions the importance of urbanism and contends that differences in crime rates across the urban-rural dimension may be attributed to the differences in the compositions of the populations residing in these areas," Laub (1983: 183) suggests that there is a con-founding effect between urbanism and race. Using National Crime Survey (NCS) data,[3] Laub examined only personal crimes (rape, robbery, assault, and personal larceny) in a comparison of urban and rural area crime rates. To determine whether personal crime rates were related to "race or place," Laub found that in comparisons of urban versus rural areas, place is important in accounting for the variation in rates, but as places increase in size, race becomes more important (ibid.: 193). Laub speculates that "urbanism acts to reduce and weaken the restraints to crime and delinquency among blacks and other groups," conclud-ing, "These data strongly suggest that both ecological factors such as size, den-sity, and heterogeneity and individual attributes of population aggregates such as race, sex, age, and socioeconomic status be examined conjointly in a study of criminal behavior. *The crime problem is a problem in the city, and mainly of the city*" (ibid.: 194; emphasis added).

A survey of persons aged fifteen or over in New Jersey, Iowa, and Oregon, reported in 1989 by Tittle, challenged the assumption that the size of a place is associated with deviant behavior and found that four of the five subcultures (illegal gambling, roguishness, tax cheating, and rebelliousness) were positively and significantly affected by size of place, whereas a subculture of violence was not (Tittle, 1989: 287).[4] After additional statistical analyses, Tittle decided that "size-of-place seems to be irrelevant to the effect of subcultural involvement on the probability of any particular kind of deviance being committed," or "the effects of the urban environment on the character and consequences of subcul-tures" (ibid.: 293). Thus, Tittle (ibid.: 292) concludes, "the effect of subcultural involvement on deviance is no greater in larger than in smaller places."

Noting that "there is conformity in the slums and deviance in affluent sub-urbs" and that most people who live in really bad slums are not deviants, recent ecological theorizing by Stark (1987: 904) targets deviant places. His argument is that an ecological theory of crime should depend not on "kinds of people" (compositional effects), but rather on specific aspects of urban neighborhoods. Through the application of thirty integrated propositions to five characteristics of urban neighborhoods that are typical of high deviance (density, poverty, mixed use, transience, and dilapidation),[5] Stark (ibid.: 905) finds that "high black crime rates are, in large measure, the result of where they live."

ECONOMIC INEQUALITY

The findings of contemporary cross-national studies that examined income in-equality provide a basis for understanding the rationale of this concept as ap-plied to United States minority populations. Avison and Loring (1986) studied the influence of income inequality and ethnic heterogeneity on the homicide rates of thirty-two nations. Support was found for conflict theories of crime[6] and the idea that "both ethnic heterogeneity and income inequality are impor-tant in accounting for variations in rates of homicide across nations" (ibid.: 746). The researchers emphasize that structural factors, such as inequality which can lead to social conflict, and cultural differences have an impact on crime.

Messner (1989) used both INTERPOL and World Health Organization homicide data in his study of fifty-two nation-states to test two hypotheses derived from Peter Blau's macrostructural theory:[7]

> (1) the level of economic discrimination should be positively related to national homicide rates, (2) the level of economic discrimination should be a stronger predictor of homicide rates than is income inequality. This latter hypothesis follows from the theoretical claim that *consolidated* inequality is especially likely to produce the diffuse hostility responsible for high levels of violent crime. (Ibid.: 599; emphasis in original)

Put another way, Messner (ibid.: 597) hypothesized that "nations with intense and pervasive discrimination will exhibit comparatively high levels of homicide, and that the effects of discrimination will exceed those of income inequality." Both hypotheses were supported by the multiple regression analyses Messner employed. A momentous additional finding is that the type of inequality and the way economic inequality is generated ("in terms of ascribed social characteristics") are more influential on homicide levels than the magnitude of the inequality itself (ibid.: 607).

The following attempt to condense the substantial amount of research on African American crime in urban areas into a coherent picture of the phenomenon is reminiscent of the ancient "chicken-egg" quandary in that it is difficult, if not impossible, to state which comes first, urbanism or poverty; poverty or lower socioeconomic level; unemployment, then poverty, and then lower socioeconomic level; or any combination of these social/structural characteristics. As Blau and Blau (1982: 121) observe, "the important question is whether this relationship indicates an influence of poverty on violent crime or merely reflects the fact that much inequality entails much poverty, and inequality is what fosters criminal violence."

Of course, there is the additional possibility that none of these variables is the primary factor influencing African American crime in urban areas.[8] In order to provide a logical framework to describe the research addressing these social structural features, an arbitrary schema is created wherein *economic inequality* is the basic premise—since this body of knowledge has produced the most consistent findings—and unemployment, poverty, and lower social class status are generally viewed as consequences of the original inequitable economic condition of African Americans and other minorities. Considering the intercorrelations frequently found between these urban attributes, one could begin with any one of them and demonstrate a connection to the other variables—a process, in fact, undertaken precisely by many of the researchers who address the topic of African American crime and elements of the social structure.

Jacobs (1981) used multiple regression techniques in his analysis of 1970 Standard Metropolitan Statistical Areas (SMSAs) to examine the association between economic inequality and theft rates (burglary, grand larceny, and robbery) in a test of relative deprivation. Several potential causal factors controlled for were percentage of African Americans, population size, economic development, educational level of residents, percentage of the male population aged fifteen to twenty-four, and percentage of families below the poverty line (absolute poverty). The independent variable, economic inequality, was measured by the Gini index.[9] Economic inequality was found to have strong independent effects on two of the theft measures, burglary and grand larceny, but not on robbery, leading Jacobs (ibid.: 22) to conclude that his results were "consistent with an assertion that contrasts in economic privilege give rise to property crimes."[10] However, the problem is not economic need, since unemployment and measures of absolute poverty did not seem to have independent, positive effects on the theft rates. In sum, Jacobs (ibid.: 23) demonstrated that pronounced differences in economic resources and affluence in unequal metropolitan areas are easily observed by those with "little to lose and much to gain" who, in a society stressing economic success, steal from those who "have," particularly from victims in close proximity.

Blau and Blau adopt a macrosociological approach to test the relationship between inequality and violence:

> The hypothesis inferred is that socioeconomic inequalities that are associated with ascribed positions, thereby consolidating and reinforcing ethnic and class differences, engender pervasive conflict in a democracy. Great economic inequalities generally foster conflict and violence, but ascriptive inequalities do so particularly. Pronounced ascriptive inequalities transform the experience of poverty for many into the hereditary permanent state of being one of the poor. (1982: 118-119)

Thus, the "resentment, frustration, hopelessness, and alienation" resulting from living in poverty are felt by those experiencing ethnic inequality (e.g., the ascribed status of race), and viewing the great riches of others leads to deep hostility, and ultimately criminal violence. Blau and Blau drew upon data from the 125 largest SMSAs in 1979, using arrests for major violent crimes (murder, forcible rape, robbery, and aggravated assault) as the dependent variable. Population size, percentage African American, percentage poor, geographical region, income inequality, percentage of divorces, and racial socioeconomic inequality were the independent variables.[11]

Support was found for their hypothesis that inequality, particularly ascriptive inequality, engenders violence. Thus, the higher violent crime rates among African Americans, according to Blau and Blau, have nothing to do with genetic characteristics or family makeup, i.e., single-parent families, but reflect the socioeconomic inequality between African Americans and Euro-Americans, particularly in SMSAs with high proportions of African Americans. Blau and Blau further suggest that intraracial murder and assault, the most prevalent victim-offender combination, can be explained by within-race economic inequality, especially between acquaintances, friends, or relatives.

Without a doubt, the seminal research of Jacobs (1981) and the Blaus (1982) has influenced contemporary studies of the effects of racial and economic inequality and violent crime. At the root of the possible consequences of economic inequality and crime is the *conflict perspective,* which perceives the dominant, powerful (white) groups in society as attempting to control culturally dissimilar groups (in this case, nonwhites) who are seen by the dominant group as a threat to the political and social order benefiting them. Domination of nonwhites, who are also viewed as racially and culturally dissimilar and subordinate, is achieved through agents of social control such as the police. Thus, according to conflict theory, "nonwhites have a substantially higher arrest rate than whites because, relative to whites, they are less able to resist arrest and because authorities share common stereotypes linking them with crime" (Liska and Chamlin, 1984: 384). Another means of social control takes place in the isolation of worrisome groups into inner-city ghettos and barrios; racial segregation has the additional benefit of reducing the costs of crime control (ibid.: 385).

In order to examine the social structural effects of racial/economic composition on crime control in a test of conflict theory, Liska and Chamlin examined the arrest rates for personal (homicide, aggravated assault, and rape) and property (robbery, larceny, burglary, and auto theft) Index crimes using "macrosocial units" for analysis. Consistent with the conflict thesis, property arrest rates in the seventy-six cities studied were found to be strongly affected by income inequality. Substantial effects on arrests were also indicated by segregation, proportion nonwhite, and reported crime rates. Independent of police size and reported crime rates, Liska and Chamlin attribute variations in arrest rates among U.S. cities to their economic/racial makeup (ibid.: 394).

The Marxian approach extends the conflict perspective. As Sackrey observes in *The Political Economy of Urban Poverty:*

> According to these Marxists, market discrimination is not just an important cause of the relative disadvantage of blacks, but an outward manifestation of a "thoroughly saturated" racist social order. . . . It implies an attitude on the part of whites and a resultant attitude on the part of blacks which have become strong elements of the "human nature" of each race. A competitive order intensifies the kinds of racist tendencies which people seem to have had throughout human history. In other words, in the view of these Marxists, and most other radicals, black poverty reflects racism. . . . Capitalism, because it is competitive and aggressive exacerbates whatever racial or other prejudices one may have to begin with. (1973: 60)

Studies of economic inequality and African American crime rates are usually concerned with some measure of income inequality and/or poverty. As the studies outlined above indicate, *absolute poverty,* or "low income," is generally what the average citizen would consider as poor, destitute, or without the basic necessities of life. Being below the federal Social Security "poverty line," or the annual income required for a family of four to subsist, is often used as the economic yardstick to determine absolute poverty. Although both types of poverty have been viewed in terms of criminogenic contexts, *relative poverty,* or "lagging income," is deemed more pertinent to the study of crime, because this concept suggests that a perceived difference in income and a lagging economic level compared to that of others leads to resentment, hostility, and, eventually, violent crime (Messner, 1982; Messner and Tardiff, 1986; Krahn, Hartnagel, and Gartrell, 1986).

Assuming that these measures of deprivation are equal to measures of economic inequality, Messner (1982) studied homicide rates for 204 Standard Metropolitan Statistical Areas as geographically described by the FBI's Uniform Crime Reports. Messner found the absence of a significant effect of the poverty measures "quite perplexing," since offenders who commit homicide "are recruited disproportionately from the ranks of the poor, yet a large poverty population appears to be associated with a low homicide rate" (ibid.: 112). The strongest associations with homicide were found for the proportion of the population that was African American. In a replication and extension of Messner's investigation, Bailey (1984) used cities, not SMSAs, and three years, instead of one year, but did not consider Messner's findings "perplexing" in light of the extensive number of studies finding a connection between low income and crime. Instead, Bailey (ibid.: 534) felt that the problem rested in Messner's use of SMSAs as the unit of analysis, because SMSAs are "quite diverse sociodemographically," they are not homogeneous social communities, and, more important, "aggregation at the SMSA level has the effect of ignoring theoretically important variation in homicides and other factors of interest within the SMSA. But such variation clearly does exist" (ibid.: 535). For two of the three years studied, Bailey consistently found that poverty (both absolute and relative) and homicide rates were positively and significantly related. He also notes that even after income inequality, poverty, and low income were controlled for, the percentage of African American population was still one of the best predictors of city homicide rates over all three time periods studied (ibid.: 541).

Robert J. Sampson's work (1985a) clearly indicates that using aggregate crime rates as the dependent variable confounds individual-level and aggregate-level effects by failing to differentiate racial composition effects from environmental context. He emphasizes two main points tangential to this discussion: (1) most recent studies of racial composition and city violent crime have reported strong positive relationships between proportion African American and criminal violence (particularly homicide); and (2) Wolfgang and Ferracuti's (1967) subculture of violence thesis seems to be the most popular theory applied to explain the race-crime relationship. To test the subculture of violence perspective, Sampson (1985a: 54) focused on fifty-five of the largest (>250,000 population) U.S. cities as the units of analysis and predicted that "the size of the black population will have a positive effect on black violence, independent of population concentration, inequality, poverty, and other city characteristics." The dependent variable was arrests for homicides. Except for racial income inequality, all of the independent variables in the model had significant effects, with percentage black as the strongest predictor of homicide. But when Sampson disaggregated by race of offender, percentage black no longer demonstrated a significant effect on homicide for whites or blacks—a finding that tends to refute the subculture of violence theory. Nonsignificant results were found after further analyses were made by substituting the absolute size of the black population for percentage black in order to reach the "critical mass" of blacks necessary for "viable subcultures." Sampson concludes from these findings that there is no support for the subculture of violence thesis of black homicide based on either relative or absolute racial composition (ibid.: 63). In fact, "the data do suggest that blacks in cities with large black ghettoes do not have higher violent offending rates than blacks in cities with a small black population" (ibid.: 72).

Next, Sampson utilized income inequality and percentage black as the major independent variables in fifty-three of the fifty-five cities in which violent crime (murder, rape, aggravated assault), robbery, and burglary rates were disaggregated by race and age (1985b).[12] Again the subculture of violence thesis was disconfirmed, while support was indicated for relative deprivation (poverty) and conflict theories:

> Overall, the data support the notion that structural economic factors are important in predicting offending patterns. Specifically, a general pattern emerged in the data whereby income inequality had consistent and relatively strong effects on black offending. Indeed, in 10 out of 12 regression models, income inequality had a significant positive effect on black criminal offending, net of the influence of region, racial composition, poverty, and structural opportunity. Importantly, however, in not one equation did the absolute level of black poverty influence the black crime rate. (Sampson, 1985b: 666-667)

Messner and Tardiff (1986) approach the question of economic inequality and homicide from a microlevel of analysis. They dismiss larger political and statistical units of analysis in favor of *neighborhoods,* which "are more likely to constitute meaningful frames of reference for social comparisons," and reflect "natural" groupings of urban populations. In their test of the hypothesis that "a high degree of economic inequality in a neighborhood will give rise to high levels of relative deprivation and high rates of homicide," Messner and Tardiff sampled twenty-six Manhattan, New York neighborhoods (ibid.: 297). If relative deprivation functions as a catalyst for hostility and violence, one must presumably compare oneself with others who are more advantaged; if one comes up short in the comparison, the result may be hostility, aggression, or ultimately homicide. A series of multiple regression analyses did not support the hypothesis, but size of the poverty population (percentage below the poverty line) and the percentage divorced or separated, which Messner and Tardiff see as "mutually reinforcing," were significant predictors of homicide rates (ibid.: 312). Racial composition (the relative size of the African American population in a neighborhood) had no effect on homicide rates, nor was there support found for the theory that African Americans "adhere to a distinctive subculture of violence which manifests itself in high levels of homicide" (ibid.).

This review of research demonstrates that poverty is an integral component of economic inequality. Some definition of poverty, i.e., absolute or relative (also referred to as "deprivation" in many studies), is included in each of the studies described. In addition to poverty, a study by Wiltz (1985) added the influence of family structure in an examination of state homicide rates among African Americans. Earlier path analyses described by Carroll and Jackson (1983) showed a relationship between female-headed families, economic inequality, and crime. Wiltz defined "family structure" as female-headed families, specifically the percentage of African American households in each state headed by females. At the state level, Wiltz reports that differences in African American homicide rates among southern African Americans are due to differences in the proportion of the population living in urban areas. However, among all categories of African Americans, the poverty variable was a stronger and more consistent predictor of African American homicides than the female-headed household variable, which turned out to be the least effective predictor. "Therefore, our findings bring into question the imputed significance that female-headed families have on black homicides. It can be argued then that the socialization, supervisory and disciplinary problems of children in these families do not manifest themselves, to any significant extent, into black homicides" (Wiltz, 1985). Actually, the female-headed household variable was found to be *a better predictor for white homicides,* which, according to Wiltz, makes it appear that "the deleterious consequences imputed to families headed by women may hold true for whites when homicides are considered." Since poverty has a "substantially greater influence in predicting homicides among blacks than does family structure," Wiltz suggests that "violence may be a response to the various economic constraints that are experienced by many blacks in American society."

In their discussion of the conservative view which stresses a culture of poverty that reproduces itself and perpetuates "the moral depravity of the lower classes," Balkan, Berger, and Schmidt (1980: 19) are critical of an approach that "tends to stress human inadequacies rather than institutional constraints." This blaming of the victim by conservative theorists ignores possible causes of crime associated with economic conditions and the fact that "many Americans hate the poor, and many more especially hate minority poor" (Sackrey 1973: 135).

It seems apparent that more recent investigations of social structural influences on African American crime rates in central cities are disconfirming the subculture of violence thesis put forth by Wolfgang and Ferracuti (1967). On the other hand, economic inequality appears to have sound support in studies that increasingly apply more rigorous and highly sophisticated statistical methods of data analysis. The influence of unemployment and socioeconomic status level is not as clearly defined on the basis of these research efforts as is economic inequality:

Blacks have been kept at the bottom of the social order since their first step onto this land; thus, they are the latest immigrants to the city, having been kept in the South first as slaves for cotton-based southern feudalism, then as marginal tenant farmers and domestic service workers after Reconstruction. They live in central cities today, with no access to the suburbs, first because they are relatively un-skilled, second because they are black. (Sackrey, 1973: 62)

UNEMPLOYMENT

In a brief review of the few studies addressing the effects of population density and unemployment on urban crime rates, Kvålseth (1977), while noting that the findings were generally contradictory and inconclusive, found the unemploy-ment rate to have a positive effect on the crime rate: "(1) the total urban em-ployment rate has a positive influence on the rates of burglary and larceny, (2) the male unemployment rate exerts a positive influence on the robbery rate, and (3) both the male and female unemployment rates have a positive effect on the rate of rape" (ibid.: 109). More recently, a review and in-depth analysis of sixty-three aggregate studies, the majority involving data from the 1970s, when unemployment increased strikingly, also lends support to a positive, frequently significant relationship between unemployment and crime (Chiricos, 1987).

In contrast, Jacobs (1981) is numbered among those who did not find a very strong connection between property crime and level of unemployment. These discrepancies could be linked to a number of research problems identifed by Allan and Steffensmeier (1989: 108-109), who note that (1) few studies have focused on the effect of employment conditions on crime; (2) there are statisti-cal or measurement flaws in the research design; (3) the unemployment-crime relationship may differ by types of crime, social groups, or age groups; and (4) there has been "inadequate conceptualization and operationalization of labor market conditions."

Other research efforts appear to have avoided some of these shortcomings, with varying results. For example, Davis (1983) used an *econometric model*[13] as the appropriate method to measure the impact of unemployment on crime in his sample of 1978 and 1979 closed misdemeanor cases in New York City. Several assumptions were made: American society views employment as a dominant value; one cause of poverty is unemployment; and poverty is seen as a cause of crime. In his analysis, the variables Davis employed were number of arrests, employment, seriousness and disposition of prior arrests, prior correctional pro-gram, jail, marital status, age, ethnicity (white or African American), and inter-action of employment, jail, and prior correctional program. Although about one-half of the variance was explained, 50 percent remained unexplained. With controls for the other variables, Davis found that even though the "more one is employed, the less he is arrested," employment had little effect on arrests.

Thornberry and Christenson (1984) utilized a linear panel reciprocal model to overcome the pitfalls of the traditional, unidirectional model most frequently used in studies of unemployment and crime. They argue that "unemployment, like criminal activity, is not an enduring status of the individual but occurs at intermittent intervals over time" (ibid.: 400). Their hypothesis suggests that crime also influences unemployment, or that the two are reciprocally related, with neither viewed totally as a cause or an effect of the other. The sample studied was taken from a Philadelphia birth cohort study in 1945, with the 567 subjects interviewed at age twenty-five at the time of the study. Thornberry and Christenson's results indicate strong support for the reciprocal model of crime and unemployment, a relationship that was found to operate mainly through lagged effects.[14] In other words, "unemployment exerts a rather immediate effect on criminal involvement, while criminal involvement exerts a more long-range effect on unemployment" (ibid.: 405). When delinquency, race, and status of origin were held constant, the model fit less-advantaged groups (delinquents, blacks, and blue-collar subjects) better than more-advantaged groups (nondelinquents, whites, and white-collar subjects). Thornberry and Christenson (ibid.: 409) turn to *strain theory*[15] to explain why less-advantaged subjects may be more susceptible to such reciprocal effects: "it is their tenuous hold on legitimate avenues to success that renders them vulnerable to increased levels of unemployment and crime, in the first place, and in turn, to the feedback effects of each variable on the other."

Sampson (1987) probed the possible relationship between urban African American violence, male joblessness, and family dissolution within the African American "underclass." The purpose was to see whether a structural factor such as joblessness is linked to family disruption and ultimately crime among African Americans because of the resultant female-headed household and poverty. Sampson first points out the dramatic difference between African American and Euro-American family structures: 42 percent of black families with children are female-headed, but only 11 percent of white families are, a difference that may be attributed to the increasing rate of joblessness among African American men. Thus, there is a suggested negative link between African American marital instability and unemployment (ibid.: 351).

In order to explain the crime rates of urban African American communities in line with this thesis, Sampson offers three ways that family dissolution resulting from male joblessness can lead to crime: the negative effects of broken homes can produce juvenile delinquents; family disruption may reduce formal community social controls; and informal community controls are attenuated (ibid.: 352-353). His major hypothesis is that

> variations in rates of black family disruption in urban areas are positively related to rates of black criminal offending, independent of those factors (e.g., poverty) associated with families headed by females and frequently hypothesized as providing motivation for crime. To the extent that the disruption of families is linked primarily to the social control of juveniles and their peer groups, the effect of family structure should be strongest for juveniles. But since family disruption is hypothesized to increase generally the opportunities for crimes, and since disproportionate numbers of those who are divorced or separated in a population may be indicative of much instability, disorientation, and conflict in adult personal relations, community family disruption is expected to be significantly related to adult criminality as well. (Ibid.: 354)

The units of analysis in the Sampson study were United States cities with populations over 100,000 (N = 153). The variables were percentage of total female-headed black households and those with children under age eighteen; the number of employed black males per 100 black females (a "male marriage pool index"); black per capita income (an economic deprivation measure); population size; density of housing units; the mean public assistance payment to black families, by city (a control variable); median age of the black population (a control variable); and controls for region and percentage black (racial composition). The dependent variables were race- and age-specific rates for homicide and robbery, which, according to the literature, are the most serious and reliably recorded Index crimes.

As predicted, the results of the multiple regression analyses reveal that "the effects of black male joblessness and economic deprivation on crime appear to be mediated in large part by family disruption" (Sampson, 1987: 377). In sum, joblessness has little or no direct effect on crime but strongly impacts family disruption, which itself convincingly predicts African American murder and robbery, especially by juveniles. Also, contrary to prevailing beliefs, Sampson found nothing "inherent in black culture that is conducive to crime," and, like many other researchers (Loftin and Hill, 1974; Laub, 1983; Sampson, 1985a; Messner and Tardiff, 1986; Tittle, 1989), he found no support for the subculture of violence thesis.

Duster (1987) reminds us that unemployment among black youth has quadrupled in the last twenty-five years, to a rate of almost 50 percent, but there has been little change in white youth unemployment over that time period. Of equal importance, Duster stresses that African Americans have been so long on the "bottom rung of the American economic and political order" that the "permanence of this structural status has led to the emergence of an 'underclass'" (ibid.: 303). The problem, he adds, is not found in the hiring practices of the manufacturing sector, which distributes jobs fairly equally, but in retail establishments that discriminate against African American youth. Duster feels that the problem of African American youth unemployment and the development of the African American urban underclass is structural: "Whereas the nation used the cheap labor of young Blacks for centuries, the new generation faces for the first time both the rejection and the massive irrelevance of their labor. One of the major factors is the decision by a substantial segment of the American business community to relocate to areas where Black youth are not located and thus cannot be employed" (ibid.: 306). Duster admits that unemployment does not directly cause crime, but emphasizes the strong connection between crime and structural economic factors such as the movement of capital to foreign markets where labor is cheap, or from cities to suburbs, and from the northern cities to Sunbelt areas.

SOCIAL CLASS

The relationship between class and crime is almost as controversial as that between unemployment and crime. Central to the debate are both definitional and methodological problems. Social class has been defined many ways, for example, as lower class, as working class, or as occupying a low socioeconomic level.

Whatever nomenclature is used, the definition almost always is seen as a status that is "relatively low on the social class continuum" (Braithwaite, 1981: 37). Measures used to determine the social class of individuals have variously included unemployment, occupational level of an adult (unskilled or semiskilled), or, in the case of a juvenile, the father's occupation. Other yardsticks are percentage of adult males in lower-class jobs, percentage unemployed, percentage on welfare, percentage below a poverty line, percentage living in substandard housing, percentage with a below-average educational level, or a composite of these (ibid.). A large proportion of minorities located in urban areas could be described as fitting most of these characteristics.

More than twenty years ago, Green (1970) reported on the relationship between social class among African Americans and crime in the small industrial city of Ypsilanti, Michigan during 1941-1965. Although it was found that compared to Euro-Americans, the higher official rate of crime for African Americans was related to a disproportionate distribution of lower-class characteristics (e.g., unemployment, lower-level employment, rural southern migration), Green concluded that "the effect of socioeconomic status on arrest rates . . . appears to operate independently of race" (ibid.: 490). Nor did Green find any support for individual racial or cultural characteristics or racial conflict as explanatory for the differences in black-white crime rates.

More recently, in a study of social class and juvenile violent behavior, Brownfield (1986) measured violence by self-reports and official police records. The independent variable, social class, was defined in four ways: (1) neo-Marxist ("social relations of domination and appropriation"); (2) "disreputable poverty" (father's unemployment and welfare status); (3) gradational measures (occupation and education); and (4) ecological measures (lower-, middle-, and upper-class areas defined by housing criteria). The association and strength of the relationship between class and violence depended primarily on the social class measure Brownfield used: for the neo-Marxist definition, no significant effects were found; moderate correlations were observed in the cases of gradational and ecological measures of class; while indications of disreputable poverty revealed a relatively strong correlation with violent behavior (ibid.: 435).

In 1978, Tittle, Villemez, and Smith reported a review of thirty-five studies examining the relationship between social class and crime and delinquency that resulted in a flurry of response after their determination that such a relationship was a "myth." Noting that an inverse relationship between social class and crime was once widely accepted as an explanation for concentrations of delinquency and crime, the authors state that this view was attacked in the late fifties and sixties and replaced by a focus on *stratification theory*. Their examination of both self-report and official statistics studies suggests that

for the past four decades there has been a monotonic decline in association between social class and crime/delinquency, with contemporary (those done since 1970) self-report and official statistics studies finding essentially no relationship between class and crime/delinquency. Moreover, these historical changes are found to be attributable to changes in findings by studies using official data. (1978: 654)

A response by Clelland and Carter (1980: 319) takes Tittle, Villemez, and Smith to task by challenging their reanalysis of the empirical studies on the basis of six flaws in their evaluation: "paucity of evidence; lack of specification of theoretical relationships; faulty specification and measures of class; inadequate operational definitions of 'crime'; faulty analysis of evidence; and failure to examine all evidence." Clelland and Carter appear to adopt a neo-Marxian perspective when they state their belief that some types of crime may be based on class relations, but others are not. For example, they point out that the corporate crimes of the bourgeoisie and the managerial class, as well as other "white-collar" crimes, are class-based: "the social definition of these offenses, as well as differential enforcement and sentencing, reflects the social relations of production" (ibid.: 332). Clelland and Carter find no theory explaining the relationship between class and the commission of trivial offenses. Yet, they believe that disproportionate numbers of serious predatory crimes and crimes of violence are "crimes of accommodation" by "marginal factions of the working class" (ibid.) and, in contrast to the position of Tittle, Villemez, and Smith, they feel that the empirical evidence supports such a notion of lower-class crime.

Finally, Braithwaite (1981: 37), who is also critical of the Tittle, Villemez, and Smith (1978) review, states that their finding of a total of thirty-five studies indicates that "they did not look very hard," since Braithwaite's review includes forty-seven self-report studies and fifty-three official records studies on the relationship between social class and juvenile crime, forty-six official studies of social class and adult crime, fifty-seven official records studies on the relationship between social class and the area in which individuals live, thirteen official records studies on social class of area and adult crime, and eight self-report studies on social class involving juvenile crime and area. Consequently, Braithwaite (1981: 49) comes to the "inescapable" conclusion from "the voluminous, though not always satisfactory, evidence available at this time that lower class people do commit those direct interpersonal types of crime which are normally handled by the police at a higher rate than middle class people."

Unlike Tittle, Villemez, and Smith (1978), Braithwaite does not feel the study of crime should shift from class-based theories, nor does he overlook the crimes of the powerful: "What we require are class-based theories which explain why certain types of crime are perpetrated disproportionately by the powerless, while other forms of crime are almost exclusively the prerogative of the powerful" (1981: 49).

From the previous discussion of the major reviews of empirical studies of the relationship between social class and crime/delinquency (Tittle, Villemez, and Smith, 1978; Braithwaite, 1981) and the Brownfield analysis (1986) of social class and violent behavior, there seems to be little doubt that there is an association between economic level (however defined) and crime commission, and certainly for the lower classes, excessive social control enforcement for their crimes or delinquencies. But a recall of the above treatise on the social structural elements of unemployment, poverty, and economic inequality suggests that the question of causation is highly complex.

In a provocative article, " 'Street' Crime—A View from the Left," Tony Platt (1978) warns us that despite established evidence of the link between "street" crime and economic conditions, crime is "not simply a matter of poverty," nor is "street" crime explained by poverty. Instead, "street" crime is largely an intraclass and intraracial phenomenon whose victims are predominantly African Americans and Chicanos living in metropolitan areas. In his words, "Historically, 'street crime' has tended to be concentrated in the marginalized sectors of the labor force and in the demoralized layers of the working class, irrespective of skin color or ethnic origin" (ibid.: 30).

Theories of Asian American Crime

It is not surprising that there is scant information on Asian American crime causation because of the paucity of studies of Asian American criminality. What little is known seems to suggest that "the extent of criminality among Orientals in America seems to vary inversely with the extent to which they are incorporated in closely integrated family and community groups" (Hayner, 1938: 908). However, we will see later that this perspective has been challenged. As Hayner (ibid.: 900) observed more than fifty years ago, none of the diverse Asian American groups demonstrate important differences when compared with whites, but they do show interesting variations in involvement in crime when compared with one another. It was noted in Chapter 2 that Japanese Americans have consistently had lower rates of crime than Chinese Americans. What appears to account for this difference is the stronger filial piety and feeling of kinship found in Japanese American families, the efficiency and organization of the Japanese community, and the fact that the Japanese are a proud people who hate to "lose face." Therefore they do as much as possible to maintain a high status for their family or community (ibid.: 911-912).

In China, the family is also the dominant social group, in which "all social relationships and all values are tied up" (ibid.: 913). As a result, the early United States policy measures and laws that prohibited Chinese men from having their wives with them in this country are believed to have contributed heavily to their crime history. The absence of family controls "undermined the characteristic Chinese temperance in the indulgence of their two vices of gambling and the use of opium products" (ibid.: 914), while the lack of female companionship led to the bootlegging of Chinese girls and, possibly, to prostitution in the Chinatowns of America (see Chapter 2).

Another major difference between Chinese and Japanese crime in America is seen in the fact that the secret societies, or tongs, that existed in China and other overseas Chinese communities also existed in the American Chinatowns (Sowell, 1981: 140). Their use of the hatchet as a weapon led to the name "hatchet men," a term applied to numerous other activities, even after these hatchet men began to use revolvers, machine guns, and, today, Uzis as they assimilated into American society. To provide the homeless and womenless men of the early Chinatowns and the steady influx of white clientele seeking vice with "exotic" prostitutes, gambling, and opium, the tongs divided up the territory and frequently had bloody tong wars, which continued until 1931 in some Chinese communities.

Over time, modification of restrictive immigration laws that permitted some wives from China to join their husbands, and other females of marriageable age to enter the country, helped to ease the sex-ratio imbalance, thus allowing the development of more family life (ibid.: 143). As a result, the Chinese American crime rate dropped significantly, only to rise again slowly in the 1960s with the increasing numbers of Chinese street gangs, particularly in New York and San Francisco.

In 1973 there were about two hundred youth gang murders in New York's Chinatown (Sowell, 1981), a result of the gangs' shift in focus from self-protection from other minority gangs to working as protection for the gambling operations of the tongs (Chin, 1990). By the 1980s, however, the tongs were unable to control these youths. There had been some earlier retaliation against these new youth gangs by tongs in San Francisco. The tongs issued a public warning to those who engaged in "unruly behavior harmful to the commercial and social life of our community," which apparently went unheeded until the "bound bodies of five Hong Kong Chinese youth were shortly thereafter found floating in the San Francisco Bay" (Sowell, 1981: 151).

Unfortunately, crime and violence have recently increased dramatically in the Chinatowns of the United States (Flowers, 1990: 139), from Hawaii to New York. Young immigrants from Hong Kong who have formed Chinese youth gangs are the basis for the increases in "vandalism, violence, extortion, theft, terrorism, and murder" (Sowell, 1981: 151). These gangs also harass, insult, and rob the tourists upon whom the Chinatown economy relies. Yet, according to Sowell, many Chinese restaurants in New York still serve gang members free meals, and they and other Chinese businesses pay them protection money.

These immigrant teenagers face "poverty, rejection, discrimination, unemployment," social conditions that are exacerbated by a "combination of lack of knowledge of English, minimal occupational skills, cultural discontinuity, overcrowded homes, and lack of opportunity in both the ethnic and the larger communities" (ibid.: 129). Commenting on recent Chinatown concerns over the "increasing rebelliousness, criminality, and radicalism of many Chinese youth," Parrillo observes:

The growing problem of youthful militancy and delinquency appears to reflect the marginal status of those in the younger generation who experience frustration and adjustment problems in America. Recent arrivals from Hong Kong are unfamiliar with the language and culture, they are either unemployed or in the lowliest of jobs, and they live in overcrowded, slum-like quarters with no recreational facilities. Gang behavior serves as an alternative and a means of filling status and identity needs. (1985: 251-252)

Despite a description of conditions that might suggest a social/structural approach to Chinese American crime and delinquency causation (e.g., under- or unemployment, economic inequality, poverty), a neo-Marxist perspective (conflict theory), or even racist (discrimination) theory, many theorists rely upon the traditional gang viewpoint ("status and identity") to explain the youthful Chinese criminality. Takagi and Platt (1978: 13-14) have long protested against the idea that assimilation/acculturation and culture and personality are the dominant explanations for Asian American crime. They point out that in recent years, arrests of Chinese juveniles have increased, but not arrests of Japanese youths. Also, they object to the ascribed term of a Chinatown "gang," because it "fails to discriminate youth involved in political activities from those lumpen elements that engage in criminal behavior" (ibid.: 20). Takagi and Platt further state that there is no evidence to support the many accusations against Chinese youths, such as drug dependency and international drug trafficking, and that their rackets and delinquency are uniquely Chinese.

The implications of weakened family and community life alternatively suggest that *social control theory* might be applied to Asian American crime causation both in the historical sense and in the light of recent immigration. Control theorists do not ask what causes deviance, but what causes conformity (Thio, 1978). According to this perspective, what causes deviance is the absence of what causes conformity, and correspondingly, what leads to conformity is social control over the individual.

One of the proponents of control theory, Travis Hirschi (1969), assumes that we are all animals endowed with the ability to commit deviant acts, but most of us do not take advantage of this ability because of our strong bond to society. This bond ensures our conformity, but if our bond to society is weak or broken, we will commit deviant acts. Because of the emphasis on the bonding process, this social control perspective is sometimes referred to as "bonding theory."

If the elements of his or her bond to society are strong, an individual is likely to conform. If they are weak, deviance may result. According to control theory, then, the strong emphasis on the family and the community that is historically a part of the Asian tradition would lead to strong bonds to society and subsequent conformity. Since the Asian American experience in the United States led to the weakening or actual destruction of families, deviance might have resulted. Few Chinese had families here or the possibility of starting a family. The recent Hong Kong, Vietnamese, Cambodian, and other Oriental immigrants, particularly the young, either had to sever former bonds or had no prior bonds at all. Noting that the nature and volume of Chinese crime have changed conspicuously in recent decades, Pao-Min suggests that the Chinese have become "increasingly American" (1981: 363) and emphasizes the "waning role of the traditional Chinese family as an effective agent of social control, apparently as a result of the decline of the extended family system and the rise in the number of broken homes" (ibid.: 367). Additionally, Pao-Min introduces other possible contributors to contemporary Chinese crime: congested urban environments, the lack of recreational facilities in Chinese communities, poor job prospects, and social and linguistic diversity within the Chinese population itself that may lead to factional conflicts and tensions (ibid.).

Beginning with the internment of Japanese Americans in World War II and the disintegration of those families through the undermining of the authority of family heads and the later assimilation of the Sansei and Yonsei generations into the American youth subculture, some deterioration of the bonding to society may be indicated, but it is clearly not as severe as the weakening bonds seen in the Oriental groups without family ties. Thus, the traditional approach of social control theory might explain why Japanese Americans have consistently had the lowest rates of crime of all Asian American groups.

But social control theory could be seen as simply another form of the *assimilation/acculturation theory,* which Takagi and Platt find most objectionable since they feel that "racist stereotyping has long been used in the United States to intimidate and discipline new immigrants, as well as to create antagonisms and divisions within the working class as a whole. The 'crime of historical distortion' is the rule, not exception, of bourgeois propaganda" (1978: 21).

In their alternative analysis of crime in the Chinese community, Takagi and Platt (ibid.: 22) decry "racist explanations of Chinese crime" and offer instead a picture of "superexploitation" which resulted from "over a hundred years of brutal labor practices, institutionalized racism, discriminatory legislation and extralegal repression." The people of ghettoized Chinatowns in this nation, like African Americans and oppressed Hispanic and Native Americans, experience extremely high unemployment rates, depressing poverty, and disheartening living and social circumstances as a result of the capitalistic "labor market practices and labor processes" which are reflective of the exploitation of a "capitalistic political economy" (ibid.: 22).

The dearth of research or other information on the extent of Asian American crime was noted earlier in this section; obviously, until more study is available on this subcultural group, further theorizing about causation is premature.

Theories of Native American Crime

A content analysis of a sample of twenty-four books with themes about the struggles against racism in the 1960s (Martínez, 1989) found "a massive omission of activism by peoples of color other than African Americans" (ibid.: 175), with not a single bibliographic listing involving Native Americans, Asians, Chicanos, or Puerto Ricans. Nor was Thomas J. Young able to uncover any mention of Native American crime, or crime causation, in his examination of a dozen frequently used introductory criminal justice textbooks over a ten-year period (1980-1989), leading him to comment:

For the most part, however, criminal justice scholars have ignored issues relating to Native Americans. This tendency probably reflects the marginal social, political, and economic status of Native Americans. Unfortunately, this lack of scholarly research means that Native Americans commonly are viewed in terms of narrow, ethnocentric stereotypes (e.g., drunken savages). (1990: 112)

The paucity of information on Native Americans is generally reflected in a lack of empirically supported theoretical perspectives addressing causes of Indian crime. May (1982a: 233-234) has identified several themes of explanation for American Indian crime: adjustment/acculturation; social disorganization; social organization; that Indians are a more criminal group; that Native Americans are victims of discrimination; and that oversurveillance in Indian communities involves them more in the criminal justice system.

American Indians from virtually all tribes appear to have difficulty relating to the dominant United States culture because it is so different from their own tribal traditions. According to Cummings and Harrison (1972: 82), the Bureau of Indian Affairs (BIA), specifically, and the federal government, in general, view the Indian native culture as antagonistic to American culture and have consistently instituted policies to "adjust the Indian to the dominant society." Friction and stress are the direct results of the attempt to exchange Indian values for those of mainstream America. Adjustment is especially difficult for Indians in urban areas where value orientation and problems of social and economic survival persist. For example, a study of American Indians living in Seattle, Washington found a fairly low level of assimilation into that urban environment (Chadwick and Stauss, 1975).

These adjustment/acculturation problems result in more frequent arrests, often for such escapist behaviors as drinking. An early study by Charles Reasons of Native American arrest rates from 1950 to 1968 revealed a substantial disparity in arrest rates for drinking-related offenses (drunkenness, driving while intoxicated, and liquor law violations) between Native Americans and all other racial groups (1972: 81-82). Reasons attributes the excessive drinking of Native Americans to frustration and cultural indecision as a result of increasing contacts with the dominant American culture, noting also that drinking may lead to crime. Along this line, in his review of explanations of Native American drinking, May suggests that the binge drinking of Native Americans was adopted by some Indians after having originated as the normative model of white traders:

> Not only did Indians have role models to present the idea of binge-drinking behavior, but in addition this type of drinking behavior was readily encouraged by the fur traders who wanted a steady market through the use of liquor by Indians. By exposing Indians to alcohol and encouraging its use, many traders utilized liquor not only as a profitable trade item, but also as a method of cheating Indians. By refusing to trade unless alcohol had been partaken by all parties, many traders could trick particular Indians into becoming intoxicated and then make unfair exchanges. (May, 1977: 227)

Social disorganization as an explanatory factor for Indian crime is seen as the result of historical events, culture conflict, and other pressures on Indian society that led to the disorganization of their traditional social and cultural systems. Because of this breakdown, the perspective suggests that many Native Americans suffer from anomie or unclarity of behavioral norms, with resultant higher rates of crime and deviance. Earlier works on Indian alcohol use and suicide often attributed these deviances to such causes. In their study of the relationship between alcoholism, homicide, and suicide and theories of social disorganization and anomie among Indians, Levy and Kunitz (1971) found that enduring characteristics of the Navajo and Hopi cultures were more explanatory predisposing factors of the social pathologies than responses to acculturation and social disorganization. Their examination of historical records suggests that high suicide and homicide rates existed during the pre-reservation period and are not necessarily responses to recent social disorganization. Further, suicide and homicide occurred in all areas of the reservation at no higher frequencies than in border towns or more acculturated communities (ibid.: 104).

Levy and Kunitz (ibid.: 102) acknowledge that the white man introduced alcohol to most Indian tribes north of Mexico, but are reluctant to attribute the excessive use of alcohol either to stress associated with acculturation or to escapism, since they note some variation by tribe in the extent of drunkenness. Among the Navajo, for example, the highest level of alcohol use was found among the most traditional and least acculturated, whereas the lowest use was found among the most acculturated Indians who were not on the reservation (ibid.: 109). While noting that the Hopi Indians are renowned for their resistance to alcohol use and their lack of aggression, Levy and Kunitz also found that Hopi suicide and homicide rates were similar to those of both the Navajo and the general U.S. population. Further, Hopi drinking patterns differ from those of Navajos and whites in that Hopi Indians hide their drinking (ibid.: 117). In sum, Levy and Kunitz feel that deviance was present in pre-reservation society and doubt that Indian social deviance is high or even increasing in all instances compared to earlier time periods. Instead, they suggest that the notion of social disintegration and lack of acculturation to white goals are "the products of certain traditions of Western social thought" rooted in cultural values and having "certain practical and political implications" (ibid.: 119-120).

Another application to Native Americans of the *anomie theory* of deviance is discussed in terms of blocked access to legitimate opportunity structures. Reasons (1972: 89) notes that Native Americans were more economically advantaged but had fewer normative controls against deviance and more anomie than Chicanos. Conceivably, since both minority groups had less opportunity than whites, Native American deviant behavior may be the result of cultural conflicts. Closely related to differential access to opportunity structure are economic factors such as poverty (Stewart, 1964). Native American poverty on reservations and in rural areas is extensive, and "compared with other minority groups caught in the midst of urban poverty, the life of the urban American Indian represents a new dimension in wretchedness in American urban life" (Cummings and Harrison, 1972: 84). However, even though the economic position of Native Americans is more desperate than that of any other minority group, Reasons (1972: 89) observes that such economic factors are "not necessary or sufficient" conditions for deviance, since many people experiencing poverty are not involved in crime.

Patterns of Indian behavior or extensions of traditional cultural behavior typical of their social organization are offered as another explanatory theme of Indian crime. According to this perspective, the types of deviant behaviors that are encouraged or allowed vary from tribe to tribe. If, for example, a tribe places a low value on the possession of property and material goods, that tribe will have low property crime. On the other hand, tribes characterized by a low degree of social integration will manifest higher rates of drinking violations, homicide, and other crimes against persons.

Implicitly, or in some cases explicitly, suggested in a number of early works on Indian crime is the idea that Indians are simply *a more criminal group*. Virtually all early studies found that arrests, convictions, and incarceration rates were higher for Native Americans than for most groups in the United States (e.g., Stewart, 1964; Reasons, 1972). Reliance upon such official statistics led to the conclusion that Indians were highly criminal, a form of racial stereotyping found for all racial minority groups.[16] In contrast, Stewart states that reliance on racial factors to explain Indian criminality must be rejected and defines American Indians as a social-legal group: "This specification is necessary because many of the people enjoying legal privileges of American Indians are, in fact, biologically part Negro or part Caucasian. The extremely large portion of individuals with mixed ancestry among the Indians indicates that hereditary racial factors are too complex to explain Indian behavior" (1964: 61).

Self-report studies reveal few differences between Indians and whites in frequency of crime and indicate that some Indians are highly criminal in only a few deviant areas (May, 1982a). Numerous and repetitive arrests among a minority of Indians greatly inflate the rates of arrest and incarceration for all Indians. Thus, in spite of high overall Indian crime rates, a very small proportion of individuals account for the bulk of the offenses (ibid.).

Like other historically disadvantaged minorities in this country, Indians are the victims of prejudice and discrimination at all levels of the criminal justice system. Although few studies produce solid statistical evidence, since Native Americans differ in a racial, cultural, and behavioral sense, racial discrimination against them has been described as existing in arrest situations, courts, and the laws, and as a contributing factor in high arrest rates (Reasons, 1972: 89). Indians may be perceived by the larger society and the police as a deviant group and consequently labeled formally or informally as deviant, thus resulting in more arrests and harsher treatment, particularly in non-Indian towns which are adjacent to reservations.

Again, as in the cases of African Americans and other minorities, oversurveillance of Native Americans is a predominant theme. Many authors suggest that both on and off the reservation, Indians are overpoliced and more carefully

watched than other groups. Additionally, Indians are subjected to an extra police force and court system to which other American citizens are not. Like most
Americans, Native Americans are under the legal purview of federal, state,
county, and city jurisdictions, but on most reservations they are additionally
responsible to tribal police and courts. Tribal police are the only racially specific
police force in the United States, who in most cases have the power only to
arrest Indians belonging to their tribes as well as to other tribes, and no authority to arrest whites. Such extensive law enforcement influence results in more
Indian arrests.

The fact that many Indians on reservations tend to rely upon tribal police
in ways that local police in other areas of the country are not utilized only
compounds the problem. Tribal police are frequently called about or become
involved in minor family situations such as slight domestic quarrels, minor
drinking incidents within a family, disciplining a child regarding a routine delinquent incident, and other civil and personal matters. In other words, tribal
police are frequently used as referees in situations which elsewhere would not
come to the attention of the police or be recorded in official statistics (May,
1982a).

Since Native Americans often do not know of or take advantage of free
services such as legal aid, they are less able to escape convictions or secure lesser
sentences. This infrequent utilization of legal advantages and services not only
leads to more severe treatment in their relationship with the criminal justice
system but also contributes to the inaccurate accounting of the extent of their
criminality (ibid.).

Theories of Hispanic American Crime

There is little information to draw upon in attempting to explain Hispanic
American crime causation because of the dearth of empirical research that addresses Hispanic Americans as a group or investigates any of their specific subgroups. This diverse minority group includes people of Mexican heritage, Puerto
Ricans, Cubans, Dominicans, and a variety of Latin and South Americans, all
with their own unique cultural histories and customs. In addition, Hispanic
Americans have not been studied to any degree as individual groups or even as a
single entity because they are so often categorized as "white." As pointed out in
Chapter 2, typical official statistics only compare Hispanics with non-Hispanics,
thus omitting valuable nuances of heritage. Despite this shortcoming, several of
the explanatory crime themes offered parallel those for other racial minorities,
particularly those outlined in the previous discussion of Native Americans.

Since many Hispanics are recent arrivals to the United States, problems of
adjustment/acculturation and social disorganization, particularly in urban areas,
are offered to explain Hispanic involvement in crime. One appropriate exemplar
is the 1980 Mariel Cuban "Banditos," who were identified as a "danger to law
enforcement and society in general" (Benderoth, 1983a: 32). Despite the fact

that most of these Cuban refugees were urban working-class and lower-class persons (Parrillo, 1985: 370), they did not receive the warm welcome bestowed upon the previous influx of middle- and upper-class, predominantly "white" Cuban professionals from 1959 to 1961. Some Cubans received the same disparaging treatment as other poor Spanish-speaking subgroups such as Puerto Ricans, because non-Hispanics could not differentiate between them (ibid.). Largely because of racial attitudes, stereotyping, and prejudice, the Mariel immigrants in New York City were not assimilated into the dominant society and were generally assumed to be criminals (ibid.: 33). Ironically, these Marielitos had previously experienced racial prejudice in Cuba because of their darker skin color. In New York City, police were made aware of special "identifiers" to allegedly differentiate Mariel Cubans from other Hispanics: missing teeth, body scars, and tattoos associated with the Santeria religion, a religion with origins in Africa (Benderoth, 1983b: 45-46).

Hispanics are viewed as "different" from the majority group, and since they most often speak a different language, the prejudice, discrimination, and oversurveillance found in other minority communities are also typical in their communities, particularly in the urban "barrios." The misunderstandings that develop because of the inability to communicate with police officers and the tendency of some officers to interpret the speaking of a foreign language as an act of defiance (Bondavalli and Bondavalli, 1981: 56) add fuel to the fire of prejudice and discrimination. Such practices often result in the "net widening" that leads to more Hispanic involvement in the criminal justice system.

Low economic status and concomitant poverty are also mentioned as factors responsible for Hispanic crime, since as Flowers (1990: 99) notes, "Hispanic unemployment, income, educational, occupational, and median age levels are below or lower than those of the general population." Puerto Ricans and Mexicans usually occupy low-status jobs requiring few skills that pay little and offer little mobility (Parrillo, 1985: 348). In a comparison of the poverty rates of Hispanics, African Americans, and whites, Parrillo (ibid.: 350) reports a ratio of Hispanic to white poverty of 2.7, and Hispanic family income as 70 percent of white family income in 1981.

Many of the unemployed and underemployed Hispanics are youths; therefore a great deal of the stigmatization and stereotyping of Hispanics centers on gang members and machismo, particularly the Mexican (Chicano) gangs in Los Angeles. As with African American violence, the subculture of violence thesis has also been applied to Hispanics. In reference to the theory as proposed by Wolfgang and Ferracuti (1967), Erlanger discusses the importance of values as causative in violent behavior:

Subcultural values, it is argued, define certain circumstances and stimuli that appropriately evoke physical aggression, especially on the part of young black and Hispanic males. Within the subculture, failure to respond violently to physical or verbal challenge may well lead to negative sanctions, while violent response to such challenges is said to be supported, encouraged and at times directly required. (1979: 235)

In his exploratory study of thirty-five Los Angeles Chicanos, two-thirds of whom had gang experience, Erlanger concludes that even though Chicano culture stresses male courage and dignity, how these values are expressed in behavior is largely determined by the level of estrangement in a community (ibid.: 246). Chicano values in the barrio are independent of and differ from those of the dominant Anglo society, but "they do not directly require or condone violence" (ibid.: 235).

Joan Moore (1985) invokes *labeling theory* when she points to the isolation of Chicano gangs, gang members, and their families in East Los Angeles. In her case history of the development of Los Angeles Chicano youth gangs, Moore speaks of "ascribed deviance," or the ascription of deviance to young minority males based upon stereotypes held by Anglos:

> Stigma involves a stereotype, and for minorities the stereotypes include perceptions of deviance. The larger society certainly does label some minority persons, a priori, as "probably deviant." Thus to be young, male, and black or Chicano in white America is to be a suspect person. To be a visible member of a population that many Anglos associate with violent crime is to evoke hostile and fearful responses. (Ibid.: 2)

Moore reports that aggressive Chicano male youth groups have existed since the nineteenth century, and although they were not necessarily delinquent, they were labeled as such. Of the four "critical turning points" in the reputation of Chicano gangs in East Los Angeles,[17] Moore (ibid.: 9) notes that "three of these four turning points involved further isolation and intra-community stigmatization of the gangs. Across these four periods, media coverage of the gangs has always been negative." The final outcome of the isolation and stigmatization resulted in an underclass "left to the attention of law enforcement" (ibid.).

Once brought into the criminal justice system, many Hispanics, like Native Americans, do not know of and consequently do not utilize the available free legal and other social services that might help them to avoid the harshness of conviction and severe sentences, a problem that is exacerbated by the language barrier.

A Minority View

It is ironic that so many of the explanations of minority crime focus on minority violence when American history is filled with violence, particularly as directed against its minority citizens. Chapter 1 detailed the violent treatment of Native Americans, African American slaves, Chinese, and Mexicans at the hands of Euro-Americans. The prolonged tradition of racial conflict, which at this writing is on the upswing, resulted in thirty-three major urban race riots between 1900 and 1949, over two hundred major riots between 1964 and 1968, and a return to urban burnings and rioting in the 1980s and 1990s. Today, race-related hatred, intimidation, and violence, largely directed toward minorities, has been referred to as a "national epidemic" (Hyer, 1988), and special police units have been established in some urban areas to classify and record such incidents. Boston's Community Disorders Unit, instituted in 1978, and similar special data-collection divisions in New York, Pennsylvania, and Maryland have been mandated by state legislation or initiated to comply with state civil rights laws.[18]

The number of nonmember sympathizers who donate to the Ku Klux Klan, attend Klan rallies, and read Klan literature is well over 100,000 (Padgett, 1984). A 1982 survey in the nine-county Chattanooga, Tennessee area revealed that over 32 percent of the white respondents liked the Ku Klux Klan or some of its aspects, almost 55 percent supported the idea of an organization to "stand up for the rights of white people," and 48 percent would restrict the rights of African Americans to demonstrate (ibid.: 116-117). Other neo-Nazi hate groups such as the "Skinheads," the White Aryan Nation, and the White Aryan Resistance (WAR) also glorify the violence they direct at racial/ethnic minorities.

The extreme of such violent expression is the lynch mob, a racist, violent phenomenon, commonly associated with the Ku Klux Klan, which emerged in the back country of South Carolina in 1767, and was later named after the notorious Colonel Charles Lynch of Virginia. Lynch mobs were most common in the post–Civil War south and were used as a means of maintaining white supremacy. It is estimated that between 1882 and 1903, southern lynch mobs killed 1,985 African Americans. Lynching is not an obsolete phenomenon; today there are isolated lynchings of minorities reported across the country.

Further, the United States has the bloodiest and most violent labor history of any industrial nation in the world. Other indicators of a violent tradition in this country are the wars that raged between whites and American Indians almost continuously from 1607 to 1890; the ongoing great blood feuds between families in the mountains of Kentucky, Virginia, and West Virginia and in central Texas; the gang murders and other violent actions of organized crime (between 1919 and 1967 there were 1,000 gang murders in Chicago alone); and the United States government's use of deadly force, for example, the National Guard's killing of Colorado strikers in 1912 and their killing of unarmed Kent State University students in 1970.

In general, the frontier tradition (see, e.g., Cash, 1941; Pettigrew and Spier, 1962) has been proffered as characteristic of the American approval of violence and contributory to contemporary violence. Under this perspective and in the exploitation of land, emphasis is on reliance on one's own initiative and resources for almost everything. When the law is broken, decisions are made on the spot in vigilante style. The values of such a tradition include:

1. The idealized version of manhood, typified by the "John Wayne syndrome," including characteristics such as confidence in one's physical

prowess and in man-to-man confrontations, being rough and ready with one's fists, and standing tall against affronts and danger.

2. The tradition of gun ownership, where guns are the symbols of the independent spirit and masculinity.

3. The feeling of independence from authority, evidenced in the aforementioned vigilante right to avenge wrongs, to be armed, and to be the enforcer of the law if one believes the authorities are not performing satisfactorily.

4. The belief in violence as a successful solution to problems. In 1969, for example, a survey of American males revealed that a large proportion approved of extreme violence in situations not involving danger to life or property (Ball-Rokeach, 1973).

MINORITY THEORISTS ON MINORITY CRIME

In his in-depth treatise on the "colonial model," African American sociologist Robert Staples emphasizes the pervasiveness of violence in the fabric of colonial society. African Americans in American society, and in all societies where they are oppressed, are not the instigators of violence; it is already there, since the maintenance and perpetuation of colonialism are dependent upon violence (Staples, 1975). In line with the observations of the West Indian African psychiatrist Frantz Fanon (1963; 1967), Staples demonstrates that through slavery, the colonized native is introduced to violence by his colonial oppressor. The brutalities of slaveholders in the antebellum South, for example, presented models of atrocity and violence to the slaves who were the victims of such maltreatment. After the Civil War, violence was also used to intimidate and control African Americans. Thus, according to Staples, the colonial system teaches, maintains, and perpetuates violence.

To test whether decolonization on the Caribbean island of St. Vincent would lead to a reduction in intragroup black violence, Roy Austin (1983a) compared violence rates before and after British decolonization. His findings tend to support the colonial model, except for the two most serious violent offenses— murder and manslaughter. Austin speculates that more lethal weapons may have become available, along with more willingness to use them.

As previously indicated, Darnell Hawkins (1983; 1986a) feels that the subculture of violence theory ignores or underemphasizes a variety of historical-structural, situational, and economic factors that might explain the high rates of African American homicide. He proposes several explanatory concepts:

Proposition 1: Under American criminal law, black life is cheap, whereas white life is valuable (Hawkins, 1986a: 114). The rates of criminal violence among African Americans, in comparison to other nonwhite and Euro-American ethnics, are attributable to their unique history of slavery and oppression. The historical behavior of American law, especially in the South, created a hierarchy of the seriousness of criminal violence based primarily on the racial identity of, and the relationship between, the victim and offender. During slavery, and in the immediate post-Reconstruction South, offenses committed by African Americans against Euro-Americans were seen as attacks on the racial social order.

To test this proposition, Hawkins offers two hypotheses: (1) Past and present indices of official sanctioning of homicide offenders will reveal harshest penalties for offenses of African Americans against Euro-Americans who are in positions of authority and/or who are strangers to the offender. The least severely sanctioned will be offenses occurring among interracial acquaintances or family members where whites are offenders. (2) Studies of African American public opinion will reveal that African Americans believe that the behavior of the law protects the lives of whites more than the lives of African Americans.

Hawkins's second proposition (ibid.: 119) suggests that past and present racial and social class differences in the administration of justice affect African American criminal violence. In other words, the response of police, prosecutors, and courts to prehomicide types of behaviors (e.g., ignoring previous assault histories) influences the rate of homicide. Official responses to prehomicide behaviors, such as assault, are affected by such factors as the race and social class of the victims and offenders. Like homicide, prehomicide behavior among the poor and African Americans is likely to be perceived by law enforcement authorities as "normal" and inevitable.

Hawkins (ibid.: 124) finds that "economic deprivation creates a climate of powerlessness in which individual acts of violence are likely to take place." To the extent that criminal violence is caused by economic deprivation and powerlessness, homicides will occur at a higher rate among the African American underclass than among the African American middle class.

Concluding that the causation of African American homicide cannot be examined apart from "the study of racial discrimination and bias in the administration of justice" (ibid.: 127), Hawkins offers three theoretical propositions as guides for future research on African American homicide: (1) the historical devaluation of African American life; (2) official responses of the criminal justice system to prehomicide behavior among African Americans; and (3) the direct effects of economic deprivation as important causal factors in such homicides.

A recent study of trends in racial inequality and African American involvement in violence by Roy Austin (1983b) examined whether African American progress toward equality and the Black Power Movement contributed to a reduction in African American violence. The belief that egalitarian trends and the Movement could have ameliorative effects on violence is supported by the colonial model of Frantz Fanon (1963; 1967) and other social scientific statements, such as the propositions offered by Hawkins (1986a). Austin found the trends consistent with the belief: structural changes, indicated by educational and political progress, were associated with violence reduction. But, contrary to Hawkins's hypothesis, an effect for economic progress was doubtful. Cultural changes related to the struggle for black power seem likely to have contributed to the reduction in violence. These findings are contrary to the purely structural explanation of those social scientists who tend to emphasize changes in the economic structure.

The myopic Euro-American research focus on violent crime is not peculiar to African Americans; violent crime has been disproportionately linked to all four of the racial minority groups discussed. The majority of the research on Native and Hispanic Americans also stresses the violence theme. In a monograph, *The Hispanic Experience of Criminal Justice* (1979), Peter L. Sissons refers to the application of the subculture of violence theory to Hispanics by some theorists who view violence as preexisting in the Hispanic culture, instead of considering that "other forms of violence associated with the achievement of certain criminal goals may be expressions of the failure of an individual to retain his grasp upon a culture which is slipping away from him in a new highly industrialized and socially complex society" (ibid.: 9).

In the early 1940s, Hayner (1942: 613) reported "exceedingly high rates for murder and assault" within some Indian tribes, which he attributed to "the intensity and character of contacts with white civilization, on the one hand, and . . . the source and adequacy of sustenance, on the other" (ibid.: 602). Fifty years later, Young (1990: 112) finds that the aggravated assault rate of Native Americans on reservations is about six times the United States rural rate, while the murder rate on reservations is three times the rate for the rural United States.

Yet, one wonders why so little attention has been devoted to research that might determine why there are so few minority mass murderers, serial killers, or sex murderers, killers who frequently commit heinous, pathological, and sexually perverted acts of violence.

While not contesting the fact that the poor, particularly urban African Americans and Chicanos, are overwhelmingly the victims of "street crimes," Bernard Headley challenges the prevailing notion that "the physical survival and well-being of the black community in America is threatened more by blacks killing or stealing from other blacks ('threats from within') than from external or systemic forces ('threats from without')" (1982-1983: 50). In essence, Headley questions the study of African Americans apart from "the larger social reality of crime in the United States," by noting that it is not the ecology of African American criminality but the social and economic forces that produce the criminal that are at issue (ibid.: 57-58). Headley argues that the myth of "black-on-black" crime should be put into perspective with "the larger and more serious crimes committed against black and poor Americans by the ruling sectors of the society" (ibid.: 60). Headley finds that the only long-term solution is through

> a radical overhaul of the American political economy and the ideology that directs and guides the criminal justice system. An economy that generates gross levels of inequality and consequently relegates a substantial proportion of its population to permanent unemployment, joblessness, and demoralization—then uses its criminal justice system to control this surplus population—cannot hope to "free" itself of the menace of predatory crime. (Ibid.: 61)

After a review of the most prominent minority and nonminority perspectives of minority crime, one logical conclusion reached is that there is an inordinate interest in minority crime causation, while we have yet to uncover the causes of nonminority crime. In the previous chapter, it was demonstrated that within-group comparisons of crime commission, as measured by arrests, reveal little variation by racial/ethnic status, which suggests that American perpetrators from all groups commit the same offenses. In proportion to each subgroup's total crime, minorities were as likely as whites, for example, to steal, kill, fight, use drugs, gamble, get drunk, or prostitute themselves or others. However, between-group arrest percentages varied dramatically. As political activist Angela Davis (1991) recently noted, this observation suggests that "criminality is a social construction." Thus, the task is to find the common threads that weave the pattern of minority stereotyping which ultimately involves them unequally in the criminal justice system.

A review of the literature reveals four general perspectives offered to explain minority crime: adjustment/acculturation, economic realities (e.g., deprivation, unemployment, poverty, class level, economic inequality), social disorganization, and the subculture of violence. As seen in Table 3-1, within some minority subgroups only specific subcategories are ascribed by some theorists (e.g., rural African Americans), while other minority subgroups are not represented by certain theories at all (e.g., subculture of violence). Further, it seems that the only theoretical perspective that appears to be representative of all racial minority subgroups is social disorganization (or differential social organization). Another commonality shared by these minorities is color. It is suggested that the two are notably intertwined.

TABLE 3-1: Common Perspectives of Minority Crime
(by major subgroup)

Adjustment/ Acculturation	Economic	Social Disorganization	Subculture of Violence
Rural African Americans	African Americans	African Americans	African Americans
Hispanic Americans	Hispanic Americans	Hispanic Americans	Hispanic Americans
Native Americans	Native Americans	Native Americans	
Asian Americans	Some Asian Americans	Asian Americans	

Daniel Georges-Abeyie is highly critical of the current Eurocentric approach to criminological/criminal justice theories of African American criminality because they

1. Lack a social ecological perspective;
2. Too often focus on the formal decision in the processing of Blacks; and
3. Analyze African Americans as an ethnic monolith who are often caught up in a

criminal justice system which is really a morass of disjointed, interconnected agencies involving both an informal and formal decision-making process. (1989: 37)[19]

In line with the previously discussed appraisal of Mann and Selva (1979), Georges-Abeyie finds that these contemporary approaches lack sensitivity to a diverse African American ethnicity, a result of Euro-Americans' deficient ability to recognize the "cultural-social-spatial identities" and origins of African Americans from Africa, the Caribbean, Central America, and South America[20] and the concomitant "nexus of profound cultural variables" such as religion, color, and hue (1989: 38). Most important, he develops the concept of color/hue "identifiers," which is totally ignored in research on African American crime causation:

Thus, should social distance be significant within and between Black ethnic groups, then is it not possible that social distance between Blacks and whites might impact every phase of the processing of Black ethnics? Is it not also conceivable that different Black ethnic groups are more involved in extralegal and illegal activity than are others, and that certain Black ethnics dominate certain criminal activities (or are believed to) and are thus viewed as more threatening than are other Black ethnics (e.g., Jamaican versus Hispanic, African American versus British West Indian, "dark-skinned" Negroids versus what some Blacks have derisively labeled "high yellas" and "brights")? (Georges-Abeyie, 1989: 39)

The notion of color or shade of color has generally been overlooked by researchers of minority crime causation. However, Charles E. Silberman opens an exploratory door that suggests the possibility of two very important explanatory concepts: (1) the relationship between color and crime, and (2) the variation in treatment of specific minority groups: "Rural black migrants to metropolitan areas face all the problems of acculturation that other rural migrants have faced; but they carry two additional burdens: their color and their heritage of slavery. Prejudice against black people is more virulent and intractable than is prejudice against Orientals, Chicanos, Native Americans, Catholics, or Jews" (1978: 170).

For many decades African American social scientists have pointed to the connection between skin color and the status of African Americans in this country. In a test of the theory of human ecology proposed by the Chicago School (e.g., Park and Burgess, 1925; Burgess, 1926; Park, 1936; Wirth, 1938), E. Franklin Frazier examined the processes of social selection and segregation in the African American community in Chicago. Earlier, Park (1926: 8-9) had noted the creation of "natural social groups" in urban "natural social areas" due to racial segregation. Frazier's analysis identified seven areas or zones within the "Negro community," finding that one of the most arresting characteristics of the selection and segregation process was the "variation in the percentage of mulattoes in the population of different zones" (Edwards, 1968: 123). The highest concentration of mulattoes was in the zone with the largest concentration of higher occupational classes. In a later work, *Black Bourgeoisie,* Frazier further defined how in segregated cities a class structure slowly emerged which was based upon social distinctions such as education and conventional behavior. At the top of the social pyramid there was a small upper class. The superior status of this class was due chiefly to its differentiation from the great mass of the Negro population because of a family heritage which resulted partly from its mixed ancestry. . . . The members' light skin-color was indicative not only of their white ancestry, but of their descent from the Negroes who were free before the Civil War, or those who had enjoyed the advantages of having served in the houses of their masters. (1965: 20)

Social isolation because of skin color, or "differentness," has also been reported by other African American theorists: for example, Kenneth Clark (*Dark Ghetto*, 1965), psychiatrists James Comer (*Beyond Black and White*, 1972) and William Grier and Price Cobbs (*Black Rage*, 1968), and psychologist Sterling Plumpp (*Black Rituals*, 1972). In referring to the "white mind," Grier and Cobbs demonstrate that through rationalization and justification, whites have denied that African Americans' constitutional and human rights have been violated over the years. Since, in the "white mind," whites and blacks have had the same basic experiences since the end of slavery, whites "comfortably assume that blacks have special problems in America only because they are either inferior or lazy" (Grier and Cobbs, 1968: 118). When asked to explain the black-white gap in socioeconomic status, whites surveyed from 1977 to 1989 emphasized the lack of motivation among poor blacks and blamed blacks for their economic condition (Kluegel, 1990: 524). It is argued that such Euro-American mindsets apply not only to African Americans but to other racial minorities as well.

In response to his own provocative question: "Can it be shown conclusively that blacks, for example, have experienced racism to a proportionately greater degree than Asians to account for crime differentials between them?" Flowers states:

A likely explanation is that while racism is certainly not solely responsible for minority crime, it is equally certain that as an intrinsic part of the American heritage, its effect has been indelible in the behavior of those most victimized by it. In other words, although minority crime may be a product of many societal and personal conditions, *it is the minority's general place in society as established over centuries that is the undercoating of his or her circumstances.* Differential rates of crime among minority groups may be less a matter of disparity in racism or discriminatory treatment than a difference in subsequent adjustment and reaction by racial and ethnic minority groups to its effects. (1990: 75-76; emphasis added)

But it is conceivable that African Americans *have* been the victims of institutionalized racism to a greater extent than Asian, Hispanic, and Native Americans, beginning with the institution of their status as slaves and extending over time until today in disorganized urban communities, primarily because they are a more visible minority. They are more racially "different" from Euro-Americans than the other minority subgroups because of their darker skin color. By the same token, "black" Puerto Ricans, dark-skinned Cubans, and darker-hued

Mexican Americans have also experienced more virulent racism than their Hispanic counterparts with lighter complexions (see Chapter 1).

Racism and discrimination, as well as the adaptation and response to such practices, do vary among the minority groups, but only in proportion to the extent of the racism and discrimination experienced. Actually, the problem lies with Euro-Americans, since it is they who experience fear of the "different," specifically those of different color. In his early treatise on the bases of race prejudice, Robert E. Park observed:

> On the whole, we may define the situation in which races meet, as one of vague apprehension tinged with and qualified by curiosity. The first effect is to provoke in us a state of tension—a more vivid awareness and readiness to act—and with that a certain amount of reserve and self-consciousness which is incident to every effort at self-control. . . .
>
> . . . It is in such situations, I suspect, that those antipathies arise which seem to constitute the most irrational, and at the same time the most invincible, elements in racial prejudice. (Turner, 1967: 178)

If a white woman is walking her dog in the dark of night in a middle-class neighborhood and encounters an Oriental man jogging toward her, she might momentarily hold her breath until he has passed. But if the jogger is an African American man, especially one of darker complexion, she will probably feel anxiety and fear, and may even cross the street in avoidance. It has been demonstrated that in an identical scenario, white police officers would stop and question the African American jogger about what he was doing in the neighborhood. To them, it is of little consequence whether the man is a medical doctor, an attorney, or a university professor; he is a black man.[21] Since this is the type of experience faced by middle- and upper-class people of color, the implications of such negative episodes for their minority counterparts in the socially isolated urban Chinatowns, barrios, ghettos, and reservations are obvious.

The long history of discrimination against minorities, rooted in institutional racism, according to African American sociologist William Julius Wilson, is buttressed by "the complex interaction between the economic and social position of blacks on the one hand and their personal and familial modes of adaptation on the other that has produced such social problems as high crime rates" (Wilson and Herrnstein, 1985: 485). Each of the minority groups discussed also conforms to Wilson's etiological description. Further, differential treatment because of their skin color is not unique to American racial minorities. In many multicolored nations (e.g., most of the Caribbean islands, Central and South America, South Africa), whites are at the top of the economic and social ladder, while people of darkest skin color are at the bottom, with the spectrum from light to dark on the rungs in between. Put another way, at the top are the "haves"; at the bottom are the "have nots."

How can one study and test a hypothesis that suggests there are significant interrelationships between skin color, institutional racism, and minority crime?

Noting that it has never been done, Wilson and Herrnstein offer a partial plan, "a prospective, longitudinal study of black and white children growing up in a big city, a study that attends closely to constitutional factors; early familial and school experiences; the ways in which young people come into contact with peers, the labor market, and the criminal justice system; and the development of a set of values and an orientation toward the larger society" (1985: 485). As presented, it could be predicted that not much more novel data would be obtained than were reported by the Chicago Area Project (Shaw and McKay, 1942) or the National Youth Surveys (e.g., Gold and Reimer, 1975). A refinement of the study would include cross-cultural components: the inclusion of other minority children of color; the study of children in integrated neighborhoods, in suburban and rural areas, and near Indian reservations. A final prediction is that the immediate response of potential funding agencies, particularly governmental sources, would be negative. This is not necessarily because of the costs and magnitude of such an endeavor, since one day's expenditures for the Persian Gulf War would have more than adequately covered the research expenses, but if the hypothesis is valid, such resistance would be due to the entrenched institutionalized racism in the political structure itself.

Finally, and most important, any research addressing the etiology of minority crime should be undertaken predominantly by minority researchers, or by those who understand the nuances of the subject matter. For as Barak so insightfully notes:

> The suggestion here is that culturally hegemonic white bias in criminal justice/criminology literacy (CJCL) has had the effect of suppressing the understanding of important historical and social contexts for making sense out of the African American (or other ethnic and feminist) experiences in relationship to the processes of crime and justice. In turn, this suppression of an African-American interpretation in CJCL education leads to a limited and distorted view of criminal justice and criminality, serving to further isolate the urban underclasses and street criminals. It also contributes to those prevailing negative trends that are not only increasing social stratification and polarization, but that are simultaneously reinforcing the class, racial, and gender divisions throughout American society. (1991: 9)

Part Two

The Response to Minority Crime

4

Law and Its Enforcement against Minorities

When whites talk of "criminal justice"
To minorities it means "just us."
—Anonymous

The Lawlessness of American Law

Throughout its history, American law is replete with evidence of discrimination against racial minorities in employment, housing, public and private education, political power, health care, and marriage. These types of legal action reflect the social-structural condition that leads to criminal behavior by minorities, particularly when the issues of color and economics are introduced. Law has been defined by Donald Black as "governmental control" that varies directly with rank in that "people with less wealth have less law" (cited in Gottfredson and Hindelang, 1979: 3). Chambliss and Seidman (1971: 65) respond more acutely to this perspective when they state, "In all societies, regardless of how the interest groups vary in number, those which are most likely to be effective are the ones that control the economic or political institutions of the society. The most influential groups will of course be those which control both. As a consequence, legislation typically favors the wealthier, the more politically active groups in the society."

Clearly, Native Americans, Asian Americans, African Americans, and Hispanic Americans historically have been in positions of less wealth; therefore, according to the above perspectives, they have less law and less access to the law, and have been and currently are abused by the law. The inequalities accruing to minorities under our system of law and justice not only are present in the contemporary operation of our legal system, but also have existed since its origin.

What sociologists (and other social scientists, for that matter) who try to explain the "law in action" frequently overlook or, according to Quinney (1974: 24), "fail to realize" is that the law of American society has been formulated by only a few, those "representing the power elite with similar interests—who dominate the political process." The evolution of American law, especially criminal law, clearly demonstrates how the "minority crime problem" developed and has been exacerbated throughout the history of this country. In his espousal of a radical humanistic perspective in criminology, Friedrichs (1982: 214) finds that "the principal danger for a humanist criminology is that it exposes and condemns injustices in the criminal justice system without sufficient attention to the structural roots of these injustices."

This section examines the genesis of American law as related to racial minorities and focuses on two basic aspects in the social structure which influenced law development—minority labor, specifically "the exploitation of numerous and varied forms of labor including slave labor, forced labor and bonded labor as well as wage labor" (Schwendinger and Schwendinger, 1977: 6), and "legal" violence, or how "the legal system provides the mechanism for the forceful and violent control of the rest of the population" (Quinney, 1974: 52). As is the practice in this book, in order to understand the inequities applied to racial minorities within the American legal system, it is necessary to examine the historical record. Therefore, this section traces the process of customizing the criminal law for American minority members through several time periods, depicted in Table 4-1: the colonial period, the constitutional era through the time of the Civil War, the postbellum period to the First World War, and the time of World Wars I and II and the post–World War II era until today.

THE COLONIAL PERIOD
No other minority has had as many laws, opinions, or treaties directed at controlling their welfare as the American Indian. The Schwendingers ably describe the law in this context:

> One can say that certain bourgeois laws themselves have undermined pre-existing production relations together with the customs, laws, and lives of people everywhere. For example, not only were slave relations secured by such laws but treaties were imposed on American Indian tribes legalizing the wholesale and violent theft of natural resources, and the transformation of these resources into bourgeois property. (1977: 6)

In contrast to the Mexican government, which does not legally view Indians as a separate and distinct group, the Canadian and United States governments signed treaties with the Indians or defined their legal status through legislation which recognized them as a separate group. The U.S. treaties guaranteed the Indians permanent occupancy and use of certain areas in exchange for the ceding of lands to the federal government (Wingspread Conference, 1973). In addition to treaty making, in 1789 the federal government "asserted criminal jurisdiction over Indians" (Peak, 1989: 394).

Prior to the signing of these "agreements" with the government, the Indians were battling to retain their tribal lands, since the "notion of racial inferiority" had become "an excuse to push Indians off their lands" (ibid.). But Indians were

TABLE 4-1: Major U.S. Legislation Affecting Racial Minorities (1690-1976)

Historical Period	Legislation by Type of American			
	Native	*African*	*Asian*	*Hispanic*
Colonial (1619-1776)	Treaties (1754) Rape laws	Slave Codes (1690) Rape laws	—	—
Constitutional-Civil War (1776-1865)	*Cherokee Nation v. Georgia* (1830)—ousted from lands	U.S. Constitution ³/₅ of a human being (1776)— *Dred Scott* (1857)— blacks unequal to whites Emancipation Proclamation (1863) freed slaves	Oregon Constitution denied vote (1857)	Texas annexed (1857)
Postbellum to World War I (1865-1917)	Appropriations Act (1871) eliminated treaties	Black Codes 13th Amendment (1865) abolished slavery Civil Rights Act (1866) 14th Amendment (1868) accorded citizenship 15th Amendment (1870) granted right to vote *Pace v. Alabama* (1883)— anti-race mixing *Plessy v. Ferguson* (1896)— "separate but equal" Jim Crowism	State laws similar to Black codes Chinese Exclusion Act (1882) prohibited immigration California Alien Act (1913) denied Japanese land ownership	—

TABLE 4-1 (*continued*)

Legislation by Type of American

Historical Period	*Native*	*African*	*Asian*	*Hispanic*
World War I to 1976	1924-citizenship granted	Civil Rights Acts (1964)	Immigration Law of 1924—excluded immigration	1930's Immigration laws—excluded immigration
	Public Law 280 (1953) states' rights over crimes	Voters Rights Act (1965)	1930's Immigration laws	Bracero Program (1942) "stoop labor" permitted immigration
	Native American Church v. U.S. (1959) Tribal law higher than state law	*Loving v. Virginia* (1967) anti-miscegenation unconstitutional	President's Executive Order (1942) internment	
		Civil Rights Acts (1968)	Exclusion Act repealed (1943)	
	U.S. Code (1976) states' rights over criminal and civil cases			

sorely losing their fights with encroaching settlers and traders who were subsequently aided by the military. As described in Chapter 1, the ensuing demand for land "spurred the federal government's decision for 'removal' of the Indians to unwanted lands West of the Mississippi" (Gubler, 1963: 207). Meanwhile, "the Indians improved daily and wonderfully by their intercourse with whites. They took to drinking rum, they learned to cheat, to lie, to swear, to gamble, to quarrel, to cut each other's throat, in short to excel in all that marked the superiority of their Christian visitors" (Peak, 1989: 394).

Two important factors inherent in these earlier "treaties" should be noted: "the imprecise legal definition of Indian territory for criminal definement and prosecution," and the lack of a precise legal definition of "Indian" for the same purposes (Gubler, 1963: 209-210). In earlier times, everyone knew what an Indian was, but with blurred bloodlines, "eyeball" definitions and other methods of defining Indians rapidly became inadequate. As we shall later see, if an Indian cannot "prove" his or her heritage, it is difficult, if not impossible, to claim ancestral rights. By the same token, it has recently become popular for Euro-Americans to claim "Indian blood" and the benefits that might accrue to that status.

The criminal injustice of being kidnapped from one's native country, transported hundreds of miles under horrendous conditions like cattle, and enslaved, marks the origins of the unequal treatment experienced by African Americans[1] that resulted in a dual system of justice which continues to exist in America on the basis of skin color. Forced to work on plantations, these African slaves first encountered "law" as "plantation justice," typified in the 1690 slave codes. "These codes, a group of laws designed specifically for the discipline and control of the slave, clearly delineated the social and legal relationship of the black man to the white man. . . . They all were generally designed to prevent slaves from carrying weapons, owning property, and having rights or legal protection" (Owens and Bell, 1977: 7).

More important, since these slavery laws gave the Euro-American plantation owners and overseers (or any "white" man, for that matter) enormous power "to determine and give meaning to the situation of the inferiority of the black man, there was no real need to justify nor be concerned with equal justice and treatment" (Mann and Selva, 1979: 171). The dispenser of "plantation justice" specified the punishments to fit the "crimes" of the slaves, punishments that were cruel and brutal—whipping, hanging, branding, castration, and death.

Castration and death were frequently used for such crimes as attempted rape or rape of a white woman, and sometimes just for striking a white person (Owens and Bell, 1977; Jordon, 1974). Early eighteenth-century laws in Pennsylvania and New Jersey prescribed castration of African American men solely for the attempted rape of a white woman, while Virginia's provision for castration covered a variety of serious offenses. Although repealed in 1769, the Virginia statute maintained the provision that castration of African American men might still be applied in the attempted rape or rape of a white woman (Jordon, 1974).

During one period of time, sexual mutilation was almost exclusively reserved for blacks and Indians accused of interracial sex crimes (Burns, 1973: 160).

THE CONSTITUTIONAL ERA THROUGH THE CIVIL WAR

The General Crimes Act, enacted in 1817, provided a system of criminal justice for the American population, Indian and non-Indian alike. This act gave to federal and state courts concurrently the jurisdiction to try cases involving offenses committed on Indian lands—such offenses "would be adjudicated the same as offenses committed anywhere under the exclusive jurisdiction of the United States" (Peak, 1989: 394).

Meanwhile, the United States Constitution and the laws following it continued to sustain racial inequality, compromise African American rights, and ensure white dominance and control. While not explicitly alluding to race or slavery, by considering a black slave as equal to only three-fifths of a human being, in effect the Constitution sanctioned slavery in the states upholding the practice (Miller, 1966), and "the false principle of the inferiority of black people because of their race or color, which over the years had become imbedded in our national consciousness, now became part of our country's fundamental law" (Crockett, 1972: 7). Once established by law and internalized in the national mind, the results of such legislation persisted, and as Miller (1966: 63) accurately notes,

> Americans simply have a double standard of judgment as to rights of white persons as contrasted to those of Negroes. To them, white persons are born vested with that vast array of rights and privileges vaguely thought of as natural rights. Negroes, on the other hand, are regarded as entitled to such rights as the white majority grants them. It is commonly said that Negroes must "earn" the rights they would enjoy. That attitude is deeply rooted in our history. (1966: 63)

It is commonly believed that the original Constitution and the Bill of Rights protected the rights and liberties of all Americans. However, "in truth, the equalitarian guarantees explicit and implicit in the Constitution and amplified in the Bill of Rights offered absolutely no protection to the approximately 700,000 persons held in slavery at the birth of the nation and, as the Supreme Court was to hold later, little more protection for some 60,000 free Negroes of the North and South" (ibid.: 64). On the contrary, the Constitution protected slavery in those states which practiced it by the inclusion of a fugitive clause providing for the return of slaves who escaped to other states ("Justice Thurgood Marshall's Dissenting Opinion," 1979: 57). Further, it provided legal provisions for preserving the "migration or importation" of slaves until 1808 (Hindelang, 1969: 306), and prohibited Congress from "taxing slavery out of existence" for the same period of time (Long, Long, Leon, and Weston, 1975: 31). In essence, "the writers of the United States Constitution reduced blacks to the level of chattel" (Marshall, 1979: 57). To defend their slave property interests, individual states passed the Slave Codes, a notion of the African slave as property that was later reinforced by the United States Supreme Court in the *Dred Scott* decision.

The benchmark decision in *Dred Scott v. Sanford* in 1857 demonstrates early racist interpretations of the precarious relationships between the races by reflecting the dogma held by society and the law that blacks should not be accorded equal rights with whites. The question asked in *Dred Scott* was:

> Can a Negro whose ancestors were imported into this country as slaves, become a member of the political community formed and brought into existence by the Constitution of the United States, and as such become entitled to all the rights, and privileges, and immunities, guaranteed by that instrument to the citizen? (Todd, 1979: 65)

The Court answered:

> We think they are not, and that they are not included, and were not intended to be included, under the word "citizen" in the Constitution, and can therefore claim none of the rights and privileges which that instrument provides for and secures to citizens of the United States. On the contrary, they were at that time considered as a subordinate and inferior class of beings, who had been subjugated by the dominant race, and whether emancipated or not . . . had not rights or privileges but such as those who held power . . . might choose to grant them. . . . (Stampp, 1970: 17)

Accordingly, since African Americans had no rights which the Euro-American needed to respect, their "less than human status," and thus unequal justice, was secured.

Constitutionally, racial classification is suspect, and in fact, it was later forbidden by the Civil War Amendments, which were to eliminate "all invidious racial distinctions tolerated by the original Constitution, as interpreted by the Supreme Court, and to provide a new constitutional basis for congressional action to establish equality whenever states or individuals were laggard or insisted on imposing racial disabilities" (Miller, 1966: 66). But, as we will later see, the Supreme Court revised the meanings of those amendments.

The Constitution did little for the Indians, either, since only three provisions referred directly to them—Article 1, Section 2, clause 3 and Section 8, clause 3, and the Fourteenth Amendment, Section 2—and these stipulations left "untouched the general field of national authority to assert criminal jurisdiction over Indians and Indian territory" (Gubler, 1963: 207); instead, "the new Constitution contained four important statutes that invoked federal authority over Indian matters. They included the power to make war, to govern territories, to make treaties, and to spend money" (Peak, 1989: 394). The Emancipation Proclamation (1863), which was issued in the midst of the Civil War, freed the slaves, but it did not relate to the Indians.

THE POSTBELLUM PERIOD TO WORLD WAR I

In the immediate post–Civil War period, two significant amendments to the Constitution were ratified: the Thirteenth Amendment (1865), which abolished slavery and involuntary servitude, and the Fourteenth Amendment (1868), which provided citizenship to the former slaves and guaranteed them equal protection of the law previously extended to other citizens (Vetter and Silverman, 1986: 452). Although they were no longer in slavery, the oppression of African Americans, which was rooted in economic self-interest, did not abate with their new "freedom." They were still subjected to a different measure of justice: since "total control through the institution of slavery could no longer be effected, more subtle forms of coercion and control were needed" (Mann and Selva, 1979: 171).

The first Civil Rights Act (1866) was enacted by Congress after the ratification of the Thirteenth Amendment as a response to the Black Codes which threatened to reduce African Americans to a status of semi-slavery. These codes, initiated by the provisional legislatures of many southern states, were similar to the earlier Slave Codes and included restrictions: limiting the rights of African Americans to own or rent property, providing imprisonment for breach of employment contracts, and denying African Americans the right to testify in court against Euro-Americans. Under the Black Codes, in some towns African Americans could not be on the streets after dark, and they could hold only menial jobs (Miller, 1966; Todd, 1979).

In his historical review of punishment for rape in Virginia, Donald Partington highlights one of the more ingenious means of ensuring control of African American men. Prior to 1866, the Virginia Code contained a rape punishment disparity—African American men could be put to death; Euro-American men could not be sentenced to more than twenty years in prison. After 1866, purportedly the statutes were amended to eliminate this racial disparity—a person convicted of rape could be punished either by confinement in prison for not more than twenty years, or by death. Such a determination under the altered statute included this provision—at the discretion of the jury—which, considering the prior racial discriminatory track record of the rape statute, in effect continued the old policies (Partington, 1965: 50-56).

Another subtle form of control was found in the laws concerned with the sexual relationships of African American men and Euro-American women. In the South, laws enacted to "prevent intercourse between the Black man and the white woman were specially legislated at an early date and in language reflecting the white man's abhorrence toward this mix" (Johnston, 1970, cited in Mann and Selva, 1979: 172). There were also situations where a Euro-American woman who married an African slave became the property of the slave's master—in essence, a slave herself.

Challenges to statutes which prohibited interracial marriages and statutes providing more severe sanctions for illicit interracial sexual intercourse than for illicit intercourse indulged in by persons of the same race suggest that such laws "contravened the equal protection guarantee of the Fourteenth Amendment" to the U.S. Constitution (Mann and Selva, 1979: 172). In Pace v. Alabama (1883),[2] the Court held constitutional an Alabama statute that imposed two to seven years' punishment for fornication between a black and a white, but only six months when fornication was committed by persons of the same race. The Court found that since whites and blacks were punished, equal protection was provided, and further, relied on the grounds that it was "a legitimate exercise of the state's police power" (Mann and Selva, 1979: 172). Similar discriminatory laws existed in this country until the 1960s. The extraordinary legal powers of the individual states over the lives of U.S. minorities have not been emphasized in most legal analyses, yet

> in every generation, state laws on race have been of crucial significance—laws that not only defined who is a Negro and then determined his status, but also controlled the Negro's relationship to all important social and political institutions within the society and even entered into the most intimate recesses of his personal life. . . .
>
> Those who argue that it is not proper for state governments to intervene in race relations conveniently forget that from the end of the Reconstruction period many states enacted laws requiring the rigid segregation of the races in nearly every aspect of public life, including public accommodations, schools, jury trials, housing, suffrage, transportation, and, in some instances, as in South Carolina, employment. (Hill, 1965: 95)

The ratification of the Fifteenth Amendment in 1870 gave African Americans the vote.[3] Congress had the right to enforce the Thirteenth, Fourteenth, and Fifteenth amendments through legislation; thus, during the Reconstruction era a great deal of legislative activity took place, which culminated in the Civil Rights Act of 1875. This act was an attempt to use federal power to prevent racial discrimination by specifying that there were only "citizens," not "blacks" or "whites" (Miller, 1966: 67).

Beginning with the *Slaughter-House Cases* in 1873,[4] and over the next few years, through a series of racist decisions the Supreme Court managed to declare the Civil Rights Act of 1875 unconstitutional (1883) and gut each of the constitutional amendments. As Long et al. note,

> The lawmakers of the federal government who had supported the anti-slave movement through the Civil War years and the Reconstruction labored diligently on the explicit language of the Civil War Amendments. The 1873 decision of the Supreme Court in the Slaughter-House Cases contradicted the legislative intent to prevent racial discrimination, and the judicial double-talk in the majority opinion over who were citizens and whether United States or state citizenship protected the basic right to work was an insult. (1975: 35)

Through its decision in the *Slaughter-House Cases,* the Court restored the *Dred Scott* doctrine of two classes of citizenship, national and state, thus threatening the privileges and immunities clause of the Fourteenth Amendment; in *United States v. Cruikshank* (1875),[5] the Court restored control of civil rights to the states; the Fifteenth Amendment granting voting rights was restricted in *United States v. Reese* (1875),[6] and *Virginia v. Rives* (1879)[7] "validated the indictments and verdicts of all-white juries," which led to "extensive discrimination in jury selection" and racial exclusion on juries (Miller, 1966: 67). But the death blow to the Civil War Amendments and African American equality came in *Plessy v. Ferguson* (1896),[8] when the Court upheld a Louisiana railroad law requiring "separate but equal" accommodations for African and Euro-Americans. This single case provided an extensive constitutional basis for segregationist state laws (Hill, 1965: 96) and "made lawful for over fifty years the doctrine that black Americans could be denied equal protection of the laws by compelling racial segregation and forcing blacks to accept separate accommodations" (Long et al., 1975: 35). Thereafter, separate but equal became the law of the land, and Jim Crowism—"the pervasive segregation laws and discriminatory practices"—flourished (Sowell, 1981: 72).

> The Jim Crow laws regulated every dimension of social contact between blacks and whites. Separate building entrances and exits, seating arrangements in theatres (or separate theatres), public transportation, waiting rooms in railroad stations (and later, separate bus stations and airports), toilets, drinking fountains, hotels, restaurants, and other accommodations were required for blacks. (Long et al., 1975: 35)

In the two previous decades, the Indians had been steadily pushed westward; thus, when the railroad opened up the West in 1870, in their efforts to take Indian lands, Euro-Americans totally ignored previous treaties (Washburn, 1976). Congressional law (1830) authorized the president to move any eastern tribe west of the Mississippi by military force, if required. When, in 1830 (*Cherokee Nation v. Georgia*), the Cherokee nation petitioned the U.S. Supreme Court to intervene and prohibit state agents from "harassing them and taking possession of their lands," the Court rejected their plea, and like all the other tribes they were ousted from their lands and escorted west (Long et al., 1975: 21).

The alleged federal paternalism was vividly expressed through another act of Congress: the Appropriations Act of March 3, 1871, which stated that "hereafter no Indian nation or tribe within the territory of the United States shall be acknowledged or recognized as an independent nation, tribe, or power with whom the United States may contract by treaty" (Gubler, 1963: 212).

Stripped of their lands, segregated on reservations, and with their previously promised sovereignty removed by the elimination of treaty making, Native Americans found Congress assuming the legal power of legislating directly for them (Gubler, 1963; Long et al., 1975). It is no wonder the Indians fought back—during this period of American history, the Indian battles of 1870-1880 were waged, and lost.

The ultimate blow came in the *Kagama* decision of 1886, when the Court ruled that the national government would have authority over "these remnants of a race once powerful, now weak and diminished in numbers,"[9] for their own protection, thus making the Indians wards of the federal government while simultaneously declaring that they "owe no allegiance to the states and receive from them no protection. Because of the local ill feeling, the people of the states where they are found are often their deadliest enemies" (Hall, 1979: 50).

Two outstanding critical reviews of the status of the Chinese during this period masterfully depict the plight of Asian Americans in the West: Paul Takagi and Tony Platt's (1978) examination of the Chinese in California, and Charles Tracy's (1980) treatise on the Chinese in Oregon from 1871 to 1885. Takagi and Platt (1978: 4) remind us that since the average Chinese laborer could not pay the passage to this country, he came under a signed three-to-ten-year labor contract, and his servitude, like that of the African slave in the South, was auctioned off by commission merchants. The Chinese laborers who worked the gold mines until they panned out and undertook the back-breaking labor of laying the Central Pacific Railroad tracks were victims of harassment that ultimately turned into violence and massacre. In addition to racial discrimination at the hands of Euro-Americans, the legal system also became harsh toward the Chinese, who had once been welcomed as a source of labor the Euro-American had shunned.

Laws which discriminated against the Chinese were similar to the Slave Codes and Black Codes experienced by African Americans in the South. In many instances, since the Chinese were "free," the laws were especially oppressive. Both California and Oregon, the states where Chinese were most numerous, prohibited a Chinese person from testifying against a Euro-American, a status that frequently left them helpless victims of robberies and beatings. Interestingly, in Oregon, although not permitted to bring legal action against "whites," Chinese could, and did, press charges against African Americans and other Chinese in city, county, and state courts (Tracy, 1980: 14).

The first Constitution of the Oregon Territory (1857) prohibited African and Asian Americans from voting and banned nonresident African Americans from even entering the Territory (Tracy, 1980)! In California the legislature denied citizenship to the Chinese through its rejection of the Fifteenth Amendment, and simultaneously excluded Chinese children from public schools (Takagi and Platt, 1978). A flurry of local ordinances were enacted in both states to prohibit Chinese ownership of land, exclude their entrance into certain occupations, and rigidly tax them out of entrepreneurship. As Takagi and Platt (ibid.: 3) comment, "Race and racism are parts of this history and cannot be separated from the transformation of labor process that channeled the Chinese into particular occupations."

The West Coast Chinese were damaged economically by such racially discriminatory laws as the 1857 statutes in Oregon that required every Chinese miner to pay a monthly tax to the local sheriff for property protection. If it was not paid, the result was seizure and sale of all property within the hour. Other laws prohibited Chinese immigrants from owning real estate or working a mining claim (Tracy, 1980). California ordinances even more precisely structured the occupational choices for the Chinese: business and occupation licenses were denied to "any alien ineligible for citizenship"; laundry deliveries by foot (the Chinese method) were taxed at the rate of fifteen dollars a quarter, while deliveries by a horse-drawn vehicle required the payment of a two-dollar license fee; aliens were not permitted to catch fish for sale in any state waters; laundries had to be of stone or brick construction and, according to another municipal ordinance, could not operate between 10:00 P.M. and 6:00 A.M. (Takagi and Platt,

1978). At the national level, the Chinese Exclusion Act of 1882 effectively prohibited Chinese immigration to this country through repeated renewals for fifty years, until its repeal in 1943. Thus, the expansion of the "Chinese Menace" was temporarily halted.

The Japanese, who were also located predominantly on the West Coast, received similar discriminatory treatment because of their racial/color status, but did not suffer these early injustices for as long a period of time as the Chinese, since the Japanese did not begin to arrive in the United States in sufficient numbers to pose a threat until 1869. Japanese contract laborers who went to work on the plantations of Hawaii in 1868 faced many of the hardships indicative of coolie labor, but it was on the mainland where the law impacted them most negatively. Just as racist legislation had been directed at the Chinese, for decades anti-Japanese laws affecting property ownership and school segregation were passed in California. The final degradation against the Japanese Americans was not to come until World War II, with laws designed to ensure their internment in relocation camps.

Although no specific statutes were enacted against Mexican Americans during this period of time, they were exploited for their "stoop labor," kept in poverty and primitive living conditions, and otherwise maltreated because of their color, language deficiency, and "differentness." Thus, at this time in American history, the status of Mexican Americans was essentially the same as that of African Americans, Asian Americans, and Native Americans—an oppressed minority.

FROM THE WORLD WARS TO TODAY

Federal legislation, state statutes, and municipal ordinances up to this time appeared to be a response to the perceived economic threat posed by the racial minority sector. But there were clear indications that American law functioned just as fiercely against other levels of social interaction between the majority (white) and minority (peoples of color) groups. Of all the segregationist laws that had ensured the power of states' rights resulting from *Plessy v. Ferguson*—or those laws related to schools, colleges and universities, public halls and theaters, hospitals, transportation, and penal facilities—the laws indicating the most fear on the part of Euro-Americans were the ones against mixed marriages.

In 1949, thirty states and our national capital continued to forbid the marriage of a "white" and a "black" or "mulatto"; five states banned "white" and Indian marriages, and fifteen states legislated against mixed marriages between "whites" and "Orientals" (Murray, 1950). As late as 1957, twenty-two states still had such miscegenation laws, some with penalties of up to ten years in prison, while Maryland and Nevada continued to legislate against fornication between the races (Greenberg, 1959). The Maryland law, which was not declared unconstitutional until 1957 in *State v. Howard*, was not only racist but also sexist, finding that any "white" woman "who shall suffer or permit herself to be got with child" as a result of fornication with a "negro" had committed a felony which carried a penalty of not less than eighteen months or more than five years in the penitentiary (Murray, 1950: 206). The Nevada anti-fornication statute was even more racist, since it prohibited sexual activity between "whites and blacks, mulattos, Indians, Malayan or Mongolian persons" at the risk of a $100 to $500 fine, six months to one year in jail, or both (ibid.: 266).

Recall that this all began with the U.S. Supreme Court's decision in *Pace v. Alabama* (1883), when anti-fornication statutes banning sexual intercourse between "whites" and "blacks" were upheld. The *Pace* decision was not overruled by the Court until 1964 in *McLaughlin v. Florida,* when it was judged a violation of individual rights.[10] Anti-miscegenation statutes were determined unconstitutional, as well as morally abhorrent, three years later by the Court in a case ironically named *Loving v. Virginia* (1967).[11]

The various segregationist states' legal definitions of "Negro" patently indicate the racist attitudes of this country extant in 1949; for example, "any blood of African race" (Tennessee), "any person who has in his or her veins any negro blood whatever" (Arkansas), "all persons with an appreciable mixture of negro blood" (Louisiana), or the most common measure, "one-eighth or more of African or Negro blood," which was the established "amount" among those fifteen states which attempted to define "Negro" (Murray, 1950).[12]

The first fifty years of the twentieth century were replete with national and state legislation directed against racial minorities—the California Alien Law Act of 1913 denied Japanese ownership of land; legislation excluding Japanese immigration was passed in 1924; immigration laws of the 1930s prohibited Mexican entry into the United States; a 1942 presidential executive order interned Japanese Americans in veritable concentration camps; and there were racial segregationist statutes and laws denying the right to vote—no person of color was spared.

As minority legal oppression became increasingly unbearable, particularly when minority members were literally denied control of their own communities, many rebelled. The ensuing racial protests, or, as they were viewed by the dominant majority, "riots," and their suppression led to a shocking series of brutal, violent, and lawless acts perpetrated by law enforcement representatives throughout the country. It is at this point in history that racist applications of the criminal law and the resultant incapacitation of minorities through imprisonment became the intensified means of minority control—the current practice.

It is not suggested that the consistent discriminatory application of the criminal law in a fashion that results in the abuse of peoples of color in this country is solely a recent phenomenon; quite the contrary. American federal, state, and local governments have always enacted and enforced criminal laws which were custom-made for specific racial minority groups. When the more flagrant, systemic means of economic and political control of minorities used in the past were no longer feasible or morally acceptable, particularly in the eyes of the rest of the world, criminal law began to be used to warehouse American minorities and maintain their unequal status. The employment of this method introduced an expanded new industry—the criminal justice enterprise—which created more jobs for the majority group as law enforcers, probation officers, lawyers, judges, clerks, prison guards, and numerous other occupations supplemental to the criminal justice system. Nor can we overlook the enhanced capitalistic (ruling-class) opportunities: the construction industry that builds jails and prisons; private entrepreneurs who benefit from the cheap (slave) labor in the production of their products through prison industries; and the profiteers who function as suppliers to this multi-billion-dollar business. The criminalization of minority peoples supplies the human fuel to maintain this constantly expanding enterprise.

American Minorities and Criminal Law

In their discussion of the developmental stages of law, Vetter and Silverman (1986: 15) describe the last stage as occurring when the state assumes the obligation to punish wrongdoing to protect the citizenry; thus, crimes become offenses against the state, and the domain of the state is enlarged to prevent them. Once the state has obtained this control, according to Sheley (1985: 67), "the acts and people we call 'criminal' and our concern with crime at any given time reflect the work of various interest groups within society's current power structure. The ebb and flow of law is the ebb and flow of interest groups." There is substantial historical evidence that racial minorities in this country have consistently been exploited for the economic benefit of the majority (or Euro-American) group through such measures as slavery, bonded labor, forced labor, "coolie" labor, and other forms of cheap wage labor. In fact, an abundance of documentation suggests that this country was built through such forms of minority labor. Needless to say, the fruits of their labors have not been fully realized by the minority members. It is through the domination by the majority (white) economic interest groups that the rewards have been effected, and it is these groups who have consistently profited from minority labor.

Over the many decades when Native Americans, African Americans, Hispanic Americans, and Asian Americans were denied ownership of land and property or what they thought they owned was seized, various legal measures were effected to ensure the subordination of each of these groups. The laws, statutes, and local ordinances that once were effective are no longer efficacious today; therefore, to maintain its hegemony, the majority group has turned to the criminal law as a final means of legal control. Richard Quinney succinctly describes this process:

> Criminal law is used by the state and the ruling class to secure the survival of the capitalist system, and, as capitalist society is further threatened by its own contradictions, criminal law will be increasingly used in the attempt to maintain domestic order. The underclass, the class that must remain oppressed for the triumph of the dominant economic class, will continue to be the object of crime control as long as the dominant class seeks to perpetuate itself, that is, as long as capitalism exists. (1977: 86)

Since the American "underclass" has always had a disproportionate share of racial minorities within its ranks, it is reasonably argued not only that many American criminal laws were devised expressly for these minorities, but also that criminal laws not specifically addressed to them were more frequently applied to them. This is not to deny that there are not "real" criminals among the minority underclass, although how they became criminals is debatable, since "criminal behavior can be comprehended as a rational response of persons who are exploited by the way capitalistic society is organized" (Selva, 1985: 341).

FEDERAL LAWLESSNESS

The role played by the federal government in the oppression of American minorities through the use of criminal law is unique. For the most part, in earlier decades the federal role could be called "law by omission," since federal agents tended not to support the guarantee of individual rights to peoples of color. Greenberg (1959: 313) describes how the law can be used as a "weapon of persecution" through such elements as rules about lynchings and police brutality. Whenever the topic of lynching is broached, the victim viewed immediately in the mind's eye is an African American male hanging grotesquely from a cottonwood tree. Excluding the lynching violence in the nation's frontier period and the antebellum period following the Civil War, two and a half times as many African Americans as Euro-Americans were executed by lynching between 1882 and 1951 (Long et al., 1975: 8). This pattern became fixed during Reconstruction, with the southern states responsible for over nine-tenths of the lynchings; more than 80 percent of the victims were African American (Myrdal, 1944: 64).

One study reports that approximately five thousand African Americans were lynched by mobs between 1865 and 1955 (Demaris, 1970: 115). But as Joel Kovel (1970: 68) notes, "before there were lynchings in the South, there were laws to do what mobs took upon themselves to perform after the Civil War." The intensely violent treatment of the Chinese at the hands of mobs and the decimation of Native Americans in the lust for their tribal lands are further indications that the federal government and its "treaties" and laws did not protect minorities in America, but instead contributed to their systematic genocide.

The Civil Rights Act (1866) passed after the Civil War was an attempt by Congress to protect minorities from such lawless, violent actions, but the laws were not enforced. Section 241 of the act covered mobs which seize a prisoner from a federal marshal or kill a prisoner in public custody and contained a fine of $5,000 and/or ten years for the offense. The other principal federal sanction against "willful acts committed under color of law which deprive inhabitants of any state or territory of rights protected by the Constitution and the laws of the United States," found in Section 242 of the Civil Rights Act, applied to state officers and private citizens in collusion with officials (Greenberg, 1959: 316). Being "tried by ordeal" was (and still is) a risk that a member of an unpopular minority accused of a crime might face, i.e., "third-degree" pressure or beatings to obtain a confession. This section of the Civil Rights Act was ignored and virtually unapplied from Reconstruction until 1945, when in *Screws v. United*

States the federal government prosecuted a Georgia sheriff who had beaten to death an African American prisoner in his custody, thereby depriving the victim of the constitutional right to be tried and punished according to due process of law and not by "ordeal."

The treatment of Native Americans by the federal government constitutes a special case where criminal law is concerned. Constant changes in the body of law and Indian domestic policy have occurred since 1832, when in *Worcester v. Georgia* the U.S. Supreme Court declared that Indians, as dependent sovereigns, were not subject to the laws of the national and state governments or to the jurisdictions of their courts unless expressly made so by Congress (Gubler, 1963: 210).[13] The fact that the legal status of the Indians did not originate in the Constitution but in international law and power politics presents an additional problem of providing Indians with a just and responsible system of criminal law. There is also a question of the extent to which the United States Constitution controls tribal governments and provides individual Indians with criminal procedural and substantive protections. In addition to the uncertainty of his or her constitutional guarantees, a Native American is subjected to the racial discrimination faced commonly by other peoples of color in our society when prosecuted by either state or national governments (Krulitz, 1979: 1).

On August 14, 1953, through Public Law 280, the 83rd Congress gave the states exclusive jurisdiction over crimes and offenses committed by or against Native Americans in the Indian country within their states. Yet the Court found in the 1959 *Native American Church of North America* case[14] that Indian tribes had a higher status than states. However, in 1976, in Subchapter III, which covers jurisdiction over criminal and civil actions, the United States Code declared that

> the consent of the United States is hereby given to any State not having jurisdiction over criminal offenses committed by or against Indians in the areas of Indian country situated within such State to assume, *with the consent of the Indian tribe* occupying the particular Indian country or part thereof which could be affected by such assumption, such measure of jurisdiction over any or all of such offenses committed within such Indian country, or any part thereof . . . and the criminal laws of such state shall have the same force and effect. . . . [15] (Emphasis added)

Apparently many Indian tribes gave consent to this form of "double jeopardy" (they also have tribal laws), since by 1971, seventeen[16] of the twenty-nine states[17] containing federal and state Indian reservations, trust areas, or native villages assumed some measure of criminal jurisdiction over Indian country. In a few states, criminal jurisdiction was retained by the U.S. courts when offenses were committed by or against Indians on reservations. Arizona's 1985 revised statutes are typical of the confusion on this issue:

> Indian tribal courts lack criminal jurisdiction over non-Indians. The laws and courts of Arizona have jurisdiction over offenses committed on an Indian Reservation in Arizona between persons who are not Indians, but the laws and courts of the

United States, rather than those of Arizona have jurisdiction over offenses committed there by one who is not an Indian against one who is an Indian.

Jurisdiction of federal government over Indians accused of crime is derived from the fact that Indians are wards of federal government and dependent upon it until fully emancipated; when emancipated, Indian is subject to jurisdiction of state in which offense is committed.[18]

The congressional intent of overcoming "the problem of lawlessness on Indian reservations and the absence of adequate tribal institutions for law enforcement" under Public Law 280 did not prevent Indian tribes from enacting their own codes of law and order, establishing tribal courts, and enforcing the tribal laws through tribal police, but it took a series of cases to accomplish this status (Krulitz, 1979: 2). Thus, it is also in the obfuscation of the criminal law where the federal government has poignantly demonstrated its lawlessness toward Native Americans. Many an Indian has languished in jail awaiting a determination of which criminal jurisdiction he or she is subject to.

More recently the federal contribution to the legal maltreatment of the minority underclass has been through the passage of omnibus, net-widening criminal laws directed, in large part, at racial/ethnic minorities. The stigmatization and incarceration of American minorities as a result of federal narcotics legislation was described previously (see Chapter 2). In *The American Disease: Origins of Narcotic Control,* David Musto points out the federal lawlessness related to minorities and drugs:

> American concern with narcotics is more than a medical or legal problem—it is in the fullest sense a political problem. The energy that has given impetus to drug control and prohibition came from profound tensions among socio-economic groups, ethnic minorities, and generations—as well as the psychological attraction of certain drugs. The form of this control has been shaped by the gradual evolution of constitutional law and the lessening limitation of federal police powers. . . . The most passionate support for legal prohibition of narcotics has been associated with fear of a given drug's effect on a specific minority. (1973: 244)

Musto clearly demonstrates that the (Euro-American) majority's fear was of a loss of social control over certain minorities because of a belief that the drugs had certain powers only over minorities! African Americans were thought to be invincible to .38 bullets and stimulated to rape under the influence of cocaine. The typical fear of sexual activity between Euro-American women and men of minority races was reinforced by the absurd notion that opium acted as a catalyst for sex between Chinese and Euro-Americans. Violence was associated with both marijuana and the Mexicans, and heroin and urban gangs. Another of the underlying reasons for such persecution is revealed in *Outsiders*, where Howard Becker (1963) vividly describes how the federal government, in this case the Bureau of Narcotics, orchestrated the propaganda campaign that resulted in negative public opinion against marijuana, and ultimately the Marijuana Tax Act, in order to stay in existence as an agency.

Finally, the federal government clearly displayed its indifference and criminal lawlessness toward American peoples of color by turning its back on the violent treatment minorities received in the states, counties, and municipalities of this country. It was not until the 1960s that legislation in civil rights for minorities was enacted, legislation that was the result of major acts of violence. The Civil Rights Acts of 1964 followed the killing of Euro-American civil rights workers in Mississippi, the 1965 Voters Rights Act resulted from the beating and killing of civil rights workers in Alabama, and the Civil Rights Act of 1968 followed the brutal assassination of Martin Luther King, Jr. (Todd, 1979: 73). The lessons of the Civil Rights Acts of 1866 demonstrate that the acquisition of civil rights does not guarantee that those rights will be upheld or that there will be protection for the due process rights associated with minority offenders' criminal liability. Most peoples of color know that the word or letter of the law does not coincide with the practice or implementation of the law where minority Americans are concerned.

STATE AND MUNICIPAL LAWLESSNESS

In broaching how state and municipal laws lead to the stigmatization and criminalization of minorities by precipitating their entry into the criminal justice system, our concern is with the *substantive* criminal law which defines those acts prohibited to citizens—felonies and misdemeanors. Throughout this chapter, mention was made of the laws passed predominantly by southern and western states which legally discriminated against racial minorities: the Black Codes, the segregationist Jim Crow laws, statutes against miscegenation and interracial fornication, and the Oregon and California statutes against the Chinese and Japanese. Violation of any of these laws resulted in arrests, incarceration, and often the deaths of minorities.

Carey draws a distinction between criminal acts that are evil (e.g., murder) and not evil (e.g., traffic violations):

> The criminal codes of the eighteenth century dealt mainly with behavior that was evil in itself. Since the eighteenth century, however, criminal law has been used more and more for the purposes of regulating those acts not evil in themselves. The criminal codes have continually been expanded so that in the United States some state penal codes run to thousands of sections and attempt to regulate almost every conceivable kind of behavior. (1978: 14)

It is contended that not only were "special" laws written to control and subjugate minorities, but also, in an overreach of the criminal law, an ever-increasing number of mundane, non-evil laws were enforced against minorities. Chapter 2 revealed that the vast majority of crimes for which minorities are arrested are "victimless" or public-order crimes such as gambling, drunkenness, disorderly conduct, drug abuse, vagrancy, and prostitution. A portrayal of the criminal justice experiences of the nineteenth-century Chinese in Oregon provides a typical example of how such "municipal ordinances are relatively easy to enact and can be quite responsive to community attitudes and problems" (Tracy, 1980: 19).

Chinese were over 60 percent of all persons arrested for violations of Portland's ordinances during the period studied (1871-1885), and these arrests did not include disorderly conduct, gambling, assault, opium, prostitution, and drunkenness! Chinese accounted for 68 percent of all gambling arrests during the fifteen-year study period; such arrests peaked in 1883, with a Chinese/non-Chinese ratio of 29 to 1. Comparable arrest ratios for prostitution were 8.5 to 1 (1878). Even more ludicrously racist was the "cubic air" ordinance passed in 1873, which resulted in mass arrests of Portland Chinese. This law, allegedly enacted to protect the health of the city, required the arrest of all persons occupying a building containing less than 550 cubic feet of air per person (Tracy, 1980: 17). Other ordinances directed at the Chinese during this time prohibited carrying things suspended from poles on or across the shoulders (the Chinese method), the "smoking, buying, possessing or bargaining for opium" (a predominantly Chinese practice), and playing any musical instrument other than a stringed one in any theater after midnight (the "Chinese Theater Ordinance"; ibid.).

Although data are not available as to the nature of the offenses, Takagi and Platt (1978: 10) report that during this period of time, Asian Americans had one of the highest incarceration rates of any of the minorities in California prisons. At the turn of the century, the rates per 10,000 penal inmates ranked in order were: Native American (55), Chinese (38), "Negro" (33), and "white" (10). Although the rates for prisoners of Mexican origin were not given, Takagi and Platt (ibid.: 10-11) note that in 1860, persons with origins in Mexico constituted 15.7 percent of the California prison population, which was 6.5 times their proportion in the general population.

Whereas these examples highlight the discriminatory application of the criminal law toward the Chinese at one small point in time, an in-depth historical analysis of the statutes and municipal codes of the majority of the states would undoubtedly expose thousands of similar laws resulting in the criminalization of American minorities. In *Sense and Nonsense about Crime*, Samuel A. Walker (1985a: 209) finds that "it is not the criminal justice system but society as a whole that is criminogenic. People commit the crimes that are available to them." It could be added that minority people commit crimes that are created for them.

The Law Enforcers

Since the early days of this nation, peoples of color have complained of differential, primarily disrespectful and brutal, treatment by the police, particularly white police officers. Their voices have largely been unheeded. Tragically, many white social scientists—those funded almost exclusively to research law enforcement and other criminal justice practices affecting racial minorities[19]—not only appear blind to the pervasive problem of white police maltreatment of peoples of color, but also disregard documentation proffered by the abused as "anecdotal" and belittle the opinions of experts in the field, particularly racial minorities with experience and expertise:

> In the absence of more empirical data it is common to find in the literature testimonials from "authorities" asserting that police brutality is a fact and that the race of the victim is a primary motivating factor in such beatings. These statements are often given by commissions or investigators of riots, social scientists, black leaders, and black police administrators. (Wilbanks, 1987: 71)

Perhaps the recent visual recording and nationally televised accounting of the prolonged beating of an African American motorist in Los Angeles by four white police officers, while at least twenty-three other officers looked on, will bring awareness to those oblivious to the plight of peoples of color at the hands of the police in the United States. The victim, twenty-five-year-old Rodney King, was shot with a stun gun, beaten with police batons, kicked, and stomped, an attack involving fifty-six blows which "left him with brain damage, internal bleeding, missing teeth and a broken ankle" (Leerhsen and Wright, 1991: 53). One of the assailants wrote in his police report that Mr. King had "minor" injuries; however, the doctors' report revealed that "his face is partially paralyzed and that, among other injuries, he has nine skull fractures, a broken cheekbone, a shattered eye socket and a broken leg" (Baker and Wright, 1991: 19). Los Angeles Chief of Police Daryl Gates called the assault "an aberration" despite the facts that in the previous year the Los Angeles Police Department had paid out $8.1 million in similar cases of excessive force (Turque, Buckley, and Wright, 1991: 32) and that the police have "always been brutal and lawless to the powerless" (Reich, 1973: 150). In 1990, more than 600 complaints were made against Los Angeles police, and an additional 127 were lodged with the Police Misconduct Lawyer Referral Service in the first two months of 1991 (ibid.). The American Civil Liberties Union in southern California reports receiving 55 complaints against police each week from African American and Hispanic American citizens (Baker and Wright, 1991). The figures from Los Angeles and the state of California represent only a fraction of the number of such police practices taking place daily nationwide.

When the criminal trial of Rodney King's four police assailants was moved to Simi Valley, a predominantly white, middle-class suburban area where many Los Angeles police retire, most African American social scientists with whom I talked were shocked. We assumed that the officers would be acquitted and predicted that the oppressed minority citizens in South-Central Los Angeles would negatively respond to what they saw as another indication of unequal justice. It is amazing that both the local and the national government officials were unaware of the potential for revolt that such a miscarriage of justice would instigate. It is such indifference to the plight of minorities in the ghettos, barrios,

Chinatowns, and on the Indian reservations of this nation that hardens the attitudes of the minorities toward the majority group.

Any attempt to understand the prevailing attitude of minorities toward law enforcement and, conversely, police attitudes toward minorities entails an examination of both subgroups. Earlier chapters wove a historical picture of each relevant racial/ethnic minority group; this section addresses the development of a police entity that has taken on the character of a subculture—one that is frequently in conflict with each of the United States minority subcultures. There is an abundance of literature describing the "police subculture" that will not be detailed here. On the other hand, it is contended that the existence of a police subculture predominantly reflects a standardized and entrenched police personality that is the basis for the "police problem" as minorities view it. Such a perspective also helps to explain why minority law enforcement personnel, despite having racial/ethnic difficulties within their occupation and being largely excluded from the white-dominated police subculture, on many occasions are almost as problematic for minority groups as nonminority police officers.

POLICE PERSONNEL STATISTICS

The most recent available data indicate that among those cities and agencies reporting, there were a total of 793,020 police employees during fiscal year 1990, of which 595,869 were sworn police officers (Reaves, 1992: 2). It comes as no surprise that the police organization today is "typically white and male": the overall breakdown of officers is 83.0 percent white, 10.5 percent African American, 5.2 percent Hispanic, and 1.3 percent other racial/ethnics (ibid.: 1). These more recent figures reflect a dramatic reduction in African American and Hispanic officers as reported earlier by Carter and Sapp (1990: 66). A 1983 survey revealed that in the forty-seven largest cities responding, the percentage of African American officers ranged from a low of 0.7 in Honolulu to a high of 50.1 in Washington, D.C. (U.S. Department of Justice, 1984: 64). No city had a proportion of African American police officers equal to or higher than the percentage of African Americans in the community. The employment of Hispanic American police officers presents a similar picture, with the exception of Toledo, Ohio, where 3 percent of the residents and 3.6 percent of the officers were Hispanic. The city reporting the highest proportion of Hispanic officers was El Paso, Texas (56.9 percent), but despite having Hispanic American populations, five of the cities (Memphis, Tennessee; Columbus, Ohio; St. Louis, Missouri; Charlotte, N.C.; and Birmingham, Alabama) had no Hispanic police officers. Sworn personnel in local police agencies (83.0 percent white, 17.0 percent nonwhite [Reaves, 1992: 1]) have more minority representation than either sheriffs' agencies (86.6 percent white, 13.4 percent nonwhite [Reaves, 1989: 1]) or state police forces (87.1 percent white, 12.9 percent nonwhite [Reaves, 1992: 1]).

Although the prejudice toward Asian Americans is not as intense as toward African Americans, according to one researcher, "racism seems to play a part in the recruitment of orientals just as it does with the recruitment of other minority groups" (Hoffman, 1981). Despite the fact that there are substantial populations of Asian Americans in several large cities—e.g., Los Angeles, San Francisco, Chicago, and New York City—and that 50 percent of the Hawaiian population is Oriental, nationwide there are only a handful of Asian American officers, most of whom are of Japanese and Chinese descent. As in the case of other minorities, the right to be policed by "one's own" suggests the need for increased numbers of Asian American officers, particularly since new immigrant populations introduce a language barrier, and there is an additional need for officers to understand the "life style problems and rationale for behavior" of this American subgroup (ibid.: 31-32). More important, in New York City alone, an estimated 70 percent of the street heroin is supplied by ethnic Chinese and Asian drug rings, which indicates the acute need for Asian American Drug Enforcement Administration (DEA) agents ("Desperately Seeking Oriental DEA Agents," 1988: 1). Despite intensive recruitment efforts, not a single one of the seven hundred DEA applications received over a fourteen-month period was filed by an Asian American. There are unique problems in the recruitment of Asian American agents and police officers: (1) in some law enforcement units, a lower priority for Asian American recruitment than for other minorities; (2) past experience with police officials in their former countries, which leads to ambivalence and negativism toward the police profession; (3) the language barrier; and (4) racism (Hoffman, 1981: 32).

LAW ENFORCEMENT EXPENDITURES AND DEPLOYMENT

A special report on police expenditures and employment in eighty-eight large U.S. cities released by the Bureau of Justice Statistics in 1986 found a thirty-seven-fold increase in spending for police services between 1938 and 1982 (U.S. Department of Justice, 1986: 1). In dollar figures, the increases were from $80 million in 1938 to more than $3 billion in 1982, reflecting a steadily rising police share of total city budgets from 8 percent (1940) to 14 percent (1980); the figure had increased to more than $41.5 billion by 1990 (Reaves, 1992: 2). By 1988, operating and capital expenses of local, sheriffs', and state police agencies totaled more than $28 billion (U.S. Department of Justice, 1988: 1).

Aside from the obvious increase in crime over this time period,[20] there is evidence to suggest that the rise in per capita municipal police expenditures is positively related to the racial/ethnic composition of U.S. cities. Confirmation for this position has been found through examination of the number of minority group members in a city and the extent of their civil rights activities. Using these variables as independent predictors of expenditures, Jackson and Carroll (1981: 303) report: "Our evidence that police expenditures are a resource which is mobilized when a minority group appears threatening to the dominant group underscores the need for an examination of the role of police in determining the political balance between members of minority and majority groups. If the acquisition of policing resources is in part a response to perceived threat, the use of these resources may affect the civil liberties of minority-group members." The relative size of the African American population was a significant predictor in the Jackson and Carroll study.

Parallel results were also found in a study of all U.S. cities of 25,000 or more population size in Jackson's (1985) investigation of the significance of Hispanic visibility as a determinant of the fiscal commitment to policing. Regional comparisons of southern and western cities (N = 175) with larger proportions of Hispanics (12 percent), and northern and north-central areas (142 cities) which averaged only 3 percent Hispanic populations further illustrate the significant influence of relative size of Hispanic population on the primary measures of policing expenditures (salaries and operations, capital expenditures, and total police expenditures). Such findings appear to indicate that the more visible a minority group is, the more it is viewed as a social and economic threat by the nonminority community, which then responds with increased willingness to control the minority group's activities: "The curvilinear relationship between the percent Hispanic populations and capital police expenditures, which persists after the fiscal capacity of the community and the likelihood of social service activity by the police are taken into consideration, provides direct support for the importance of minority group threat as an influence on the collective commitment to policing" (Jackson, 1985: 193).

Further evidence in support of a relationship between minority status and police hiring is reported by Huff and Stahura (1980) in their study of 252 suburban areas. Despite the low percentage of African Americans in the northern and northeastern city suburbs examined, these researchers found that "suburban residents and community leaders view blacks as high crime populations which necessitate a greater degree of community police activity; i.e., in suburbs of the same size and density, a higher police employment rate is expected in suburbs with larger black populations" (ibid.: 465).

When more police are employed in relation to the perceived numbers of minorities in a specific population and the subsequent response of the dominant group's publicly expressed desires, they are deployed to the ghettos and barrios of that city. As a result of such assignments, the members of minority communities are subject to disproportionate patrols and excessive surveillance. Such law enforcement infiltration results in police witnessing the commission of minor law infractions and what they believe to be crimes (the minorities may not view it the same way) and a concomitant increase in minority arrests. Because of mutual antagonism between the police and minority citizens, too often an inquiry, an attitude, or even a posture, on either side, escalates into a confrontation that leads to arrest.[21]

POLICE PERSONALITY AND PRACTICES

The American police system has its roots in the British prototype developed in 1829 by Sir Robert Peel, whose first model police force, the Metropolitan Police of London, bore little resemblance to the law enforcement organizations in the United States today. As the former governor of colonial Ireland, Peel realized that in a free society, the support of the general public was requisite for police to function effectively, and he therefore produced a carefully thought out and structured plan. However, when the first police departments were started in

Boston (1822), New York City (1844), and Chicago (1851), comparable and careful consideration was not given to the American system.[22]

Originally the American police were involved in peacekeeping or order maintenance and a variety of social services to the community, and did not practice law enforcement, or the catching of criminals. Further, in early police organizations, specialization was minimal, learning was largely by apprenticeship, and there was little deference to the police hierarchy. These are still the characteristics typical of many police departments (Wilson, 1974). Of utmost concern to minority involvement in the criminal justice system is an organizational feature unique to the police structure—as one moves *down* the police hierarchy, discretion increases.

POLICE DISCRETION

Full enforcement of the law requires police officers to enforce all laws, at all times, against all offenders, and denies police the authority to ignore violations or simply warn offenders. Taking into consideration a variety of factors, discretion permits an officer to decide the degree of effort necessary to enforce particular laws and recognizes the use of actions short of arrest in order to achieve the desired goal (Goldstein, 1975). If a criminal or municipal code is so broad or ambiguous that a clear definition is difficult, if not impossible, to interpret, or if a law is obsolete, the police officer is in a laissez-faire position to stop or arrest, based upon a personal interpretation of the forms of conduct subject to the criminal process.

Often the police perception of community standards and attitudes influences the decision to arrest. Minority Americans may be stopped for questioning in sections of cities where they are not often seen, or for driving a car which seems beyond their means or is assumed by the police to be of doubtful legal possession; minorities are often hassled simply for having a conversation on the street (Wilkins, 1985). Pepinsky comments on the influence of racial stereotypes in police decision-making:

> The principle of the use of status identification as a criterion for decision-making is divisible into two parts. If the decision-maker perceives the status of a subject of his decision to be desirable, the decision-maker will act to carry out the subject's wishes as the decision-maker perceives them. If the decision-maker perceives the status of a subject to be undesirable, the decision will be to act against the perceived wishes of the subject. (1975: 37)

Several early studies of juvenile-police interaction suggest "a dual system of American justice—a system that is at times more punitive when applied to blacks than to whites" (Georges-Abeyie, 1984a: 132).[23] In most cases, the youth's attitude or personal and social characteristics were influential in negatively affecting police discretion. Although Black and Reiss's (1970) observational study of police-citizen encounters in Chicago, Boston, and Washington, D.C. did not support an allegation of prejudicial police discretion based on race, in a similar study of "street-level justice" in the Tampa/St. Petersburg area,

Rochester, New York, and St. Louis, Missouri, reported by Smith and Visher (1981), it was determined that African American citizens were the victims of police racial discrimination.

Since the few available studies of this issue offer support to both sides of the question, perhaps a better measure of the problem is found in police attitudes toward minorities and the police notion of "street justice," or order-maintenance policing. In a recent article, Sykes (1986: 506) defends such peacekeeping activity by law enforcement as a "means by which a community can achieve order if its police institution is limited by the administrative and procedural due process." Sykes (ibid.: 503) views order-maintenance policing as having a functional role related to community expectations because it articulates the community norms "when other supporting institutions fail or are inadequately developed to insure social peace." The problem with this rationale for "street justice" is that it assumes that the police are a part of the communities which they monitor, which is a false assumption.[24] In a response to Sykes, Klockars (1986: 514) states that police "understand 'street justice' to be appropriate and necessary (i.e., morally justifiable and socially desirable) in situations where the law and courts would be likely to refuse to punish with the severity that police themselves believe the offense warrants." Street justice, Klockars adds, is most frequently provoked when an offense is against a police officer:

> Any act which openly defies police authority, insults a police officer or causes a police officer to lose face merits "street justice" to even up the score and teach the offending party a lesson. . . . For example, running away from a policeman and making him give chase through back yards, over fences and down back alleys is an offense that warrants the "little street justice" of at least one or two good punches when the offender is finally caught. By extension, police morality also holds that the more serious the offense against police authority, the more severe the street justice that is warranted. Assaulting a police officer justifies street justice severe enough to require a trip to the hospital. Shooting or shooting at a police officer justifies street justice severe enough to require a trip to the morgue. (Ibid.: 514-515)

Contrary to Wilbanks's (1987: 69) assertion that "there is little evidence that white police officers make different decisions with respect to arrest than black ones," the ordeals of African American and other minorities at the hands of law enforcement suggest otherwise. Wilbanks rejects such minority experience as relying on anecdotes, "common-sense" scenarios, or "statements from authorities such as black judges who assert that racism is pervasive in law enforcement" (ibid.: 70). In essence, Wilbanks spurns the opinions of African Americans at any occupational or experiential level. Such a stance flies in the face of numerous studies demonstrating that "lower income minority groups have less favorable attitudes toward police than do middle income whites, that white non-ethnics tend to have less favorable attitudes towards police than do white ethnics, and that young people tend to have less favorable attitudes than older people" (Scaglion and Condon, 1980: 486).

In a survey of attitudes toward police and police service in four Pittsburgh,

Pennsylvania neighborhoods—low-income black, low-income white, low-income racially heterogeneous, and white upper-middle-class—Scaglion and Condon (1980) report that the significant determinant of attitudes toward police officers is actual personal contact in previous encounters. Satisfaction with the police and police service was found to be related to positive interactions, notwithstanding racial or income statuses, a conclusion that refutes "the opinion that certain segments of the community will have negative opinions of police regardless of how patrol officers behave" (ibid.: 493). Thus, minority persons are disapproving of police officers based on past personal experiences and the similar experiences of their friends and relatives.[25]

Dennis Powell, a former police officer and trainer of other officers, administered a questionnaire to 171 police officers from two urban and three suburban police agencies in northwestern Indiana to "evaluate the effects of race, if any, on the application of discretion in conjunction with the legal or departmental requirements of these agencies" (Powell, 1981: 384). The results of Powell's study indicate that police were significantly more punitive against African American offenders than white offenders, particularly the police in the white suburbs. Not only was more personal discretion employed when the offender was African American, but also police tended to use more personal discretion than their supervisors required. Powell concluded:

> The results of this study indicate there are significant differences among police agencies concerning how they use their discretionary powers, and these differences are influenced by the racial mix of both the community being policed and the police agency itself. Considering these findings, it also seems appropriate to suggest that there may be a considerable amount of racial discrimination prevalent within policing. (Ibid.: 388)

Two possible interrelated characteristics of the law enforcement institution appear to explain police discrimination against minority subjects—the police personality, and the police-minority relationship that is the result of the expression of specific characteristics of that police personality.

THE POLICE PERSONALITY

If there is a distinct police personality, according to Balch (1972), there is insufficient hard evidence to confirm its existence. He criticizes the methods used in studies of the police personality for not utilizing control groups or follow-up studies, as fraught with sampling problems, and for using inadequate measuring instruments. In fact, police *applicants* have been found to be healthier than the normative population:

> They are generally less depressed and anxious, and more assertive and interested in making and maintaining social contacts. . . . They have a greater tendency to present a good impression of themselves than the normative population. . . . They are a more homogeneous group than the normative population. The greater homo-

geneity is probably due to the sharing of personality characteristics which lead one to desire becoming a police officer. (Carpenter and Raza, 1987: 16)

Apparently, once such applicants become police officers, they change. Other researchers claim to have found a police type that they attribute more to personality characteristics and social backgrounds than to the frequently acknowledged socialization into an organizational or occupational structure and police subculture.[26] While there is also the view that there is a model police personality but it is not pathological (Lefkowitz, 1975), the preponderance of available evidence suggests otherwise.

One observational study of law enforcement involvement in the minority ghettos and barrios of this nation led the researchers to identify the "ghetto cop": "Emotionally and psychologically, the ghetto cop is only a little better off than the people he must watch over. For if the truth be known, he is being oppressed, too; and ultimately his psyche becomes damaged in ways similar to the ghetto residents" (Wilson and Cooper, 1979: 33). These researchers suggest that "ghetto cops" have somehow become assimilated into the ghetto and become "ghettoized." But overall, it is the homogeneity among police attitudes and beliefs that is thought to be related to personality and social factors in their backgrounds.

In *Police Riots* (1972), Stark finds that religious and economic conservatism and beliefs about the cause of crime and criminality affect the nature and quality of the police ideology. Such convictions, which Stark feels include right-wing extreme views (because of the large numbers of right-wingers on police forces), result in the belief that the commission of crimes is primarily volitional, involving free will and choices by intentionally bad people, and is not due to social-structural and cultural circumstances such as poverty, inadequate education, poor life chances, and similar negative influences. Closely related to such opinion is the personality trait of cynicism so frequently associated with police officers, or the idea that everyone is always trying to "get over," and that except for fear of the police, everyone would commit crimes (Niederhoffer, 1967a).

O'Connell, Holzman, and Armandi (1986: 308) studied two dimensions of police cynicism, organizational and work. Mistrusting the organization constitutes organizational cynicism, whereas "a disparaging mistrust toward the service of the people and the enforcement of the law" describes work cynicism. One indicator of work cynicism appears to be related to police line officers' middle-class status and the stress, tension, and resentment derived from performing services for persons of lower class (ibid.: 312). In contrast, a study of police chiefs measured three dimensions of cynicism—cynicism directed toward the police organization, toward outsiders, and toward commitment to work (Crank, Culbertson, Poole, and Regoli, 1987). Of salient interest here is the cynicism expressed toward outsiders, namely in departmental relations with outside interest (community) groups, and particularly focused on sociocultural characteristics (ibid.: 45). These two studies suggest that cynicism on the part of police toward the residents they are "to serve and protect" is systemic.

Authoritarianism is a second personality characteristic believed to be overly represented among law enforcement personnel, particularly among the lower echelons, or line officers. While admitting the possibility of a self-selection process that predisposes those with authoritarian personalities to enter police work, Niederhoffer (1967a) feels that experience and socialization in the police system lead to the development of this trait. The tough-mindedness, power, and force typical of the authoritarian police personality working the streets are probably most clearly seen in conjunction with the almost paranoid concern with what Skolnick (1966) calls *symbolic assailants*. Certain people, especially members of racial/ethnic groups, are viewed with suspicion by the police because of the way they are dressed, their language, the use of certain gestures, or their skin color, often regardless of their economic status. In a fascinating analysis of police authority, Howard Cohen cites the following exchange between a rookie cop and a seasoned officer:

> I saw movement as two black figures stepped slowly from behind the crates and stood in the spotlight's glare. They begin walking toward us.
> "Watch the one on your right," D'Angelo instructed.
> I could see them both clearly now for the first time—two black youths in their late teens. "What did they do?" I asked as I watched the pair approach us.
> "Don't know," he said, still without taking his eyes off them. "They was walking along being real cool back there. Then they seen us coming and ducked into that alley." "On the car," he said simply to the man on the left as he walked up. (1987: 52)

As it turned out, the experienced officer's suspicions were correct, and a weapon and drugs were found:

> All of his street sense told him they were probably drug users and dealers. The last thing he wanted to do was give them the message that they were safe from him. He intimidated, threatened, searched one of them illegally, and arrested them. (Ibid.: 53)

Other police personality traits identified are assertiveness, rigidity, aggressiveness, and punitiveness, with officers variously described as impulsive risk takers, racially prejudiced, emotionally maladjusted, and lacking in self-confidence.[27] Finding psychologically sound police recruits is often hindered by disagreement over the merits and utility of psychological tests, particularly the personality inventory tests currently in use (Nislow, 1988). Most screening tests are used to identify psychological pathologies such as schizophrenia and are not designed to detect racial prejudice, the police characteristic most criticized by all racial/ethnic minorities.

POLICE PREJUDICE

It is usually estimated that police devote no more than 10 to 15 percent of their time to activities which are directly related to criminal law enforcement.[28] Since the majority of their time is spent in order maintenance and service calls, with far less time devoted to crime fighting, it is illogical to assume that the discriminatory police attitude toward and treatment of minorities is related to alleged criminal activity and not to race. A number of perspectives attempting to explain such differential handling are found in the literature on police-minority relations:

(1) the police are not racially prejudiced;
(2) the police are racially prejudiced;
(3) police practices reflect the attitudes of the larger society;
(4) the police response is related to the socioeconomic status, not the race, of the suspect;
(5) the police differential response to minorities reflects cultural biases.

There are numerous studies which offer some degree of support for each of these positions, but the preponderance of the literature suggests that racism or prejudice is the major reason for harsher treatment of minorities compared to whites.

The police are not prejudiced. The most frequently cited argument against police racial discrimination draws upon the 1966 observational study of police-citizen encounters in Boston, Chicago, and Washington, D.C. reported by Black and Reiss (1970). It is widely reported that Black and Reiss found no connection between racial attitudes of police officers and their behavior toward minority suspects. In fact, *demeanor* was deemed to be more influential in the arrest decisions. Considering the hostility between police officers and minorities, demeanor is a crucial variable in police–minority citizen encounters and does not negate the possibility that the demeanor may be a reaction to racial prejudice initially exhibited by an officer. It has been noted that Black and Reiss failed to demonstrate whether the disrespect toward the police took place before or after the arrest was made, suggesting that "arrest may cause disrespect as much as disrespect causes arrest" (Sherman, 1980: 80). Since over three-fourths of the policemen studied expressed prejudice against blacks (Campbell, 1980: 478), in the face of antagonism and disrespectful demeanor from black suspects, an arrest reaction is not unexpected. A later analysis by Sherman of the Black and Reiss data linked specific officers' attitudes with their behavior, and although the relationship was weak, "the more white officers disliked blacks, the more likely they were to arrest black suspects" (Sherman, 1980: 76).

The police are prejudiced. Among the many studies finding an association between police racial prejudice and minority arrests, the following selected research best describes the extent and nature of such differential minority treatment by law enforcement personnel. In a study of marijuana arrests in three metropolitan areas—Cook County (Chicago), Illinois; Douglas County (Omaha), Nebraska; and Washington, D.C.—the black arrest rate was four times that of nonblacks in Chicago, although not appreciably different in the other two areas (Johnson, Petersen, and Wells, 1977). Most of the arrestees were young black males involved in a police-citizen encounter where no marijuana violation was seen, but during police stops for other purposes, the marijuana was produced by a search based on suspicion. Similarly, DeFleur's study of drug arrests in Chicago over a thirty-year period (1942-1970) found "systematic biases in the operations of police assigned to the Narcotics Division" (1975: 88). In calculations of white and nonwhite arrests for each census tract over the time period, in the 1950s nonwhites "were often charged with loitering or other minor offenses," and "many were arrested at the same locations again and again" (ibid.: 92-93). By the 1960s and 1970s, black hostility and lack of cooperation had become so great that it influenced the decisions of narcotics police with regard to the areas where they would work and whom they would arrest. In other words, demeanor that resulted from violations of arrestees' rights and admitted police brutality became an influential factor in law enforcement.

A final study in this genre compared independent samples of the drinking/ driving population: unsanctioned drinking drivers and sanctioned drinking drivers (DUIs) in a "medium-sized Georgia city" (Hollinger, 1984). Although race was not a significant indicator, significantly more nonwhite than white DUIs were arrested in areas of medium/low police patrol intensity, since they were "off their turf." Further, the race of the driver might have been influential in an officer's decision to stop the vehicle and/or effect an arrest after the stop. While not mentioned by the researcher, it is possible that since drinking was involved, hostile or belligerent demeanor might have been an influence in the arrest decision.

In episodes involving perceived police malpractice in Los Angeles, Mexican Americans had the highest percentage of arrests for interfering with the police (58 percent) when compared to blacks (24 percent) and Anglos (18 percent). Morales (1972: 11) asks, "Can this behavior be explained historically that because of a long standing experience of living in an environment of alienation, feelings of disrespect and distrust toward American law enforcement–legal institutions have intensified to the degree that Mexican-Americans have been 'conditioned' to respond in this manner for survival purposes?"

Among the racial stereotypes and prejudicial beliefs held by some police officers are that Mexican Americans are "a child race," "sly, treacherous, wily, undependable," and knife carriers (ibid.: 35-37). Former FBI director J. Edgar Hoover said, "You never have to bother about a President being shot by Puerto Ricans or Mexicans. They don't shoot very straight. But if they come at you with a knife, beware" ("J. Edgar Hoover Speaks Out with Vigor," 1970: 16).

In a Denver study, Bayley and Mendelsohn (1968) found the police to be prejudiced against blacks and Hispanics. Almost half of the minority people in Denver had had recent significant contacts with the police, and one-third of the surveyed police officers, especially patrolmen, felt that blacks and Hispanics required stricter law enforcement procedures than the rest of the population:

They are suspicious of minority people, believing that they are more likely to be involved in criminal activity than Dominants. They consider violence against persons more common among minority people and are therefore more concerned for their own safety when intervening. Policemen believe that hostility is greater toward them in minority neighborhoods, and they expect a greater incidence of resistance in making arrests. (Ibid.: 195)

A study undertaken in the Bay Area in Coast County, California by Swett (1969) found that physical appearance, such as skin color, contributed to the police view of minorities as "culturally different," and governed their actions. Police stereotyping resulted in suspicion, increased surveillance in minority communities, and a "self-fulfilling prophecy." For example, the national high Indian arrest incidence for offenses involving drunkenness made officers "more prone to look for evidence of drunkenness in cases involving Indians and to see sufficient evidence to warrant arrest" (ibid.: 93).

In her discussion of the right to privacy and search and seizure issues, Johns comments that such tactics, as well as other law enforcement procedures, predominantly affect minorities and the poor:

Many have argued that the "profiles" used by local as well as federal authorities to stop and search suspected drug couriers are racially biased. The darker the skin, the more likely the person is to be stopped. In Mississippi, for example, a newspaper reporter examined police files on people stopped on one interstate highway. Fifty-five of the fifty-seven stops were of blacks or Hispanics. In another study conducted by a Rutgers University statistician, 80 percent of the arrests on one stretch of the New Jersey Turnpike were of black males driving late model cars with out-of-state license plates. Only 4.7 percent of the total traffic fit that description. . . . In New York, all but two of the over two hundred people arrested in 1989 in a drug-interdiction program at the Port Authority Bus Terminal were Hispanic or black. Critics of drug profiles argue that since the Supreme Court upheld the use of profiles in selecting people to be questioned, the arrests of black and Hispanic suspects have increased. (1992: 91)

Direct observations of police-citizen encounters with and without complainants in St. Louis, Missouri, Rochester, New York, and the Tampa–St. Petersburg, Florida area found that race was a significant factor in arrests—"the differential racial composition of lower-status neighborhoods creates a significant racial disparity in population of arrested persons"—but that the poverty level of a community was more influential in such decisions (Smith, Visher, and Davidson, 1984: 246). Even though there was weak evidence of racial prejudice against suspects, Smith, Visher, and Davidson (ibid.: 248) uncovered "a more invisible form of police discrimination," that of making arrests in incidents involving white complainants while denying black complainants such legal protection in similar situations. The authors speculate that this differential police response toward victims may be "one manifestation of a generally unsympathetic police posture toward minority groups generally, and blacks specifically," or that police may see black complainants as "less deserving of legal protection" (ibid.). Along that line, Bynum, Cordner, and Greene (1982: 314) found that the police decision to follow up citizen complaints with investigations and the effort put into investigations of incidents that came to the attention of the police were influenced by race: "cases of minority victims are less likely to be extensively investigated, while those of female, higher economic status, older, and employed victims tend to be slightly better investigated."

Police practices are a reflection of society. Closely related to police racial prejudice is the idea that police practices reflect the attitudes of the larger society. In a sense, this is a class issue, and there are varying accounts of the status level of police officers as representative of the majority of Americans. In a Denver study, the police viewed themselves as "on the borderline between middle-class and working-class status" (Bayley and Mendelsohn, 1968: 8), and a Bay Area, California study found that law enforcement personnel were recruited primarily from the lower-middle and upper-lower classes, with middle-class applicants coming generally from "police families" (Swett, 1969: 83). In his study of the Gary, Indiana police, Greer (1978a: 49) notes that urban policemen are generally viewed as "manifesting traits of authoritarianism and racism endemic to the working class from whose ranks they are recruited," but actually have social origins from the lower middle class and come disproportionately from families of white-collar workers, skilled craftsmen, and foremen.

The salient point is that U.S. police forces, particularly in urban areas where large numbers of minorities are located, are recruited from a social group which is racially prejudiced. Morales (1972: 33) believes that police recruited from the dominant society "reflect the values, attitudes and prejudices of the majority community," and observes: "There is the general belief that the poor commit more crime than the affluent. Also, poor people who are of darker skin are under greater suspicion of committing crime—even more so if they communicate in a 'foreign' language. Needless to say that Mexican Americans meet all of these criteria."

In Denver, police officers were found to share the racial prejudices of the community as a whole and when surveyed, indicated that "revulsion against mixing is strongest with respect to marriage and least strong with respect to eating together at the same table" (Bayley and Mendelsohn, 1968: 145). Whereas 84 percent of the public in the survey stated that they would be upset if an immediate family member married a black, 85 percent of the police revealed this sentiment. The authors observed that "the quality of the gap between Negro and Dominant seems less bridgeable and more emotionally involved than the gap between the majority community and any other ethnic group. Between Negroes and Dominants there is not only the sense of difference, but a strong suggestion that contact itself is somehow contaminating" (ibid.: 146).

If racism is as prevalent in this country as the above accounts indicate, and if police officers are recruited from the most racially prejudiced class level, it follows logically that law enforcement personnel would reflect the biased attitudes of the larger society from which they came, and "the officer having internalized the motivation and goals of middle-class America and incorporated the value profile of middle-class America as subsidiary to his focal values, measures cultural difference against the yardstick of this internalized ideal" (Swett, 1969: 88-89).

Police respond to socioeconomic level, not race. Some researchers attribute the differential treatment of minorities by police to economic status level and not race by demonstrating that harsher law enforcement is directed at the poor, regardless of race. Since the police generally believe that lower-class people are more disreputable and commit more crimes, there is more surveillance in poor neighborhoods, and consequently there are more arrests. A review of the findings of quantitative research on police behavior reported by Sherman (1980: 83) noted that "the frequent observation in the qualitative studies of policing that lower-class suspects receive harsher treatment from the police is generally supported by the limited quantitative observational evidence."

More recently, Hollinger (1984) found support for a "conflict model" of criminal justice in his study of DUI cases involving proactive police arrests. The lack of status and power of both black and white drinking drivers from the lower social classes, who were largely in blue-collar occupations, increased their liability for arrest. Both black and white offenders in poorer neighborhoods were observed to "suffer from discriminatory application of the law by police" in the three-city study of police-citizen encounters reported by Smith, Visher, and Davidson (1984: 243). The finding that the race effect disappeared when the neighborhood poverty level was introduced "suggests that socio-economic status rather than suspect race is the axis around which arrest discrimination revolves" (ibid.).

There are at least two problems associated with explanatory models of police discrimination which focus on class level in lieu of race. First, in metropolitan areas, there are disproportionate populations of minorities located in the urban barrios and ghettos. While Smith, Visher, and Davidson (ibid.: 249) note that more selective, punitive treatment is accorded offenders in lower-status neighborhoods, they also admit that a larger proportion of blacks reside in such neighborhoods and are disproportionately represented among those arrested. Furthermore, police field practices function to widen the arrest net in slum areas:

> Police field interrogation has become a prime public issue because patrol officers have been accused of indiscriminately stopping and frisking persons. Some police forces routinely search known criminals, shabbily dressed persons, or minority groups. Some police field interrogations are conducted primarily in slum communities, where persons may be questioned indiscriminately rather than for objective reasons, and where some patrolmen have asked questions in an unfriendly and abusive fashion. As a result, field interrogations are a major source of friction between police and minority group members. (Long, Long, Leon, and Weston, 1975: 120)

A second difficulty with the socioeconomic explanation of police discrimination is more compelling. A few studies reveal that minorities of higher status levels are just as likely to have negative encounters with the police as low-income-level minorities. In their Denver study, Bayley and Mendelsohn (1968) found that education provided no insulation for minorities in police decisions to stop and arrest. Although more blacks (82 percent) and Hispanics (68 percent) with eighth-grade educations were stopped and arrested, 75 percent of the blacks and 50 percent of Hispanics with some college also had that experience (ibid.: 115). The researchers conclude that "class is unrelated to the incidence of bad treatment. This finding gives credence to the charge of well-to-do Negroes with professional status that they are subjected to the same kind of humiliations that all Negroes experience. Professional attainments do not hide the color of their skins" (ibid.: 127). Also, Sherman's analysis of the Black and Reiss data indicates that in reactive encounters with the police, white-collar blacks were more likely than blue-collar blacks to be interrogated.

Hundreds of cases of police maltreatment of minority members at all status levels were documented across the country by the study of the National Minority Advisory Council on Criminal Justice (1980). This authentification of discriminatory law enforcement practices provided support for allegations minorities have made for years about their treatment at the hands of the police, which some criminological researchers had often dismissed as "anecdotes," and as lacking empirical evidence.[29]

Police response reflects cultural biases. Although it is difficult to separate race/ethnicity from culture, some researchers attribute the differential treatment of minorities by law enforcement officers to biases against the various minority cultures. The primary thrust of the culturally biased viewpoint is the tendency of police to stereotype minorities. Clearly, the difference between such racial stereotyping and prejudice and racism is a matter of nuance.[30] Further, this perspective necessarily involves a consideration of class level, particularly the class level of law enforcement personnel. The concept of a police culture, or subculture, and its ideologies is also an intervening factor in the cultural bias equation.

According to Morales (1972: 33), in addition to other demeaning stereotypes, American society tends to view Mexican Americans as a "child race" and has even gone so far as to suggest that there is a biological proneness to criminality, with the effect that "those law enforcement agencies believing these stereotypes of Mexican Americans respond by placing significantly greater numbers of police in Mexican American communities, even though their own statistical facts reveal comparable felony crime rates as compared to more affluent, white, non-Spanish surname communities."

Another common stereotype held by law enforcement officers and reinforced by arrests, convictions, and imprisonments that make the belief a "fact," is that Mexican Americans are narcotics users. This erroneous belief is maintained despite the fact that there is little difference between their alcohol or drug usage and that of any other American group. The stigmatization as drug users negatively affects all minorities in this nation.[31] Through the emphasis on the immorality of drug use and drug users prevalent since the turn of the century and the mistaken association of this stereotype with minorities, police feel that their detection efforts and questionable practices in the enforcement of anti-drug laws are justified (DeFleur, 1975: 90).

In his discussion of cultural bias in the American legal system, Swett (1969: 88-90) describes the perceptions of cultural difference by police officers as both "ethnocentric and stereotypical," with police suspicion increasing according to this mindset:

> When physical appearance and dress of the subject indicated conformity to middle-class standards, suspicion decreased. . . . Similarly, if physical appearance and dress indicated nonconformity to middle-class standards, such as the long hair and exotic garb of the hippie, the African styles of the black nationalist, or the slick hair and "sharp" apparel of the Chicano, suspicion would be high initially, then decrease or increase according to the evidence of recognition or rejection of the police culture's focal values. . . . The propensity for police suspicion to increase according to ethnocentric perception of cultural difference is reinforced by stereotypes.

Whether individual police officers are personally prejudiced toward minorities or are reflecting the racism, classism, or cultural biases of the larger society, peoples of color in the United States consistently report discriminatory treatment by law enforcement personnel that contributes greatly to minority animosity, resentment, and lack of respect for the police.

Police Interactions with Minorities

More than twenty years ago, Kuykendall (1970) described "negative contacts" between police and minority groups, or those situations in which minorities perceive unequal treatment by the police. Today, Georges-Abeyie more accurately describes such informal aspects of the criminal justice system as "petit apartheid realities," seen, for example, in the stop-and-question and stop-and-frisk practices of the police:

> A case in point is the 1988 City of Philadelphia American Civil Liberties Union (ACLU) agreement to halt the Philadelphia Police Department's practice of stopping and questioning Black males . . . 20 to 40 years of age, ranging in height from five-feet-four inches to five-feet-ten inches, and weighing from 120 to 160 pounds, who happened to be in Philadelphia's Center City. The practice became more pervasive when the police were investigating the Center City "stalker incidents." The unofficial search-and-question technique was initiated in an attempt to apprehend a slender Black male who was suspected of raping eight females, one Hispanic and seven white. Petit apartheid appears to have also been the reality in suburban Pittsburgh during 1987, when the Homestead Police Department officers made late night, door-to-door requests of all Black males in the township to voluntarily submit to fingerprinting and blood tests. The initiative was in response to a series of rapes of elderly white females (and one elderly Black female) by a man wearing a ski mask who had a "Black-sounding voice." Petit apartheid may have also been the reality of the Lower Providence Township (Montgomery County, Pennsylvania) Police De-

partment's alleged practice of stopping automobiles with "black interiors," that is, with Black motorists. (1989: 46-47)

A number of studies of police-minority relations describe the rudeness, insults, lack of understanding, posturing, and brutality that police officers exhibit toward blacks and other minorities. Any response or protest to such demeaning behavior is quickly suppressed through arrest. A police officer maintains "the sole right to halt, question and search any individual who he (not the law) considers 'suspicious' " (Wilkins, 1985: 250).[32] In her examination of race as it relates to the decision to detain a suspect, Johnson (1983) identifies a number of instances in which race may be a factor in law enforcement detention decisions: (1) when a victim or witness has described the perpetrator's race, and race appears to be the sole factor sustaining the detention; (2) when minority members are questioned because they are somewhere they do not "belong" (incongruity); (3) when race, usually Hispanic or Asian, is used as the identifying criterion for an illegal alien; (4) in drug courier profiles, "the newest and most sophisticated use of race as a factor in probable cause determinations"; and (5) when the police officer believes that "minority race indicates a general propensity to commit crime" (ibid.: 225-236).

The reports of extensive police oversurveillance and excessive patrolling in minority communities detailed earlier are augmented by other frequent complaints by minority citizens: derogatory name calling, discourtesy, harassment, brutality on the street and in the jails, choke holds, and lethal force. Hundreds of complaints of such maltreatment are made annually to national and state civil-rights organizations and commissions, but obtaining information about and proving such accusations is burdensome (Reiss, 1968).

Wingspread, in Racine, Wisconsin, was the site of a symposium on crime and the Hispanic held by the National Council of Raza in 1979. In their deliberations, they concurred with the findings of the 1970 federal report "Mexican Americans and the Administration of Justice" on patterns of police misconduct toward Mexican Americans, which included excessive police violence, discriminatory treatment of juveniles by law enforcement officers, discourtesy toward Mexican Americans, discriminatory enforcement of motor vehicle ordinances, and excessive use of arrests for "investigation" and of "stop and frisk" (Rubio-Festa, 1979).

Spanish-speaking Americans often have difficulty communicating with the police, particularly under stressful circumstances, yet they frequently find that police officers speak enough Spanish to call them such names as "pancho" or "muchacho" (Kuykendall, 1970). In fact, belittling name calling by the police has been reported by every minority group in the country.

Although Chinese and Japanese Americans have generally indicated little discrimination by the police toward them, the other historically disadvantaged U.S. minority groups collectively register the same complaints against police: (1) excessive and suppressive patrolling of their neighborhoods; (2) more severe treatment compared to that given whites; (3) lack of attention or response to minority complaints; (4) violation of constitutional rights;[33] (5) unnecessary interrogations and searches; (6) oppression, brutality, and use of excessive force (Kuykendall, 1970; Rubio-Festa, 1979).

There has been little empirical research on Chicano/police conflict despite the fact that "urban unrest and police confrontations have been common occurrences in chicano urban barrios since the 'zootsuit' riots of the 40s."[34] Mirande's (1980) study of attitudes in a southern California barrio found that Chicanos were more fearful and less supportive of police than blacks. Mirande (ibid.: 530) describes the Chicano/police relationship: "The police have traditionally been viewed not only as outsiders but as representatives of the dominant, oppressive anglo society. Over the past seven or eight years prior to the survey, there had been about one chicano shot per year. Residents complain of extensive police abuse and harassment."

As previously noted, an earlier survey of police-citizen encounters in Denver revealed that almost half of the minorities had had personal contacts with the police, leading Bayley and Mendelsohn (1968: 116) to comment: "Thus, when minority people speak about the police they do so with considerable personal authority." Compared to only 4 percent of whites so reporting, 10 percent of the blacks citing their own personal experience and 24 percent of the Hispanics surveyed reported that either they or a family member had received bad treatment at the hands of the police, or that they had personally witnessed a minority person being badly treated (36 percent black; 40 percent Hispanic) (ibid.: 117-118). Further, 27 percent of black respondents and 36.8 percent of Hispanics in the survey said they had been treated with "disrespect, cursed, manhandled or roughed up" (ibid.: 126-128). Even more appalling is the finding that 53 percent of the police officers surveyed said they had witnessed what might be considered police brutality, while 27 percent admitted witnessing incidents that they considered harassment or the excessive use of force (ibid.: 128-129).

Commissions in Jacksonville, Florida and San Jose, California report similar findings. Until 1968, the Jacksonville police department was segregated and had a long history of ill treatment of blacks by the police:

Henry Adams, a private attorney, claimed that many times when police use excessive force, they often charge the arrestee with resisting arrest with violence—a felony carrying a possible 5-year penalty. He felt that such charges were made to justify the use of force during the arrest, and thereby discourage the filing of complaint charges or law suits against individual officers or the department. (Florida Advisory Commission, 1975: 29)

Up to 1976, a minority was killed by law enforcement almost every two years in San Jose, California, and "community members expressed fear that any contact with a law enforcement officer would end in a beating or death" (Pilla, 1980: 8). One interviewed outreach worker testified that "police show their guns even on a (stop for a) minor traffic violation. They approach cars with their guns drawn and shoot and kill people on the slightest provocation" (ibid.).

For Hispanics in the southwestern states, the problem of police brutality is of long standing. For example, in 1859, a Mexican American in Brownsville, Texas stated:

> Many of us have been robbed of our property, jailed, persecuted, murdered and hunted like wild beasts because our work was fruitful. Their avarice was incited and led them to frightful crimes against our people. These monsters are not punished because the gringos do not apply their law against gringos and use it to persecute Mexicans because, they say, our people are not worthy to belong to the human race. (Morales, 1972: 12)

More recent accounts of police brutality are mixed. The U.S. Civil Rights Commission continues to receive increasing volumes of complaints of police abuse, which is allegedly escalating in seriousness and appears to be institutionalized, not an isolated problem (U.S. Commission on Civil Rights, 1981). There are still periodic reports in the media of excessive force by individual police agencies. Despite these daily accounts of police brutality against minorities all over the country, there are few recent empirical studies of the problem.

Over the years, however, there have been a number of studies of police use of lethal force that resulted in minority deaths, with few prosecutions of the law enforcement perpetrators indicated.

POLICE USE OF DEADLY FORCE AGAINST MINORITIES

In a discussion of the police use of force, Schultz and Service (1981: 62) support the need for an officer to be able to exercise force in order to maintain peace and order, but also note that the use of a nightstick or baton, flashlight, or fists "may in a given situation be potentially as deadly or injurious as a firearm." To this list could be added the latest police physical control mechanisms: the carotid sleeper, which is "designed to compress the carotid arteries on both sides of the neck, reducing the flow of blood to the brain and incapacitating the individual," and the choke hold, which is "designed to block the air passage by forearm compression on the airway" (Reay and Mathers, 1983: 13). The FBI warns that officers should have proper training in the use and effects of such measures, since "neck holds must be considered potentially lethal whenever applied" (ibid.: 15). Warnings notwithstanding, several recent newspaper accounts suggest that these tactics are more frequently used against minorities and that minorities predominate among suspects who have died from the police use of such neck holds. A class action suit brought against the city of Los Angeles because of deaths caused by the use of such measures revealed that in the eleven cases where race of the victim was identified, seven (63.6 percent) of the persons who died as a result of choke holds by Los Angeles police officers were African American (Koiwai, 1987). L.A. Police Chief Daryl Gates blamed the black victims for their own choke hold deaths, "for not having veins in their necks 'like normal people'" (Turque, Buckley, and Wright, 1991: 33). The investigation also revealed that until their adoption by law enforcement officers, no deaths had occurred through the use of these techniques (*shime-waza*) since the sport of judo was begun in 1882 (Koiwai, 1987: 419).

Noting that there is a significant correlation between community behavioral characteristics and the police use of deadly force, Kania and Mackey (1977) attribute such violence to police exposure to the violence in the communities where they work. Their fifty-state ecological study of vital statistics over a ten-year period (1961-1970) removes the focus of police abuse of citizens from "an image of a violent police establishment," which stigmatizes conscientious officers, to one of response to the community (ibid.: 27). Kania and Mackey found that among a number of community characteristics, police-caused homicides had the strongest relationship with levels of public violence and homicide. Although there is the risk in such a model of "blaming the victim," the Kania-Mackey perspective offers a reasonable rationalization for minority officers' use of deadly force:

> The police officer working within a given community does more than just observe its patterns of behavior. He develops his on-the-job demeanor in direct response to what he observes. When he works in a community in which the resort to violence is a common, appropriate, or functional response to conflict and tension, the police officer will be more inclined to use violence in pursuit of legitimate ends. *This development may take the form of an internalized value system, or may be represented as a peer-group normative system.* (Ibid.: 46; emphasis added)

While admitting that the relationship is spurious, in a number of publications from his dissertation on shootings by the New York Police Department (NYPD), Fyfe (1981b: 381) contends that his data "clearly do not support the contention that white police have little regard for the lives of minority citizens; indeed, whites are underrepresented among NYPD shooters." Whereas little attention is focused on his finding that NYPD blacks and Hispanics are less likely than whites to inflict injuries in shootings,[35] Fyfe reports that minorities killed and wounded by police in New York City are the victims of minority, not white, officers. However, Fyfe (ibid.: 377) does note that "the primary reason for the disproportionate shooting of on-duty black and Hispanic police officers and detectives is their disproportionate assignment to department units and to those areas of New York City in which the likelihood of police shooting is greatest." He further acknowledges that "the reasons for this differential assignment pattern, in turn, generally involve the perception of black and Hispanic officers as blacks or Hispanics first, and as police officers second" (ibid.). Moreover, Fyfe points out that "white officers more often live and spend their off-duty hours in outlying areas that are largely white, and that black and Hispanic officers more often live in and spend their off-duty time in the inner city" (ibid.: 379). More important, no conclusion may be drawn from these data regarding a white officer's propensity to kill a minority suspect. Although the intraracial rates of NYPD police slayings of citizens show blacks killing other blacks at a rate of 19.6 per 1,000, the white rate of killing blacks (8.2) hardly differs from the

Hispanic rate of killing blacks (8.9). White officers who were not assigned to and did not live or spend time in black inner-city communities could be viewed as targeting black citizens in New York City for lethal force.

Fyfe's (1988: 194-195) analysis of Memphis police shootings from 1969 through 1976 determines that "Memphis police used their broad authority to shoot in elective situations when their targets were black, and that typically they refrained from doing so when white subjects were involved."

At the request of the National Organization of Black Law Enforcement Executives (NOBLE), the U.S. Department of Justice in 1978 conducted a workshop in St. Louis, Missouri on the police use of deadly force as a problem "particularly acute for black, Hispanic, and Native Americans" (Brenner and Kravitz, 1979: ix). NOBLE was concerned that members of these minority groups account annually for over half of police killings. In the workshop proceedings, a summary of extant research on the police use of deadly force by Sulton and Cooper (1979: 92) revealed that "the number of civilian deaths by legal intervention of the police is increasing and that the death rates for blacks and Hispanics remain disproportionate to the numbers of blacks and Hispanics in the general population." Also, the Mexican American Legal Defense Fund (MALDEF) documented fity-six cases of police brutality, excessive and deadly force involving Hispanic victims, between 1974 and 1978, with western and southwestern states, especially Texas and California, leading all others (Sulton and Cooper, 1979).

A few of the researchers in the NOBLE workshop believed that the increased number of civilian deaths resulted from the dangerousness of police work, but findings from other studies challenged that position by noting that (1) the danger of the police job was exaggerated compared to other occupations; (2) there was "no upward trend in police death rate trends to accompany the upward trend in civilian rates"; (3) minority civilian death rates exceeded minority arrest rates; and (4) there was significant involvement of off-duty officers—between 17 and 20 percent—in shooting incidents (ibid.: 92-93).

In the decade since the NOBLE symposium, a number of studies have suggested that police use of deadly force against minorities has decreased as the result of a number of social factors: public concern and outcry about the police use of deadly force and its effect on society,[36] an increase in specialized law enforcement training, changes in police administrative directives on the proper use of weaponry, and the U.S. Supreme Court decision in *Tennessee v. Garner*.[37]

Grounding its argument in the Fourth Amendment reasonableness requirement, in March of 1985 the Supreme Court ruled that the "statutory and administrative rules governing shootings of fleeing suspects must restrict officers to firing only when the officers have 'probable cause to believe that the suspect poses a threat of serious physical harm either to the officers or to others'" (Geller, 1985: 155). At issue was the killing of a slightly built (5'4" tall and around 100 or 110 pounds), unarmed, fleeing black fifteen-year-old male who, while trying to climb a six-foot chain link fence, was shot in the back of the head by a white Memphis police officer, Elton Hymon. As Justice White noted in his opinion, "With the aid of a flashlight, Hymon was able to see Garner's face and hands. He saw no sign of a weapon and though not certain, was 'reasonably sure' and 'figured' that Garner was unarmed" (*Tennessee v. Garner,* 85 L ED 2d, p. 5).

Prior to the decision in *Tennessee v. Garner,* some police jurisdictions had issued administrative policies on fleeing felons that appear to have contributed to reduced citizen fatalities at the hands of police. In August 1972, for example, the New York City Police Department instituted shooting guidelines and incident review procedures which were more restrictive than former statutes concerning fleeing felons and defense of life and resulted in substantial decreases in shots fired, shootings, and suspect injuries (Fyfe, 1979). An examination of national trends of police use of lethal force from 1964 to 1974, reported by Kuykendall in 1981, found that over the time period studied, police decreasingly used deadly force. Another study by Lawrence Sherman (1986) found that urban police killed half as many citizens in 1984 as they had in 1971, with much of the decline seen in black deaths. Other researchers attributed the reduction in black homicides to restrictive shooting policies by new progressive police leaders, yet concluded that the variable rates of police killings among cities "demonstrate that police shootings are still highly discretionary, and greatly dependent on local police practices and customs" (*Crime Control Digest,* 1986: 4).

In a summary statement of their review of lethal police force, Binder and Fridell (1984: 265) suggest that "there are alternative plausible hypotheses to the racial discrimination hypothesis" to account for the differences found in cities studied. However, they also state that "nobody could reasonably doubt that there has been organizational discrimination in shooting behavior on the part of whole departments in the past, or even, in isolated cases, at the present time, or that there has been and continues to be individual discrimination on the part of one, a few or several officers in many or most police departments." However, the following observation seems more accurate:

> As long as discretion is used to the disadvantage of a group because of race, culture, or economic level, blacks will continue to be discriminated against in the criminal justice system. It is highly unlikely that the attitude of the majority race in this country toward blacks will change sufficiently to cause them to be truly concerned with black crime and the black offender. It is much easier to remove from the larger society those persons who have outlived their usefulness than to seek the means to insure their meaningful participation in such a society. (Banks, 1977: 44-45)

Minority Police Officers

Reiss (1968) found little difference between the degree of force used by white and black policemen in his early observational study in Chicago, and noted that one in ten policemen in high-crime city areas sometimes used force unnecessarily. He also pointed out that policemen are most likely to exercise force against members of their own race, primarily because those are the persons whom they police. Referring to the Reiss data, Sherman (1980: 74-75) adds that "black officers in three large cities in 1966 patrolled more aggressively, initiated more citizen contacts, and reported crime contacts more often than white officers." Fyfe's (1981b) examination of the most extreme form of violence—police killings of citizens—found higher intraracial rates among black and Hispanic officers than among their white counterparts. More important, each of these researchers, as well as the bulk of the extant research on arrests, police use of force, and police use of deadly force, indicates clearly that not only do most minority officers live in minority communities, but they are also disproportionately assigned to minority and other high-risk police districts. These are critical intervening factors that influence the extent of a minority officer's exposure to confrontational and dangerous situations.

In addition to unequal exposure to liability, some authors suggest that by virtue of their occupation, minority police officers may be coopted by the police "subculture." According to Greer's (1978a: 56) study of the Gary, Indiana police, "It is true that in urban settings where ethnic machines dominate the police, and where black officers are a distinct minority, the latter have substantially accommodated themselves to the dominant police patterns." Swett (1969: 92) discusses the marginality of ethnic minority officers and includes the observation that these officers internalize the police value system because they identify more with the police culture than with their own cultures.[38] He attributes the minority officer's cooptation to upward social mobility, the police selection process, and the use of police training methods which foster police culturalization. Swett adjudges the ethnic minority officer as marginal within the police subculture:

Despite this marginality in the police culture, or perhaps because of it, the ethnic minority officer tends to overconform by measuring cultural differences on an even stricter middle-class standard than his nonminority colleagues, and to subscribe with at least equal force to their stereotypes. In consequence, the ethnic minority officer often displays a greater degree of suspicion of the culturally different, particularly members of his own ethnic group, than the nonminority officer. (Ibid.)

A more recent survey of 576 African American metropolitan policemen challenges the marginality theory. Campbell (1980) defines marginality in two ways: strong racial identification/strong police identification, and weak racial identification/weak police identification, concluding that the data did not generally support the theory. Instead, she suggests that the black officer may be comfortable in both his occupation and his racial group and not be psychologically harmed by the double negative status: "It is possible that this group of police officers represent a new breed of police whose conception of blackness is much less negative than that of their predecessors since they may have been influenced more by the black consciousness movement of the late 1960s" (ibid.: 482).

A similar study reported by Buzawa (1981) involved officers from Detroit, Michigan and Oakland, California. She found variations between the two samples and significant differences in the work attitudes of black and white officers from Detroit and Oakland. In the interviews, Buzawa (ibid.: 73) reported that "virtually every white respondent stated that affirmative action effectively inhibited realistic opportunities for rapid advancement," and felt that his or her department was experiencing low morale, performance, and personnel quality. In contrast, black officers were more enthusiastic about their departments and felt that their occupation and their departments were generally respected. This view was particularly expressed by the black Detroit officers, who felt esteemed by the community.

There is some empirical evidence to justify the minority officers' convictions that citizens view their performance positively. In their Denver public opinion survey, Bayley and Mendelsohn found that

> there do not seem to be strong negative reactions among minority people to minority policemen. Only 8% of the Negroes and 5% of the Spanish-named said they thought of such officers as traitors or did not respect them. Over 70% of all minority people said they thought they were doing a good job, respected them, and thought they were helping the cause. (1968: 122)

There are many indications that minority officers are believed to have developed greater rapport with minority citizens than have white officers. Minority officers are also thought to understand certain types of behavior and view it as routine and normal. On the other hand, in the same situation, the white officer might see the same behavior as deviant or hostile (Bannon and Wilt, 1973). Carter (1986) surveyed and interviewed members of a Texas police department, 70 percent of whom were Hispanic, and as a result, developed a concept of external discrimination which reflected the relationships of officers and citizens in the course of policing. After stating that most Anglo officers did not like Mexicans, Hispanic officers "significantly believed that Hispanic citizens were the recipients of intentional discrimination" by white officers (ibid.: 208). Based on his findings, Carter suggests that white officers were suspicious of Hispanics more because of "cultural symbols" such as appearance, language, and dress than because of substantive facts. The Hispanic officers strongly believed that they "served the Hispanic community better than Anglo officers" (ibid.: 209).

Apparently Native Americans are also very dissatisfied with law enforcement. They decry "the discriminatory and inadequate treatment and protection from federal law enforcement agencies" (Feinman, 1986: 194). The Native American criticism centers on the increasing power of the federal system on Indian reservations and the concomitant restriction of the power of tribal justice systems (ibid.). An ethnographic study reported by Clarice Feinman, who lived on a New Mexico Navajo reservation for eighteen months, describes the Navajo police and citizen problems:

Navajo police officers deal with several problems that are unique to reservations. They must understand and perform their duties under three levels of law enforcement jurisdiction: federal, state (New Mexico, Utah, and Arizona), and tribal. They must contend with the cultural conflicts between Indian values and methods of social control and Anglo values and criminal laws. (Ibid.: 194–195)

As a result of having to learn five law enforcement jurisdictions, and after undertaking the initial investigative work on all reservation cases, Navajo officers are required to turn their cases over to either state or federal authorities. Navajo officers view such practices not only as frustrating but also as insulting, since they "resent the fact that they are not considered capable of handling crimes committed on their reservation if non-Indians are involved or if the crime is a felony and only Indians are involved" (ibid.: 196). The Navajo police are restricted to handling only those misdemeanor cases including offenses by Indians against Indians (ibid.). In light of the ascribed position of the Navajo police, it is no wonder that the Navajos are suspicious of their tribal police and give them little cooperation or respect (ibid.: 197).

INTRA-POLICE RACIAL CONFLICT

African American and other minority police officers may be comfortable with themselves, and even with their constituents, but there is increasing evidence that they justifiably share some of the hostility toward white officers that minority citizens have repeatedly expressed.

Noting that previous studies revealed a majority of African American police to have negative feelings toward their white colleagues, which were reciprocated, Beard (1977) studied the job-related attitudes and perceptions of the total population of black officers in Washington, D.C. The respondents, who were overwhelmingly found in the lowest police rank (84 percent), indicated that they rarely socialized with their white counterparts, and 65 percent of them trusted few or none of their fellow white officers (ibid.: 50).

Two reports by Teahan (1975a; 1975b) offer clues to understanding this internal law enforcement friction. During the twelve-week academy training of black and white officers, role playing and small-group interaction techniques were used to improve communication, openness, and trust between the two groups. Instead, the posttest results indicated that although the white officers became sensitized to black-white problems, they seemed to become more prejudiced toward blacks (1975a: 41) and foreigners (ibid.: 45). A backlash effect of the program apparently occurred, since white officers felt more strongly that blacks were more criminal than whites, and as a result of this belief, the officers were more likely to assume that blacks were guilty. In contrast, the black officers in the experimental group demonstrated more positive feelings toward whites and felt that the relationships between them and the white officers were better than they had been at the beginning of the academic training. Black control group members, however, felt that black-white relationships worsened and reported more negative feelings toward whites. Whites in control groups also indicated more prejudice toward blacks in posttesting.

Additional posttesting of these subjects (97 whites, 24 blacks) took place eighteen months after their graduation from the police academy, and after they had worked "on the force" (Teahan, 1975b). Attitudes between the races reflected "extreme polarization," specifically in negative attitudes toward blacks, decreased white interest in equality, and "dramatic rises" in white ethnocentrism (ibid.: 53). A tremendous increase in white officers' prejudice and negative feelings toward both black officers specifically and black people generally was uncovered:

> Whites are not even bothering to give lip service to the importance of police-community relations any longer, nor are they as willing to admit, as they had previously, that verbal abuse of citizens is bad. In addition, they no longer insist, to the same degree as during the academy, that they are trying to understand black people. Instead, they agree more than ever, that separate police associations and more segregated duty may be the best course of action. (Ibid.)

Posttested black officers expressed greater dislike for whites, and also tended to defend blacks less than in the earlier testing: "They seem to shift from support to condemnation of other blacks, which suggests that they must feel under constant pressure from the opinion of the white majority with whom they work" (ibid.: 52). As with their white counterparts, black officers' disillusionment about black-white departmental relationships led to increased interest in segregated patrol car duty and police associations.

Carter (1986: 207) reports that Hispanic officers also felt that department recruitment practices and procedures were discriminatory and favored Anglo applicants because the recruitment and personnel officers were all Anglo and the employment selection board was largely Anglo. Further, Hispanic officers felt that promotions were based on ethnicity, again favoring Anglos. Carter concludes that in the Texas police department studied, "there appears to be a form of institutional discrimination born in homeostatic prejudice against the Hispanic" (ibid.).

However, at the same time Hispanic officers believed that officers discriminated against citizens based on ethnicity, it was suggested that Hispanic officers may discriminate against Hispanic citizens more than against Anglos, when Carter (ibid.: 209) intimates that "the occupational socialization of officers which creates the well-documented 'police subculture' may give the officer a psychological self-perception of being a member of a group that is uniquely distinct from any ethnic or racial association. The result is a closer identification with the occupational culture than with the socio-ethnic culture."

Similarly, Teahan (1975b: 52) noted that black officers seemed to defend fellow blacks less after being on the force than when they were in the academy: "Here again we are confronted with the ambivalence of black officers. They seem to shift from support to condemnation of other blacks, which suggests that they must feel under constant pressure from the opinion of the white majority with whom they work."

Feinman (1986: 197) also points to the fact that "historically, Indian police officers were tools of the U.S. Army or the BIA, an Anglo invention following Anglo values and laws used to control and punish Indians and deny them their sovereignty." Such attitudes interfere with effective law enforcement on the reservations and lead to Navajos' hiding offenders, concealing information, and not seeking police assistance.

Another factor that leads to friction between minority and nonminority officers is the belief by white officers that Hispanic, African, and Native Americans are not as capable as white officers in carrying out their law enforcement duties (Teahan, 1975b; Carter, 1986; Feinman, 1986). This prejudice is held in spite of the fact that minority officers are more highly educated than white officers, and that law enforcement administrators (police chiefs and sheriffs) believe that officers who are college-educated "perform more effectively, have fewer disciplinary problems, are named in fewer citizen complaints, use discretion more wisely, show greater initiative, and communicate better with the public" (*Criminal Justice Newsletter,* 1989: 4).[39] A recent national survey of all state police and highway patrol agencies, all city departments serving populations greater than fifty thousand, and all county sheriffs' departments having more than one hundred sworn officers, revealed the following percentages of officers earning undergraduate degrees by race/ethnicity: white, 62 percent; black, 63 percent; Hispanic, 68 percent; other, 73 percent (Carter and Sapp, 1990: 66). Furthermore, the distribution of graduate degrees is more disparate: white, 4 percent; Hispanic, 5 percent; other, 8 percent; black, 9 percent (ibid.).

The rising hostility between minority and white police officers has resulted in minority withdrawal from "traditional" police organizations and a concomitant proliferation of minority police organizations established in major cities as well as nationally.[40] Within the police departments of our nation there is turmoil: "Major disagreements over affirmative action and the department's response to the needs of the black community reveal increasingly diverse attitudes and are predictive of mounting internal tension" (Buzawa, 1981: 66). There may be "law," but today, at least among the law enforcers, there is precious little order.

A Minority View

This chapter has demonstrated throughout how the law and legal system has perpetuated and continues to maintain an ingrained system of injustice for peoples of color:

The dominant experience has been one in which the law acted as the vehicle by which the generalized racism in the society was made particular and converted into standards and policies of subjugation and social control. Most white Americans tend to view the historic role of the law in this country as that of a tool for the expansion of liberty, and they are largely correct as to themselves—especially if they are not poor (which most are not). However, etched deep in the collective consciousness of American blacks is the role that the law has played in their oppression. It is a present perception which comports with both the historical and contemporary reality. (Burns, 1973: 157)

As Reich (1973: 449) points out, there are different sets of laws depending upon one's "status, class, and position in society," to which could be added, depending upon one's skin color in this society. Earlier sections of this chapter documented how "colonial laws were written to guard production by slaves"; "treaties were imposed on American Indian tribes legalizing the wholesale and violent theft of natural resources, and the transformation of these resources into bourgeois property" (Schwendinger and Schwendinger, 1977: 6); and all black, brown, red, and yellow people were denied the basic human, economic, and due process rights guaranteed to white members of this nation. This second-class status has been extended and exacerbated by additional encroachments on freedoms by means of the "get tough"-on-crime policies instituted by an ever-widenening, extremely conservative administration, legislatures, and Supreme Court. New federal laws—for example, omnibus crime laws, federal sentencing guidelines, the federal death penalty; and questionable legal practices—drug courier "profiles," urine testing, changed Miranda warnings, stop and frisk, search and seize, and executing children and the mentally retarded, to name but a few—reflect the mean-spirited, punitive, and institutionalized racist perspectives of those in power.

This country has not evolved very far from the literacy tests and poll taxes that prohibited African Americans from voting. Today, large-acre zoning laws effectively put certain geographical areas off limits to blacks. In addition, the law continues to be used as a tool for depriving black people of effective political participation through the exercise of the franchise, for example, where "at-large" systems of voting can be used to assure that a black minority will never be in a position in the particular locale in question to elect a political representative of its own choosing (Burns, 1973: 161). As a result, African American and other racial minorities lack adequate representation as lawmakers, and laws are made subsequently by persons who are not members of the groups directly involved in what has become legal persecution of peoples of color. The significance of this disenfranchisement is obvious:

State legislatures have always played a central role in the criminal justice system. Traditionally this role focused on defining the scope of the criminal law and setting limits for criminal sentencing. State legislatures also establish budgets for many criminal justice agencies, and therefore shape the priorities of statewide criminal justice policy. (McGarrell and Flanagan, 1987: 102)

At this writing, only about 8 percent of national lawmakers politically represent racial minorities—twenty-five African Americans (5.7 percent), ten Hispanic Americans (2.3 percent), and a lone Asian American from Hawaii ("A Not So Simple Game," 1991: 21). After a long and distinguished career, Justice

Thurgood Marshall, the only person of color ever seated on the U.S. Supreme Court, recently announced his retirement. Because of the current conservative administration and the existing national "backlash" climate, Justice Marshall was replaced by the reputedly conservative African American jurist Clarence Thomas, whose confirmation hearings were a shameful and blatant example of the institutional racism in this nation.

During the Senate subcommittee confirmation hearings on Justice Thomas's nomination to the United States Supreme Court, it became obvious that some members of the committee were frustrated at Thomas's extremely articulate and very adroit handling of their questions. What followed was, as Justice Thomas called it, "a lynching." The introduction of alleged sexual harassment testimony by African American law professor Anita Hill resulted in character assassinations of both of these theretofore unblemished African Americans. Explicit sexual probing and innuendo were obviously embarrassing to Justice Thomas, to Professor Hill, and to every African American viewing the hearings. In light of the plethora of sex-related and financial scandals that are continually associated with the United States Congress and the upper echelons of our government, the indisputable conspired public "lynchings" of these two respected African American citizens served to expose the covert racism endemic to this country at even the highest levels.

The proliferation of new laws that directly or indirectly affect significant numbers of peoples of color leads to the selective enforcement of the law and reinforces the fact that "the greater the number of laws, the greater the resulting discretion, and the more lawless the official part of the state becomes" (Reich, 1973: 450).

Personal contacts and experiences mold the impressions and opinions of both citizens and police officers. Nonminority police, who are by choice isolated from the community in the first place, appear to be unable to differentiate between citizens and lawbreakers; therefore, most problems between the community and the police are with average citizens, and not with criminals (Bell, 1983). We have already seen substantial evidence indicating that, for numerous reasons, minorities view the police more negatively than whites.[41] At least nineteen studies have been identified which establish that fact (Peek, Lowe, and Alston, 1981).

Noting that blacks are more likely than whites to have negative opinions about the police and also experience more police maltreatment than whites, Apple and O'Brien (1983) studied the influence of racial composition on views held toward police in a moderate-income neighborhood in Akron, Ohio. They hypothesized that "changing racial composition of the neighborhood sets in motion a different set of social psychological processes for blacks and whites which produces different effects on the way each racial group views the police" (ibid.: 77). Although there was little difference between black and white mean scores of police quality, the data supported the hypothesis that an increased proportion of blacks in the neighborhood resulted in increased negative citizen evaluations of the police. The two possible explanations Apple and O'Brien offered for this finding were that the increase in blacks led to more hostile exchanges between blacks and the police, or that associations with more blacks having negative opinions of the police were reinforcing to other blacks. It would appear that both factors might have contributed to the greater black negative sentiment toward police.

Since surveys of black attitudes toward police typically involve household residents, street respondents' views are usually omitted. Most polls have indicated that higher-status blacks hold more contrary attitudes toward the police, or that "social status did not serve as an insulator" (Boggs and Galliher, 1975: 394). In an innovative study of a midwestern city police district, Boggs and Galliher compared blacks at different status levels (street and household) on their evaluations of police-initiated contacts and respondent calls for service. The police ratings for neighborhood service were in the expected direction, with more negative evaluations by household persons of higher status. Overall, 80.1 percent of the black household respondents rated combined contacts with police and neighborhood police service as poor (33 percent) or fair (47.1 percent). A total of 84.7 percent of black respondents with high-school or more education (higher status) viewed police contacts and service as poor (40.3 percent) or fair (44.4 percent). Also, as expected, street respondents were far more likely to have experienced police-initiated contacts than household respondents, resulting in 88 percent of street interviewees' overall ratings of police as fair (47 percent) or poor (41 percent). The proportion of poor assessments of police by blacks was found to be larger than national surveys report, and much higher than the figures cited in a similar survey in Denver.

The early Denver study found that almost half of the minorities in that city, largely blacks and Mexican Americans, had had recent personal, significant, negative contacts with the police. The researchers found that respect for the police was declining, and that only 22 percent of blacks and 31 percent of Hispanics, compared to 54 percent of whites, rated the reputation of the police as high (Bayley and Mendelsohn, 1968: 41) Even the surveyed police recognized their image problem among minorities, since 56 percent admitted that minorities, especially Hispanics, had particularly unfavorable opinions of them (ibid.: 45).

Hispanic residents in the Miami/Dade County, Florida area, who are predominantly of Cuban descent, were more likely to rate their local police as "good" (46.9 percent) than black residents (35 percent); however, both minority groups were less likely than whites (57.1 percent) to give such ratings (Florida Bureau, 1981: 19). A possible explanation for the difference of opinion of the two types of Hispanic groups, Mexican (the Denver study) and Cuban, may be related to the length of residence. For the most part, Miami Cubans have come to this country in the last two decades, whereas southwestern Mexican Americans have been here more than two centuries. Overall, Miami/Dade County residents demonstrated less confidence in police performance than other Florida urban or rural respondents.

A more recent survey of minority attitudes toward Miami police queried multi-ethnic neighborhood residents (Alpert and Dunham, 1988). The five Dade County neighborhoods included upper-middle-class African Americans, low-income African Americans residing in a housing project, middle- and upper-class Anglos, 1960 Cuban entrants, and 1980 (Mariel) Cuban entrants. Even though they differed on some points, despite class level, African Americans and 1980 Marielitos were found to be much more negative and suspicious toward police as agents of social control than whites or 1960 Cubans. The opinion of the Marielitos is especially notable, since they are predominantly of lower-class status, are also of darker skin color, and exhibit more African physical characteristics. Further, these 1980 Cubans had the highest percentage of negative opinions toward the police (24 percent) of any group, followed closely by lower-income blacks (22 percent), middle- to upper-income blacks (14 percent), upper-level whites (6 percent), and 1960 Cubans (2 percent),[42] who are generally described as middle- to upper-class, based upon their previous status in Cuba and their rapid assimilation in this country (ibid.: 96, Table 6-1).

The major determinant of disapproving attitudes toward police is the nature of the personal interaction, particularly the actual contact with a uniformed officer on patrol. Respondents interviewed in Pittsburgh, Pennsylvania reported more satisfactory contacts with and better opinions of police when they had spoken with police in an informal way, such as asking for information or directions, or when they had had sociable contact with them at parties or other social functions (Scaglion and Condon, 1980). In a field test of exchange theory—i.e., the police-citizen encounter is a two-way exchange—Wiley and Hudik (1974) found that among the police/citizen interactions, one of the touchiest was field interrogation. Referring to the Black and Reiss (1970) data, they note that only 14 percent of the observed field interviews resulted in arrests, leaving 86 percent of those stopped by police as presumably innocent people. Wiley and Hudik feel that hostility displayed by people who are stopped may be related to an officer's lack of explanation for their detainment. Their interview data, collected on the predominantly black south side of Chicago, supported their hypothesis that citizens who were given no reason for being stopped were "least likely to reward the officer either with willing cooperation or supportive comments" (Wiley and Hudik, 1974: 125).

It is evident that the results of surveys and polls on how minority groups perceive law enforcers reveal a very negative image of police. Also, far too often it is the rule and not the exception that harsher police actions are directed at minority citizens whether they are suspects in criminal activities or not, and despite their class level or professional status. Thus, minorities' negative views of law enforcement are partially a response to reciprocal negative attitudes police hold and demonstrate toward minorities. The long history of negative interactions between agents of law enforcement and persons of color in the United States provides another explanation for the poor image of police consistently held by minorities.

Early in the chapter, the standard description of the origin of the United States police (see "Police Personality and Practices") was briefly presented, but there is another history of racial oppression by police that has been largely ignored until recently. In a brilliant and informative monograph, Williams and Murphy (1990: 3) find that "the first American modern-style policing occurred in the 'slave patrols,' developed by the white slave owners as a means of dealing with runaways. Believing that their militia was not capable of dealing with the perceived threat, the colonial State governments of the South enacted slave patrol legislation during the 1740's."

Williams and Murphy add that all southern states eventually enacted similar statutes which gave these "new police" the total power to break into blacks' homes, punish slaves or runaways, whip slaves who challenged their authority, and apprehend any slave suspected of a crime. They comment: "Understandably, the actions of such patrols established an *indelible impression* on both the whites who implemented this system and the blacks who were the brunt of it" (ibid.: 4; emphasis added).

It is this "indelible impression," reinforced over more than 250 years, that forms the basis of the minority citizen–police problem today. Minorities' resentful attitudes toward agents of social control are rooted in a long and bloody history of minority oppression. We have already seen (Chapter 1) that since the birth of this nation, peoples of color have been enslaved, segregated, discriminated against, and killed. Indian patrols, slave patrols, border patrols, or some form of law enforcement personnel has consistently reflected a Eurocentric, racist society whose "laws" are upheld and whose beliefs, prejudices, and practices have become institutionalized. As Williams and Murphy argue:

> The fact that the legal order not only countenanced but sustained slavery, segregation, and discrimination for most of our Nation's history—and the fact that the police were bound to uphold that order—set a pattern for police behavior and attitudes toward minority communities that has persisted until the present day. That pattern includes the idea that minorities have fewer civil rights, that the task of the police is to keep them under control, and that the police have little responsibility for protecting them from crime within their communities. (1990: 2)

5

Unequal Justice

A QUESTION OF COLOR

Injustice anywhere is a threat to justice everywhere.
—Martin Luther King Jr. (1963)

The Pretrial Experiences of Minorities

A great deal of criminological attention and research has been devoted to final sentencing outcomes for minority offenders; however, there has been scant concentration on portentous actions and decisions occurring earlier on the route to court after an arrest has been effected. This oversight is particularly misleading, since it has been found that "when racial differences in processing occur, they are likely to occur at stages prior to final sentencing" (Farnworth and Horan, 1980: 381). The assignment of bail and preventive detention demonstrate that either minorities are denied the opportunity to make bond and thereby secure release from jail, or bond is frequently set at such an exorbitant amount that a minority defendant is unable to raise it and remains in detention until the case is heard. In both events the accused is deprived of precious freedom and simultaneously denied the right to assist in the adequate preparation of his/her case. The exclusion of minority group members from grand juries and trial juries has been and continues to be a central problem in the administration of justice. The need for minority legal representation and opinions of defense attorneys held by minority defendants are rarely discussed but are additional important pretrial issues.

The far-reaching influence and excessive discretion of the prosecutor frequently have detrimental effects on minorities at each step of the criminal justice process, ranging from charging and grand jury indictments to plea bargaining and final court dispositions. Poor and minority defendants are more likely to waive the constitutional right to a trial and thus tend to plea bargain in hopes of obtaining more lenient sentences, although there is some doubt that plea negotiations are really "bargains." Each of these stumbling blocks has its own deleterious effect, and by the time of the court date, collectively, they can be devastating for the minority defendant.

Bail and Detention

After a suspect has been taken into custody, one of the most important discretionary decisions is whether the accused will be held or released before trial (Levine, Musheno, and Palumbo, 1986: 342). The major factors involved in a bail decision center on (1) whether the suspect has to put up bail, (2) the amount of bail required, and (3) the consequences of detention if bail is not granted or cannot be met. Since bail is a guarantee that a criminal defendant will appear in court as required, appearance results in return of the security; failure to appear forfeits the bail (Inciardi, 1984: 443). Pretrial release suggests a risk that a defendant who has been arrested and subsequently determined a suspect by prosecutors may commit additional offenses (Rhodes, 1985: 1).

The original intent of bail was to ensure that a person accused of a crime would appear for trial. In the medieval era, it was traditional for a friend or neighbor to assume responsibility for the defendant's appearance; however, if the accused failed to appear, the "surety" or third party was tried in his or her place (Zavitz, Mina, Kuykendall, Greenfeld, and White, 1983: 58; Sorin, 1985: 1). As a result of massive urbanization in the United States, by the late nineteenth century, "money bail came to virtually total domination when an increasing number of individuals were not well-known in the community, and there was no other manner deemed forceful enough to ensure the appearance of the accused at trial" (Ozanne, Wilson, and Gedney, 1980: 148).

Somehow the purpose of bail—to ensure the accused's appearance for trial—loses its significance when minorities are the defendants. The reliance on money bail was widely condemned in the 1960s because of apparent discrimination against the poor and minorities, specifically because those incarcerated before trial were frequently sentenced more severely than similarly charged defendants who were freed before their trials (Bynum, 1982: 68). In a study of trial courts in Chicago, Lizotte (1978: 572, 577) found that it was economically more difficult for nonwhites and defendants of lower occupational status to make bail, and an indirect effect of not making bail was "outright discrimination and longer prison sentences."

The Manhattan Bail Project, undertaken by the Vera Institute of Justice in New York City from 1961 to 1964, tested whether indigent defendants released on their own recognizance (ROR) would appear for trial (Sorin, 1985: 1). By substituting "objective criteria for the arbitrary and discriminatory practice of bail," the Vera project found that the majority of ROR defendants did appear for trial, and the practice of ROR quickly spread across the nation (Bynum, 1982: 69). A recent experiment comparing defendants under supervised pretrial release (SPR) with felony defendants having similar characteristics found that 90 percent of the SPRs—75 percent of whom were minorities—did not flee and were not rearrested (Austin, Krisberg, and Litsky, 1985).

The criteria established for pretrial release may still be discriminatory on the basis of economic status or skin color. In a study of a large western city, Bynum (1982: 77) identified six groups of variables as potentially influential in release on recognizance and found that blacks and Native Americans were less likely to receive ROR than nonminority defendants with the same characteristics. The most significant variable influencing the ROR decision was access to financial resources; minority status was the fourth-strongest predictor. A Florida study revealed that, among the variables studied, demeanor had the greatest effect and seriousness of offense the least effect in ROR decisions (Frazier, Bock, and Henretta, 1980: 177). The relative importance of these two variables was reversed where amount of bail was concerned. Although race and demeanor/appearance were not reported, an earlier description of the sample indicates that about 46 percent were African American, and few persons appearing in the court were from the middle or upper classes (Frazier, 1979: 208).

The implications of the "repressive application of bail laws" are enormous for minority defendants. The National Minority Advisory Council on Criminal Justice, a national fact-finding body, found that minorities experienced the imposition of (1) legal maximum bail settings; (2) exorbitant bail for alleged major crimes and conspiracies; (3) extremely high bails for minor offenses; (4) overcharges at arrest with concomitant high, impossible bail; and (5) the application of multiple charges, with bail imposed at the legal maximum for each separate charge (NMAC, 1980: 204).

Judges often use criteria such as crime prevention and retribution or punishment to assign bails that are unrelated to guaranteeing court appearances, "since they do not want to look bad in the public's eye when they have released people who commit new crimes while awaiting trial" (Levine, Musheno, and Palumbo, 1986: 346). In addition to a judge's concern with maintaining a positive political image, there is also the problem of judicial bias. In her study of criminal defendants prosecuted in New York, Nagel (1983: 481) found that in decisions concerning alternatives to cash bail, judicial identity appeared to be as explanatory as the combined legal and extralegal variables studied: "Among the extra-legal factors that affect pretrial release decisions, the effects of status characteristics of the defendant pale in comparison to the effects of bench bias and measures of the defendant's dangerousness." The evidence also revealed discrimination against minorities, particularly Hispanics, in the determination of the amount of bail. Although legal variables (prior criminal record, seriousness of charge) were most important, Nagel (ibid.: 509-510) notes that such variables may be a biasing influence on the judge because of the suggestion of dangerousness.

The issue of the public perception of dangerousness and an insistence upon the protection of society often leads judges to set bail so high for some defendants that, in practice, it becomes a mechanism for preventive detention (Inciardi, 1984: 445). Scholars are divided on the matter of preventive pretrial detention, but the public generally supports the concept, especially when violent crime is involved (Nagel, 1983: 486). The stereotyping of African Americans and other minorities as dangerous puts them more at risk of this type of social and judicial bias.[1] The injustice incumbent in such practices is frequently overlooked:

> The due process notion of presumption of innocence requires that criminally charged defendants be treated as innocent until guilt has been established. Thus, a glaring affront to due process is offered by the very existence of the practice of pretrial detention. To the defendant, pretrial detention is essentially punitive; it institutionalizes the punishment of persons who theoretically are presumed innocent. More troublesome to due process principles than the mere existence of pretrial detention is the use of bail for the purpose of detaining persons deemed dangerous by bail judges. (Goldkamp, 1980: 183)

Although the Eighth Amendment to the U.S. Constitution specifies that "excessive bail shall not be required," in reality, minority suspects, particularly in political protest or riot situations, have often been assigned impossibly high bails for both preventive and punishment purposes; for example, during the ghetto riots occurring in the 1960s in Chicago, Detroit, and Los Angeles, bail was set very high ($50,000 for those accused of looting, and $200,000 for those accused of assault). Obviously, disproportionately large numbers of those arrested were jailed. But the percentage of convictions was far below normal, and relatively few of those convicted received jail sentences (Levine, Musheno, and Palumbo, 1986: 347).

> In the Detroit ghetto rebellion of 1967, discriminatory courtroom practices were overt and well-documented. A total of 7,200 persons were arrested. Virtually all of these were low-income or indigent blacks. Of the 4,260 persons brought into Recorder's (Detroit Municipal) Court, 3,230 were charged with looting, a five-year felony, a charge which also was the basis for high bail and extended delay in processing the cases. (NMAC, 1980: 201)

Ultimately almost half of these cases were dismissed for lack of evidence, but in the interim, even African Americans with "long residence records, regular jobs, and with no previous police records found themselves isolated in maximum security prisons, without benefit of counsel or any semblance of due process" (ibid.). Aside from minority protests, the National Minority Advisory Council on Criminal Justice found that the bail bond system discriminates against minorities and poor people on a daily basis.

Typically, only three factors are considered in setting bail—the most important is the seriousness of the crime. The assumption is that the more severe the offense, the greater the likelihood of forfeiture of bail. Second, prior criminal record provides a rationale that repeat offenders, or recidivists, have a higher possibility of forfeiting bond. The third factor considered is the strength of the state's case based on the premise that the greater the chance of conviction, the stronger the interest in fleeing (Inciardi, 1984: 446-447). The first two assumptions are clearly questionable, since seven out of eight persons released (87.5

percent) return for final dispositions in their cases (Sorin, 1985: 3). A major examination of pretrial releases in eight urban jurisdictions on the state and local levels concluded that of the 85 percent of defendants released, only about 15 percent were rearrested while on pretrial conditional release; an additional 15 percent failed to appear at the time of the trial.

Because of the way the money bail system operates, minority suspects who are poor are jailed for inordinately long periods of time, while whites go free: "Both are equally presumed innocent; money is the discriminating factor. As a result, the country's jails are packed to overflowing with the nation's poor—with red, brown, black, and yellow men and women showing up in disproportionate numbers" (Burns, 1973: 161). The consequences of such bail malpractice can be overwhelming for minorities. In addition to the possibility of being convicted and receiving a more severe sentence as a result of pretrial detention, other serious repercussions can result from incarceration pending trial. Pretrial detention prevents the accused from locating evidence and witnesses and having more complete access to counsel. It disrupts employment and family relations. If pretrial incarceration results in the loss of employment, the families of the detained accused may require public assistance for survival (Bynum, 1982: 68).

Detention subjects people to what are often ghastly jail conditions. Defendants awaiting trial are indiscriminately mixed with convicted felons, many of whom are violent offenders, and scores of detainees each year are beaten, raped, and murdered (Inciardi, 1984: 451-452). Pretrial detention also limits defendants' ability to help with their own defenses, and stigmatizes them if they indeed go to trial (Levine, Musheno, and Palumbo, 1986: 342). It coerces defendants who are detained in jail into plea negotiation in order to settle the matter more rapidly (Inciardi, 1984: 451). Finally, as previously noted, sentence severity is greatest for defendants who are detained prior to trial. Research has demonstrated repeatedly that detainees are more likely to be indicted, convicted, and sentenced more harshly than released defendants.

Privately secured bail typically involves bondsmen who charge defendants a fee for the service: "A bondsman signs a promissory note to the court for the bail amount and charges the defendant a fee for the service (usually 10% of the bail amount). If the defendant fails to appear, the bondsman must pay the court the full amount. Frequently, the bondsman requires the defendant to post collateral in addition to the fee" (Zavitz et al., 1983: 58).

There are several ways an accused minority can be abused when at the financial mercy of a professional bondsman. First, since substantial capital is a necessary prerequisite for the occupation, the majority of bondsmen are Euro-Americans. Consequently, those who harbor racial prejudices will not accept minority defendants. Second, whether or not a defendant gains release depends on the discretion of the bonding agent, who may not select poor (or minority) defendants because of the low fees associated with low bails (Goldkamp, 1980: 182). A third possibility of refusal to assume the bonds of minorities may be that the bondsman adopts the stereotypical attitude that minorities are poor bail risks who will abscond and forfeit the bondsman's money. Fourth, some bondsmen, who are as crooked as the persons they represent, are reputed to gouge minorities by taking what few possessions they have as additional collateral and never returning them.

In 1984, two federal legislative acts—the Bail Reform Act and the Comprehensive Crime Control Act—resulted in significant changes in federal pretrial release and detention practices that negatively impacted African Americans and other minorities. After the Bail Reform Act of 1984 became effective, a comparative study of the pretrial experiences of defendants in 1983 and 1985 suggested that "pretrial detention has largely been used as an alternative to bail as a means of holding defendants" (Kennedy and Carlson, 1988: 1). Before the Act, 7 percent were held in pretrial detention, whereas after the Act, about two-thirds were (ibid.). Among these comparison groups, detention of African Americans had increased from 1.7 percent in 1983 to 19.1 percent in 1985. Comparable increases for Hispanics were from 2.7 percent to 33.2 percent, and for other minorities from 1.2 percent to 22.9 percent (ibid.: 4).[2] Persons held who were charged with immigration offenses, predominantly minorities, increased over this two-year time span from 51 percent to 67 percent (ibid.: 3). In addition to the substantial increase in minority defendants held before trial, after the Act the average time held also increased 5 percent, from fifty to fifty-three days (ibid.: 5).

An examination of the offenses for which the defendants were detained until trial clearly suggests that peoples of color are disproportionately and increasingly held in pretrial detention under the new legislation. Although type of offense by racial/ethnic status is not provided in the report, the following offenses constitute 72.7 percent of the reasons defendants are held until trial—the most frequent offense, drugs (39.8 percent), is commonly recognized as a crime for which minorities are unequally arrested, immigration offenses (19.4 percent) typically involve persons of Hispanic or Asian extraction, and African Americans and Hispanics are disproportionately arrested for violent offenses (13.5 percent).

Under the Comprehensive Crime Control Act of 1984, federal defendants may be detained *without bail* if it is determined in a special hearing that no financial or other conditions will reasonably ensure their appearance as required, and that such detention will guarantee the safety of other persons in the community (Rhodes, 1985: 2). When bail is set, those defendants accused of the most serious crimes and who have lengthy criminal histories and weak social and economic ties are accorded the highest bails (ibid.: 5), a profile that fits many minorities. Since "the probability of posting bail increases with the defendant's annual income, his education, and his ability to hire a private attorney," given the economic status of minorities in the United States, it is not surprising that with other variables held constant, "non-Caucasians" are far less likely than Caucasians to be able to post bail in federal cases (ibid.: 3-4).

Jury Selection

The methods used in empaneling and composing a jury can result in unfair treatment of minorities during the jury selection process. Since grand juries have almost unlimited power to hand down criminal indictments, the lack of minority representation on grand juries, as well as on juries in trials where minorities are defendants, indicates an abrogation of the Sixth Amendment constitutional right to an impartial jury trial in criminal cases—that is, to be tried by one's peers.

A grand jury can arrive at its indictment decision on its own initiative through accusations based on its observations or knowledge; or, as is common practice, it can indict a person solely on evidence presented by the prosecutor (Inciardi, 1984: 459). In either case, an indictment is returned on the basis of a majority vote and arrived at privately and secretly without the accused or accused's defense counsel being present (ibid.: 460). A grand jury can refuse to criminally indict, in which case the accused is released; it can alter or reduce the charges; or it can hand down the indictment presented by the prosecutor, the customary practice, since "a grand jury rarely disagrees with the recommendations of the prosecution" (Barlow, 1984: 443). The implications of such an enormous amount of discretion and power in the hands of a simple majority is discomforting; for a minority suspect, the ramifications of the grand jury selection procedure can be petrifying.

Grand juries are generally composed using the "key man" method. Key men are prominent members of the community, usually white, propertied males whom the court chooses for the purpose of selecting perspective jurors (NMAC, 1980: 206):

> The State of Texas used a "key man" system to select persons for the jury panel. This system gave the local sheriff, the key man, the authority to identify and select persons for the jury panel from anywhere in the county. More often than not the sheriff selected persons that he knew or used names recommended to him by these persons. . . . Because the sheriff knew few Mexican-Americans, few of them were ever chosen for jury panels, thereby causing a significant underrepresentation of Mexican-Americans on trial juries. (Joyner, 1982: 109)

The subjective bias of such a system is obvious—key men select men like themselves, not persons of color or poor people.

Jury selections using other, more objective methods, such as lists of registered voters, automobile registrations, or property tax rolls, also have built-in biases that favor the middle class, specifically the white middle class. Jury lists derived from such sources often "do not result in a given jury panel representing an ethnic, economic, racial, and cross-cultural section of the population in the court's jurisdiction" (NMAC, 1980: 206) because they exclude racial minorities, those in lower socioeconomic statuses, and the less educated. Minorities who through a variety of methods have been kept from registering to vote can never serve on juries in areas that use voter status as a criterion. "Redlining" voting districts and other means of preventing minority voting reduce the numbers of African Americans, Hispanics, Native Americans, and Americans of Asian descent on the voter rolls. The National Minority Advisory Council on Criminal Justice (1980) points out that many minorities will try to avoid jury duty because, as lower-level, blue-collar employees, they cannot afford the loss of hourly wages that jury duty entails. The result of these and other barriers is that most empaneled juries consist of white, middle-class, middle-aged persons whose beliefs and cultural attitudes mirror those of the dominant (white) political and economic structure, and ultimately prove potentially damaging to a minority defendant's right to an equitable trial (ibid.: 207).

In addition to these possible initial obstructions to fair trials for minorities, the selection of jurors can introduce other pitfalls. For decades, peremptory challenges, in which the prosecutor and the defense each have a specified number of exclusions for which no reasons are necessary, have been detrimental to minority defendants (Vetter and Silverman, 1986: 503). Such exclusions generally ensure the probability of a white, middle-class jury, since "each challenge of a member of an underrepresented group by the prosecution decreases the relative representation of that group on the panel to a greater degree than does challenge of a member of the overrepresented group" (ibid.: 206). The notorious Angela Davis trial, which took place in one of the most conservative Northern California counties, found the lone African American on the jury list removed early through peremptory challenge by the prosecuting attorney, which "eliminated any possibility that Angela Davis would realistically be afforded a trial by her peers" (Hilliard, Dent, Hayes, Pierce, and Poussaint, 1974: 56).

In *Swain v. Alabama* (1965), the Court allowed prosecutors to eliminate all prospective African American jurors from a jury with an African American defendant. The absurd notion that "prosecutors are suggesting that they often attempt to exclude blacks from the jury because of prejudice by blacks and not because of their own prejudice" (Wilbanks, 1986: 94) apparently did not convince the U.S. Supreme Court, since it recently barred prosecutors from disqualifying potential jurors based on their race. The nationwide exclusion of African American jurors in trials of African American defendants resulted in *Batson v. Kentucky* (1986), in which the Court ruled 7 to 2 that prosecutors "have the burden of proving their peremptory—or automatic—challenges to potential jurors are not based on race" ("Court," 1987: 1B). Until Batson it was found that in some jurisdictions, up to 82 percent of African American jurors had been struck from criminal cases (Murphy, 1988: 182).

Jury size has been found to be a discriminatory factor in felony cases of African Americans and other minorities in the half-dozen states that permit less than twelve-person juries.[3] In 1970, the U.S. Supreme Court decided in *Williams v. Florida* that a panel of fewer than twelve jurors was as reliable a fact-finding body as a panel of twelve as long as unanimity was maintained (Vetter and Silverman, 1986: 504). Ironically, the 1980 riots in Miami erupted because an all-white, six-member Tampa jury acquitted four white ex–Dade County (Miami) policemen charged with the beating death of an African American businessman. At issue is the reduced probability of minority empanelment. If twelve-person juries rarely include African Americans and other minorities, selection of a jury of six from an already unrepresentative pool will be less likely to provide a cross-section of the community (NMAC, 1980: 208). As one African American attorney on a national Courts Task Force observed,

> I question whether the smaller jury will not have the effect of easing the prosecutor's burden of proof. It would seem that it would be easier for him to convince six rather than twelve, that he has met his burden. Moreover, the reduced size of the jury would make the possibility of a hung jury less likely. I am of the opinion that the possibility of a hung jury is an integral part of the concept of reasonable doubt, which, in turn, is the very cornerstone of the criminal process. (Ibid.)

The Legal Actors: Defense and Prosecuting Attorneys

The right to counsel is one of the most vital due process rights an individual in a criminal court proceeding is constitutionally assured. Such legal representation is necessary in an adversary system of justice such as ours. The defense of accused persons has a legal mandate in the Sixth Amendment of the U.S. Constitution, which provides the "assistance of counsel for his defense" (Gaskins, 1984: 1). This lawful charge has been restructured through a number of Supreme Court cases. *Johnson v. Zerbst* (1928)[4] required that counsel be appointed in federal criminal cases but was not applicable to the states. This oversight was rectified in a 1932 case, *Powell v. Alabama,*[5] when the U.S. Supreme Court held that the due process clause of the Fourteenth Amendment "required a state court to appoint counsel for indigent defendants who were charged with a capital offense" (ibid.: 2). In 1963, in *Gideon v. Wainwright,*[6] the indigence doctrine was expanded to include anyone accused of a felony; and in 1972, the Sixth Amendment due process right to counsel was extended in *Argensinger v. Hamlin*[7] to misdemeanor cases that could lead to incarceration (NMAC, 1980: 211; Gaskins, 1984: 2). Over time, the Court broadened the right to counsel in criminal cases by including every critical step in the prosecution journey: arraignment, preliminary hearing, plea entry, and sentencing. Legal assistance to indigent defendants in the preparation of their first appeals was confirmed in *Douglas v. California* (1963),[8] although discretionary review was not included in state courts or the U.S. Supreme Court (Gaskins, 1984: 2). Individual states also offer unique legal defense programs; for example, Florida provides legal representation in postconviction capital cases (Spangenberg, Kapuscinski, and Smith, 1988: 7).

The latest available data indicate that in 1986, almost $1 billion was spent on indigent defense services in the 4.4 million cases tried in local and state courts, an increase of 60 percent over the sum spent in 1982 (ibid.: 1). These cases utilized one of three primary types of indigent defense systems—*assigned counsel systems, contract systems,* or *public defender programs.*

There are at least two potentially serious and discriminating flaws inherent in the assigned counsel and contract methods: the original selection of an attorney and the quality of the attorney selected. In the first instance, there is little research or literature available, a finding that is in itself questionable considering the millions of dollars allocated annually to these private-practice lawyers. The bulk of extant research addresses the caliber of provided legal counsel in indigent cases, not the selection procedure.

Under an assigned counsel system, it is often judges who have the immense authority and discretion to appoint attorneys, a situation that is conceivably more discomforting because the judges also ultimately hear the cases.[9] Judges, like states attorneys, are also subject to ethnocentricity or to having personal racial prejudices. Even under the coordinated, administrative method of assigning counsel, a sole administrator has this authority. It should not be overlooked that the southern and midwestern regions more frequently use these methods and are renowned as the areas of the country most likely to face charges of racism in the administration of justice. Whether racially biased or not, there is still the danger of the "good old boy" system, where such appointments are rooted in favoritism or nepotism, thereby screening out minority attorneys or those nonminority lawyers who are inclined toward civil rights concerns and justice.

Contract attorney programs could also be accused of partisanship, particularly since this method of indigent defense selection is peculiar to small counties. Under this system, a single lawyer or law firm, a bar association, or a nonprofit organization receives a fixed sum or "block grant" through direct negotiations with the county (Gaskins, 1984: 5-6; Spangenberg, Kapuscinski, and Smith, 1988: 3). This method is in contrast to both the use of public defenders who are salaried and the voucher systems used in assigned counsel programs. The enormous political autonomy in small counties is legendary. Every potential abuse of power identified in the other systems—local politics, bigotry, other-culture ignorance, favoritism, and nepotism—is likely to be exacerbated in smaller communities using the contract system. Although this type of program has been adopted in only 10.7 percent of the counties, its growth by nearly two-thirds from 1982 to 1986 attests to its increasing popularity, particularly in the West.[10]

The implications for racial discrimination under public defender systems are most appropriately centered upon the political system in a community. A chief public defender is an appointed figure who, in turn, generally has license to hire the public defenders on his/her staff. The possible misapplication of such power and discretion is obvious: if the administrator has personal biases against, or ignorance of, indigent peoples of color, such attitudes and beliefs could be influential in the selection of attorneys and the climate of the public defender's office, and could eventually filter throughout the entire judicial system, that is, become institutionalized.

Under any of these systems, political or financial dishonesty is always possible in such appointments. The public generally likes to think of the legal profession as honorable; nonetheless it is conceivable (and media-exposed scandals often so indicate) that many attorneys who defend the indigent in criminal cases do it simply for the money, are appointed for political favors owed to them, or represent such cases for other types of monetary reasons (e.g., "kickbacks"). Too often the results of these unlawful liaisons are shoddy legal defenses of clients.

THE QUALITY OF CRIMINAL DEFENSE

The quality of service provided by assigned counsel systems is generally thought not to be as high as that of privately retained counsel:

> Many lawyers assigned to indigents are young, often right out of law school, with no experience in criminal cases. The low fees for this type of practice make it tempting for a court-appointed lawyer to plead his client guilty to save the time and work necessary for a long trial. Funds are rarely provided for the expenses of investigation or calling expert witnesses. (NMAC, 1980: 212)

Although the public defender system has a more complete available staff, including investigators, and the legal files of previous cases, it also has its problems. In fact, several studies on the performance of public defense systems for indigent defendants have yielded mixed results. Some studies are highly critical of public defenders, others question the ability of assigned counsel, and some researchers find that privately retained counsel does not offer the best defense to an indigent client charged with a felony.

Skolnick (1967: 59) observed judges, prosecutors, and public defenders in a California county and found that public defenders represented more than 60 percent of the accused felons and were also the most important defense attorneys. What mattered most to the prosecutor was not the type of attorney but whether he or she could be relied on as a "cooperative" defense attorney. This "cooperative" category included only a few public defenders and leading private attorneys. All of the leading white defense attorneys insisted that the "cooperative" position was in their clients' interest and settled 90 percent of their cases in this manner. The one African American lawyer settled only about half of his cases this way, because his clients expected a posture of challenge in defense and mistrusted attorneys who appeared to cooperate too closely with the prosecutor and the police. Skolnick (ibid.: 60-61) notes that "cooperating" with the prosecution is in a lawyer's interest as well as a client's, since lawyers usually charge a set fee whether there is a trial or not. Thus, it is economically advantageous for attorneys to plead their clients guilty.

In research on the application of the "two wrestler syndrome" to public defenders—when two combatants who routinely face each other develop a symbiotic relationship and cooperative arrangements to make everyone's job easier—Battle (1971: 61) suggests that the pressures toward cooperation are equally strong for private attorneys. His interviews with Texas attorneys revealed that political considerations and fee limitations result in more concern to preserve relationships within the criminal justice system than is shown in the transitory relationship with the client.

The public defender has greater flexibility to maintain an adversarial position than the private defense attorney. It has also been pointed out that since public defenders must deal with the same prosecutors and judges on a daily basis, they become "coopted" or fight less in one case to get a better deal in another one. This is especially true if they know that a particular judge may be irritated by requests for jury trials (NMAC, 1980: 213). Oaks and Lehman (1970: 166-167) studied lawyers for the poor and noted that either work pressure or the desire to please the judge with whom they work every day may influence public defenders to encourage guilty pleas instead of trials. Sometimes a trial is not in the best interest of a defendant, particularly a minority defendant, since pleading guilty may result in more lenient treatment. Privately retained attorneys may go to trial to demonstrate that they have earned the fees that they accepted. Oaks and Lehman (1970) found that public defenders went for guilty pleas in 75.4 percent of their cases, compared to 53 percent of cases with private counsel and 63.1 percent represented by the Bar Association committee. Among those lawyers who went to trial, public defenders were more successful in obtaining acquittals (55 percent) than private attorneys (20 percent) in bench trials. The reverse was true in jury trials, where there were only 18 percent acquittals by public defenders, compared to 30 percent by private attorneys (ibid.: Table 2).

"Client control" is a concept frequently used in studies of type and quality of defense attorneys for indigent defendants. Since the attorney is responsible for both the strategy and the tactics in the case, under this system, if a client does not accept the attorney's interpretation of the counsel's role, the attorney feels that his reputation may be damaged. Although it can be problematic for any type of defense attorney, this dilemma can be particularly acute for a public defender because he was not chosen by his client (Skolnick, 1967: 65-67). Further, the public defender finds his clientele more distrustful and suspicious than clients of private defense attorneys because the public defender is known to be paid from the same source as the district attorney. Indigent defendants are more numerous, are less able to make bond, are more likely to be inarticulate and unable to aid in their own defense, lack knowledge of constitutional rights, and, as noted, since they have not engaged their own counsel, they tend to be suspicious, hostile, and critical toward their attorney from the beginning of the case (Skolnick, 1967). Despite all these handicaps, Skolnick feels that critics of the public defender fail to consider the socioeconomic differences between the clients of public defenders and those of private attorneys and therefore underestimate the quality of defense provided.

Nagel (1973: 414-415) reported that defendants received more favorable treatment with hired counsel than with provided counsel at all stages of the criminal justice process, except on matters of delay and shortness of prison sentence. He attributed his findings to the inability of public defenders to devote sufficient research and investigation to each case, their youth and inexperience, and the greater likelihood that they would be understaffed and overworked (ibid.: 417). However, as noted above, several years later the National Minority Advisory Council on Criminal Justice (1980) questioned these characteristics of assigned attorneys in minority defendant cases. In contrast, Wheeler and Wheeler (1980: 329) found that in Texas convictions and jail dispositions, regardless of race, appointed counsel were as effective as retained attorneys in felony cases.

The research of Eisenstein and Jacob (1977) offers further support for the work of public defenders. Although their conviction rate was slightly higher than that of private or assigned counsel, the researchers found that public defenders do better for their clients than the other two types of counsel in the receipt of shorter sentences. Eisenstein and Jacob (ibid.: 285) conclude that the "evidence does not support the charge that public defenders neglect their clients or sell their clients short."

More recently, a Maryland study reported by Jendrek (1984) examined the interaction effects between race and other independent variables, including type of lawyer. She hypothesized that race interacts with type of counsel; therefore blacks would be more likely than whites to be treated harshly for using court resources, i.e., court-appointed attorneys (ibid.: 572). Unexpectedly, the prediction was not supported; net of all other variables, court-appointed attorneys obtained shorter sentences for their clients than private attorneys. Jendrek suggests that public defenders' familiarity with court procedures may yield advantages to their clients.

Whereas the bulk of past research on sentencing suggests that having a private attorney in criminal cases affords the defendant the best opportunity for more lenient treatment by the court, an observational court study found that women felons were more favorably treated when represented by public defenders than private attorneys (Mann, 1984). A significant difference was found between the court performances of the two types of legal representation when prison was the final outcome. Only 10 percent of the cases represented by public defenders received prison sentences, whereas 50 percent of the women represented by private attorneys were sentenced to prison. The direction of this finding holds when type of offense is controlled for, although the relationship is no longer significant. An examination of sentencing outcomes by type of legal representation controlling for race revealed that African American women with public defenders were not likely to receive a prison sentence (only 14.3 percent did), but the converse was true when a private attorney was engaged: 53.8 percent of these women were sentenced to prison. On the other hand, white women were not likely to receive prison sentences whatever type of attorney represented them, but there was slightly more likelihood of prison with a private attorney.

Differences between public defenders and assigned counsel have been identified. The aforementioned study by Nagel (1973: 420) found that assigned counsel seemed to exert more effort for their indigent clients, and the more vigorous representation that they provided resulted in more of their clients being released on bail and receiving suspended sentences or probation. In contrast, Casper (1972: 102) is critical of assigned counsel because in some localities a few attorneys dominate the assigned counsel systems, and since their fees are so small, in order to make a living, they have a large turnover of cases. This process precludes their spending much time on any single defendant.

A Missouri study for the American Bar Foundation found that all attorneys, regardless of whether retained, assigned, or public defender, were more successful in representing whites than blacks. "But whether this was because they were consciously less concerned, or because unconscious biases affected their conduct, or because juries discriminated irrespective of the quality of representation, is unknown" (Gerard and Terry, 1970: 437).

Obviously the research on quality of legal defense by type of attorney is currently inconclusive, especially where defense of minorities is concerned. It is also premature to dismiss racial discrimination as the underlying cause of the poor quality of defense for minority defendants. The opportunity to have the best possible defense in criminal cases should be afforded to all indigent defendants, and minorities are disproportionate recipients of "free" counsel. Whether such attorneys provide better legal counsel is not the entire issue. It has been shown that no matter how zealous public defenders may be, they are the most frequently utilized form of indigent defense for minorities, and they are young and inexperienced and lack money for expert witnesses and investigations. Such handicaps too often impede positive court outcomes. Since these limitations are acknowledged, what possible reason other than discrimination (or disinterest, which is almost identical) could explain the disproportionate use of such a system for minority defendants?

THE DEFENDANT'S VIEW OF LAWYERS

> Indigent defendants, in general, have low opinions of public defenders:
> "Did you have a lawyer when you went to court the next day?"
> "No. I had a public defender."
>
> —A Defendant, 1971 (Casper, 1972: 101)

In a Connecticut study of defendants' attitudes toward three types of lawyers, Casper (ibid.: 105) found that in answer to the question "Do you think (your lawyer) was on your side?" only 20.4 percent of the defendants represented by public defenders replied in the affirmative, compared to 100 percent in privately retained cases and 70 percent in legal assistance cases. One of the major complaints was that the typical defendant was granted only five to ten minutes to confer with his public defender attorney. The private lawyer was viewed as giving advice, providing information, and offering suggestions, whereas the public defender was highly distrusted because most defendants studied felt that he or she was trying to tell them what to do.[11] Concern was also expressed because they could not fire their public defender and thus had no control over the matter. Pay and source of income were also critical variables in distrust of the public defender. Since "he gets his money either way," defendants felt that public defenders have no financial incentive for fighting for their clients. Also, "paying a lawyer not only provides some assurance that he is on the defendant's side, but also gives the defendant a sense of leverage over his attorney, a sense that he is in a position of some autonomy" (ibid.: 112). But the most important distrust factor was that the public defender is an employee of the state, and as one felon commented, "They got to be on the state's side in order that they can work for the state" (ibid.: 110).

A later study by Casper that included interviews with 812 indigent male felons in Phoenix, Baltimore, and Detroit showed that defendants "do not trust public defenders to the same extent as private defense attorneys" (Casper, 1978: iii). In fact, there was little trust in assigned counsel, since they are also paid by the state. The majority of those interviewed were minorities (73.7 percent), mostly African American (64 percent); therefore it is conceivable that the low satisfaction with state lawyers expressed reflects predominantly minority opinions.

Despite conflicting evidence about the effectiveness of public defenders and assigned counsel, minority defendants have a higher opinion of and more trust in privately obtained, or hired, counsel. Minority defendants criticize public defender attorneys because they are white, middle-class professionals who they feel have more in common culturally with the prosecutors (and judges) than they have with the majority of indigent defendants, who are minority, poor, and of a different social and economic class from that of the defense attorney (NMAC, 1980: 213).

THE PROSECUTOR

The other legal actor in the adversarial court process is the prosecutor who indicts and tries a criminal defendant. Depending upon the jurisdiction, this individual is variously known as a district attorney, county attorney, state attorney, or U.S. attorney (Inciardi, 1984: 396). Whatever the appellation, he or she has "virtually unlimited authority" to decide who will be prosecuted and "sole discretion" to determine the prosecution charges, since after an arrest is made, prosecutorial discretion begins (Abadinsky, 1987: 319-320). For minorities, the inequities ensuing from this absolute and unrestricted authority center on the increased likelihood of being charged, overcharged, and indicted.

A cross-city comparison of felony case processing, for example, found that one-third of the cases were dropped after filing (Brosi, 1979: 15). Most of the reasons for such case attrition were related to problems with court appearances of witnesses or to insufficient evidence. Although the study did not distinguish the cases by race, postfiling dismissal and nolle prosequi were most evident in jurisdictions with typically high proportions of minority cases: e.g., Los Angeles (76 percent), New Orleans (64 percent), and the District of Columbia (49 percent). Similarly, a California study of reasons for release on felony charges which did include race found that "if we combine the reasons for police and prosecutor release, we see that insufficient evidence accounted for *approximately 95 percent* of those released" (Petersilia, 1983: 25; emphasis added). The discriminatory practice originated with the arresting officers and was compounded further by the prosecutor. These data revealed racial disparity in both filing and release—of those arrested, only 21.2 percent of whites were not charged, compared to 31.5 percent of blacks and 28 percent of Hispanics, leading the researcher to conclude: "These data suggest that blacks and Hispanics in California are more likely than whites to be arrested under circumstances that provide insufficient evidence to support criminal charges" (ibid.: 26).

A more poignant example of the abuse of prosecutorial discretion was seen recently at the highest level of government when the United States attorney general used sex to entrap the African American mayor of the nation's capital. As one reporter observed:

> Never had the federal government stooped so low to make a case. But the mayor was suspected to be a user; the government had millions of dollars and thousands of hours invested in an investigation that would not otherwise result in a conviction; a seduction on videotape would help make valid all the other evidence. . . . (the attorney general) gave the approval of the nation's highest law enforcement official to the sleaziest entrapment yet perpetuated on a suspect. The end, he decided, justified the unprecedented means. (Safire, 1990: A-8)

According to the reporter, while the U.S. attorney general zealously pursued the African American mayor's cocaine case, he simultaneously neglected to investigate the alleged frequent cocaine use of one of his own close friends, who was also his special assistant. There was no sex trap, surveillance, or harassment in that case. This type of sensational incident pales in comparison to the thousands of such inconsistencies faced daily by African American, Asian American, Hispanic, and Native American citizens because of their skin color.

As "an elected official, the local American prosecutor is responsible only to the voters" (Zavitz et al., 1983: 55), and his/her decisions are generally not subject to court review (Brosi, 1979: 11); therefore, the potential influence and pressures of the communities which elect them "may even determine whether they choose to prosecute in a given case" (Reid, 1979: 471). When a society is racist, through public criticism and other pressures, society's views can be appeased and readily acted upon through the office of the prosecutor (Inciardi, 1984: 401).

Aside from influences from the community, prosecutors have been shown to have agendas related to their personal career objectives that demonstrate little attention to justice for minority defendants. As Forst, Lucianovic, and Cox (1978: 65) accurately note, "It is as natural for the prosecutor to assess his own performance by counting convictions as it is for the police to assess their performance by counting arrests." Others point to the link between prosecutors' conviction rates and their professional success and career advancement (Albonetti, 1986; Blumberg, 1967) or to the ideas of not jeopardizing a "good batting average" (Albonetti, 1986: 632) and of prosecutorial "wins" (Uhlman and Walker, 1979: 219). Perhaps, as the American Bar Association observed, the duty of prosecutors to seek justice, and not just convict, has instead become a self-serving game. Another observer has described the practice of law as "a confidence game" (Blumberg, 1967). In such games, African Americans, Hispanics, and other racial minorities are too frequently the losers.

PLEA "BARGAINING"

Although outright dismissal—refusal, nolle prosequi, and dismissal by the prosecutor or judge—is the most common disposition of criminal arrests, the most common disposition once a case is accepted for prosecution is a plea of guilty; such pleas account for almost all convictions (Brosi, 1979: 35). Plea bargains were permitted as far back as the time of the Roman Empire, when they were known as "judicial confessions" (Steinberg, 1984: 585). The American experience in such "bargains," which came to the fore in the late nineteenth century, evolved into the primary method of case resolution today (Sanborn, 1986: 134). Sanborn (ibid.: 111) defines plea negotiation as "the defendant's agreement to plead guilty to a criminal charge in exchange for a charge and/or sentence consideration from the prosecutor and/or judge."

Today, the majority of felony defendants plead guilty to offenses in order to avoid trial and to achieve a lesser charge or a reduced sentence. A negotiated plea by the defendant is the major pawn in the aforementioned "game" played by defense attorneys and prosecutors. The prosecutor, who plays the principal role in the plea bargain, determines the concessions, and in most jurisdictions there are no procedures to control that decision (Inciardi, 1984: 404). Prosecutors can make two types of concessions in negotiating a plea: a reduction of the charges against the defendant, and a sentence recommendation to the judge (Brosi, 1979: 38). In inducing a defendant to plead guilty, the prosecutor is able to select either minor charges or multiple charges if he or she decides to indict in the first place (NMAC, 1980: 209). Overcharging, a prosecutorial practice of initially indicting a defendant with the most serious charge—one that is usually unsustainable—is commonly used as a lever to induce a plea of guilty on a lesser charge in minority cases (ibid.: 210).

The value of reputation and success in prosecutors' careers was mentioned earlier as a motivator for convictions. Prosecutors with "shaky cases may accept guilty pleas for 'lesser included offenses' and save the time and money of a risky trial for the major crime" (Vetter and Silverman, 1986: 500). Since this form of negotiation between the prosecution and the legal defense is also the primary technique for disposing of criminal cases on overcrowded court dockets (NMAC, 1980: 211), the percentage of convictions that result from guilty pleas has been found to range from 68 percent to 100 percent (Brosi, 1979: 35). Zatz (1985: 173), for example, found that 95 percent of the guilty pleas in her sample resulted in convictions.

Others in the criminal justice system also contribute to the plea bargain practice. In the previous chapter we noted that police officers routinely overcharge at arrest; furthermore, "all court personnel, including the accused's own lawyer, tend to be coopted to become agent mediators who help the accused redefine his situation and restructure his perceptions concomitant with a plea of guilty" (Blumberg, 1967: 19-20).

Public defenders prefer the quick disposition involved in the guilty plea because of overwhelming case loads and pressure from judges who wish to dispose of as many of their cases as quickly as they feasibly can (Abadinsky, 1987: 338). Private, hired counsel have different reasons for persuading their clients to plead guilty.

Since most criminal defendants can afford only modest fees, attorneys prefer the dependable income from spending a modest amount of time with a large number of clients rather than the risk of devoting many hours on a few clients who may not be able to pay them. Under the circumstances, private defense counsel is likely to recommend that his or her client plead guilty in exchange for leniency. (Ibid.: 337-338)

In contrast to the legal actors, the accused is rarely involved in direct negotiations and plays only a small role, limited to an acceptance or rejection of the prosecutor's offer (Inciardi, 1984: 404). Recent data from a study of fourteen large jurisdictions (200,000 or more population) found that in order to obtain either a reduced sentence, a dismissal, or a reduction of other charges in the case or other cases, 60 percent of the defendants pled guilty to the *top charge* filed by the prosecutor (Boland and Furst, 1984: 3).

This abrogation of the adversarial process in order to accommodate the justice system is more appalling when "many pleas to reduced charges are not the result of negotiations between the prosecutor and defense counsel, but rather reflect a decision on the part of the prosecutor" made in early felony case-processing stages (ibid.: 1). Pleas are not "negotiated" in some jurisdictions but, after case screening, are presented on a "take-it-or-leave-it" basis to the defense (ibid.: 3). Further, "the innocent are often encouraged to enter a plea of guilt and accept a certain but slight penalty rather than run the risk of a more serious conviction" (Farrell and Swigert, 1978: 446). Under such a process, the defendant surrenders numerous constitutional rights guaranteed by the Fifth and Sixth amendments—the rights to remain silent, to confront witnesses, to be proven guilty beyond a reasonable doubt, and to a trial by jury (Inciardi, 1984: 467). The fear of a determination of guilt and a harsh sentence if they go to trial often convinces minorities to plead to a lesser charge (NMAC, 1980: 211), especially when it is known that more severe penalties are exacted as a result of jury trials (Uhlman and Walker, 1979: 231).

When a defendant makes bail, it seriously handicaps the prosecutor in conducting plea negotiations, since the defendant will experience less pressure to plead guilty (Lizotte, 1978: 572). Earlier, it was pointed out that minority arrestees are less able to make bail. Therefore, it follows that there is more pressure upon incarcerated minorities to plead guilty and thereby obtain release from deplorable county jails. Lizotte (ibid.: 572) observed that in order to dispose quickly of a case, both public defenders and privately hired attorneys "may be less inclined to help their clients make bail."

Clearly, part of defense strategy is often the plea of the defendant. In a study of convicted felons, Kelly (1976) examined guilty pleas by racial or ethnic identity of the defendants (Mexican American, African American, Indian, or white) and found that while the defense plea strategy was more influential in sentence length than race, the "only significant relationships" were found between type of plea and being black, leading Kelly (ibid.: 247) to conclude: "For the present, the influence of defense strategies and racial attitudes does appear operative in determining sentence length, and in striking ways detrimental to the notions of due process and equality of treatment in the system of criminal justice."

A later study of male defendants also focused on the effects of race on negotiated outcomes, but across judicial jurisdictions in six U.S. municipal areas, finding that "nonwhite burglary defendants who plead guilty are 20 percent more
likely to be imprisoned than are their white counterparts" (Humphrey and Fogarty, 1987: 179). This finding was more pronounced for southern jurisdictions.

Despite the fact that "a plea is no bargain" (Uhlman and Walker, 1979: 230),
especially for minorities, in Santobello v. New York (1971),[12] the U.S. Supreme
Court ruled that "plea negotiation is a legitimate means of securing a guilty plea
from a criminal defendant," a decision that widened prosecutorial discretion.
Later, in Bordenkircher v. Hayes (1978),[13] which extended new prosecutorial
license, the four dissenting U.S. Supreme Court justices[14] were critical of the
overcharge, described by the National Minority Advisory Council on Criminal
Justice as among "the most serious aspects of prosecutorial abuse against minorities" (NMAC, 1980: 210). In this Kentucky case, Hayes, the defendant, was
indicted for check forgery. The punishment was two to ten years, since the
amount of the check was $88.30. The "plea bargain" by the prosecutor was an
offer to recommend a five-year prison term for Hayes's guilty plea. Since Hayes
had two prior convictions, if he did not accept the "deal," the prosecutor would
additionally charge him as a habitual criminal, which could result in a life sentence. Hayes refused the deal, was convicted, and received the life sentence. The
appellate judge overturned the sentence, but the U.S. Supreme Court subsequently reversed the appellate decision as "mutually advantageous" to defendants and prosecutors (ibid.: 210). The dissenting justices felt that "prosecutors
should be required to decide the appropriate charge to bring against defendants
before starting plea negotiation" (ibid.; emphasis added).

> Even experienced defendants who know their lawyers have bargained for a sentence
> at the so-called rate can be left with contempt for the incapacity of the criminal
> justice system to accommodate to their sense of what they have done and of what
> they face, with people and circumstances which may never appear in a trial record.
> It is not merely a matter of a defendant's understanding that the deal obtained is a
> normal or even better than normal one. In and outside the court, the defendant's
> sense of justice rests on many levels of awareness that what matters to the defendant
> affects outcomes which extend far beyond the jail door, both in time and in space.
> (Pepinsky, 1991: 2)

Minorities in Court

Information secured most recently by the Bureau of Justice Statistics (BJS) on all
3,235 felony courts in the District of Columbia and the fifty states reveals that
1.5 million felony cases were filed in 1985, and of this number, 69 percent were
disposed of through conviction (Bessette, 1989: 48; Dillingham, 1990: 66). In
1986, an estimated 583,000 offenders were convicted of felonies in state courts;
46 percent of them were sentenced to state prisons, and 21 percent to local jails

(Zack W. Allen, 1989: 1). Among all felons convicted in 1986, 40 percent were black, and about 1 percent were American Indian, Alaska Native, Asian, or Pacific Islander (Langan and Dawson, 1990: 1).[15] At the federal level, between July 1, 1985 and June 30, 1986, 40,740 offenders were convicted, 51 percent of whom were sentenced to prison (Kaplan, 1987: 1). A disproportionate number of these federally and state-sentenced felony offenders were (and continue to be) racial minorities.

As noted in Chapter 4, some of this imbalance can be attributed to discriminatory law enforcement and, as described earlier in this chapter, to pretrial inequities. There is also ample evidence that racial discrimination is an integral component of United States courts and their participants—the courtroom actors, or "repeat players" (Phillips and Ekland-Olson, 1982).

The Courtroom Actors

In addition to the sentencing practices of judges and juries, the courtroom milieu and its occupants contribute to a scenario that does not generally favor minorities. We looked at the roles played by prosecutors and defense attorneys as courtroom actors; we now turn to the parts played by judges and probation officers—other members of the courtroom "workgroup."[16] The arrangement of "repeat players" in courtroom "worksites" has been well established as a "community that responds to organizational concerns" in trial courts (ibid.: 530). The constant interaction between courtroom actors leads to the development of informal relationships that exist inside and outside the courtroom. Whether on the golf links, at the bridge club, or in the course of any other middle- to upper-class socializing, the key "players" in this scenario are socially intertwined at a socioeconomic level far beyond that of the average criminal court defendant, particularly the minority defendant.

THE JUDGE
The most recent available data indicate that of the estimated 583,000 felony cases processed in state courts in 1986, 89 percent of the defendants convicted pleaded guilty, 8 percent were found guilty by juries, and 3 percent were found guilty by judges. In convictions decided by a judge alone, 50 percent resulted in sentences to prison, as compared to 71 percent of the felons convicted by juries and 44 percent of those pleading guilty. A judge's average assigned prison sentence was 103 months, whereas the sentences for defendants convicted by juries averaged 159 months, or twice as long as the 72 months received by felons who pleaded guilty (Gaskins, 1990: 1). On the average, felony defendants in noncapital trials received more severe punishment when they were convicted by juries rather than by judges in bench trials; however, a higher percentage of the jury convictions were for violent offenses (ibid.: 5). Six states permit the jury that convicted to set the sentence in a noncapital case.[17] Arizona, Colorado, Indiana, and Wisconsin allow the jury to make sentencing recommendations to the trial

judge. In the remaining forty states and the District of Columbia, the trial judge has sole responsibility for determining the sentence, including those cases where a defendant's guilty plea has been accepted by the judge (ibid.: 8). These statistics indicate the omnipotence of judges.

The method of selecting judges practically ensures the introduction of class bias into the trial courtroom. Often the selection ignores such characteristics as "professional incompetence, laziness, or intemperance which should disqualify a lawyer from becoming a judge" (Abadinsky, 1987: 313). Inciardi (1984: 391) has noted that those who have judicial authority of the highest order "are not always the most qualified or best trained," and some have no legal training or a college or law degree. Although the criteria for appointment to the highest court in the nation are extremely unassuming, because of "informal" criteria so far all of the nominees have been lawyers. It has been only since 1957 that the Supreme Court has consisted of law school graduates (ibid.: 394): "There are, to be sure, no constitutional or statutory qualifications for serving on the U.S. Supreme Court—there is no age limitation, no requirement that the justices be native-born citizens, nor even the requirement that the justices have a legal background."

The problem of incompetence comes about because trial judges are usually either appointed or elected, and both methods are potentially contaminated by class and/or political influences. If elected, a judge is reflective of the community that put him/her on the ballot and secured that election. If appointed, as is the case in the federal system, the political message is clear: "The appointment of a judge by a chief executive is often a highly partisan act, meaning that only persons who have made political or financial contributions are likely to be chosen. . . . Political considerations, as opposed to selecting the best qualified candidate, are the norm for judicial appointments" (Abadinsky, 1987: 315).

The "merit selection" of judges, also known as the Missouri Plan because it was adopted there initially, offers no better justice than election or appointment, since the method resembles the "key man" method of jury selection. A "blue ribbon" committee (or commission), in this case composed of lawyers, submits a list of candidates for consideration by the governor for judicial appointment. "Known as the ABA Plan or 'merit selection,' it calls for a gubernatorial appointment to be made from a list of nominees drafted by a commission of lawyers, members of the lay electorate, and an incumbent judge. The appointee then serves one or more years, or until the next election, and then must be confirmed by the people in a *plebiscite* (vote of the people)" (Inciardi, 1984: 393-394; emphasis in original).

For the most part, the sentencing studies discussed later in this chapter do not take into consideration either the method of judge selection or the qualifications of the judges selected. The handful of studies that do examine judges suggest quite clearly that influential factors in judicial deliberations have been consistently and erroneously overlooked or ignored. Vetter and Silverman comment accurately that disparities in sentencing among judges may be ascribed to a number of factors: the conflicting goals of criminal justice; the fact that judges are a product of different backgrounds and have different social values; the administrative pressures on the judge; and the influence of community values on the system. Each of these factors structures to some extent the judge's exercise of discretion in sentencing offenders. In addition, it may be suggested that a judge's perception of these factors is dependent on his or her attitudes toward the law, toward a particular crime, or toward a type of offender. (1986: 511)

In Mann's 1981-82 observational study of criminal courts in Fulton County (Atlanta), Georgia, among the many events recorded, interviews and court observations illustrate how personal background can influence a judge's perception and decisions.[18] One Superior Court judge who was observed to make every effort to be fair and impartial commented to Mann that he was "white and middle-class," whereas 95 percent of the defendants before him were black, and he knew "absolutely nothing about their culture." This judge freely admitted his frustration and concern about sentencing blacks about whom he knew little, since he felt that there might be characteristics in their backgrounds of which he was unaware that could be pertinent to their cases. Another Superior Court judge had been the victim of two home burglaries in which cherished silver heirlooms had been stolen. Both prosecutors and public defenders informed Mann that this judge was "death on the mention of 'silver.'" When a black defendant came before him for stealing a watch from a victim's wrist, although the watch was a silver-colored Timex, the prosecutor repeatedly used the adjective "silver" in describing it. As a result, the judge was observed to become visibly upset with each deliberate use of the word and eventually imposed a sentence disproportionate to the seriousness of the offense. Court personnel told Mann that the prosecutor, a white female, had used an unfair tactic to add to her "wins," since everyone knew "silver" was a taboo word for that particular judge.

In an earlier study of the same Georgia criminal courts, Gibson (1978) found no sentencing differences based on race when the data were aggregated, but an examination of the individual judges revealed three sentencing patterns: pro-black, anti-black, and nondiscriminatory:

Anti-black judges are strongly tied to traditional southern culture, concerned about crime, prejudiced against blacks, and relatively punitive in their sentencing philosophies. In addition, they tend to rely more heavily on the defendant's attitude and prior record in making sentencing decisions. Thus, discrimination seems to flow from both the attitudinal predispositions of the judges and the process they employ to make decisions. (Ibid.: 455)

Seven Florida judges examined by Frazier and Bock (1982) were all white, all Democrats, and all born in the South, and with one exception they had obtained their law degrees from the same university. Although the sentencing patterns of the judges varied substantially, the authors attributed the differences to the types of cases individual judges heard, and not to differences in sentencing styles. Such an interpretation seems logical, since the judges' backgrounds were so homogeneous. But Frazier and Bock's findings of judges' tendencies not to sentence women and whites to prison, and to favor them with lenient sentences, "lend some support to claims of discriminatory treatment in the criminal justice system and . . . suggest differential treatment on bases of offenders' traits may occur in the final stages of the sentencing process" (ibid.: 270).

Unfortunately, most studies of the social backgrounds of judges do not assess how a judge's personal values are transposed into court decision-making, but instead are either simple compilations of background characteristics or hypothe-sized and tested relationships between such variables and decision-making pat-terns. The personal characteristics of judges "are generally treated as if they represented relatively stable, precise, and identifiable personal values and ideol-ogies," thereby ignoring the influences of courtroom socialization that might change old values (Grossman, 1967: 345). Closely enmeshed with a judge's social and political background, social values, and attitudes is the formulation of nega-tive stereotypes of minorities that could impact upon court decisions.

Along this line, Bernstein, Kelly, and Doyle (1977) explored the processing of male felons in New York State, 88.5 percent of whom were black or Hispanic, and found that judges significantly dismissed minority defendants charged with assault, judicial actions which "may reflect the lesser value placed on interper-sonal violence when it occurs *among* minority groups" (ibid.: 751; emphasis in original). Such judicial attitudes appear to mirror the stereotype of minorities as typically violent, dangerous, or threatening (Farnworth and Horan, 1980; Zatz, 1984), and the assumption that "nonwhites commit crimes because the non-white subculture accepts such behavior" (Bernstein, Kelly, and Doyle, 1977: 753). Bernstein and her colleagues (ibid.: 753, 754) also noted the effects, though small, of "negative status labels," such as prior criminal record, that defendants bring with them from prior decisions in earlier stages of their deviance processing.

In her three-state study (California, Michigan, and Texas), despite controls for relevant variables influential in sentencing, Petersilia (1985: 28) still found that blacks and Hispanics were more likely to be sentenced to prison, with longer sentences, and less likely to be accorded probation than white felony offenders. The treatment of California Hispanics particularly reflects "racial disparities in sentencing," in spite of the fact that the whites and minorities sampled had almost the same annual crime commission rates once they became involved in crime (ibid.: 30-31). Petersilia (ibid.: 28-29) hypothesizes that judges may be reluctant to send whites to predominantly minority prisons where they might be victimized, or it is possible that judges feel that whites are more capable of rehabilitation than minorities. Obviously, either position could indicate minority stereotyping and/or racial prejudice, that is, reflect views which contradict the expectation that judges should be less racially biased or at least control their biases better than jurors (Johnson, 1985: 1623-1624).

Peremptory challenges that eliminated minority jurors were described earlier as among several points in the criminal processing system at which minority defendants are disadvantaged. Judges also have unique prerogatives in the selection of prospective jurors for criminal trials. During the *voir dire*, the judge questions each prospective juror in open court to uncover biases and has the option to dismiss a person if, in the judge's opinion, a bias is exposed. Further, when there is challenge for cause by a prosecutor or a defense attorney, the judge determines the validity of the challenge (Abadinsky, 1987: 247). The wide discretion encompassed in such determinations is overshadowed only by the potential expression of racial prejudice or cultural biases.

In addition to different backgrounds, potential racial prejudices, and cultural stereotyping, administrative pressures can play an integral role in judges' decisions. Skolnick (1967: 55, 62) observed that judges in California were unhappy when overcharges were so severe as to discourage guilty pleas, noting that because of administrative pressure, a judge will rarely reject a plea of guilty or fail to cooperate with "deals" made by the prosecution and defense.

Responses of trial court administrators to a recent national survey of judges and trial court administrators indicated their belief that judges needed training in stress management (56 percent), management training (58 percent), and time management (57 percent), and that new judges needed training (50 percent). In contrast, only 35 to 45 percent of the judges cited such training needs (Nugent and McEwen, 1988: 5, Exhibit 7). This type of egotistical elitism concerns peoples of color in this nation, since it is generally felt that nonminority judges could greatly benefit from cultural diversity and human relations training.

Most of the studies of the influence and effects of judges' characteristics focus on black and Hispanic defendants, to the neglect of the abysmal circumstances found in Native American courts on Indian reservations. Peak (1989: 403, citing Olney) reports the results of a survey of Native American courts on twenty-three major reservations where the " 'system' of justice usually consisted of the assignment, trial, and sentencing; discovery, hearing, and motions were rarely used." To qualify as a judge, one had only to be a tribal member, at least thirty years of age, and to have no prior felony convictions, and no misdemeanor convictions within a year. Judges served at the pleasure of the tribal council, and many older judges spoke only the native language, often acting as both prosecutor and defender during trials. Admission of hearsay was the norm, and only three courts employed rules of evidence. Under such a system, it is not surprising that today some Native Americans refer to jail as the "home of the braves" (ibid.: 405).

PROBATION OFFICERS

Considered among the most important "players" in the court workgroup, probation officers wield a huge amount of influence over defendants' fates. The evaluation of a defendant recorded in a presentence investigation report (PSR) is usually undertaken by a probation officer or his/her equivalent. Generally this report, which contains recommendations for sentencing from the victim, the prosecutor, and the presentence investigator (Inciardi, 1984: 523), is designed to "assist the court in implementing its mandate to seek individualized justice" (Walsh, 1985: 290). Even if a sentencing recommendation is not accorded a great deal of merit, the report itself can entail serious repercussions for the minority defendant if probation officers exhibit a lack of cultural sensitivity and/or racial prejudice. As Murphy (1988: 179) notes, "Minorities often do not show up well in PSR indicators of recidivism such as family stability and unemployment. As a result, probation officers and parole boards are likely to identify minorities as higher risks, and therefore candidates for harsher sentences, and longer time served."

Most studies of courtroom activity and sentencing emphasize the fact that the majority of judges follow the sentencing recommendations of the probation officers assigned to their court: "In sentencing and in parole decisions, the probation officer's presentence investigation report plays a key role. Judges follow the probation officer's sentencing recommendation in 80 percent of cases, and the report also becomes the heart of the parole board's case summary file" (Cockrell, 1983: 1).

New information from a study by a former fifteen-year probation officer refers to these recommendations as "ceremonial," stating that in about half of the cases, the sentence has already been determined (Rosecrance, 1985: 542). Further, Rosecrance (ibid.: 544, 547) suggests that probation officers not only maintain their credibility with judges, prosecutors, and their probation supervisors by "structuring recommendations compatible with current sentencing concepts and policies," but in their investigation they also selectively seek information which justifies their original, preformed recommendation. According to Rosecrance, the primary objective of a probation department is to avoid controversy. Since judges "favor presentence recommendations that reflect their personal sentencing policies," probation officers are clearly compromised when they tailor their PSRs to accommodate judges (ibid.: 545) .

On the other hand, a carefully designed study by Walsh (1985) finds that probation officers are not "judicial hacks" who "second guess" judges, nor do they perceive themselves as such. After controlling for crime seriousness and prior record and still finding that probation officers' recommendations accounted for 65 percent of the variance in sentence severity, Walsh (ibid.: 301) concludes that probation officers "play an important role, perhaps the major role, in the determination of sentencing outcomes."

Other possible influences on probation officers' decisions center on their movement up the career ladder. Judges exercise substantial control over probation officers' careers, since judicial praise is often the basis for promotion. Further, judicial criticism can halt career advancement when, for example, one or more presiding judges must approve the upward move in a probation department, particularly to an administrative position (Rosecrance, 1985: 545).

There is wide variation in the preparation and skills of probation officers. In some states, untrained high-school graduates work in probation; in others, inexperienced college graduates are recruited, and "probation becomes an entry-level position for employment in the criminal justice field" (Inciardi, 1984: 708).

Many jurisdictions offer low salaries and have large case loads, and limited advancement opportunities exist, with resultant "frustration, dissatisfaction, cynicism, and high staff turnover" that "often results in apathy toward client needs and problems" and "an avoidance of responsibility" (ibid.). It is highly unlikely that minority clients could benefit under such a system.

Race and Noncapital Sentencing

There are substantial differences among the states in their laws and sentencing practices; however, more recent tendencies emphasize mandatory sentencing.[19] Research efforts on this subject document positions which support the notion of differential sentencing because of race, as well as the contrary position that there is no discrimination in sentencing because of racial status. Such mixed and controversial findings continue to make the question of racial discrimination in sentencing inconclusive. In a sense the issue is like being "a little bit pregnant"— one either is or is not—and the implications of the various sentencing practices, those in the past as well as those indicated by recent evidence, continue to suggest racial discrimination in sentencing. The related literature indicates four major approaches to the topic: (1) reviews of early studies;[20] (2) criticisms of the early reviews; (3) recent studies finding no racial discrimination in sentencing (NDT);[21] and (4) recent studies finding discrimination in sentencing (DT).

REVIEWS OF RACE AND SENTENCING STUDIES[22]
The first summary review by Hindelang (1969) was equally divided between four studies that supported racial discrimination in sentencing and four that did not (two were by the same researcher). Hindelang is highly critical of the DT studies that found support for the differential treatment of blacks, for a number of reasons: they utilize data from five southern states, do not control for pertinent nonracial variables, are ten years older than the nondiscrimination studies, and primarily examine homicide. In contrast, the NDT studies took place in two northern states, controlled for other variables such as previous felonies, were more recent, and largely examined property crimes.

In an assessment of the influence of "extralegal" characteristics on criminal sentencing (the dependent variable), Hagan (1974) reviewed twenty studies undertaken between 1928 and 1973 that used race as one of the salient independent variables. Ten of the studies focused on capital punishment, and ten on noncapital cases. Because of his concern with the statistical analyses and lack of controls for other variables, namely type of offense and defendant's prior record, Hagan reanalyzed seventeen of the studies, including nine noncapital cases. When offense was held constant and there was no prior record, the relationship between race and disposition was no longer statistically significant in the noncapital cases. However, when there were previous convictions, the significance was sustained in two of three studies (ibid.: 378). After noting the "weakness" of evidence supporting "unjust discrimination" by the original researchers, Hagan concludes that "while there may be evidence of differential sentencing, knowledge of extra-legal offender characteristics contributes relatively little to our ability to predict judicial dispositions" (ibid.: 379).

Gary Kleck (1981: 785) provides an "exhaustive assessment of all scholarly empirical studies of race and criminal sentencing of adults in the United States published through 1979," finding that the DT was supported in eight studies, the NDT was justified in twenty studies, and there were mixed results in the remaining studies. "Mixed" findings were indicated if one-third to one-half of a study's findings favored the discrimination thesis, for example, where more than one crime or more than one sentencing outcome was studied. Under this method, a determination of NDT could be assigned if there were more instances of nondiscrimination on a particular variable even when there was evidence of bias against black defendants on the same variable (ibid.: 789). Like Hagan, Kleck (ibid.: 792) found that "the more adequate the control for prior record, the less likely it is that a study will produce findings supporting a discrimination hypothesis." Two of the eight DT studies (25 percent), eight of the twelve "mixed" studies (66.7 percent), and thirteen of the twenty NDT studies (65 percent) controlled for prior record. Viewed another way, control for prior record was used in 50 percent of the combined DT and "mixed" research results, whereas in the studies finding nondiscrimination in noncapital sentencing, 65 percent used this control (ibid.: 792, Table 3).

Kleck feels that his examination of racial discrimination in noncapital sentencing in the forty studies contradicts the discrimination thesis in terms of extensive "overt" discrimination against black defendants. However, he also states that "there is evidence of discrimination for a minority of specific jurisdictions, judges, crime types, etc.," and that none of the findings are inconsistent with the possibility of "overt discrimination at earlier stages in the criminal justice process" or with "the assertion of institutional racism or income discrimination in sentencing" (ibid.: 799). Noting that "neither this nor any other study of sentencing per se could reject the hypothesis of institutional racism in sentencing," Kleck suggests that institutional racism is seen in the use of prior record as a basis for sentencing—a practice that results in less favorable outcomes for minority defendants because they are more likely to have prior convictions (ibid.: 784).

A review of fifty-one studies using data "through 1968 and from 1969 on" that included findings on race and sentencing was reported by Hagan and Bumiller in 1983. As both Hagan (1974) and Kleck (1981) found in previous reviews, the earlier studies were less likely to control for offense and prior record (44 percent did) than the studies from 1969 on (76.9 percent did). Studies with such controls were found to have fewer findings of discrimination than those without such controls, but in both time periods discrimination was more frequently found than not. In fact, the studies in the second time period that used controls for offense and record were more apt to find discrimination (50 percent) than those in the first time period (27.3 percent). Without controls, these proportions were 66.6 percent (after 1968) and 78.6 percent (to 1968), respectively (Hagan and Bumiller, 1983: 21). To explain this glaring discrepancy, Hagan and Bumiller suggest that in addition to more sophisticated statistical techniques, researchers also "focused more selectively on those structural and contextual conditions that are most likely to result in racial discrimination" (ibid.).

CRITIQUES OF THE EARLY REVIEWS
Marjorie Zatz (1987) contributes a sage and thoughtful historical analysis of racial/ethnic[23] discrimination in criminal justice processing through the identification of four waves of research on sentencing disparities. Wave I, conducted through the mid-1960s, revealed overt discrimination against minority defendants. In Wave II, the studies reported in the first wave were reanalyzed in the late 1960s and 1970s and criticized for poor research designs and analyses. Wave II studies determined that the early noncapital sentencing discrimination findings resulted from artifacts of research flaws. Wave III research, reported in the 1970s and 1980s, consisted of data collected in the 1960s and 1970s that indicated overt discrimination as well as subtle forms of bias against minority defendants. Subtle prejudice against defendants of color continues to appear in the studies on determinate sentencing that began in the early 1980s and make up Wave IV (ibid.: 69-70).

We will return often to Zatz's informative and fascinating account of these research periods throughout the following sections, but we will now focus on her appraisal of the reanalyses of Wave II. The paramount interpretation during that era was that the relationship between race and sentence outcomes was relatively weak (Hagan and Bumiller, 1983: 32), or that more minorities are harshly sentenced because they are more criminal (e.g., Hindelang, 1978; Wilbanks, 1987), and not because the system is biased.

Zatz points out that in their reanalyses of racial discrimination studies, critics such as Hagan (1974) and Kleck (1981) concluded with two heretofore ignored caveats:

The first was that race might have a cumulative effect by operating *indirectly* through other variables to the disadvantage of minority group members. The second was that race and other extralegal attributes of the offender could *interact* with other factors to influence decision making. . . . These caveats were usually lost on readers who later placed such studies squarely in the "no discrimination found" side of the debate. (Zatz, 1987: 73-74; emphasis in original)

Further, Zatz (ibid.: 74) observes that in Wave III, Hagan himself found racial disparities in his sentencing studies of black and white draft resisters between 1963 and 1976 (Hagan and Bernstein, 1979), and again in cases of black and white New York drug offenders (Peterson and Hagan, 1984). If the data had not been disaggregated, Hagan and Bernstein would not have found racial differences showing black resisters as more likely than white resisters to be imprisoned in 1963-1968 (Hagan and Bumiller, 1983: 24). Although the nonwhite ordinary drug offenders in the second study received shorter sentences than their white counterparts, nonwhite big dealers averaged nineteen months longer than white big dealers because they "were likely to be perceived as inflicting their evil on an already victimized population: nonwhite users" (Peterson and Hagan, 1984: 67).[24]

Kempf and Austin (1986) are even more critical of the Hindelang (1969), Hagan (1974), and Kleck (1981) reviews when they suggest that the reviewers did not carefully examine the studies finding no racial discrimination, and thus they missed the real evidence that demonstrated interaction effects. In contrast to these earlier reviewers, Kempf and Austin more carefully re-evaluated some of the same studies and report that the empirical evidence favors widespread racial disparity more than either Hindelang, Hagan, or Kleck allows: "There were *more* non-Southern studies and non-capital offense studies showing discrimination than the viewers claimed. Further, methodological controls, especially for prior record, did *not* have the claimed effect of eliminating findings of racial bias in studies specified by the reviewers" (Kempf and Austin, 1986: 43; emphasis added).[25]

In an earlier version of their analysis, Kempf and Austin (1983: 6) were particularly concerned with Kleck's classifications of DT and NDT studies because he used "an arbitrary and unusually strict standard for inclusion in the supportive category." The standard Kleck used affirmed discrimination only if one-half of the offenses studied showed racial disparity, thereby suggesting that a rate of discrimination as high as 49 percent could occur by chance alone.

After controlling for both seriousness of offense and prior record, Kempf and Austin (1986) found that more recent noncapital offense data for Pennsylvania provide evidence of racial bias against blacks at every level of jurisdiction (urban, suburban, rural). Urban courts showed the greatest racial disparity in incarceration, and greater sentence lengths were accorded blacks in suburban jurisdictions. Not only is racial discrimination not "a thing of the past," but apparently it is alive and well in the northern state studied.

Barlow (1984: 466) observes that the "accumulated disadvantages" of being black (or a member of any minority) and lower-class may also be influential social considerations in criminal court decisions; further, "prior record is itself a product of *previous* discretionary judgments."

The insistence on the importance of a prior criminal record, or even worse, a prior juvenile record,[26] as a control in studies of sentencing discrimination against minority defendants has attracted a number of critics who claim that even when evidence of prior record accounts for a great deal of the variance in sentencing procedures, this does not exclude race (ibid.). Farrell and Swigert (1978: 445) analyzed the differential treatment of homicide defendants and determined that even when prior record was controlled for, lower-status defendants were still more severely sanctioned. They note that black defendants usually have lower status, acquire lengthier records, and receive harsher dispositions because race "operates in the legal process through its association with occupational prestige" (ibid.). Farrell and Swigert (ibid.: 451) add that prior record, as "partly a product of discretionary treatment, becomes a salient factor in the accumulation of additional convictions," not only directly affecting the disposition but also influencing access to private attorneys and bail—the lack of which also circumscribes court outcomes.[27] Indirect racial discrimination is possible when minority defendants are poor because they are unable to engage private counsel or obtain pretrial release and as a result receive more severe sentences (Spohn, Gruhl, and Welch, 1981-82: 85).

A series of articles based upon a seven-city comparison evaluated the influence of prior record on sentencing decisions (Welch, Gruhl, and Spohn, 1984; Welch and Spohn, 1986; Spohn and Welch, 1987). The researchers note that prior record is typically second in importance to charge in the determination of sentence severity. As a result of their carefully controlled analyses, the authors conclude that prior incarceration is the best criminal history measure, convictions are the second safest control variable, and prior arrests have the weakest effects on sentencing: "When judges decide whether to impose a prison sentence or probation term, any type of prior record apparently tips the scales toward incarceration. . . . In determining the severity (length) of the sentence, on the other hand, judges are influenced by previous prison terms but not by previous arrests or convictions" (Spohn and Welch, 1987: 293-294).

RECENT STUDIES ON RACE AND SENTENCING[28]

So much attention and criticism was directed toward previous research designs of racial discrimination in sentencing that contemporary studies attempt to overcome the earlier errors through the use of longitudinal data sets that permit the examination of persons from arrest through sentencing—for example, Offender-Based Transaction Statistics (OBTS) and the Prosecutor's Management Information System (PROMIS). Unfortunately, these data also have problems, such as selection of the sample studied (*selection bias*) and *specification error,* or the omission of other indirect variables which might affect sentencing outcomes, i.e., type of counsel, pretrial detention, plea vs. trial, and so forth (Pruitt and Wilson, 1983; Zatz, 1987). Even research efforts to define minorities[29] and the subsequent coding of race/ethnicity have serious drawbacks: white-nonwhite designations group all nonwhites together, and white-black dichotomies eliminate other minority groups (Zatz, 1987: 82).

Normally, the standard aggregate method (*additive model*) is used in sentencing studies. This approach tends to conceal racial differences and consequently assumes there is no differentiation in sentencing according to race/ethnicity. Miethe and Moore (1984) indicate that a *race-specific* approach offers a better model, since racial effects may be determined by other social and legal variables. Their application of both models to each stage of criminal processing of a midwestern statewide sample of felony offenders revealed no racial differences at any stage under the additive model, but significant racial differences under the race-specific model. Blacks were found not to receive sentence negotiations and to be allocated longer sentences than whites. The blacks who were most severely sanctioned were profiled as being single, coming from an urban area, having a prior felony record, and committing multiple and serious offenses; "possibly because they are perceived by criminal justice officials as especially 'dangerous' or 'threatening,' single blacks are particularly vulnerable to discriminatory treatment at all pre-sentencing stages" (ibid.: 22).

Kleck (1985) criticizes the methods of summarizing evidence of racial discrimination in sentencing because such summaries, common to textbooks, journal articles, and other professional publications, mislead the nondiscriminating reader. Specifically, Kleck identifies biased, selective citation of previous studies that support one's adopted view; making general assertions while leaving readers to reach their own conclusions; lumping together a variety of studies concerned with different points in the criminal justice process as indicative of race; giving equal credence to studies regardless of methodological strength; and exhibiting "magnanimous neutrality." Kleck (ibid.: 282) defines the latter as claiming that an author's summary reveals findings that are "mixed," "contradictory," or "equally divided pro and con or that no tentative conclusions either way are merited."

It is not the intention here to classify, or even evaluate, the following research efforts to accommodate the concerns of either Kleck or Zatz, but the caveats they propose should be kept in mind. The subtleties and compulsive tenor of Kleck's criticisms of previous summaries of studies showing racial discrimination in sentencing are especially disconcerting when the far-reaching effects of such a sensitive issue as mistreatment of minorities in *any* institutional or organizational analysis are addressed. Even a single verified case of unequal sentencing because of racial status serves to illuminate flaws in the criminal justice system, and indeed ample research demonstrates that there are thousands of such cases—can we dismiss the real world issue of juridical injustice toward minorities because of a lack of the precise methodological rigor demanded by some quantitative researchers?

In an effort to avert some of the problems with methods found in other studies of race and sentencing, Pruitt and Wilson (1983) drew upon longitudinal data in a Milwaukee study of convicted robbers and burglars. Numerous controls were used to overcome the problems of measurement errors (e.g., prior record, if a weapon was used, if there were injuries, the victim-offender relationship), specification errors (e.g., plea vs. trial, ability to post bail, type of attorney), and sample selection bias (use of data over a ten-year period). Although race effects were evident in prison sentences and lengths in the earliest period (1967-1968), no such biases were found in the two later periods of 1971-1972 and 1976-1977.

More recently, Klein, Petersilia, and Turner (1990) analyzed data for 11,553 adult males from urban counties in California who were convicted of assault, robbery, burglary, theft, forgery, or drug crimes. The study, which was a one-year effort funded by the state legislature to evaluate the impact of California's 1977 Determinate Sentencing Act, suggests "some tentative support for racial disparity" even after implementation of the Act (ibid.: 813).[30] In addition to race, a large number of independent variables (prior record, crime characteristics, offender demographics, criminal justice process variables) were included in the multiple regression analysis. Imprisonment and length of prison term were the dependent variables.[31] Although black and Latino offenders were more frequently sentenced to prison for assault and drug offenses, with the exceptions of robbery and drugs, further statistical adjustments revealed that "racial disparity in sentencing does not reflect racial discrimination" (ibid.: 815). Additional statistical manipulations did not diminish the fact that race influenced the probability for imprisonment, especially for Latinos (ibid.: 816).

In a similar study, Petersilia (1983: 32) had found that after conviction, Hispanics and blacks were treated more harshly by the courts than whites. These minority groups were more likely to be sentenced to jail on misdemeanor charges, and to prison if convicted of felonies. Blacks and Hispanics also received longer sentences than whites. In a later report, Petersilia (1985) notes that it is mainly at the sentencing stage that minorities experience the differential treatment, since minority status alone accounted for an additional sentence length of one to seven months, especially in Texas for both blacks and Hispanics, and in California for blacks. Although Michigan also imposed longer sentences, the parole process apparently benefited blacks, who did not serve longer terms than whites. Petersilia suggests that such findings represented discrimination against minorities that apparently diminished after determinate sentencing was initiated in California (Klein, Petersilia, and Turner, 1990). The researchers further state that there is no evidence of racial discrimination in the length of prison term accorded for any of the crimes. But one is left to wonder about the real significance of these minority group sentencing outcomes in California when the study categorized 10 percent of racial/ethnic minorities as white.

Another study using sentencing data after the first year of determinate sentencing in California continued to find that Chicanos were treated differently by the court. Lamenting the paucity of data on Hispanic defendants despite their being the third-largest racial-ethnic group in the criminal justice system, Zatz (1984) found no *overt* racial/ethnic discrimination in sentencing. Observing that the majority of studies routinely stop at this point and report that there is no racial disparity in sentencing, Zatz (ibid.: 156) looks beyond the main effects "to unravel the complex relations between race/ethnicity and criminal sentencing." She concludes that stereotyping of Chicanos as specializing in drug trafficking, and concomitantly as especially dangerous, causes evidence of a prior record to be used more harshly against them than against white or black defendants. This is particularly so because California views prior record as an aggravating factor in such instances and lengthens sentences accordingly. Zatz makes a strong argument against classifying Hispanics as white or nonwhite, a contention we find is also valid for the classification of other minorities such as Asian Americans and Native Americans as white.

A study in two southwest jurisdictions—Tucson, Arizona and El Paso, Texas—found differing results in the official processing of minorities by geographical area. Compared to whites, Hispanic defendants were treated more leniently by the courts in Tucson, an area with only 21 percent Hispanic population. In El Paso, a "border town" where 61 percent of the citizens are Hispanic, Hispanic defendants were less likely to receive pretrial release, were more likely to be convicted, and received harsher sentences after conviction than white defendants charged with the same crimes—burglary and robbery (LaFree, 1985). Although not the primary study focus, blacks were similarly sanctioned in El Paso. LaFree's results tend to corroborate those of an earlier study of the same jurisdictions reported by Holmes and Daudistel (1984), who also compared sentence severity among whites (Anglos), Hispanics (of Mexican origin), and blacks in robbery and burglary convictions and found that blacks and Hispanics were "considerably more likely" to receive a severe sentence than whites. Further, in Arizona, "judges appear to punish inordinately the relatively small number of minority defendants who exercised their right to a jury trial" (ibid.: 273).

Returning to the problems of studies done at different times and employing different research methods, Welch, Spohn, and Gruhl (1985: 68) intimate that since "most of these studies were done in different places, the discrepancies in their findings could indicate that different jurisdictions treat defendants differently." Accordingly, while undertaken in six different states,[32] their study examined convictions and sentences by race with the same methodology, at the same time. Once controls for legal and extralegal variables were introduced, except for Norfolk, Virginia, where blacks were sentenced at a higher rate and received significantly lengthier sentences than whites, Welch, Spohn, and Gruhl found few racial differences in conviction rates or sentence length. However, in all six cities, blacks were sentenced to prison more frequently than whites, and significantly more in cities in the southeast and southwest (El Paso, New Orleans, and Norfolk). This discrimination was especially true for blacks who pled guilty, which suggests that "the harsher treatment of blacks who plead guilty, vis-à-vis whites who plead guilty, is due to the more severe sentence accompanying a given final charge or set of charges against blacks. That is, blacks are incarcerated more often because of discrimination in the sentencing process itself" (ibid.: 75). A significant difference in the likelihood of conviction was the only difference found between Hispanics and whites, and only in El Paso.

Concomitant with the paucity of sentencing studies on Hispanics, there is a dearth of such information on Asian or Native Americans, but what little has been published indicates that Native Americans also face differential treatment by the courts. Hall and Simkus (1975: 200) compared the sentencing of Native Americans and whites in a western state and found that Native Americans were only 3 percent of the state population but 22 percent to 25 percent of the state's inmate population. They noted that stereotypes appeared to play a role in Native Americans' disproportionate sentences, since controlling for the type of offense did not influence the differential outcome. Hall and Simkus (ibid.: 215, 216) describe the Native American's "subjection to the remaining influence of old negative stereotypes as a 'drunken, brawling, (horse) stealing' Indian." Such stereotypes may influence the court's perception of this minority group as a threat to the community, as unable to benefit from rehabilitation, or both.

THE NEW SENTENCING SYSTEMS AND RACISM
The judge usually has the power to decide whether or not an offender will be

sent to prison. A judge can suspend a prison sentence or assign probation and/ or a fine, or select an alternative to incarceration such as requiring the offender to make restitution or perform community service. This discretionary power is now far from absolute. As of January 1983, forty-eight states and the District of Columbia had enacted laws mandating a prison sentence for certain serious offenses or under aggravating circumstances.

State sentencing systems include *indeterminate sentencing,* under which the judge has control over whether a defendant goes to prison and the length of the sentence assigned according to statute, but the time served is determined by a parole board. Within specified boundaries, a judge is permitted to set the length of sentences under *presumptive sentencing,* including adjustments for aggravating and mitigating circumstances; however, the sentence length is set by each offense or offense class. Although the judge sets the type and length of prison sentences under *determinate sentencing,* within statutory limits, parole boards cannot release prisoners before their sentences have ended. *Mandatory prison terms* reflect those prison sentences predetermined by legislative statute after convictions by certain offenders or for certain crimes (Bessette, 1989: 51; Galvin, 1983: 1).

In recent years, mandatory and determinate sentencing practices and the eradication of parole boards have become the primary means of dealing with convicted felons. As Zatz (1987: 78-79) accurately notes, "it was the initiation of a policy change to determinate sentencing that distinguishes research during this period from its predecessors." Such methods were allegedly intended to curb the wide discretion of judges and parole boards, and to reduce racial disparity, but instead, within the new sentencing systems there is still potential for racial discrimination that reflects the fear and sentiments of the larger society.

During the first year of determinate sentencing in California, Zatz (1984) found no *main effects* of race/ethnicity, but *interaction effects* identified subtle disparities associated with factors which legally enhanced or mitigated sentence lengths, especially for Chicanos. Another examination of the effects of determinate and mandatory sentencing from thirty-eight states found that the increase in prison populations was not influenced by these reforms, but "the data suggest that sentencing practices may have become more stringent during the 1970s in states with relatively large black populations concentrated in metropolitan areas" (Carroll and Cornell, 1985: 488).

In a test of the conflict model of incarceration over three recent years, McGarrell (1992) reports rather stable effects of both social structural characteristics and the crime rate over the three time periods examined. McGarrell finds that states with disproportionately large African American populations are more punitive and respond to crime with more incarcerations, findings that "are consistent with models positing institutional racism at the structural level." He adds: "In brief, social structures characterized by racial heterogeneity, at least in terms of percent black in the U.S., incarcerate at higher rates even after holding constant the effects of the violent crime rate. Further, these results hold for a subsample of states excluding those of the deep south" (ibid.: 19).

A former parole board member, Oscar Shade, asks: "But, what if the purpose of current criminal justice reforms is not to equalize and individualize sentences, but rather a means to get black criminals off the streets?" (1982: 63). Shade suggests that a law-and-order backlash led to sentencing reforms and more repressive punishment, particularly for black offenders. Prior to the 1960s, Shade notes that black crime was directed toward other blacks and restricted to the black community, actions society considered "normal" for blacks and appropriately located. However, with media-generated depictions of black protests, riots, and attacks on whites and their properties, these actions "further polarized white attitudes and behaviors towards blacks" (ibid.: 62).

Ironically, according to Blumstein (1984: 130), the change from indeterminate (individual punitive treatment) to determinate (aggregate punitive treatment) sentencing resulted from a union of political left and political right proponents. The left thought that determinate sentences would reduce racial disparity and discrimination by reducing individual discretion. Liberals viewed such discretion as an "abridgement of rights"; radicals saw it as "a repressive expansion of social control" (Zatz, 1987: 79). Being of the "just deserts" or retribution persuasion, the right felt that the existing system was too lenient. In his historical review of sentencing reforms, David Rothman (1983: 643) cites the adoption of a determinate sentencing code in California as an example of this right-left coalition. The ACLU and conservative groups both supported the code initially, but when the final bill inflated the sentencing time frames, the ACLU reversed its position and fought the code, the conservatives who continued to support it won, while the ACLU and, ultimately, minority defendants lost. Donald Cressey (1980: 56) quotes Chief Justice of the U.S. Court of Appeals for the District of Columbia David Bazelon, who warns us that "mandatory incarceration, determinate sentencing, and the like are the first steps in a thousand-mile journey, but in precisely the wrong direction, towards repression."

The Capital Punishment Controversy

One of the most controversial and divisive subjects that inflame public emotions today is the death penalty. Recent public opinion polls show that a majority of the United States population favors capital punishment; the latest Gallup Poll indicates that 79 percent of U.S. citizens favor the death penalty for those convicted of murder (Jamieson and Flanagan, 1989: 223). Even more disconcerting is the finding that 51 percent also support the death penalty for convicted rapists; interestingly, more males (55 percent) than females (48 percent) expressed this opinion. Not surprisingly, nonwhites are twice as likely as whites to oppose capital punishment for murder (28 percent vs. 14 percent). Compared to 1972-1974 polls, when 64 percent of blacks were found to oppose the death penalty, only 31 percent do now. This statistic reflects a trend toward greater approval of capital punishment by blacks that is possibly related to increased social status as well as their higher likelihood of being victimized (Combs and Comer, 1981: 351, 359).

Neely (1978: 270) suggests that the influence of the mass media in a capitalist system might contribute in two ways to these types of opinion. First, it is an advantage to advertisers to use the media "to convince people that they should aspire to live like the upper and middle classes rather than attempt to restructure the social system." And a restructuring to secure equality for peoples of color would be threatening to the dominant group. Second, the mass media present "stereotypes of criminals from minority groups without the balance of deviants from the dominant group. . . . The media are used as instruments to create a generalized criminal mythology which reinforces stereotypic conceptions of criminal types" (ibid.).

The United States, the only Western industrial country in which the state continues to execute its people without restrictions (Bohm, Clark, and Aveni, 1990: 185), has more persons on death row than any other country except Pakistan (Bienen, 1987). One wonders why the United States maintains this bent to kill. Most Western industrial nations which abolished capital punishment did so "because it failed to measure up to evolving standards of decency in Western culture" (Lundy, 1985: 1). In contrast, the enthusiastic American support of state killing is exemplified by those who organize tailgate parties at prisons to cheer when a person is executed. The tenor of such barbarism and the glee exhibited by these celebrants are sadly reminiscent of early lynch mobs and mirror the underlying current of violence directed against racial minorities described previously in Chapter 1. A number of studies addressing the contemporary American attitude toward the death penalty highlight the ignorance and emotionality of the U.S. public (e.g., Bohm, 1987; Finckenauer, 1988). Since most people have little personal experience with murder, murderers, or murder victims, and are not familiar with empirical research on the topic, they rely on politicians, law enforcement officials, and the news media for their information. In a perverted circular sense, politicians purport to rely on public opinion, through polls, for their decisions. However, there are strong indications that the capital punishment stance of politicians may run counter to the public wish.

Although the last juvenile execution in the state of Indiana took place in 1920, according to Hamm (1989), Indiana continues to maintain the lowest minimum execution age (ten years) in the United States and the world's harshest juvenile death penalty code.[33] Hamm's survey of the Indiana General Assembly in 1986 revealed that the typical legislator, "a white male Republican who lives in an urban or suburban area of the state," favored the death penalty for adults (69 percent), and almost half (47 percent) supported capital punishment for juveniles (ibid.: 225-226). However, the position of these legislators does not reflect the will of their constituents, since less than 30 percent of the public supports the execution of juveniles (ibid.: 228).

A second example of egregious political decision-making concerning capital punishment is seen in the reliance of policy makers on erroneously interpreted public opinion surveys. Harris (1986) notes that in its decision to restore the death penalty, the U.S. Supreme Court may have been influenced by state leg-islative actions, which in turn were based on public opinion polls. Harris (ibid.: 437) contests the prevailing view that public support for capital punishment is increasing—polls that simply categorize people as for or against capital pun-ishment have "inadequately measured" and "oversimplified" death penalty sup-port. Of those polled in conjunction with a 1984 Associated Press national poll, Harris reports that only 27 percent felt that the death penalty should be allowed in all murder cases, and 57 percent would permit it only under certain circum-stances (ibid.: 441, Table 1).

While admitting that there is unfairness and discrimination against minorities and the poor in the implementation of the death penalty, the majority of Ameri-cans continue to support this practice and are "prepared to tolerate some degree of injustice" (ibid.: 454). Or as Bohm (1987: 389) puts it, "For many people, attitudes toward the death penalty do not change in light of reasoned persua-sion." Bohm and his colleagues empirically tested this contention in an experi-ment in which college students were presented with forty hours of intensive information on both sides of the death penalty issue. The subjects in the experi-mental group were better informed about the death penalty after exposure to the informational stimulus, whereas the control group hardly changed. Overall, participation in the experiment did not significantly affect or influence five out of six opinions about capital punishment, leading Bohm, Clark, and Aveni (1990: 184) to conclude that "reasoned persuasion only polarizes people further on this issue and contributes to the entrenchment of their generally uninformed opin-ions and of the reasons that support those opinions. Biased assimilation is a likely explanation for the limited influence of the class on all of the reasons in this study except administrative considerations."

Such intolerance is also apparently unaltered by the execution of the inno-cent. In this century, out of 350 cases of innocent people convicted of killings or rapes in the United States, 139 defendants received the death sentence, and 23 of them were executed for crimes they did not commit. More than 40 percent of the executed innocent were black (Ost, 1987). Those who were later proved innocent were originally found guilty as the result of errors made by the police (82), prosecutors (50), or witnesses (193).

U.S. DEATH ROW INMATES

Many sentencing studies have focused on whether the ultimate sentence, death, is disproportionately applied to nonwhites, especially African Americans. The current percentage of minority inmates on the death rows of this nation suggests confirmation for such an argument.

For several decades, the NAACP Legal Defense and Educational Fund (NAACP-LDF) has undertaken the remarkable task of monitoring the capital treatment of African Americans and other racial minorities. The latest available statistics from their resourceful effort (NAACP-LDF, 1992) indicate that among the 2,588 defendants on death row, almost half (48.6 percent) are minorities: African American (38.9 percent), Hispanic American (7.1 percent), Native American (1.8 percent), Asian American (0.73 percent), and unknown (0.50 percent). The federal government now also imposes the death penalty, and four out of six federal death row inhabitants (66.7 percent) are African American (ibid.: 6). An examination of the thirty-five states with capital punishment statutes reveals extraordinary disproportions of racial/ethnic minorities awaiting death. For example, 86.7 percent of the death row inmates in Maryland are minorities, and comparable figures are found in Delaware (71.4 percent), Illinois (69.8 percent), Pennsylvania (63.9 percent), New Jersey (63.6 percent), and Mississippi (61.5 percent).[34] With the exception of Wyoming and New Mexico, where there were no minorities on death row, and Idaho (4.6 percent) and Kentucky (17.9 percent), none of the capital punishment jurisdictions had less than 25 percent minority death row inmates. Yet combined, these racial minority groups are only 20 percent of the U.S. population! Even more astounding is the fact that since the reinstitution of the death penalty in 1976, 45.4 percent of the 152 persons executed have been peoples of color. Almost one-third of these minority defendants (30 percent) had white victims, but not a single white defendant has been executed for killing a racial minority (ibid.: 3) in at least fifty years.[35]

Parallel to the diligent research of the NAACP-LDF, Victor Streib has relentlessly collected statistics on juveniles sentenced to death row.[36] In his latest report, Streib (1991: 4) finds that of the thirty-two juveniles on death row as of October 2, 1991, 56 percent were minorities: 50 percent African American, 6 percent Hispanic. Of particular interest is the fact that 62.5 percent of the black juveniles who committed murder had white victims, as compared to 100 percent of the Hispanic juveniles. In light of the preponderance of blacks killing other blacks today, the disproportionate assignment of capital punishment to blacks who are convicted of killing whites is inexplicable on any reasonable grounds except racial discrimination. Over the past fifty years, empirical research has consistently supported such an assumption.

RACE AND CAPITAL PUNISHMENT

It must be reiterated that the intention here was not to review or include the vast body of literature on capital punishment or race and the death penalty, but merely to highlight the general findings on both sides of the discrimination issue and the major Supreme Court cases delimiting the controversy.[37] From the outset it can be stated unequivocally that reviews of the literature and research on capital punishment reveal a preponderance of increasingly sophisticated data which indicate that racial discrimination has always been a consideration in decisions about whom the state sentences to die.

Excluding illegal lynching, of the prisoners executed under civil authority between 1930 and 1984, 54.6 percent were nonwhites, mostly African Americans; African Americans also accounted for 89.5 percent of the executions for rape[38] during this period (Wolfgang and Riedel, 1973: 123; Aguirre and Baker, 1990: 135). Prior to this time segment, there were also a disproportionate number of black executions. In a study of the application of the death penalty in America since 1800, Agresti and Dembo (1984) document the fact that executions and lynchings of blacks, particularly in the South, were a major factor as late as the early twentieth century. From 1882 to 1899 there were 1,043 lynchings for murder, from 1900 to 1929 there were 750 such lynchings, and 44 lynchings took place between 1930 and 1967. Over this eighty-five-year time frame, 73 percent of these illegal murders were of black persons.

It was not until 1972, in *Furman v. Georgia*,[39] that the U.S. Supreme Court recognized that the death penalty was capriciously and arbitrarily applied. Although the Court, in a close and divided 5-to-4 decision, decided that the death penalty was unconstitutional and constituted cruel and unusual punishment in violation of the Eighth Amendment, it paid little attention to the racial discrimination angle. Consequently, the door was left open for states desiring capital punishment to revamp their statutes and restore the death penalty, since they had the implicit approval of the highest court in the nation. The state of Georgia, in which *Furman* had been decided originally, was the first to enact a new death penalty law. This law was tested in *Gregg v. Georgia*[40] and proclaimed constitutional by the U.S. Supreme Court in 1976. By declaring that capital punishment is not cruel or excessive if it fits the crime, that it is not incongruous with moral standards if juries are willing to impose it, and that retribution provides a sufficient rationale for the death penalty, the Court in *Gregg* tragically confirmed that retribution by itself provided sufficient reason to reinstate capital punishment, and "asserted the belief that the death penalty can be imposed fairly if the sentencing guidelines are carefully followed" (Lundy, 1985: 3).

The guidelines include two trials, one to confirm guilt and a second to decide whether the death penalty should be exacted; a consideration of any mitigating circumstances of the crime and defendant; and, once the death penalty is imposed, an automatic state supreme court review to ascertain whether all criminal legal procedures have been properly met. The Court's conviction that with such guidelines capital punishment would be assigned equitably has been repeatedly and decisively proven wrong by empirical analyses in both the post-*Furman* and post-*Gregg* periods. At issue are problems surrounding the long-standing question of race of defendant and race of victim, prosecution and grand jury indictments, sentences by "death-qualified" juries, and appellate reviews.

PROSECUTION AND INDICTMENT

A previous section ("The Prosecutor") introduced the notion of possible bias by prosecuting attorneys in noncapital sentencing through selective prosecution and overcharging. Research on post-*Furman* capital sentencing reaches the same conclusion, specifically: "The race of the victim appears to be a more important consideration of public prosecutors than is the race of the offender" (Aguirre and Baker, 1990: 143; also see Riedel, 1976). Radelet (1981), for example, collected data on murder defendants in twenty Florida counties, finding that those accused of murdering whites were significantly more likely to be indicted for first-degree murder, and eventually were also more likely to receive the death penalty. Radelet concluded that decisions made by the grand jury and the prosecutor increased the jeopardy of capital punishment through indictment for the most serious homicide charge, but the evidence was not as convincing regarding receipt of the death penalty relative to race.

Along with Georgia, Texas, and Ohio, Florida[41] was again the research site in a study of the arbitrariness of *minority group oppression* and *majority group protection* as functions of capital punishment:

Minority group oppression refers to the selective or disproportionate use of capital punishment against offenders from groups in which members are subjugated, impoverished, or dehumanized by the political, economic, or social conditions they face. Majority group protection refers to the disproportionate use of the death penalty against those whose crimes victimize members, interests, or institutions of the powerful or dominant groups in society. (Bowers and Pierce, 1980: 573)

After demonstrating that earlier studies have found consistently that blacks who kill and killers of whites are more likely to receive death sentences than white killers and those who kill blacks, Bowers and Pierce test several hypotheses on arbitrariness and discrimination in the imposition of the death penalty relative to minority and dominant group statuses.[42] The results corroborate the racial patterning found in the pre-*Furman* research: "Black killers and killers of whites are substantially more likely than others to receive a death sentence in all four states," and "race of victim tends to overshadow race of offender as a basis for differential treatment" (ibid.: 595). The Florida findings were particularly striking: blacks who killed whites were forty times more likely to receive the death penalty than blacks who killed other blacks, and were also five times more likely to be sentenced to death than whites who killed whites.

Using Florida as the exemplar, Bowers and Pierce traced the four offender/victim racial combinations (black/white, white/white, black/black, white/black) through the judicial process and found a consistently clear pattern: "At each stage of the process, race of both offender and victim affects a defendant's chances of moving to the next stage" (ibid.: 608). The finding that the victim's race made a larger difference than the offender's race suggests that the black/white homicides filed by the police as nonfelony killings or suspected felonies were converted into felony killings by prosecutors. This prosecutorial "selective transformation" was augmented by the practice of charging blacks who killed whites with accompanying felonies that subsequently doubled the chance that sentencing authorities would apply aggravating felony findings in such cases.

When Keil and Vito (1989) applied the Barnett scale of homicide severity[43] as a control in their analysis of the application of the Kentucky death penalty, they found that prosecutors were more likely to seek capital punishment for blacks who killed whites, and juries were significantly more likely to sentence such defendants to death. Since Kentucky prosecutors viewed the killing of a white by a black as especially abhorrent, they filed capital charges more often in such a case than they did with any other offender/victim racial combination (ibid.: 527). In fact, no white who killed a black was charged with a capital offense in Kentucky throughout the ten-year study period (1976-1986).

A Georgia case, *McClesky v. Kemp* (1987),[44] based its appeal of the capital sentence of a black man convicted of murdering a white police officer during an armed robbery on a study of 2,484 Georgia homicide cases between 1973 and 1979. The results of what has become known as the *Baldus study*[45] showed that during this time frame, black defendants convicted of killing whites received the death penalty in 22 percent of the cases, whereas capital punishment was the sentence in only 1 percent of the cases involving black offender/black victim convictions (Aguirre and Baker, 1990: 145). Even after Baldus and his colleagues applied 230 nonracial variable controls, killers of whites were still 4.3 times more apt to receive a death sentence than killers of blacks. Of the seven persons executed in Georgia after the 1973 statute, six were black, and all seven of the victims in these cases were white (Murphy, 1988: 181). Furthermore, blacks received capital punishment 1.1 times more frequently than other defendants. These findings formed the basis of the argument in *McClesky*, which was rejected by the U.S. Supreme Court. The majority, again in a 5-to-4 vote, ruled that "McClesky would have to prove direct racial discrimination in his case rather than infer discrimination in Georgia" based on statistical analyses of other Georgia cases (Wilbanks, 1988: 21). Put another way, "defendants are required to prove that they were specifically the target of discrimination" (Keil and Vito, 1989: 513). Warren McClesky was executed September 25, 1991.

A study reported by Heilbrun, Foster, and Golden (1989) attempts to defend the state of Georgia by insisting that evidence of racial bias in capital sentencing is falsely applied to Georgia. Their position is that more aggravating factors are involved in the killing of a white than a black, thus leading to the higher proportion of death-penalty cases for white killers. In their all-male sample of 109 death-penalty murderers (54 blacks, 55 whites) and 134 life-sentence murderers (71 blacks, 63 whites), instead of using legal aggravating factors, Heilbrun and his colleagues measured "dangerousness," a construct of an intelligence test and an antisocial measure.[46] The criteria used for diagnosing "antisociality" from the prisoners' files were "school problems (e.g., truancy, fighting), running away from home, problems with police (e.g., multiple arrests), poor work history, marital difficulties, repeated rage outbursts or fighting (not in school), sex problems (e.g., prostitution, pimping), vagrancy or wanderlust, and repeated lying or use of an alias" (ibid.: 144).[47]

According to the researchers, the combination of low IQ and "antisociality" predicts dangerous criminal behavior. The obvious problems with this potpourri are exacerbated by the project's use of undergraduate and graduate students to collect the data. Since the students were aware of the race of both victims and offenders in the cases, "blind ratings to prevent judgmental bias regarding race or sentence were not obtained" (ibid.: 146). In addition, 22 percent of the death-penalty murderers (DPM) and 6 percent of the life-sentence murderers (LSM) lacked intelligence scores. Nonetheless, Heilbrun, Foster, and Golden make a quantum leap from "dangerousness" to "heinousness," and then state that DPM criminals with white victims are more dangerous than LSM criminals with white victims. On the basis of these questionable measures and equally questionable data collection and results, blacks who kill whites were determined to be more dangerous than whites who kill whites.

Recent studies in Louisiana and New Jersey mirror the numerous findings that Georgia's death penalty methods racially discriminate. When a number of mitigating circumstances were controlled for, M. Dwayne Smith (1987: 283) still found a "pattern of discrimination by race of the victim" in the post-*Furman* period (1977-1982). Louisiana murderers of whites were twice as likely to receive the death penalty as murderers of blacks, especially if the victim was female. In an ongoing New Jersey study, preliminary results reported by Bienen (1987) indicate that white victims accounted for only 34.9 percent of all homicide cases, but such cases were 61.1 percent of all death sentences. In contrast, Hispanics constituted 15.5 percent of all homicide victims, but neither a Hispanic defendant nor any other has received the death penalty for killing a Hispanic.

A review of additional current research reported by Woodworth (1985) also reveals a persistence of race and victim disparity when homicide cases are legally identical. And in Paternoster's (1985: 63) examination of studies addressing the impact of race and victim on capital sentencing, although offender-based racial discrimination is not as consistently found, he concludes that "there is considerable evidence of victim-based discrimination at several points in the processing of potential capital punishment cases." Instead of depending on possible racist attitudes of prosecutors as explanations of their discriminatory capital sentencing behavior, Paternoster speculates that prosecutors may more vigorously seek the death penalty in white-victim cases because of an interest in not wasting resources and in maximizing the possibility of a conviction, particularly in response to the majority (white) support of capital punishment indicated in public opinion polls. Such a stance cannot eliminate the possibility of systemic, institutionalized racism in prosecution offices and grand jury indictment deliberations.

As Gross and Mauro conclude from their in-depth examination of death-penalty sentencing in eight states (Arkansas, Florida, Georgia, Illinois, Mississippi, North Carolina, Oklahoma, and Virginia), in conjunction with a plethora of similar studies, the fact that "their studies and ours all show discrimination in capital sentencing by race of the victim demonstrates that this is a real and robust phenomenon" (1989: 103).

The Gross and Mauro observation was recently verified by a report to the Senate and House committees on the Judiciary by the U.S. General Accounting Office (GAO). After the GAO reviewed fifty-three studies for appropriateness and overall methodological quality, twenty-eight studies representing twenty-three data sets survived the exacting scrutiny. A critique and synthesis of the twenty-eight studies yielded the following evidence of a pattern of racial disparity in death-penalty sentencing after the *Furman* decision:

> In 82 percent of the studies, race of victim was found to influence the likelihood of being charged with capital murder or receiving the death penalty, i.e., those who murdered whites were found to be more likely to be sentenced to death than those

who murdered blacks. This finding was remarkably consistent across data sets, states, data collection methods, and analytic techniques. The finding held for high, medium, and low quality studies.

The race of the victim influence was found in all stages of the criminal justice system process, although there were variations among studies as to whether there was a race of victim influence at specific stages. The evidence for the race of victim influence was stronger for earlier stages of the judicial process (e.g., prosecutorial decision to charge defendant with a capital offense, decision to proceed to trial rather than plea bargain) than in later stages. . . .

Legally relevant variables, such as aggravating circumstances, were influential but did not explain fully the racial disparities researchers found. (GAO, 1990: 5-6)

The proportion of nonwhite offenders sentenced to death nationwide is significantly higher since *Furman,* particularly in the western region of the country (Riedel, 1976).[48] Despite the expressed rationalizations applied to such discriminatory prosecutorial actions, "specific analyses have shown that as long as individual prosecutors continue to have broad-based discretion to select which cases they will try as capital cases, racial discrimination in application of the death penalty will undoubtedly continue" (Aguirre and Baker, 1990: 148).

JURIES AND DEATH SENTENCING

Before *Furman,* juries in murder or rape cases had the power to impose the death penalty, but the existing statutes presented them no direction in making such a decision. Through a number of cases in 1976, the Supreme Court determined that some states avoided the old problems of deciding whether a defendant receives a life or death sentence by statutorily instituting "lists of aggravating and mitigating factors that must be considered in passing judgment" (Gross and Mauro, 1989: 6). But, as Neely (1978: 270) notes, these procedures, confirmed in the *Gregg* decision, provide a defendant protection during the sentencing phase, but not during the course of a trial. No procedural guidelines include mention of stereotypes that might influence the trial process; that is, "stereotypes which remain with jurors throughout the trial will affect the final verdict unless safeguards are implemented to counteract these problems" (ibid.).

Gross and Mauro (1989: 113) introduce another factor related to the minority defendant/nonminority victim circumstance that could influence juries in capital cases when they point out that jurors are more horrified by a murder if they empathize with the victim or identify with a victim similar to themselves, a friend, or a relative. Thus, in cases where the victim is white and the jurors are also white, and the defendant is a minority with whom a juror cannot identify, the horror of the murder is intensified. Consequently, the reaction is to act more punitively toward the killer of a white. Concomitantly, Bowers and Pierce comment:

Where there is animosity, prejudice, and stereotyping along racial lines—resulting, perhaps from long-standing patterns of discrimination and deeply rooted racial attitudes and fears—people will be more shocked and outraged by crimes that victimize members of the dominant racial group, by crimes that are perpetrated by members of the subjugated or subordinated racial group, and especially by killings in which a minority group offender crosses racial boundaries to murder a majority group victim. Moreover, the people who have these attitudes and fears are also the ones who serve as jurors and who elect prosecutors and judges to execute their laws. (1980: 630-631)

Attention and criticism have recently been directed at "death-qualified" juries (see, e.g., Haney, 1980; Lundy, 1985). Such juries, under the guidelines established in *Gregg v. Georgia,* attempted to provide fair trials in capital cases under the bifurcated capital trial system. Jury selection under "death qualification" entails questioning prospective jurors about their attitudes toward the death penalty and excluding those who oppose capital punishment. Unique to death penalty cases, death qualification is the only U.S. judicial method in which jurors are excluded by law based upon their beliefs about a specific legal punishment. In *Witherspoon v. Illinois* (1968),[49] the U.S. Supreme Court ruled that the "death-qualified" jury was unconstitutional. An Illinois court in this case had permitted a sentence of death by a jury where the state had "deliberately and systematically excluded all persons who had any scruples against capital punishment" (Inciardi, 1984: 535). Despite finding in Witherspoon's behalf, the Court did not resolve the problem when it determined that if a prospective juror was opposed to the death penalty, such a viewpoint might affect a determination of guilt or the imposition of the death penalty (Haney, 1980: 514). However, in its 1971 ruling in *McGautha v. California,*[50] the Court found it "quite impossible to say that committing to the untrammeled discretion of the jury the power to pronounce life or death in capital cases is offensive to anything in the Constitution" (Inciardi, 1984: 537). The question of death-qualified juries was still not addressed.

According to Haney (1980), this process is biased because death-qualified juries are unrepresentative of the larger community, are inclined to support the prosecution, and are predisposed to convict, since lengthy discussion by the judge and attorneys prior to jury selection reinforces a suggestion of the defendant's guilt. Haney adds that experimental studies also demonstrate that the acceptance of pro–capital punishment attitudes made subjects more amenable to convict and to recommend the death penalty in hypothetical capital cases (ibid.: 523).

Finally, some opponents of "death-qualified" juries feel that these juries appear to violate the Sixth Amendment right to a jury which represents a cross-section of the community (Lundy, 1985: 5), particularly since they exclude larger numbers of blacks and women, who view the death penalty less favorably than whites or males (Haney, 1980: 517). The fact that blacks are disproportionately charged with capital crimes should surely warrant their representation on death-penalty juries.

APPELLATE REVIEWS

As previously noted, after a capital defendant has been sentenced to death, *Gregg* ensures that the state must provide automatic appellate review of the case as a "safeguard against unguided discretion in the application of the death penalty" (Aguirre and Baker, 1990: 148). To date, there are no empirical indications that the cumulative indications of arbitrariness and discrimination have been corrected through appellate reviews of capital cases. Bowers and Pierce (1980: 625) examined post-*Furman* appellate review cases (through 1977) in Florida (N = 91) and Georgia (N = 90), finding evidence that "the appellate courts have failed to meet their responsibility to remove strong and systematic extralegal influences on the imposition of the death penalty." After the appellate reviews in these states, not much changed in the differential treatment by race of offender and victim as to affirmation or reversal of the death sentence: Florida showed no clear difference, but in Georgia treatment disparities according to race of offender and victim were *accentuated*, not diminished (ibid.: 622)![51]

A Minority View

Substantial evidence gathered at early stages of criminal justice processing prior to sentencing (pretrial) leaves little doubt that there are racial differences and that such differential treatment is generally detrimental to minority defendants (Farnworth and Horan, 1980; Unnever, Frazier, and Henretta, 1980). While it is true that these differences are influenced, in large part, by a lack of money—for example, in making bail and engaging a good attorney (Zatz, 1985: 171)—it is not just a question of resources. Some authors define the disparate situation as a function of class and not race (e.g., Wilbanks, 1987: 86), but "since race and socio-economic status interact in such a complex of ways, the claim that poverty but not race is the operative factor is, in effect, not to say much of any signifi-cance when it is recognized that those who are poor are so often non-white. . . . The impact of the racial variable cannot be isolated so easily from the wealth variable" (Bell, 1973: 184).

Constant reference has been made throughout this book to the fact that society and its agents define and stereotype peoples of color, or apply "symbolic connotations" to them (Zatz, 1985: 172). Zatz notes that if the public views young African Americans as violent, the reaction is to process them quickly and lock them up securely. Similarly, she points out that a form of Hispanic respect for authority of not looking authority figures in the eye may be interpreted by white prosecutors as deceitfulness. Thus, in addition to skin color and other differentiating racial characteristics, demeanor, attitude, and appearance are also measured on the basis of ethnocentric cultural ignorance and ultimately influ-ence pretrial outcomes for minorities. An observation made more than thirty years ago holds true today: "Absolute equality before the law is difficult to realize. The imprecise nature of legal norms allows the values, attitudes, and prejudices of individuals to influence their responses to criminal behavior" (Bul-lock, 1961: 413).

PRETRIAL RELEASE DECISIONS

According to Frazier (1979: 198), little research has addressed defendants' demeanor and appearance, "in spite of the fact that these two personal variables are unequivocal constants between defendants and control agents at all levels." To partially remedy this informational gap, Frazier and his colleagues directly observed first-appearance court hearings in a court serving a six-county Florida jurisdiction. They discovered that "there is a greater chance of receiving a more severe bond disposition for persons who are nonconventional in appearance and less than respectful in demeanor" (ibid.: 201). Compared to 40 percent of defendants who were released on their own recognizance (ROR) because they showed respect and remained quiet in court unless questioned by the judge, only 6 percent of those in custody who appeared "recalcitrant or deceptive" were accorded ROR (ibid.: 203). Respectful demeanor increased the chances of ROR by 35 percent, and conventional appearance raised the probability by 23 percent (Frazier, Bock, and Henretta, 1980: 171). Racial status was not reported in the Frazier study, but the implications of release from custody for minority defendants seem clear.

In the first place, there is no escaping the fact that minorities in custody look "different," not only because of skin color and physiognomy, but also, since most are poor, their speech and manner of dress do not coincide with those of the middle-class and, in many cases, highly educated judges they face. Frazier, Bock, and Henretta (ibid.: 169) defined "nonconventionals" as "those who wore their clothes sloppily, had uncombed or dirty hair, and appeared unkempt." Obviously, African American and Puerto Rican "naturals" or "Afro" hairstyles would be suspect, and the Jamaican dreadlocks and "Frankenstein" haircuts worn by young African Americans today would certainly be looked at with judicial disfavor.

A six-month direct observational study of a North Carolina courtroom reported by Austin offers the following description (1979: 12-13): "The defendant entering the courtroom typically presented a poor image—especially against a backdrop of a white-collar orientation of other court members. More often than not, the accused was shabbily dressed (occasionally having come directly from jail) and basically lacked grooming consistent with other courtroom participants." Most minority defendants undoubtedly meet Austin's description and qualify for Frazier's definition of "nonconventional" appearance—an appearance found not to augur well for release from custody and to result in more severe bond dispositions.

Frazier (1979) reports that married and employed defendants were excused if they were disrespectful because, since they met the definition of conventional and respectable, their court misbehavior was viewed as uncharacteristic. The criteria of employment and/or being conventionally married are not the usual statuses of most minority defendants. This is particularly true of Native, African, and Hispanic Americans, who tend to be young, underemployed or unemployed, and single (see Chapter 1). If, as Frazier suggests, these attributes are viewed so highly by the court that disrespect on the part of employed and

married defendants is overlooked in bond decisions, the lack of either characteristic logically has an opposite effect. Since ties to the community are measured
by such traits, the typical poor and minority defendant commences the criminal
justice process with a preestablished handicap.

Frazier and his colleagues found that demeanor was more influential in the
judge's recognizance decision than, among other legal variables, seriousness of
the offense (Frazier, Bock, and Henretta, 1980: 177). In light of the fact that the
majority of African American defendants feel that it is impossible to get a fair
trial in this country (Bell, 1973), it should not be surprising that they demonstrate evidence of disrespect such as "postures, expressions of disgust, or . . .
smirks and levity" (Frazier, Bock, and Henretta, 1980: 169). Further, in interviews reported by Hall and Simkus (1975), several district court judges repeatedly mentioned that Native American "bad attitudes" were behind their harsher
sentencing decisions. "If the native American offenders tended to expect the
sentencing decision either to be arbitrary or to be subject to racial prejudices,
the presence of undeclared contempt for the court, projected through a bad
attitude, would not be surprising" (ibid.: 219). When judges desire and expect
"passive respectfulness," and are instead met with recalcitrant disdain from minority defendants, a punitive outcome is predictable. By the same token, judges
and other court personnel should be aware that levity is frequently a facade to
cover up anxiety. "Keeping up a front," or being "macho," is also part of the
minority cultural facade. An African American New York judge describes the
situation perfectly:

> Therefore, the ferocious afro, the wearing of beads, teeth, fetish necklaces and the
> like always define a militant black radical. It is of no matter that these outer
> camouflages for the black ego and devotion to retrospective glory are no more than
> a ghetto fashion. These are the stigmata of the enemy to the police.
>
> And even worse, the judges themselves regard such men as dangerous to the
> commonwealth. If a black man is lucky enough to have made bail or be paroled
> while his case pends, his luck may end when his case is called and he summons up
> his compensatory arrogance and bops up to the bench with what the judge inter-
> prets as black insolence. (Wright, 1984: 213)

The consequences of detention status prior to court appearance are mani-
fold and have been detailed elsewhere; however, it is reiterated that pretrial
detention has been found to be the best predictor of a prison disposition
(Bernstein, Kelly, and Doyle, 1977; Wheeler and Wheeler, 1980), possibly because "judges base their sentencing decisions more on characteristics not directly related to the immediate offense or . . . time already served in jail is
viewed as insufficient incarceration" (Kempf and Austin, 1986: 43). If a minority defendant presents a negative (alien) impression because of a cultural hair-
style, the way he or she is dressed, or an unkempt and unclean appearance,
and in addition has an "attitude" in court, positive sentencing chances are
considerably diminished.

JURIES

In an earlier section, the "key man" system of grand jury selection and the selection of jurors in criminal cases demonstrated how the exclusion of minorities from these juries adversely affects defendants of color. As Bell (1973: 191) reminds us, there is a lengthy history of banning African Americans from juries: "The post–Civil War Supreme Court, generally hostile to blacks, had little difficulty holding that a black defendant charged with a crime was entitled to be tried by a jury from which members of his race had not been systematically excluded."

Despite the Supreme Court ruling in *Batson v. Kentucky* (1986) which prohibits prosecutors from using peremptory challenges to exclude African Americans as jurors in cases with African American defendants, it is still possible to exclude eligible minorities from original juror panels and jury lists. Techniques such as key man jury selection and gerrymandering registered voters (Joyner, 1982) may be used to eliminate minorities from voters' rolls. A significant underrepresentation of Mexican Americans on trial juries occurred in Texas because of the key man system and resulted in *Castaneda v. Partida*,[52] in which the Court found "unequal application of the law" (ibid.: 109). In another significant case, *Gomillion v. Lightfoot*,[53] 400 of the 405 black registered voters were gerrymandered out of Tuskegee, Alabama. The finding that no whites were affected by the redistricting led the Court to find intent to discriminate against blacks (ibid.: 108).

The preponderance of research on racial discrimination in jury selection and final jury composition has focused on the exclusion of African Americans, Native Americans, and Hispanic Americans. To a lesser extent, Asian Americans undoubtedly are also underrepresented as jurors in criminal cases in which their counterparts are defendants. Addressing the jury exclusion of African Americans, Johnson finds that

> the same right to "racially similar" jurors should be afforded to Native American and Hispanic defendants; although the empirical evidence concerning prejudice against Native Americans and Hispanics is less extensive, the available evidence does suggest that at least in some parts of the country, stereotypes of these groups are as strong as stereotypes of blacks. Moreover, these stereotypes include some traits relevant to propensity to commit crime, and thus might be expected to affect guilt attribution. . . . Prejudice against Asian Americans appears much less intense and widespread than prejudice against other minority racial groups and, even among the prejudiced, stereotypes of Asian Americans less commonly include propensity to commit crime. (1985: 1696-1697)

To remedy this situation and provide a better representative cross-section of the community on juries, multiple potential sources of racial minorities should include welfare rolls, telephone directories, driver's license lists, utility customer lists, and the like. However, current jury selection practices, even in areas where there are substantial numbers of minorities, result in predominantly white juries who make adverse decisions about minority defendants because of their color and other racial characteristics, thus compounding the problem of unequal justice: "judges send defendants convicted by juries to jail more often and the sentences meted out in jury trials are nearly twice as serious" (Uhlman and Walker, 1979: 231).

McNeely and Pope (1981b: 37-38) describe a number of racial perception studies. One revealed that whites ascribed black stereotypes when viewing pictures of various blacks, and another showed that white simulated jurors significantly voted for convictions when there was juror/victim similarity. Many studies of simulated or "mock" juries report evidence of racial prejudice exhibited by white experimental subjects. Despite the caveat that such studies have a problem of external validity, Johnson's (1985: 1625) extensive and detailed review of this research reveals that "mock jury studies provide the strongest evidence that racial bias frequently affects the determination of guilt." Johnson categorized mock jury experiments by the purpose of the investigation: race and guilt attribution; race and sentencing; and the interaction of race, attractiveness, and blame. Although not as invariable as studies which involved race and guilt determination, the race and sentencing mock juries conjoined with the race and guilt experiments "suggest that for most white subjects, bias against black defendants is based upon subconscious stereotypes" (ibid.: 1637).

Physical attractiveness of plaintiffs in mock civil suits has been found to influence simulated jurors (Stephan and Tully, 1977); therefore it is not surprising to find an association between attractiveness and guilt in simulated criminal cases. Whereas white simulated jurors are less likely to find physically attractive defendants guilty and are more lenient in sentencing them, they "have more trouble distinguishing black faces than white faces and are likely to perceive black faces as less beautiful than white faces" (Johnson, 1985: 1639-1640). After additionally reviewing case studies and conviction and sentencing data, Johnson concludes:

> Although the case studies may be questioned because of their age and limited number, and the conviction and sentencing data are accurately said to suffer from lack of control, their consistency with the results of the mock jury studies bolsters the argument that those results reflect real world phenomena. In turn, the mock jury studies supply what is lacking from the trial data: first, proof that the racial bias reported by the older case studies is not an outdated or freakish phenomenon, but still operates upon many white Americans; and second, evidence that the racial disparities found in court records are not entirely the product of spurious correlations—and may in fact underestimate the bias against black defendants due to the offsetting effects of other variables not controlled for, such as the victim's race. (Ibid.: 1643)

THE COURT "WORKPLACE"
The roles of the participants in the micro-environment of the courtroom throughout the pretrial process greatly influence criminal case outcomes. The main participants—judge, jury, defense, prosecution, and probation officer— have been discussed at some length and will be further described, after a brief

examination of how their work milieu is instrumental in a defendant's fate. Austin's (1979) critical assessment of the ecological arrangement of the courtroom and the relationship "between the bench, the prosecution, and the defense elements of the trial process" was found to work against the defense. Austin identified five features characteristic of Superior Court structure that favor prosecutors to the detriment of the defense: (1) advantageous proximity to the jury; (2) location in a favorable direction of information flow; (3) greater strength in the number of assisting persons, including police officers and other criminal justice agents;[54] (4) more "familiarity with the turf"; and (5) more opportunity to prompt or exert control over witnesses. Such a "partial ethnography" "weights in favor of the prosecution" and suggests that "the adversarial process may be contaminated from the start by the physical structure and social organization of the courtroom" (ibid.: 14).

Early mention was made of the working relationship between prosecutors and public defenders, a system of cooperative interaction that considerably determines a defendant's sentence. Courtroom observations and interviews with court personnel and attorneys led Gertz to conclude that

> extreme sentences may be the result of an uncooperative relationship between the prosecutor and public defender. The length of time needed to dispose of cases is much shorter in team-oriented courts while having many charges dropped is more likely to lead to a lighter sentence in a friendly court atmosphere. . . . Within a cooperative court, it is possible for the defendant to manipulate his environment; however, in inflexible courts, even defendants who are willing to be contrite and passive may not be able to have a significant impact on their ultimate sentence determination. (1980: 51-52)

It was also demonstrated that black defendants receive prison sentences more frequently when they are represented by a court-appointed attorney than when they are represented by private attorneys (Farnworth and Horan, 1980). Yet, we have seen that there is substantial evidence in support of the quality of the legal performance of public defenders, who constitute the largest group of court-appointed legal counsel. One possible explanation for this incongruity is that the political arena (Eisenstein and Jacob, 1977; Gertz, 1980) and physical ecology of the courtroom work setting (Austin, 1979) introduce additional factors that negatively impact minority criminal cases. Minority attorneys and judges are rarely included as meaningful participants in the political, social, and ecological milieu of the courtroom worksetting. Despite the conceivable influence of such exclusions, there is a regrettable dearth of studies addressing these issues.

As is the general case in studies of race and criminal justice processing, little empirical attention has been devoted to the race of a defendant and the race of that defendant's legal representation. Black defendants appear to prefer private attorneys because they are regarded as more efficient (Casper, 1978). Perhaps this is because a "consistent anti-black defense attorney bias" has been noted (Johnson, 1985: 1635). Johnson (ibid.) introduces the idea of indirect racial bias that may affect a minority defendant's guilt attribution because of having black legal representation: "the black defendant is more likely to be disadvantaged by bias against clients of black attorneys," or, in other words, face "courthouse racism" (Bell, 1973: 196). Since blacks are more likely to be represented by black lawyers, "it does not take a scholar to come to the conclusion that a Black defendant represented by a Black attorney could be the victim of increased racism in the court process. There are few guarantees that the racism that affects the defendant will not also affect the defendant and his Black attorney in court" (Jones, 1978: 265).

The greatest single problem of Native Americans on reservations is the lack of defense counsel for indigent defendants. U.S. Indian lawyers are extremely rare, numbering less than one hundred (Peak, 1989: 403). It was only fifty-six years ago (1936) that African Americans were first admitted to all-white law schools, and today only 2 percent of the nation's attorneys are African American (Wildeman and Sanchez, 1990). This paucity in minority attorneys undoubtedly applies to Hispanic and Asian American legal populations. Obviously, since the majority of criminal attorneys are Euro-American, defendants of color have little choice as to who will represent them in court. There is reason to believe that blacks do not want to go to white lawyers because, "rightly or wrongly, they more often do not trust a white lawyer"; moreover, "in the case of many black Americans who go to white lawyers, there is a good chance that they may literally not be understood, because the lawyer and the client come from such different and diverse backgrounds and talk such different language. Communication becomes difficult, problematic, even hopeless" (ibid.: 6). There is little doubt that such feelings are valid for other racial minorities, especially Hispanic Americans and others who face language as well as cultural barriers.

The odds that a defendant of color will come before a judge of that same color are fairly slim. Nationally, there are only about five hundred African American judges among the thirteen thousand judges on benches today (Simpson, 1988). Similar figures for Native, Asian, and Hispanic Americans are more disparate. In previous sections, a number of questions were raised concerning judicial decisions in criminal cases involving minorities; however, two salient questions remain unanswered: (1) Does the social background of a judge make a difference in sentencing outcomes for minority defendants? and (2) Does the possession of racial minority status by a judge make a difference in sentencing outcomes for minority defendants?

A few studies generally respond to the first question negatively, finding judges to be racially impartial, although these researchers hasten to add that more research is needed on judicial backgrounds (see, e.g., Gibson, 1978; Frazier and Bock, 1982; Myers, 1988). The two factors generally determined to account for such findings are the aggregation of data across courts (a "canceling-out effect")[55] and the homogeneity of jurists' backgrounds. However, an observation Grossman (1967: 335) noted twenty-five years ago still holds true today: researchers "have stopped short of providing an adequate description of the core segment of the judicial decision-making process—that portion of the process in which personal values inputs allegedly derived from background experiences are translated into policy outcomes." Grossman added two other potentially significant factors:

> No distinction is made between background "characteristics" and actual individual experiences, although common sense and common knowledge warn us of the dangers in such reasoning. And . . . some fail to make sufficient allowance for the impact of on-the-bench socialization processes. Old values frequently change, and prior experiences frequently take on new meanings in the light of newer involvements. (Ibid.: 335-336)

Myers (1988: 668) admits there is a more complex relationship between a judge's sentencing decision and his background (remember the "silver" watch?). Further, she voices concern about the influence of the offender's background, over and above the offense, in comparison to the judge's social background, an apprehensiveness that lends some support to the argument of judges' (and other criminal justice agents') ethnocentricity and ignorance of minority cultural differences stressed throughout this book. On the other hand, Frazier and Bock (1982: 270) "call into question both the existence of individual judge effects on criminal sentencing and explanations for high agreement between probation officer recommendations and judicial decisions." Their concern is with "justice subcultures" (see also Roberts, 1984), a concept that encompasses what Grossman (1967: 336) describes as "on-the-bench socialization processes" as well as those influences described above as integral parts of the courtroom worksetting.

In regard to the second question concerning minority jurists, common sense would suggest that a minority jurist who had also experienced discrimination and racism would empathize with the minority defendant standing before him/her and accordingly show leniency. For example, a black judge had faced institutional racism in his attempt to enter and attend "America's premier law schools" (Bell, 1973: 194). As a law student he found that there were faculty who felt he was "incapable of thinking"; therefore he had to be "twice or thrice as good as others," and his work had to be "flawless to be considered competitive, and even then it is not good enough" (Wildeman and Sanchez, 1990: 8). He encountered racial bias in his bar exams—instruments used to limit the number of blacks practicing law (Bell, 1973: 199). He found professional opportunities sharply restricted and important social and professional contacts limited, particularly clerkships and employment by major white law firms (Uhlman, 1979: 7). If, after overcoming all of these obstacles that serve as "an effective screening mechanism to circumscribe black participation in the legal system" (ibid.: 8), the black judge is elected to the bench (the usual method, appointment, is rare for a racial minority), once there he or she again faces discrimination, resistance, and isolation as one of the few or probably the lone minority jurist.

Such judges might be expected to empathize with a minority defendant, but their feelings and background experiences would not interfere with their judicial role! One of the few comparisons of white and black judges and defendants concluded that "earlier speculation about systematic behavioral differences between the black and white judicial elite remains essentially unsubstantiated" (ibid.: 72). Uhlman found that black judges, like white judges, tended to convict and sentence black defendants more frequently and more severely than white defendants in the single urban trial court studied. After ruling out reverse discrimination, conservative black elitism, and pressures to conform to a dominant white elite pattern, Uhlman (ibid.: 95) attributed the sanctioning anomaly to the prior criminal records of black defendants as "a reasonable but untested alternative." It is interesting that so thorough an examination was made of the reasons why black jurists reached impartial decisions when they were just doing their jobs. If studies of race and sentencing applied such close scrutiny to the deliberations of white judges hearing minority criminal cases, more accurate assessments of the extent of institutional racism might be revealed. Overall, Uhlman determined that the trial court he studied may not have contained widespread racial discrimination, a conclusion supported by a few of the black presiding judges. In noting that the trial court is just one stage in the case-disposition process, Uhlman (ibid.) cautions that "while blatant discrimination may not be evident, racism cannot be exclusively ruled out in this court or elsewhere in the city's criminal justice system."

More recently, Welch, Combs, and Gruhl (1988) analyzed black and white trial judges' decisions to incarcerate in "Metro City," a large northeastern community. After controlling for seriousness of charge and prior record (which Uhlman did not do), they found that

> black judges are more evenhanded in their treatment of black and white defendants than are white judges, who tend to treat white defendants more leniently. In overall sentence severity, where little racial discrimination has been found, white judges treat black and white defendants equally severely, while black judges treat black defendants more leniently than white defendants. While the impact of black judges is, therefore, somewhat mixed, in the crucial decision to incarcerate, having more black judges increases equality of treatment. (Ibid.: 126)

In a call for a humanistic criminology, Friedrichs (1982: 211) stresses that more attention should be directed toward "abuse and misuse of discretionary decision-making in the criminal justice system (especially discrimination re minorities)." Even more reflective of the minority view of this book, another humanist criminologist, Hal Pepinsky, is critical of conventional social research as a science of conformity when he states,

> For some time, I have had the intuition that most social research represents a social death wish. The millennial wish of multivariate analysts in particular seem to suck all the unexplained variance out of human behavior. It remains unacknowledged that success in this endeavor would be a demonstration that human beings are preprogrammed robots. In Darwinian terms, this use of statistics builds knowledge of how to decrease the life expectancy of the human race. Multivariate analysis becomes a deadly weapon when the utopian vision of the analyst is to make depen-

dent behavior or status march right down the line specified by antecedent variables, especially when the antecedent variables like sex, age and race are largely impervious to social manipulation. (1982: 233)

This somewhat lengthy chapter is an attempt to present an "objective" view, based on the extant research literature, of the criminal justice processes and practices that are daily experiences in the lives of peoples of color in this country. Almost every member of a racial minority either has been mistreated by our "justice" system or has a relative, an in-law, an acquaintance, or a friend who has endured the experience. In this chapter it was particularly frustrating to cite study after study on pretrial and sentencing processes undertaken and reported by nonminority researchers who probably have no relatives, in-laws, acquaintances, or friends who are peoples of color.[56] This frustration is directly associated with the seriousness of the outcomes attached—racial minority suspects disproportionately become defendants and as defendants are disproportionately sent to prison or disproportionately executed. These are facts most peoples of color are aware of and that most criminologists and other social scientists should be aware of. How many studies will it take to achieve the necessary and appropriate policies to alleviate the disparate treatment of U.S. racial minorities? If only one Native, Hispanic, Asian, or African American is imprisoned, shot, gassed, electrocuted, hanged, or lethally injected because of a racist system, of what use are studies after the fact? To paraphrase Pepinsky, the humanness of this issue has been empirically sucked dry; it is time to restore it through ameliorative action.

6

Warehousing Minorities

CORRECTIONS

no dammit, no!
no more chains
no more cringing in fear
no more bowing
        nor shuffling about
We, too must live . . .

        —ricardo sánchez

A record number of persons are being held in United States jails, and our state prisons are bulging with so many inmates that some states are forced by federal court order to release them before their time is served. At the end of 1989, 4,054,000 persons, or 2.2 percent of the U.S. adult population, were under correctional supervision of some kind: jail, prison, probation, or parole (Dillingham, 1991). By 1990, over 1,000,000 persons were in the nation's prisons and jails (Stephan and Jankowski, 1991; Cohen, 1991). A disproportionate number of those persons are racial minorities.

In 1986, 50.3 percent of state prison inmates were persons of color, as were 32.7 percent of the prisoners under federal correctional authority (Jamieson and Flanagan, 1989: 620). Minority prisoners in the United States on December 31, 1987 accounted for 48.1 percent of all persons incarcerated under state and federal jurisdiction (ibid.). More recently, the 1990 Sentencing Project finds that "the extended reach of the criminal justice system has been far from uniform in its effects upon different segments of the population. . . . And, as has been true historically, but even more so now, the criminal justice system disproportionately engages minorities and the poor" (Mauer, 1990: 1). Even more startling, this national study found that "the number of *young* Black men under the control of the criminal justice system—609,690—is greater than the total number of Black men of *all ages* enrolled in college—436,000 as of 1986. For white males, the comparable figures are 4,600,000 total in higher education and 1,054,508 ages 20-29 in the criminal justice system" (ibid.: 3; emphasis in the original). Mauer (ibid.: 3) further qualifies these dire statistics by stating that they understate the numbers of black males twenty to twenty-nine years old under criminal justice control, since the reported rates are for a single day, and for a total year the figures would be considerably higher than one in four.

A quarter of a century ago, in 1967, Abraham Blumberg wrote on the "issues and ironies" of criminal justice, noting:

> So acute has the fear of crime and disorder become that many Americans would welcome the savage repression of some version of a garrison state, and the scrapping of the Bill of Rights, if that would free them from the problems of living in a modern mass society. A sense of alienation and mistrust of government has led to the stockpiling of handguns and rifles, and an ominously growing vigilantism. Irresponsible politicians exploit this pervasive sense of insecurity. Like ruthless hawkers of some worthless nostrum, they have effectively sold the notion that the social ills and political conflicts that beset us can be cured through the destruction of constitutional liberty. The mass of Americans is deceived by the law and order ideology, for it promises that one can achieve "peace of mind" and the "good life" without addressing such underlying issues as poverty, racial conflict, education, health care, population pressures, and the allocation of resources. (1979: 358)

It is the public's fear of crime that has led increasingly to the demand for arrests and incarceration of those who break the law. The police response has been a concentration of manpower in high-crime, inner-city ghettos and barrios (Hatchett, 1990: 14). As a result of the purposively directed and intensive surveillance of these areas, thousands of peoples of color are arrested and subsequently end up under the yoke of correctional authority.

In a state-by-state study of 1973 incarceration rates, Christianson (1980: 617) found that thirty-eight states imprisoned blacks at more than three times the rate for whites. Addressing the "severe disproportionality" between blacks and whites in prison populations, Blumstein (1982: 1260) found that in 1979, black males in their twenties experienced a state prison incarceration rate that was twenty-five times that of the total population. The black/white ratio for males ages twenty to twenty-nine was 7.2 to 1. Not quite a dozen years later, an examination of the "new generation of adults," or those persons in the age group twenty to twenty-nine, revealed that on any given day, almost one in four black men (23 percent) and one in ten Hispanic men (10.4 percent) are in jail, in prison, on probation, or on parole, compared to one in sixteen white men (6.2 percent) in this age group (Mauer, 1990: 3).

Even the most casual observer would find these unequal black incarceration rates alarming. But even more shocking is the rarely noted fact that such disproportionate rates have existed throughout a major portion of United States history, and not only for blacks but also for other racial minorities. In "Our Black Prisons," Christianson (1981: 373) observes that in the same year the state of New York legislated the emancipation of slaves (1796), it created the first state prison; therefore, "the state prison as we know it arose in part as a replacement for slavery, in order to control newly freed blacks." A longitudinal analysis of "historiogeographic" and other data from North Carolina explored the relationship between race and imprisonment over a period of one hundred years (Hawkins, 1985a). Among the fascinating but sobering facts unearthed are statistics showing the differential incarceration of blacks from the inception of the North Carolina prison system in 1870 until 1980. When its first state-operated prison opened in 1870, the percentage of blacks in the prison population was 78 percent; by 1878 this proportion had increased to 90 percent, dropping to 51 percent in 1930. The black-white ratio in North Carolina was highest in 1880 at 17 to 1, and by 1980 the ratio was 4.2 to 1 (ibid.: 191, 195).

A social historian, Clare McKanna, examined the San Quentin prison registers for the years 1851 to 1880. Her representative sample revealed that Hispanics were the largest minority group (13 percent) in the prison population at that time and were "greatly overrepresented compared to their numbers in society, particularly after 1850" (1985: 478). The Chinese, who "encountered difficulty in courts because of language problems and intense prejudice," constituted about 12 percent of the prison population (ibid.: 479). Although Chinese were only about 8 percent of the state population, they were the second-largest imprisoned minority group.

In sum, the massive overrepresentation of racial minorities in American prisons is not a new phenomenon, but has existed throughout much of the country's history. According to Dehais, racial differences in incarceration are highly significant, "not only because they imply that the criminal justice system *may* be operating unfairly, but also because they raise fundamental questions concerning the legitimacy of a social order which relies on imprisonment to control its minority group population" (1983: 4; emphasis in original).

Minority Inmate Populations

JAIL INMATES

Since 1983, the number of convicted inmates—those awaiting sentencing, serving a sentence, or returned to jail because of probation or parole violations—has increased 48 percent, and today they account for almost half of the adults in jails (Kline, 1990). Although the average daily population for the year ending June 29, 1990 was 408,075, there were nearly twenty million admissions and releases from local jails in that year (Stephan and Jankowski, 1991). The 1990 annual census of jails recorded 51 percent white jail inmates and 49 percent nonwhite: 47 percent black, 2 percent other races (Native Americans, Aleuts, Asians, and Pacific Islanders), and 14 percent Hispanic as compared to non-Hispanic (ibid.: 2). Over a one-year period (1988-1989), the number of jailed blacks increased 6 percent, and the number of inmates of other races doubled from 1 to 2 percent (Kline, 1990). In light of the fact that minorities are 20 percent of the U.S. population, the racial disproportionality of these figures is obvious.

STATE PRISON INMATES

The Survey of Inmates of State Correctional Facilities is conducted every five to seven years; thus, the latest results reported in 1988 represent the findings of the 1986 survey. Like the U.S. jail data, the statistics concerning minority prison inmates in 1986 paint a dismal picture: of the 450,416 inmates in state correctional facilities, the percentages of nonwhites were: black, 46.9 percent; other races, 3.4 percent; and Hispanic, 12.6 percent.[1] The remaining 49.7 percent of white inmates is a seriously questionable figure, since such statistics often include large percentages of Hispanics who are "classified" as white.

State prison populations, which totaled 735,020 inmates at midyear 1991 (Greenfeld, 1992: 1), revealed stability in the numbers for African Americans (47 percent) and persons of other races—American Indian, Asian, Pacific Islander, and Alaska Native—(3 percent) but other dramatic changes in the racial and ethnic composition over the past seventeen years (from 1974 to 1990): a decline in the percentage of white non-Hispanics (45 percent to 38 percent), and a significant increase in the percentage of Hispanic American state prisoners (from 6 percent to more than 12 percent) over this time period (ibid.: 13).

Dehais (1983) makes a convincing argument that imprisoned persons of Spanish origin should be considered a separate racial, not ethnic, category. Hispanics are treated in the same discriminatory fashion as racial minority groups in this country, and they also receive differential treatment in the criminal justice system. This confounding of white and Hispanic, Dehais notes, "effectively results in counting almost 88 percent of the more than 25,000 Spanish state prisoners as if they were white and about ten percent as if they were black under the usual reporting procedures" (ibid.: 15). One consequence of such classifications, Dehais adds, is the artificial inflation of the white incarceration rate, which obfuscates the real difference between blacks and whites, and consequently underestimates the genuine disproportionality. The National Minority Advisory Council on Criminal Justice (1980: 240) estimates that if Hispanics were not enumerated as whites, this minority subgroup would represent as much as 20 to 25 percent of the inmate population, which together with African Americans, Native Americans, and Asian Americans would constitute two-thirds of the prison population.

Other sociodemographic characteristics of the 1988 state prison survey indicate that the majority of inmates were males (95.6 percent), 93 percent were under forty-five years of age (with most, 45.7 percent, between twenty-five and thirty-four), 53.7 percent had never been married, and 61.6 percent had fewer than twelve years of education (Innes, 1988: 3, Table 1). A profile of a marginal, relatively young, minority male clearly emerges from these descriptors.

About 35 percent of the inmates in the survey admitted that they were under the influence of a drug at the time of their offense, and 43 percent said they had used drugs daily in the month before the offense. Another 54 percent reported the influence of drugs and/or alcohol at the time of the offense. Whereas 6 percent of state prisoners in 1979 were drug offenders, by 1991 an estimated 22 percent of inmates were imprisoned for drug offenses (Greenfeld, 1992: 14). The "war on drugs," enthusiastically enforced by former "drug czar" William Bennett, will undoubtedly be continued by the new czar, former Florida governor Martinez, and predictably will result in higher numbers of black and Hispanic incarcerations, since the "war" is aimed primarily at "crack" (cocaine), a drug most frequently used by poor members of these racial subgroups (Mauer, 1990: 5).[2] A North Carolina study of race and type of crime interaction found that while black and white major drug dealers were both likely to receive prison sentences after convictions for selling large quantities of drugs, blacks who were convicted for minor drug sales and for major and minor drug possession were more likely to go to prison than similarly convicted whites (Hawkins, 1986b: 261). Hawkins concludes that the relationship between race and type of crime is "an important dimension of the racial disproportionality of the prison population" (ibid.).

FEDERAL PRISON INMATES

The federal prison system also reflects a burgeoning correctional population, thereby giving more credence to the observation that "the rich get richer and the poor get prison" (Reiman, 1990); or, to be more specific, the minority poor get prison. The federal prison population at the end of 1987 included a predominance (59.5 percent) of peoples of color (Hester, 1989). According to the latest available statistics, by the end of 1989, out of a total of 59,104 inmates where race was known, there were 39,483 whites (66.8 percent), 18,092 blacks (30.6 percent), 1,065 Native Americans or Alaska Natives (1.8 percent), and 464 Asians or Pacific Islanders (0.8 percent) (Dillingham, 1991: 69). The 15,692 Hispanic (versus non-Hispanic) prisoners on December 31, 1989 were 26.6 percent of total federal inmates (ibid.: 72).[3]

Problems and Effects of Minority Correctional Warehousing

In a recent critique of current correctional practices, McShane and Williams (1989: 569) take the field of corrections to task for its dearth of creative ideas, which these critics feel makes the profession "comparatively boring and unrewarding." They are particularly concerned about the articulation of meaningful goals; for example, they view the response to overcrowding as an emphasis on "speed and economy of construction," which is "reactionary," and not "creative and proactive" like the "architectural invention" of earlier eras (ibid.: 572). Noting that prisons are criminogenic because they provide inmates with an abundance of bad influences, McShane and Williams (ibid.: 573) challenge the promotion of "efficient and economical construction of human warehouses," and suggest "alternative ways to sentence so that there is minimal criminogenic effect."

OVERCROWDING

The standards set by the American Correctional Association (ACA) specify that inmates held in single-occupancy cells require an area of at least sixty square feet

(6 x 10 feet), and that inmates should not spend more than ten hours per day in the cell. For multiple-occupancy cells, the minimum standard recommended is fifty square feet per inmate (Zavitz, 1988: 108). Nonetheless, in 1989, thirty-nine states, the District of Columbia, Puerto Rico, and the Virgin Islands were under court order or a judicial consent decree because of overcrowding and other conditions of confinement that involve equal protection and other due process issues. Of most concern is the guarantee against cruel and unusual punishment in the Eighth Amendment to the U.S. Constitution (Skinner, 1990: 18). In a recent survey of wardens and state corrections commissioners, 62 percent of the wardens and three-fourths of the commissioners ranked prison crowding as the number one problem of the criminal justice system. Because of existing confinement conditions, 64 percent of the commissioners and 46 percent of the wardens reported that they were under court orders (Grieser, 1988).

Research on crowding among animal populations has shown that in the competition for space, the interaction among some animals can have adverse effects. As psychology professor Jonathan Freedman (1975: 20) writes in *Crowding and Behavior,* "the evidence is quite convincing that high density produces an overall breakdown in normal social behavior." Studies in rat populations appear to indicate that the increased aggressiveness and general social collapse resulting from overcrowding are caused by nervousness and overexcitement. As Freedman (ibid.: 37) notes, "The phenomenon also appears to be caused primarily by the intensified social interaction and in particular by the competition for a scarce resource." The scarce resource that leads to severe pathology among rats and mice is space.

On the human side, ecological analyses of crime and crime rates yield mixed results; nonetheless, the available evidence seems to indicate that *density,* a physical phenomenon, has few, if any, positive effects on crime rates, while *crowding,* a psychological phenomenon, demonstrates a positive relationship with crime as a result of overcrowding (Harries, 1980). In their study of prison crowding, psychologists Cox, Paulus, and McCain (1984: 1148) reserve the word "crowding" for "levels of density that are aversive." Under such conditions there are a large number of people (high social density) in a low amount of space (spatial density).

Cox, Paulus, and McCain studied state prison systems in Illinois, Mississippi, Oklahoma, and Texas, each of which contained several types of housing within the facility. In line with the animal research findings, they also found social interaction to be a major component in the increased pathology associated with prison crowding and concluded that "the primary causes of negative effects related to crowding may be due to cognitive strain, anxiety or fear, and frustration intrinsic to most social interactions in crowded settings" (ibid.). The negative effects of prison crowding related to cognitive load are a consequence of difficulty in making decisions; e.g., the cognitive load would be more elevated in a six-person cell compared to a three-person cell of the same size because of the larger number of interactions (ibid.: 1158-1159).

In contrast to the findings of Cox and his colleagues, the 1984 Prison Census indicates that the *kinds* of inmates housed in state prisons may be more influential than population density in understanding differences in inmate death, assault, and disturbance rates (Innes, 1987). Alternatively, improvement in the ratio of correctional officers to inmates (from 4.6 to 4.1) may have helped in controlling some of these negative incidents.

With newer, more stringent laws, a "lock them up" state of public mind that influences incarceration policy, and mandatory sentencing, prison overcrowding will only worsen. In forecasting models for the management of growth in inmate populations using the application of a difference equation model, Heard (1990) projects that at the present rate of incarcerations, by 2017 the prison system will continue to be composed of young offenders (thirty-four years of age and under) and will continue to grow. Heard warns us that "should these trends continue, without appropriate intervention, the economic, social and medical impacts of overcrowding on managing and operating correctional facilities may be devastating."

In terms of future prison crowding, the outlook is dim. Illinois, for example, legislated natural life imprisonment and habitual offender laws in 1978; in 1982, provisions permitting the sentencing of convicted mentally ill persons to prison were enacted; between 1986 and 1989, Illinois increased penalties, particularly for drug offenses, through fifty changes in criminal statutes; and in 1989 there were 131 bills or amendments before the Illinois General Assembly that would bring more people into the Illinois prison system (Vlasak, 1989).

Since the majority of the current inmate population is nonwhite, and there is every reason to believe that under the present criminal justice system their proportions will increase, blacks and Hispanics will be those predominantly "caged under increasingly crowded, violent, and disease-ridden conditions" (Skinner, 1990: 18).

Crowded jails are also viewed as a national plight (Mancini, 1988). In a 1986 national survey of jail managers, 55 percent reported their jails filled beyond rated capacity; 13 percent were between 96 and 100 percent of rated capacity; and 38 percent were under court order concerning confinement conditions (Guynes, 1988). In the jail managers' rank orderings of the most serious criminal justice problems, jail crowding headed the list. The 1988 census of jails revealed that 404 jails (12 percent) were under state or federal court order or consent decree to limit the number of inmates, and 412 jurisdictions had similar stipulations to improve specific conditions of confinement such as crowded living units (74 percent); inadequate recreation facilities (46 percent), medical facilities or services (39 percent), and library services (33 percent); inept staffing patterns (33 percent); and deficient visiting practices (32 percent) (Stephan, 1990: 7). In other words, one out of eight jails (57 percent) is a defective institution; and mostly minorities are housed in these facilities.

As a part of its responsibility for 177 Native American tribes in twenty-seven states, the Bureau of Indian Affairs (BIA) owns and operates 26 jails throughout the country and uses 141 jails. It was not until mid-1988 that American Correctional Association standards were put into effect in tribal jails, and then only "to reflect, but not mirror," the ACA criteria (Martin, 1988: 20-21). One tribal jail in Walthill, Nebraska utilized through the mid-seventies had a dirt floor and resembled a small, windowless gas station. When the Omaha tribal jail in Macy, Nebraska was closed in 1987 because of "deplorable" conditions, the BIA constructed a new facility exclusively occupied by members of the Omaha Nation, with little planning participation from tribal officials:

> The housing units were comprised of multiple-occupancy cells with no day rooms or showers. In order to shower, all inmates had to be taken out of their respective housing units to a centralized shower area adjacent to the security corridor that offered little privacy. . . . Circulation paths for certain activities caused inmates of one classification to be moved through housing areas of other classifications. (Ibid.: 20)

With only thirty-two beds, and in light of the increased sanctions written into the federal Anti–Drug Abuse Act, the tribal jail in Macy is undoubtedly at capacity, since 90 percent of persons held in tribal jails nationally are incarcerated for alcohol-related offenses (ibid.: 19).

Skinner views overcrowded prisons as a national crisis and finds that the U.S. rate of incarceration rivals that of South Africa as the highest in the world. He comments on the disastrous effects of "surging drug arrests and stiffer prison sentences":

> The result is that most prisoners spend their days in stupefying idleness, packed together with virtually no privacy in noisy, dirty, smelly, cells or dormitories. These quite stressful conditions, unsurprisingly, beget rampant inmate violence, directed against both guards and other inmates. Both penologists and long-term convicts confirm that today's prisons are much more violent places than they were twenty years ago, with the most trivial of real or imagined offenses apt to provoke an assault or killing. (1990: 18)

MINORITY INMATES AND AIDS

Since the Acquired Immunodeficiency Syndrome (AIDS) was first identified in 1981 and the human immunodeficiency virus (HIV) that causes the illness was identified in 1984, many thousands of Americans have contracted the disease, and at least 80 percent (133,232) of patients diagnosed with AIDS before 1987 have died (Hammett and Moini, 1990: 2). More than 3,000 cases of AIDS are reported each month in the United States; 206,392 Americans have AIDS, and it is estimated that over 1,000,000 are infected with HIV ("Spiraling AIDS Count Passes 200,000 Mark," 1992: A3). In the "free world," outside of prison populations, most AIDS patients are gay or bisexual men (55 percent) or intravenous drug users (24 percent). Among gay males in 1989, there were 19,652 cases of AIDS, 82,500 were infected with the HIV virus, and so far over 50,500 have died. That demographic profile is rapidly changing: between 1988 and 1989, the number of heterosexuals and newborns with AIDS increased 36 percent and 38 percent, respectively, whereas the number of new cases among gay males increased 11 percent (Cowley, Hager, and Marshall, 1990).

Among inner-city minorities who are intravenous drug users, there has been little change in the numbers contracting the virus or securing treatment for it. In 1986, the racial/ethnic distribution of AIDS cases within the general population was: white, 60 percent; black, 25 percent; Hispanic, 14 percent; and other/unknown, 1 percent (Hammett, 1987).[4] The prevalence of minorities with AIDS in correctional facilities is more alarming. The latest available information indicates that within correctional systems, the proportions of prisoners with AIDS are 46 percent black, 27 percent Hispanic, and 27 percent white (Olivero, 1990). Overall, state and federal inmate AIDS cases totaled 3,661 as of October 1989. The comparable figure for jail inmates was 1,750 (Hammett and Moini, 1990: 3). Whereas the AIDS incidence rate for the United States was 14.7 cases per 100,000 persons in 1989, for state and federal correctional systems it was 202 cases per 100,000 inmates (ibid.: 4).

The uneven distribution of AIDS cases across the correctional system is believed to reflect both sexual activity and intravenous drug abuse. The highest incidence rates were found on the East Coast, where there are unique drug cultures consisting of "heavy use of 'shooting galleries' where 'works' are rented and shared" (Hammett, 1987: 13). In the New York state correctional system, for example, 95 percent of the AIDS cases involve intravenous drug abusers, with a racial/ethnic breakdown of 48 percent Hispanic, 32 percent black, and 20 percent white cases (ibid.). It is well known that intravenous drug use continues behind bars, but to what extent, and how much needle-sharing occurs, is unknown. Shakedowns and investigations in prison systems reveal that drugs are freely obtained by means of drug rings located throughout the American prison system.

A partial scan of media data bases showed that drug investigations took place in federal institutions, the District of Columbia, and almost one-half of the states between 1981 and 1990.[5] At the Kulani Correctional Facility, a minimum-security prison honor farm in Hawaii, among other contraband, fifty-six bags of harvested marijuana, in excess of 172 marijuana plants, ten containers of pills, four syringes, three dozen rifle shells, and at least 113 weapons were found in four shakedowns (Ong, 1984; Clark, 1984). On the mainland, Michigan prisoners were caught operating a multi-million-dollar drug business within the state prison system in 1986 (Gallagher, 1986a). According to an FBI investigation of the Michigan prison drug ring, large quantities of marijuana, cocaine, and heroin were controlled and trafficked by two kingpin drug dealers believed to be "part of an international drug smuggling network involving Detroit-area organized crime figures" (Gallagher, 1986b). The drugs were procured by motorcycle gangs on the outside and smuggled into the prison by guards, administrators, and civilian personnel (Gallagher, 1986c). Apparently even heavy prison security cannot stop the flow of drugs in an institution—an inmate who was on Death Row at the notorious Pontiac (Illinois) prison died recently after overdosing on cocaine (Smith and Gibson, 1988).

A statewide investigation of drugs in the Utah prison system resulted in seventeen indictments when the probe uncovered major criminals conducting their businesses from the prison through personal contacts with prison employees, outside relatives, wives, and girlfriends, and by way of telephone and mail. Two of the indicted inmates had to be transferred to a federal prison when it was found that they were experiencing withdrawal from heroin addiction (Sorensen, 1986). It is believed that at least 90 percent of Maine prison inmates and those in other prisons are addicted (Rayfield, 1988).

Sharing needles in drug abuse and homosexual intercourse are both common practices in correctional facilities which are exacerbated by the preexisting scandalous conditions already present:

> Inmate idleness and overcrowding—with the attendant boredom, violence, and security problems—increases the propensity and opportunity to engage in these behaviors. Consequently, an inmate entering prison today faces a significant risk of seeing what may have been, say, a one-year term for a non-violent offense turn into a death sentence should he be careless in sharing his cellmate's "works" or too weak to fend off a homosexual rape. (Skinner, 1990: 20)

An estimated 30 percent of prison inmates engage in homosexual activity, and from 9 percent to 20 percent are presumed to be victims of aggressive sexual acts while imprisoned[6] (Hammett, 1987: 15). The transmission of AIDS in prison populations is a frightening reality that cannot be ignored, particularly since there has been a 156 percent increase in this disease among corrections inmates since 1985 (Olivero, 1990: 113). Unfortunately, the problem is being ignored by state legislators, who have been hesitant to adequately fund treatment and other prison programs to slow the spread of AIDS in prisons: "politicians do not wish their names to be associated with or to endorse the lifestyle of groups with a high-risk of contracting AIDS, i.e., homosexuals and intravenous drug users" (ibid.). Since 73 percent of the prisoners with AIDS are minorities, the denial of AIDS treatment in correctional facilities further compounds the discriminatory injustices they experience both inside and outside the correctional system because of their lack of political power. As Olivero (ibid.: 121) poignantly observes, "It is clear that imprisoned racial and ethnic minority members, intravenous drug users, homosexuals, etc., are among the most unlikely to force society and the courts into adopting humane treatment standards within prisons."

DISCRIMINATION TOWARD MINORITY PRISONERS

Racism and discrimination against peoples of color permeate the criminal justice system, so it is not surprising that at the end of the long journey through this structure, the final outcome at incarceration is the same as, if not worse than, the earlier discriminatory experiences of minorities. Racial minorities are only 31.3 percent of those arrested but, excluding Hispanics, account for more than 40 percent of all U.S. inmates: 29.8 percent of federal inmates, 49 percent of jail inmates, and 51.6 percent of state prison inmates.[7] In their focus upon the characteristics of those who control and those who are controlled in the correctional system, the National Minority Advisory Council on Criminal Justice commented that

> having been apprehended, charged, and processed by the police and having been adjudicated, convicted, and sentenced by the courts, the minority offender is now passed into the hands of a system that is designed to punish for the offense, prevent any future violations, and/or prepare the offender for a productive reentry into society. In addition to this obvious dilemma concerning objectives, the problem confronting minorities brought to this stage of the criminal judicial process is that the same forces which resulted in unfair and inequitable treatment by the courts and police are now operating to frustrate the hope of restoration and rehabilitation. (NMAC, 1980: 230)

In the late summer of 1989, black inmates in the Iowa State Penitentiary wrote a letter to the warden stating that they were "being discriminated against, abused, unnecessarily harassed and degraded by prison employees who obviously have come to believe that being a racist is the way to become accepted by co-workers and superiors" (Petroski, 1989: 1). They contended that guards had verbally abused, slapped, and beaten them. Most African Americans who have been in jail or prison, who have a relative who has been incarcerated, or who know someone who has been in the correctional system, have personal knowledge or experience precisely mirroring that which the Iowa inmates were protesting. Such practices are generally not found in the research literature, because "scholars have until recently ignored the impact of race and ethnicity on the culture and structure of the prison" (Carroll, 1990: 510).

In a discussion of institutional racism in prisons, Florida community psychologist Professor Marvin Dunn comments:

> Florida's Raiford prison, for example, located in one of the most rural and isolated parts of the state, is heavily black, as are many prisons around the country. The prison is run, however, by white people who have worked as guards at the facility for many, many years. Some are the children of former prison guards. The prison is the major source of jobs for the nearby poor white community. When a black person enters such an establishment, where, in his view "rednecks" control everything, what else is he (or she?) to think except that the system is racist? Should, for example, such a person assume that if he were to come in conflict with a white prisoner that his side would be heard without prejudice? (1987: 1)

One of the major contributors to racial/ethnic discrimination in the nation's correctional facilities appears to be the racial prejudice of white (Anglo) guards and white inmates. The very "whiteness" of the prison system—most personnel are white, whereas most inmates are minority—results in closer scrutiny of minority prisoners, particularly black inmates, since they are viewed by white guards as "dangerous and threatening." Thus, in addition to closer surveillance and control of black inmates compared to their white counterparts, blacks more frequently receive disciplinary write-ups[8] for those rule infractions where guards exercise the widest discretion (Carroll, 1990: 513).

A nationally representative survey of state prison inmates in 1986 revealed that if they had served less than twelve months, whites and blacks committed rule infractions at about the same annual rate (1.5 violations), but this gap widened steadily with time served. For example, black inmates who had served sixty or more months averaged 1.1 rule violations, whereas whites averaged 0.9. Other minorities imprisoned sixty or more months also displayed rates that were higher than those for whites: Hispanics, 1.4, and "other races," 1.0. Inmates of "other races"—American Indians, Alaska Natives, Asians, and Pacific Islanders—were more frequently charged with transgressing prison rules than any other subgroup (57 percent), closely followed by black prisoners (56.8 percent). Whites (51.2 percent) and Hispanics (46.9 percent) were the least likely to be so charged. Blacks (36 percent) and members of "other races" (37 percent) also had the highest percentages of multiple infractions as compared to Hispanics (28 percent) and whites (32 percent), and once charged were also more likely than whites or Hispanics to be found guilty (Stephan, 1989). It is possible that blacks and most members of the "other races" group were more racially identifiable because of their skin color than some of the Hispanics, but this conjecture cannot be verified on the basis of the information available.

Various explanations are offered for the differential assessment of prison rule infractions to minorities. Such a highly discretionary decision can result in severe punishments and ultimately affect a prisoner's release time. Wilbanks (1987: 133), for example, suggests the possibility that guards perceive blacks as more aggressive (or dangerous) than whites. On the other hand, empirical studies have shown that other factors, including the racial prejudice of white guards, affect not only black inmates but all imprisoned minorities. In a study of guards in a midwestern maximum-security prison, Poole and Regoli (1980: 221) report that "commitment to a custody orientation controls what guards perceive as well as how they respond to that perception." Their study suggests that in order to manage role stress, guards increase their custody orientation. As a result, they then become disposed to a negative conception of inmates and concomitantly practice closer surveillance and stricter enforcement of rules. Poole and Regoli (ibid.: 224) conclude that "disciplinary reports are thus a function of both inmate behavior and guards' reactions to that behavior." According to inmates, "guards' reactions" appropriately describe the dynamics of these unjust actions, since they view guards as unqualified to make such judgments:

The "correctional officer" (prison guard) who charges the offense that greatly affects the amount of time a prisoner may serve, has no training, and in most cases doesn't fully know the prison rules. Thus, the prisoner's action at best is whimsical but based upon this ill-trained prison guard's evaluation is the criterion used by the Adult Authority to determine whether a prisoner is fit for society. (Kasirika [Divans] and Muntu [West], 1971: 8)

A Massachusetts prison study was more specific and attributed blacks' greater numbers of disciplinary write-ups to official repression, particularly since those involved in political groups were far more likely to receive such negative sanctions. More than half of the blacks who were political group members at Concord Reformatory (56 percent) and 59.4 percent at Walpole State Prison were written up for violations, but only 33 percent of the nonpolitical black prisoners at both Concord and Walpole were so sanctioned (Morris, 1974: 314, 317).

In his study of race relations at Eastern Correctional Institution, a maximum-security facility in an eastern state, Carroll (1974: 144) reports that a white inmate elite is practically exempted from custodial control, and "the disproportionate number of reported infractions involving black inmates is a consequence of the under-reporting by officers of infractions by members of the white elite." In other words, while protecting the immunity of the white elite, officers meet their quotas at the expense of black inmates. A former Soledad inmate states that in its effort to destroy the unity of lower-class workers attempting to build a strong union, the federal government was highly successful through the agitation of race wars in the thirties, the tactics used by state prison systems today: "It is now apparent that the 'system' wants to keep blacks, browns and whites in constant undefined and clouded conflict solely to prevent a concerted effort on their part to expose the inimical policies of the administrators and an insensitive political system which allows such an administration unlimited power over its wards" (Rollins [Jabali], 1971: 25).

Prejudice and discrimination directed toward minority inmates from prison guards are also demonstrated through racial slurs, harassment, and brutality. A participant observation study in a large maximum-security Texas penitentiary containing 64 percent primarily urban minority prisoners (47 percent black, 17 percent Hispanic) and 85 percent mostly rural white officers revealed verbal intimidation and physical coercion as routine operating procedure (Marquart, 1990). Of the thirty cases of guard-defined "legitimized" violence recorded, twenty-four involved black inmates, and one victim was an Hispanic: "For the white guards, black prisoners represented troublesome, hostile, and rebellious prisoners who occasionally 'needed' physical coercion to 'keep them in their place.' Racial prejudice was common, and this factor helped facilitate the belief on the part of the guards that black inmates were impolite and troublesome" (ibid.: 537).

Marquart describes several types of coercion. "Tune ups," the mildest form of physical coercion, included kicks, shoves, slaps to the head and body, and verbal humiliation such as "You stupid nigger, if you ever lie to me or any other officer about what you're doing, I'll knock your teeth in" (ibid.: 531). If an inmate fought back during a "tune up," or defied, threatened, or challenged an officer's authority, an "ass whipping," the second form of physical coercion, took place at the hands of a number of guards, who used "blackjacks, riot batons, fist loads, or aluminum-cased flashlights" (ibid.: 532). Unlike "ass whippings," which normally were not brutal enough to require hospitalization or extensive medical treatment, the third type of force employed, the "severe beating," was intended to cause physical injury or hospitalization (ibid.). The guards' grounds for such inhumane treatment were to preserve control and order, to maintain status and deference, to build guard solidarity, and to facilitate promotion (ibid.: 535).

In addition to their brutal crews, the Texas guards had a cadre of inmate "building tenders" (BTs) who functioned as an extension of the uniformed personnel. The BTs were permitted to carry weapons (clubs, knives, blackjacks) and were virtually immune from disciplinary action; some were "so loyal to the staff that they said they would kill another inmate if so ordered" (Marquart and Crouch, 1984: 498). Although the BT assignments were racially distributed among the inmates (out of eighteen head BTs there were fourteen whites, three blacks, and one Hispanic), the power was not. The white head BTs had the "real" power and dominated the inmate society because the largely rural white ranking staff "were prejudiced and 'trusted' the white BTs more than BTs from either minority group" (ibid.: 500-501). This medieval practice, which permitted a "white con power structure, similar to a caste system," continued to flourish in Texas until abolished by federal court order in 1982, fully ten years after such practices were eliminated in Mississippi, Louisiana, and Arkansas. Of course, it is highly possible that similar building tender systems exist today in other states, as well as other forms of inmate power and control.

Minority prisoners also complain about their exclusion from the more prestigious work assignments—which are usually reserved for white inmates—and denial of access to educational, vocational, and treatment programs. As an early thesis on prison repression reported, "There are always unequal job assignments with blacks receiving the worse—hardest least interesting. We are given fewer chances at meaningful vocational training (if any exists) and severely punished if we decline to take part in the farce the prison administrators denote as meaningful work" (Moore and Moore, 1973: 839).

Morris (1974: 307) found that at the Concord Reformatory in Massachusetts, 36 percent of the white inmates sampled had desirable work assignments such as "clerical or counseling service jobs and jobs in the kitchen or staff dining rooms," compared to only 5 percent of the black sample, who were over-represented in the unpleasant cement-making shop. The job discrimination at nearby Walpole State Prison was more contentious: 57 percent of the black prisoners were toiling in the worst places to work (e.g., the kitchen, the metal shop, or janitorial work), whereas only 30 percent of the whites were. Conversely, 30 percent of the whites had desirable jobs, but only 10 percent of the blacks did.

More recently, Goetting and Howsen (1983) sampled 5,385 black inmates from the larger national Survey of Inmates of State Correctional Facilities conducted by the U.S. Bureau of the Census. Although this study was criticized by Wilbanks (1987) because it was a self-report survey, the authors voice confidence in the accuracy of the information provided by the inmates and cite other similar large-scale surveys supportive of prisoner integrity in self-report surveys

(Goetting and Howsen, 1983: 22, fn 2).[9] Goetting and Howsen found significant racial differences between prison work assignments and work assignment duties: blacks were less likely than whites to have work assignments, and the types of work they were allotted were significantly less desirable and more menial (ibid.: 27). For example, lower proportions of black inmates were placed in maintenance, repair, and other higher-status prison services (library, storeroom, office work), while larger proportions were assigned to food preparation (kitchen work), janitorial duties, and farming/forestry. Recognizing the interpretive limitations of their data, Goetting and Howsen (ibid.: 29) cautiously stop short of claiming racism as an influence in the differential treatment of imprisoned blacks, but do state that their findings "shed some light on the possibility of racial discrimination in type of work assignment."

Petersilia's (1983) self-report study of state prisoners in California, Michigan, and Texas examined racial differences in work assignments and attempted to ascertain the reasons minorities had such lowly work assignments compared to whites. No racial differences were found in California, but both Texas and Michigan revealed statistically significant differences in such assignments according to race, namely: (1) greater proportions of white inmates held prison jobs in both states; and (2) blacks in Texas were far less likely to have prison work than whites (ibid.: 61).[10] After reporting that minorities place a high value on jobs, Petersilia somehow concludes that "inmates without jobs do not appear to want them" (ibid.), particularly in Texas, and although "these coincidences could represent a pattern that implies discrimination," racial discrimination is not necessarily indicated (ibid.: 63). Other than reporting that the low job participation of blacks in Michigan and Texas was attributed to their being too busy, not wanting the jobs, or not being able to take the jobs for other reasons (e.g., punishment), Petersilia seems to overlook, or at least does not tell us, *the reasons that blacks gave for not wanting the prison jobs!* In light of the aforementioned findings by Goetting and Howsen (1983), it is highly conceivable that the black prisoners, who are more politically aware today, did not want the less desirable jobs in the kitchens, laundries, and fields of the prisons, known by many black inmates as "plantation work" or "slave labor." According to two black political prisoners in maximum-security facilities, "The prison system is a slave system. A slave is one who is held captive without freedom of choice and must labor until death or until his freedom is bought" (Kasirika [Divans] and Muntu [West], 1971: 7).

Religion and language are two additional areas in which incarcerated minorities face discrimination. Accounts in minority periodicals such as *The Black Scholar* and other writings of African American inmates and ex-inmate authors indicate that Black Muslims have faced discrimination and mistreatment because of their religious orientation and cultural practices—for example, diets compatible with their beliefs and materials of their faith. Morris's study of two Massachusetts prisons near Boston—Concord Reformatory and Walpole State Prison—showed that Black Muslims were targets for harassment because, according to other non-Muslim prisoners, "they were forced to go out in the yard and hold their Islam services when there was a room available and others had room for their meetings. They are now being held in a disaster area, and they have been gassed and made to stay there for disturbance other inmates had created" (Morris, 1974: 318). And from a Nation of Islam leader: "The administration was at first totally negative—we couldn't get a place to worship and practice our religion. They finally gave us the visitors room but the guards tried to discourage other inmates from joining, e.g., they told the men that they would not receive parole if they joined up and it was known that Muslims did not receive paroles" (ibid.: 319).

Similar experiences are faced by Black Muslim groups in federal prisons. David Troung, a Vietnamese political prisoner at Ray Brook, New York, relates how even the chaplain persecuted the Black Muslims and tried to refuse them the right to observe their religious holidays without any justification for the denial ("Under the Thumb of What They Call the Justice System," 1983: 7).

Compared to other black prisoners, members of political organizations and members of the Nation of Islam[11] experience more punishment through segregation and isolation. At Walpole State Prison, for example, those in political groups were significantly more likely to spend time in isolation than nonpolitical black prisoners (62.5 percent vs. 30 percent). Further, Morris (1974: 315-316) found that although the number of black prisoners who were hit or beaten by Walpole prison staff was generally small, since the preferred methods of abuse were "psychological, verbal, and social status harassment," black members of political groups were significantly more apt to receive such physical abuse than nongroup prisoners (15.2 percent vs. 1.6 percent). Morris (ibid.: 323) concludes that since their religious beliefs led Muslims to always be disproportionately well-behaved, "clearly racism must account for possible disproportionate disciplining of members of the Nation of Islam on the grounds of security." Morris also found that resistance from black political prisoner organizations rendered the suppressive social control measures used by prison authorities generally unsuccessful.

The National Minority Advisory Council on Criminal Justice illuminates the insensitivity to the Black Muslim religion:

> Rules and policies were instituted for the specific purpose of limiting the expression of the Muslim religion, the justification being that security had to be maintained within the institution. An example of this cultural indifference is seen in regulations which led to solitary confinement for a Muslim who refused to shave his beard, but brought no disciplinary action against an Orthodox Jew for the same action. (1980: 232)

When they identify with their native culture, Native Americans are more abused by the correctional system than any other minority group. Restrictions are imposed on "wearing headbands, using native languages, maintaining long, braided hair, enjoying native music, or securing culture-related leisure and educational materials" (ibid.: 233). Although some Indian religious practices are considered by corrections authorities as "weird" or "savage," in nine western states Native Americans have been successful in obtaining ritual "sweat lodges" (small, tentlike saunas), which are "essential to the Indian's religious practices" (Rice, 1989). In a recent federal court suit involving the Utah State Prison, the attorney for six Native American inmates charged that prohibiting them from building the requested sweat lodge abridged their First Amendment right to freely practice their religion (ibid.).

Native American traditions behind bars began with the American Indian Movement (AIM) in the early 1970s and led to hundreds of protests from Indian organizations and Indian-generated legal actions. The Native American Rights Fund (NARF) instituted lawsuits against nine states and the Lompoc, California federal prison in order to secure the rights of Indians to practice their traditional religions and meet their spiritual needs. In addition to the construction of sweat lodges behind prison walls, some facilities allow sacred pipe ceremonies, an occasional powwow, and visits by medicine men (Taft, 1981a). At an Indiana University colloquium in 1990 on minorities in the correctional system where the Indiana commissioner of correction was one of the speakers, a Native American woman in the audience expressed the extreme concern of Native Americans over the deliberate breaking of a sacred pipe by one of the prison staff in an Indiana prison. The sacred pipe is particularly hallowed, for as one inmate guardian of the stone pipe and tobacco pouches said, "It connects all things—all creation in all directions. . . . You use your statues in a church to interpret your prayers. We use our pipe, and the smoke reaches the universe" (ibid.: 11).

Spanish-speaking inmates, Native Americans who prefer their tribal tongues, newly arrived Vietnamese and other persons of Asian origin, and, in some federal cases, Haitians who speak a French patois all face special problems in jails and prisons because they are not proficient in English. In addition to the undue suffering of Hispanic inmates because of the "conflict between their cultural backgrounds and the culture of the predominantly white correctional staff" (NMAC, 1980: 233), language barriers impose an added hardship. Many of the speaker announcements in prison are made in English, which, combined with the lack of knowledge of the prison rules and regulations, severely handicaps the large Spanish-speaking prison populations ("Under the Thumb," 1983: 6). Considering the dearth of Spanish-speaking corrections personnel and the rapidly escalating incarcerations of Hispanics, the communication gap is especially serious.

Heated battles concerning language occur daily in the unincarcerated population because of the ethnocentric mentality of the public, as exemplified in the "America, love it or leave it" attitude largely displayed by American whites. Obviously such bigotry against the non-English-speaking is exacerbated in predominantly white-staffed American penal institutions.

Minority Political Prisoners and Prisoners' Rights

Many minorities view themselves as political prisoners. In fact, it has been said that all Black prisoners . . . are political prisoners, for their condition derives from the political inequity of black people in America. A black prisoner's crime may or may not have been a political action against the state, but the state's action against him is always political. This knowledge, intuitively known and sometimes transcribed into political terms, exists within every black prisoner. (Chrisman, 1971: 45)

There is validity to such charges. On December 11, 1978, a petition was filed with the United Nations Commission on Human Rights Sub-Commission on Prevention of Discrimination and Protection of Minorities by three organizations[12] alleging "a consistent pattern of gross and reliably attested violations of human rights and fundamental freedoms of certain classes of prisoners in the United States because of their race, economic status and political beliefs" (Hinds, 1979: 1). The seven international jurists, all of whom were experienced in human rights cases, came to the United States to investigate violations of international prison criteria and to make an independent determination of the reliability of the allegations ("Raw Racism Shocks Jurists," 1980).[13] Their task was to determine whether the petitioners had made a prima facie case that "the situations described reveal a consistent pattern of gross and reliably attested violations of Human Rights" (Hinds, 1979: 3).[14]

The international jurists' findings were described in seven classifications: (1) four categories of political prisoners; (2) abuse of criminal processes; (3) sentencing; (4) prison conditions; (5) appellate remedies; (6) Native Americans; and (7) "Olympic Prison" in upstate New York. Each of these categories met the stipulations of the prima facie case that "there exists in the United States today a consistent pattern of gross and reliably attested violations of the human and legal rights of minorities, including policies of racial discrimination and segregation" (ibid.: 10).

The investigators defined four categories of political prisoners:

Category A. "A class of victims of FBI misconduct . . . and other forms of illegal governmental conduct who as political activists have been selectively targeted for provocation, false arrests, entrapment, fabrication of evidence, and spurious criminal prosecutions" (ibid.: 11). Examples: the Wilmington Ten (North Carolina), Republic of New Afrika defendants, and American Indian Movement defendants.

Category B. "Persons convicted of crimes purportedly committed to advance their political beliefs in the need for the liberation of Puerto Rico from colonial status and who have been subjected to extraordinarily protracted sentences and unusually brutal conditions of confinement" (ibid.: 15). Example: the Puerto Rican Nationalists.

Category C. "Persons who because of their racial and economic status are arbitrarily selected for arrest, indictment, and conviction and especially during periods of unrest" (ibid.: 17). Examples: Tommy Lee Hines (Alabama), Gary Tyler (Louisiana).

Category D. "Persons who after conviction and incarceration, because they become advocates for prison reform and spokespersons for grievances of prisoners as a class, are selected for additional criminal prosecutions and unusually brutal conditions of confinement" (ibid.: 19). Examples: the Napanoch Defendants (Sing Sing Prison, New York), the Reidsville (Georgia) Brothers, the Pontiac (Illinois) Brothers. As a result of interviews with many of these minority political prisoners and an in-depth examination of their cases, the jurists state:

> Our observations force us to conclude that the circumstances of the above class of prisoners illuminate a pattern and practice singling out leaders who attempt to organize for prison reform and subjecting them to cruel and unusual punishment solely because of their political activity while in prisons. Many of the physical conditions violate the U.N. Standard Minimum Rules for the Treatment of Prisoners, and the persistent pattern of brutalization and denial of due process is in clear violation of human rights. (Ibid.: 24)

Prisoners' rights issues have long been protested by minority inmates and, in addition to complaints about poor food and inadequate facilities and programs, include the previously discussed denial of religious freedom and practices (i.e., Black Muslims, Native Americans). Racism, racial segregation, and prison brutality on the part of both correctional officers and other inmates are also frequent allegations made by incarcerated minorities in the U.S. correctional system. Although the findings reported by the international jurists are a dozen years old, there is little indication of resultant ameliorative action. Minority political prisoners are still held in solitary confinement or in "continuous and indefinite isolation" in small cells (as were Fred Bustillo in an 8 x 10 cell and Gary Tyler in a 5 x 8 cell for $23^1/2$ hours per day) without "light, bedding, or sanitary conditions," and forced to "urinate and defecate on the cell floor" (ibid.: 32).

In a letter to the *Critical Criminologist*, Oscar López-Rivera writes that the history of the U.S. prison system is replete with cases of political prisoners:

> These prisoners were and are the Native Americans who were captured and imprisoned for fighting against genocide and for their land; they were the slave and abolitionist who fought against the deleterious system of slavery; . . . they were and are the New Afrikans fighting for their civil rights and/or for their own homeland; . . . and they were and are the Puerto Ricans fighting against colonialism, for self-determination and sovereignty. (1989: 10)

López-Rivera notes that members of the Puerto Rican Nationalists were the longest-held political prisoners in this hemisphere.[15] Although imprisoned members of Puerto Rican independence groups such as the Armed Forces of National Liberation (FALN) view themselves as prisoners of war and freedom fighters, they are nonetheless treated as criminals (Vilar, 1990: 13). One of the most notorious cases of minority political prisoner maltreatment concerns a woman, Alejandrina Torres, a Puerto Rican Nationalist. Torres received a sentence of thirty-five years in prison for possession of weapons and explosives and seditious conspiracy against the government and was subsequently confined in a subterranean cell in a federal maximum-security prison in Lexington, Kentucky. She was allowed one hour of exercise per day in a fifty-foot-square yard, and strip-searched afterwards in the "high-security" facility. As part of the constant surveillance, Mrs. Torres's cell lights were left on around the clock, with no way to stop the glare (Reuben and Norman, 1987). If this is the way minority women with strong political beliefs are treated in a male chauvinist, paternalistic country, the brutal mistreatment of minority male political prisoners comes as no surprise.

An article in the fall 1991 issue of *Social Justice,* a commemorative issue devoted to Attica, describes those U.S. peoples of color (African American, Mexican, Puerto Rican, and Native American) whose "militant resistance to racial and economic oppression," prevalent in the 1960s, culminated in their political prisoner status:

> Mass organizations demonstrated in the streets and clandestine organizations and armed self-defense groups began to function in the Black community, in the Puerto Rican barrios, among Mexican people in the southwest U.S., and on Native American reservations.
>
> It is the militancy and fundamentally anticolonial character of these movements that have been the primary impetus for the implementation of counterinsurgency methods of repression, including special restrictive procedures during trials and the creation of high-security/isolation prison units. The emergence of liberation movements seeking fundamental rights of survival for oppressed communities within the United States poses the greatest potential threat to the U.S. ruling class and has engendered qualitative repressive changes in the U.S. legal system. (Deutsch and Susler, 1991: 94-95)

Instances of racial discrimination in parole decisions and length of time served are additional political prison issues that minority inmates have decried over the years. It has already been shown that Black Muslims are discriminated against in parole decisions (Morris, 1974). There is also evidence that compared to white inmates, nonpolitical black prisoners, as well as other incarcerated minorities, experience differential treatment in parole hearing outcomes. This disparity is due in large part to the fact that "the parole administration process is an arbitrary system that permits wide discretion in parole decisions" (Brown, 1979: 355). In her discussion of race and parole decisions, Brown (ibid.: 360) suggests two ways in which these disparities might occur. First, "parole boards are sensitive to public opinion against paroling high-risk inmates (serious offenders) and therefore tend to act more cautiously on such cases." When the attitude of a parole board entails the protection of society as a primary responsibility and the rehabilitation of offenders as a secondary consideration, inmates' resentment is added to their preexisting cynicism toward the entire parole process (Vetter and Silverman, 1986: 539). Second, "racism is transmitted from the institutions to the parole board by means of institutional assessments that are recorded by prisoner personnel and become part of the inmate's permanent file." It has been well documented that minorities, especially blacks, are frequently "written up" by rural white guards who are racially prejudiced, untrained, or simply ignorant of the rules and regulations of the institutions (Kasirika [Divans] and Muntu [West], 1971; Morris, 1974; Poole and Regoli, 1980; Carroll, 1990).

Brown's (1979) study of three prisons (minimum-, medium-, and maximum-security) in a single state revealed that crucial indicators for parole hearings were both the institutional adjustment rating and the counselor's parole recommendation. Further, as the custody level of the prison increased, so did the proportion denied parole. At the minimum-custody level, there was little black-white difference in parole denials, but at the medium- and maximum-security levels, blacks were significantly more likely to be denied parole than whites. Brown also reports that counselors were least likely to recommend blacks for parole compared to white inmates. Even black prisoners who were defined as "well-adjusted" fared worse in parole outcomes than well-adjusted whites at medium- and maximum-custody institutions (ibid.: 368, Table 3). These findings led Brown to conclude that

> contrary to what is commonly assumed, type of offense, juvenile history, and the amount of time served in prison had no effect on parole. The data show that parole is primarily a function of the institution of confinement and race.
>
> Clearly, the net effect of being black decreases an inmate's chances for parole because 12 percent more whites than blacks in this sample were paroled from prison (93.8 and 81.7 percent, respectively). (Ibid.: 371)

Although Brown (ibid.: 373) was unable to determine whether there were additional factors involved other than the racial bias of the parole board (e.g., a sentencing judge's failure to sanction the parole or reduced employment opportunities for blacks), her data suggest strongly that by following counselor recommendations, the parole chances of minorities are adversely affected.

Despite indications that Indians are treated more harshly by the criminal justice system than any other racial/ethnic group in the United States, little research has been undertaken on the parole outcomes of Native Americans. One notable exception is Bynum's study of an upper plains state containing a relatively large Native American population. In order to obtain a severity-of-punishment measure, Bynum (1981) combined time served with the sentence imposed in his analysis. Overall, Indians served significantly more of their sentences (86 percent) than non-Indians (75 percent). Among those convicted for burglary, the disparity was even greater—the proportion of their sentence served for Native Americans was 84 percent, compared to 64 percent for non-Indian burglars (ibid.: 80). These differences were indicated even though the original sentences imposed were significantly shorter for Indians than non-Indians and the number of prior offenses was controlled for. Further, in the regression analysis using all cases and controlling for legal (prior convictions, prison infractions) and social (age, education, race) variables, Bynum continued to find a statistically significant relationship between being a Native American and the proportion of a sentence served. These results suggest that "the race of the inmate exerts a strong and independent effect upon the proportion of time he will be incarcerated prior to release" (ibid.: 83-84). Although Bynum was unable to answer a major question he posed—"What is it about being a Native American that induces the parole board to impose a more severe sanction upon these individuals?"—he intimates that there may be cumulative discrimination at each stage of the criminal justice process.

A three-state study (California, Texas, and Michigan) of racial disparities in the criminal justice system (Petersilia, 1983: 49-50), after controlling for factors that might impact the parole decision, still found that black and Hispanic inmates in California and Texas served longer sentences than whites who committed the same crimes. In an attempt to explain the parole outcome differences between these two states and Michigan, where blacks served less time, Petersilia (ibid.: 97) offers several illuminating facts—the presentence investigation report (PSR) is "the key document" in parole decisions; minorities often appear in a "bad light" in such reports; and because of bad PSRs, minorities are consequently identified as "high risks."[16] At the time of Petersilia's study, California had instituted a determinate sentencing policy wherein the sentence length should circumscribe the time served; therefore, "any racial disparities in time served there mostly reflect racial differences in sentencing." In contrast, the Texas parole system, which lengthened minority prison time, is extremely discretionary and individualized, tending to rely heavily on PSR information. Finally, parole decisions in Michigan appear to overcome racial differences in time served because they "have been based almost exclusively on legal indicators of personal culpability, e.g., juvenile record, violence of conviction crime, and prison behavior" (ibid.: xxvii).

It has been argued that since most states now use objective criteria in parole decisions, it is possible that racial disparity no longer exists (Wilbanks, 1987: 138). Such a simplistic argument overlooks the reality of the structure and organization of the parole system (overwhelmingly white) as compared to the prospective parolees (overwhelmingly minority), ignores the fact that subjectivity cannot be eliminated no matter how objective a rating scale is purported to be (the original design can build in biases), is naive about the present racist climate in the United States, underestimates the highly punitive public view of crimes for which minorities are more frequently convicted, especially drugs and the concomitant political (and parole) backlash associated with these views, and is unenlightened about the pervasive influence of institutional racism in the criminal justice system.

Minority Prison Violence

Violence expressed by imprisoned minorities can be directed inward, as in suicide, or outward[17] against the facility (riots) or toward other individuals, staff, or fellow inmates, in some type of assault. Bowker (1985: 12) describes prison violence in terms of goals which are *instrumental* or *expressive*. Instrumental prison violence, which is transformed into dominance in interpersonal relationships, is employed to acquire power and status, gain a better living condition, secure additional goods and services, or obtain sexual fulfillment upon demand. As Carriere (1980: 210) acutely observes, "Life becomes a milieu of tension, fear, and force in which violence is an accepted response and coping mechanism. In such a life of degradation, devoid of power, sex, and identity, an act of violence or sexual aggression acts as a manifestation of power or status." On the other hand, expressive prison violence is a nonrational form of violence which has an objective of tension reduction and ranges from brief individual outbursts to long-lasting riots.

In addition to the inmate personality, contributions to institutional violence also derive from "our concept and theory of imprisonment and attitude toward prisoners" (ibid.: 209) and the structural/functional factors of correctional systems (McDougall, 1985). Prisoners are viewed as criminals who are "believed to have assumed the risk of injury or death," which, according to inmates in some states, includes the placement of prisoners in the cells of known rapists or assaulters to punish them for rule infractions (Carriere, 1980: 209-210). Insufficient prison space and the resultant close proximity and confinement lead to tension and subsequently to violence. In the face of ever-present idleness and boredom because of a lack of work, education, and treatment programs, prison violence and riots are not unexpected (McDougall, 1985). Violent deaths are often the result of these conditions, and homicide is the leading cause of deaths during imprisonment (Carriere, 1980: 201).

Prison riots have been a part of the violent history of this nation since the first riot occurred in 1774 (Mahan, 1985). The roles played by racial/ethnic minorities and their motives for participating in recent major prison riots have typically been associated with the prison's physical and social climate. Among their many grievances, prisoners have listed inadequate food, water, and shelter; the need for a healthier diet; reduction of cell time; more recreation; more educational and treatment programs; guard harassment, prejudice, and physical brutality; long-term crowding; extended periods of idleness; few work assignments; low pay for work; poor administration; frequent changes in rules and regulations; daily degradation and humiliation; inadequate medical and drug treatment; and lack of religious freedom (Carney, 1974; Inciardi, 1984; Useem, 1985; Mahan, 1985; Abadinsky, 1987).

The two most notorious examples of prison rioting took place at the Attica (New York) Correctional Facility in 1971 and at the New Mexico State Penitentiary at Santa Fe in 1980. Both facilities contained disproportionate numbers of minority inmates—at Attica the minority population included 55 percent black, 8.5 percent Puerto Rican, and 5 percent Native American. Santa Fe's prison population was almost 70 percent minority: 58 percent Chicano, 10 percent black, and 1.5 percent Native American (Mahan, 1985: 77). Conditions at the two prisons were equally deplorable and reflected the combined list of complaints outlined above; however, the actions of the minority inmates and the response by official authorities illustrate that differential treatment was accorded the rioters based on their specific minority status.

The inmate capacity at Attica was 1,200, but when the riot erupted there, the facility housed approximately 2,225 prisoners (ibid.: 80). The largely black prisoner population, which held forty hostages, attempted to negotiate, insisted on open arbitrations before the total group with decisions made by the entire group, and in general was more politically conscious than the Santa Fe inmates. The Black Muslims even protected the hostages and were "credited with keeping order and control during the long, stressful days of the takeover" (Jacobs, 1976; Mahan, 1985: 77). The shared protests and political awareness of the inmates at Attica had amalgamated previously hostile groups such as the Black Muslims, the Black Panthers, and the Young Lords (a Puerto Rican group) into a peaceful coalition designed to bring about changes in that institution. Their error was in relying on the integrity of the government:

> They failed to realize that to those in charge of state government the lives and safety of correction officers were only slightly more important than the lives and safety of inmates. In the end, neither the lives of inmates nor those of correction officers were sufficient to prevent state officials from making their point: the state is sovereign, and rebellious prisoners must not be permitted to challenge that sovereignty. (Abadinsky, 1987: 425)

As a result of the state's recalcitrant attitude and lagging negotiations, four days after the takeover, a fifteen-minute, all-out assault by heavily armed state troopers and corrections officers culminated in the troopers' slaying of twenty-nine inmates and ten hostages and the wounding of hundreds more (Inciardi, 1984: 656). One guard was beaten by the inmates during the initial revolt and died two days later from his injuries; two other injured guards and three prisoners who died at the hands of other inmates were the extent of the violence on the part of the Attica inmates.

Despite the humaneness and restraint shown by the Attica prison rioters, according to witnesses, after the inmates had been subdued and the prison retaken, men falsely accused of being the leaders were subjected to "extreme cases of brutality and torture," and other prisoners were "forced through gauntlets and beaten with sticks and clubs" by officers who were never disciplined for these brutal actions (Mahan, 1985: 80). In addition to these blatant violations of human rights, the Goldman Panel found that in the aftermath of the retaking of Attica, there was little regard for the inmates' personal rights: they had no baths for over a week, few personal and toilet articles were allowed, no paper to write their families was permitted, and only two meals a day were provided (Carney, 1974: 193).

At the time of the Santa Fe riot, 1,136 inmates were occupying a facility with a capacity of 900 (Mahan, 1985: 80). In contrast to Attica, the 1980 rebellion at Santa Fe was not political but chaotic. There was little leadership, decisions were made not collectively but from a personal perspective, and inmate coalitions comprised cliques and bands of predominantly Chicano prisoners (Mahan, 1985). The prison population echoed the same complaints as the Attica inmates, but undoubtedly because of a lack of political consciousness, their response was more volatile and unstructured. The 120 black inmates refused to participate in the violence, and instead organized to protect themselves, and later fled from the riot (Useem, 1985: 681).

The Santa Fe riot has been described as the most brutal and costly ($200 million) riot in United States history. Although twelve guards were taken as hostages, none were killed; however, some were "beaten, sodomized, and threatened with death" (ibid.: 680). Negotiations included the "trading" of hostages for personal benefits (Mahan, 1985: 78). According to the thirty autopsies in which the cause of death could be determined, thirty of the thirty-three deaths resulted from selective prisoner-against-prisoner violence. These inmate-inflicted homicides were mainly against informants or represented the vengeance of personal grudges. "Some inmates, alone and in groups, took advantage of the situation to beat, rape, torture, and mutilate other inmates. One inmate had his head cut off with a shovel; another died from a screw-driver driven through his head; several others were immolated in their cells when inmates sprayed lighter fluid on them; and still others were tortured to death with acetylene torches" (Useem, 1985: 680).

Whereas the Attica riot lasted four days, the Santa Fe uprising was quelled after thirty-six hours. Negotiations were handled by the corrections officials instead of an observers' committee as was the case at Attica. Also, sympathetic demonstrators keeping vigil outside the Santa Fe prison might have helped to prevent a bloodbath similar to Attica's. Nonetheless, it was rumored that post-riot brutality was directed against the Santa Fe inmates, and subsequent investigations exposed the habitual use of strip cells as a disciplinary measure (Mahan, 1985).

Examination of the details of Attica and Santa Fe appears to show a more ruthless handling of the black rioters at Attica than of their Chicano counterparts at Santa Fe. Perhaps this difference may be explained by the nine years' difference in time between the two events, or the differences in locale, but it is also possible that black inmates are consistently treated more harshly in riot situations than members of other minority groups. In their comparative study of personality, intellectual, and behavioral characteristics of blacks, Chicanos, and whites in the Utah State Prison, the findings of Oldroyd and Howell (1977: 191) verified "the oft repeated impression that the Chicanos pose the greatest problems in prison and have more frequently committed assaultive crimes." Yet, corrections officers and state troopers did not use tear gas and an all-out assault to dispel the Chicano insurrection at Santa Fe. It is possible that since the rioting Chicanos murdered mostly other Chicano inmates, such killings merited little concern by the state because of the devaluation of those Chicano lives.

INMATE VIOLENCE

According to the scant literature available, prisoner-against-prisoner violence appears to be related to friction between whites and minorities that is further compounded by prison conditions, minority subcultural characteristics, and white and minority gangs. Such violence is manifested in assaults, killings, and rapes. Vetter and Silverman (1986: 530) observe that if white inmates are not prejudiced or excessively racially hostile when they enter prison, they become so after they are exposed to the hatred, hostility, and violence that black inmates display toward them.

A North Carolina study of ten correctional institutions reported in 1977 by Fuller and Orsagh is frequently cited to demonstrate the alleged interracial victimization of white inmates. The data base contained all officially reported assaultive behavior that took place in the ten prisons during the last three months in 1975. A quarterly victimization rate of 1.7 percent was corrected to 2.4 percent for unreported cases (Fuller and Orsagh, 1977: 37). Interviews with the superintendents of the prisons and a sample of four hundred inmates from an earlier survey (1971) led the researchers to ultimately reach a "net victimization rate" of 5.8 percent. Despite this somewhat confused blending of data sets and a wide variation in victimization rates, Fuller and Orsagh (1977: 38) concluded that the annual rate of 2.4 percent, which represented six inmates per thousand per quarter-year, was "considerably lower than the public, and even informed observers, suppose them to be."

During this period of time, only one homosexual rape was located in the offense report data. The superintendents estimated that nine sexual assaults had actually occurred among the inmate population of 4,495 within the three-month time frame. Using the mythical nine cases, Fuller and Orsagh (ibid.: 39) produced a victimization rate of 0.2. Making projections on the basis of correctional administrative hearsay is questionable; however, there is some verification for these low rates of sexual violence. Research in the New York state prison system (Lockwood, 1980) and a study of the federal penitentiary system (Nacci and Kane, 1983) also found prison homosexual rape to be a rare event. For example, Nacci and Kane (ibid.: 35) found that 2 out of 330 federal inmates (0.6 percent) had had to perform an undesired sex act, and 1 out of 330 had been raped (0.3 percent). Although whites were more likely to be "targets" of sexual pressure, they were just as likely to commit assaults as were blacks, but since blacks grouped together for assaults, there were more black assaulters (ibid.: 35-36).

In a review essay against prison racial segregation, Walker finds "good reason to assume that interracial assaults are overrepresented" in official records:

First, as in the "free world," victims are more likely to report crimes committed by strangers (in this context, "strangers" are defined as members of a different racial group). The second factor involves the dynamics of prison gangs. As virtually all observers have noted, prison gangs are hierarchies with a clearly defined set of roles. Many members join in order to receive protection against assaults by nonmembers. This is a contractual relationship and the price is often sexual submission to one of the stronger gang members. (1985b: 492)

Asserting that violence is "not simply a one-way, black-on-white phenomenon," Walker (ibid.: 492) refers to a study in which white inmates were found to not only encourage but also assist blacks in raping white inmates in order to "break" the white victims so that they would be agreeable to sexual relations with the white inmates who had instigated the original assaults.

Fuller and Orsagh found that victims and assailants tend to be of the same race in 61 percent of the officially reported incidents; e.g., 78 percent of the white offenders had white victims, and 53 percent of the nonwhite offenders had nonwhite victims. The other 39 percent of race victimizations were "multi-racial" incidents, with blacks more likely to assault whites (47 percent) than the reverse (22 percent). Fuller and Orsagh (1977: 45) determine that "the most important variable in explaining victimization is the fact that the victim was, himself, an assailant."

Ironically, in their study of race and prison adjustment in five correctional facilities, Goodstein and MacKenzie found that, contrary to their hypothesis, blacks did not report higher levels of conflict than whites, but, in fact, the opposite was true. In addition to reporting higher levels of prisoner/prisoner conflict, white inmates also scored higher on the assertive interactions scale, and reported no greater fear for their physical safety than blacks did. Accordingly, Goodstein and MacKenzie (1984: 290) speculate that "the victimization of whites by blacks found in other studies may not be expressions of rage and retaliation by blacks for past discrimination. Instead, this may be a response of blacks to assertive posturing by whites who are not backed up by a cohesive support group."

It has been suggested that "the balance of power has shifted in American prisons from control of prisons by largely white staff members to control by minority (black and Hispanic) inmates" (Wilbanks, 1987: 135). In contrast, Goodstein and MacKenzie found no overall differences between black and white inmates in event control.

> These results lend no support to the position that the shared cultural background of blacks resulting in more group solidarity and experience with violent subcultures may enable them to successfully exert more control of events in prisons than is possible for white inmates. Rather they suggest that blacks' lower ability to control events in prison is a reflection of discriminatory treatment in the institution, as previous research has suggested. (1984: 291-292)

Certainly the riots in the Attica and Santa Fe prisons indicate that the black and Hispanic inmate populations lacked control over the conditions and daily events of their lives, a condition that precipitated the riots in those prisons as it has in many others.

Various explanations have been offered for the alleged disproportionate rates of black violence against whites in prison settings.[18] A popular claim is that blacks are "getting even" or exacting revenge for the white oppression of blacks throughout history, or on a more personal level, as a result of negative racial experiences prior to their imprisonment. Also suggested is a variation of *importation theory,* or that before their incarceration, blacks were part of a "subculture of violence," which they brought with them into the institution.[19] In his classic *Hacks, Blacks, and Cons,* Carroll (1974: 188) found that in the maximum-security prison studied, white prisoners attacked blacks because of inflammatory racial rumors spread by the guards. The black prisoners believed that if the guards did not actually instigate such racial conflicts, they certainly promoted them. Thus, black aggression against whites may also reflect black cohesiveness and solidarity when an alliance of white prisoners and white staff is perceived as threatening, particularly when blacks view both groups as racist.

Recent attention to gang activities implies that to a large extent, minorities control contraband such as drugs—an economic enterprise made possible through compliance with corrections staff.[20] On the other hand, Carroll suggests the possibility of contraband colorblindness in the unanimous view held by the inmates at Eastern Correctional Institution:

> In their eyes, race is not a bar to exchange and cooperation in the network of relationships that surround traffic in drugs. While this view is not entirely accurate, the high demand for drugs amid a limited supply secured at considerable risk does in fact minimize the significance of race. In no other activity is biracial interaction so extensive. (Ibid.: 173)

Drug trafficking in prisons by black and other minority gangs, and organized white groups and gangs, mirrors the tactics, fear, intimidation, and violence found in drug dealing on the streets. Thus, the violence perpetrated by members of inmate gangs and other forms of prison violence tend to exacerbate racial polarity in correctional settings.

Most prison gangs are established in corrections facilities on the basis of race or ethnicity; some are generated in prison, and others are introduced into the prison by convicted gang members (Abadinsky, 1987: 427). Today's prison gangs are highly dissimilar to the political inmate groups that came into prominence in the 1960s for the purpose of securing minority prisoner rights and more humane treatment through peaceful and legal means—e.g., the Black Panther Party and the religiously affiliated Black Muslims, or Nation of Islam. Allen (1989: 10) cites a former Soledad inmate, John Irwin, now a sociology professor, who finds that the "peaceful" prisons in the first half of the century were dominated by white, old-style con bosses, but as the racial balance changed in the 1950s, "Blacks started moving out of their place, as they did on the outside. There was some degree of hostility, and it gave rise to racial battles." Accordingly, the gang leaders of the 1970s were more apt to provoke violence than keep violence under control in the style of the former "con bosses." The same dethroning of the old con power structure occurred at the notorious Stateville (Illinois) penitentiary in the late 1960s (Stojkovic, 1984: 515).

Between 1970 and 1973, eighty inmates and eleven guards were killed in the California prison system. While some attributed the violence to "racist correctional staff and administrators who perpetuated racial polarization," California officials blamed most of the turmoil on four major gangs contending for power and control (Carriere, 1980: 205-206). Those gangs—the Black Guerilla Family, Mexican Mafia, Nuestra Familia, and Aryan Brotherhood—are still active in the California prisons today. At Stateville and other Illinois prisons, four gangs, three black (the Stones, Disciples, and Vice Lords) and one Latino (the Latin Kings), which are referred to as "super-gangs," predominated in 1976 (Jacobs, 1976: 477), and still do, along with white supremacist gangs. As Jacobs (ibid.) notes, at Stateville, "the racial lines are impregnable." The Illinois minority prison gangs parallel their counterparts on the streets, mostly Chicago-area streets.

Initially, the most infamous Chicano prison gang in the California system called itself the "Baby Mafia," but it later changed its name to "Family." As one cultural anthropologist explains:

A major factor that ultimately led to the formation of Family is the Chicanos' feeling that they (as well as other prisoners) are being subjected to physical and mental abuse and manipulation by staff. . . . Because of their personal experience and knowledge, Chicano prisoners seriously question the morality of many staff members and administrators. The Chicanos see gross hypocrisy in the system, and their macho reaction against it is strong. However, the reaction cannot be overt and still be effective. (Davidson, 1974: 80-81)

There are indications that most of these gangs have expanded from their original home streets and state prisons to other state corrections systems. A riot on June 29, 1988 in the Bexar County Jail (San Antonio, Texas) was connected to the Mexican Mafia prison gang. All eleven inmates charged in the riot were confirmed as members of the Mexican Mafia, a gang that from 1980 to 1988 was linked to numerous violent crimes in Bexar County: "two capital murders, 11 attempted capital murders on a police officer, 34 murders, 12 attempted murders, 129 robberies, 14 rapes, 12 escapes, 108 cases of possession of heroin or cocaine, 33 cases of possession of marijuana, 247 burglaries and 14 aggravated assaults on a peace officer" (Edwards, 1988: 1).

Among the other eight gangs known to exist in Bexar County and the Texas prisons, the largest are the Texas Mafia, the all-white Aryan Brotherhood of Texas, and the Texas Syndicate, a predominantly Hispanic prison gang. Texas inmates in California prisons organized the Texas Syndicate for protection against western gangs. These new gangs, which are extremely well organized, are more ruthless, cold-blooded, and loyal to their fellow gang members than their earlier counterparts. Their gang loyalty is demonstrated through complete obedience to the gang, which usually includes a "death oath" and the commission of a contract killing, usually of another inmate (ibid.). Among the twenty-three rules listed in their constitution, the first one is that "no blacks will be accepted in the group." However, there is an all-black Texas gang, the Mandingo Warriors (Avery, 1989).

A California gang, the Black Guerilla Family, is one of the most feared prison gangs. Like all of the larger prison gangs, it operates its criminal activities, mostly narcotics trafficking, from the prison (Cheevers and Grabowicz, 1988). Other evidence of the extensive networking and expansion of these gangs is seen, for example, in the distribution of members of the Illinois black prison gangs. Two of the major gangs in the Pontiac (Illinois) prison, a maximum-security facility in which 60 percent of the inmates are serving time for murder (Smith, 1987), are represented in the Parchman prison in Sunflower County, Mississippi! It is believed that the Black Disciples and the Vice Lords were organized at Parchman in 1986, and by 1988 included between them about five hundred gang members out of the nearly forty-eight hundred prisoners (Branson, 1988). Vice Lords and Black Disciples, along with the Black Gangsters, Mexican Mafia, Crips, Bloods, (the latter are two Los Angeles gangs), Aryan Brotherhood, skinheads, neo-Nazis, and motorcycle gangs, have surged in membership in Iowa's prisons, where in 1981, their involvement in a riot at the Iowa State Penitentiary caused a million dollars in damages (Petroski, 1990).

Inmates at the Southern Ohio Correctional Facility, a maximum-security prison at Lucasville, are armed and preparing for violence that is the result of racial hatred and competition for the prison control of prostitution, extortion, and drug dealing. For over a year, black inmates have received threats from a violent white neo-Nazi gang, the Aryan Brotherhood. The Aryan members wear tattoos of lightning bolts on their necks—"symbols akin to the insignias worn on the collars of Hitler's elite SS troops," which they earn by committing violent or other criminal acts. They view Hitler as their savior and Nazism as their religion. At least six prison guards are reported to wear the symbol of racial hatred, and there is a history of racism directed against black inmates by white guards at Lucasville. Black prisoners, who are 60 percent of the Lucasville population, allege that some of the guards have sided with the Aryans (Salvato, 1990). At this writing, the racial situation is so volatile that violence may erupt at Lucasville or Parchman at any moment.

A Minority View

There is little doubt that peoples of color, especially African Americans, have always been disproportionately represented in the jails and prisons of this nation. Some efforts to explain this gross disparity between whites and blacks admit the complexity of the issue and, while not ruling out the possibility of racial discrimination, imply that differential involvement in serious crimes accounts for the difference (e.g., Hindelang, 1978; Blumstein, 1982; Langan, 1985). Hindelang (1978) used National Crime Survey (victimization reports) and Uniform Crime Reports (UCR) arrest descriptions; Blumstein (1982) drew upon inmate survey data to determine the racial distribution of prisoners and compared these data to criminal activity and crime type as measured by arrests (UCR); and Langan (1985) utilized National Crime Surveys (NCS) in conjunction with inmate surveys and a state prison admissions census. In their attempts to test the differential involvement (in crime) versus the racial discrimination thesis, the consensus among these researchers was that blacks commit "a disproportionate number of imprisonable crimes" (Langan, 1985: 680).

Although there are diverse serious problems associated with their conclusions, these studies have been used consistently to support a nondiscrimination thesis. However, significant questions can be raised concerning the facts that[21] (1) official measures of crime are limited by the assumption that arrests are good indicators of crime involvement;[22] (2) "aggregate data do not contain measures which adequately reflect the severity of crime or which reflect an individual offender's habitual involvement in crime" (Sabol, 1989: 416); (3) incarcerated population numbers cannot be strictly compared to numbers arrested, since "the latter is a flow concept" (ibid.: 413-414); (4) incidence of crime is confused with prevalence of crime among whites and minorities (ibid.: 415-416); (5) "we do not know which of the offenders described by NCS victims are actually arrested and processed through the criminal justice system" (ibid.: 414-415); (6) the racial disparity in incarceration cannot be understood by "a comparison of the racial distribution of persons arrested and incarcerated alone" (Dehais, 1983: 24); and, most significant, (7) each of these research efforts has ignored the effects of racial discrimination in a historical sense, particularly the influence of economic factors on minority crime and incarceration consistently espoused by a number of African American and other scholars—e.g., the relationship between unemployment and imprisonment (Dehais, 1983).

The question of economic subordination cannot be isolated from the question of color in deliberations on punishment and incarceration. As the most studied group, African Americans offer the principal example, but the "coolie" labor of Asian Americans and the "stoop" labor of Mexican and other Hispanic Americans must also be kept in mind. Historically, all peoples of color have been viewed by whites as inferior, controllable, and usable. In the eyes of the dominant group, racial minorities are frequently seen as surplus populations, and according to Quinney,

> a way of controlling this unemployed surplus population is simply and directly by confinement in prisons. The rhetoric of criminal justice—and that of conventional criminology—is that prisons are for incarcerating criminals. In spite of this mystification, the fact is that prisons are used to control that part of the surplus population that is subject to the discretion of criminal law and the criminal justice system. What is not usually presented are the figures and the conclusion that prisons are differentially utilized according to the extent of economic crisis. The finding is clear: the prison population increases as the rate of unemployment increases. (1977: 136)

In earlier times in this country, unemployment was not an issue, since slave labor was free labor. In fact, there was no reason to incarcerate people of African descent in the early South because plantation justice effectively and barbarically punished them for any real, imagined, or fabricated infractions through the use of slave codes.[23] After the Thirteenth Amendment legally freed the slaves in 1865, the Black Codes were installed to keep blacks in their place of assigned inferiority, since, following Quinney's line of thought, "ex-slaves can be analyzed as surplus populations" (Adamson, 1983: 556). The upshot was that since this "problem population" was also seen as a potential economic resource, in order to increase the number of prisoners, criminal laws were passed which added a number of serious crimes: "The black criminal population represented a threat to the economic supremacy of the white race, but also a resource that could be easily exploited" (ibid.: 562). These southern crime-control measures, which were directed primarily at ex-slaves, led to a "labor-driven prison system" (Sabol, 1989: 410).

Both southern and northern businessmen profited from the convict lease system, which was "a functional replacement for slavery; it provided an economic source of cheap labor and a political means to reestablish white supremacy in the South" (Adamson, 1983: 556). Black state convicts were leased out to work in mines and factories, on plantations and railroads, and in the woods for turpentine manufacture (ibid.: 561). The prison-based labor system did not lack "employees," since during the period from 1865 to 1890, blacks were over 95 percent of the inmate populations in most southern state penal systems (ibid.: 565).

In his study of North Carolina incarcerations between 1870 and 1980, Hawkins (1985a) also explores the idea of a racially based, labor-driven prison system. Stating that his focus is not on why blacks were disproportionately imprisoned in North Carolina over those years,[24] Hawkins is more concerned with explaining changes in the racial disproportion:

It appears that such changes are more likely a result of economically based transformations in social control that differentially impact upon racial groups than the independent effect of varying conceptions of race. Something more significant than the causal ordering of obviously related phenomena is suggested. I propose that research focused on changing conceptions or patterns of social control will account for short- and long-term race-related criminal justice outcomes and anomalies to a much greater extent than research which posits a notion of changing conceptions of race. (Ibid.: 190-191)

Thus, Hawkins concludes that changes in labor practices account for the North Carolina racial trends his analysis uncovered.

The breaking of Jim Crow laws[25] was also instrumental in increasing the incarcerated black labor pool. But more illuminating is Wilson's (1978: 14) observation that the "elaborate system of Jim Crow segregation" was created because of the southern white workers' effort to eliminate black competition. Thus, Wilson suggests that there was a move from racial oppression to economic class subordination. While other African American social scientists, especially criminologists, would insist that racial oppression is alive and well in the

United States criminal justice system, the difference seems a matter of degree. Wilson recognizes white resistance to minority progress and the "unyielding importance of race in America," but more important, his thesis emphasizes the influence of economic status on blacks' life chances (ibid.: 152), an argument applicable to all peoples of color. In fact, Wilson (ibid.) argues that "racial conflict and competition in the economic sector" are the "most important historical factors in the subjugation of blacks."[26]

The coupling of prison and the labor market as applied to African Americans leads to two critical observations: (1) the uncontestable historical and contemporary connection between labor-driven imprisonment based on color, and (2) the present-day implications of such economic motivations seen in expanding prison industries and the movement toward privatization.

When racial disproportionality in incarceration is considered on a regional basis, compared to southern blacks, blacks in the North have had higher rates of imprisonment than whites from the middle of the nineteenth century through the present (Sabol, 1989). Sabol (ibid.: 418) measured "excesses of black-white imprisonments over the ratio of black-white arrests" in all fifty states and the District of Columbia for 1960,[27] 1970, and 1980 and found a continuous increase in black incarcerations from 1960 to 1980 in the majority of states and a concomitant decrease in black arrests with wide variations across states and regions: "The calculations . . . provide convincing evidence that the national increase in black imprisonment *cannot* be the result of uniform black arrests across the nation. In most states and regions the black share of arrests has been falling! And yet, in almost every region black representation among those incarcerated has increased continuously" (ibid.: 421, 423).

Today the United States spends over $16 billion annually to operate its jails and prisons, and about $3.5 billion to build new prisons (Skinner, 1990: 21). In light of "the observed relationship between growth in the inmate population and increasing racial disparity" (Dehais, 1983: 13), the ever-expanding prison capacity will predictably involve even more peoples of color. One increasingly popular solution to defray some of the growing costs of incarceration and also permit some business persons to make a profit on inmate labor is prison industries, "a new form of slavery" (McShane and Williams, 1989: 568).

It is recalled that the leasing of black inmates in southern prisons prevalent in the middle and late nineteenth century provided a cheap labor pool for plantation owners and numerous other business enterprises. The situation was no better in the northern prisons, where instead of inmates' being "farmed out," "contractors brought their tools and materials to prison" (Walker, 1985a: 182). These forms of prison industry thrived until prison reformers, organized labor, and small entrepreneurs secured laws impeding prison industry. Congressional actions to discourage prison industry were enacted thereafter through the restriction of interstate transportation of prison-made products. But in 1979, the Prison-Industries Enhancement Act effectively removed these protective state laws and consequently "revitalized prison labor and industry" (Champion, 1990: 386-387). The prison enterprises of the 1980s range from industries that pay thirty-two cents per day to programs such as Free Venture, which pay "real-world wages" (Walker, 1985a). Today all states have prison industries with gross sales in the multi-millions, and even the federal government operates a profitable corporation, UNICOR, that relies on the profits of the labor of thousands of inmates (Champion, 1990: 387).

In addition to ethical concerns over the subscale wages paid in the majority of state prisons for the profit of private businesses and industries, one egregious drawback of prison industries is that despite the overrepresentation of minorities in these facilities, peoples of color are generally denied access to the better jobs in prison industries. The latest movement, toward privatization of prison management and ownership, can only worsen their status.

Probably the most potent example of the confusion introduced by privatization is the fact that the American Correctional Association (ACA) endorses it and the American Civil Liberties Union (ACLU) opposes it. In regard to the ACA, McShane and Williams (1989: 567) point out that corrections has been good business for private industry: the design and construction of additional prisons is a billion-dollar enterprise, and a number of ACA members and supporters, including its president, have been private businessmen. Further, many of the persons now in the private sector were those least successful in publicly operated prisons (ibid.: 569). On the ACLU side, the issue is the limitation of prisoners' rights (Champion, 1990: 381).

Our earlier discussion of prison industries revealed that such enterprises have been a part of the corrections system since the first U.S. prisons existed. In recent times, for the most part, the private-public contractual relationship has been in the private vendoring of services involving health care, educational and drug treatment programs, and vocational training to public facilities, as well as the operation of a limited number of juvenile delinquent facilities (Logan and Rausch, 1985; Bowditch and Everett, 1987). Prison Rehabilitation Industries and Diversified Enterprise Inc. (PRIDE, Inc.) has controlled and managed all Florida prison industries since 1981 (Sexton, Farrow, and Auerbach, 1985; Chi, 1990).[28] In 1988, PRIDE, Inc., which is operated by the Eckerd drugstore empire, realized a $4 million profit (Chi, 1990: 219). The private business sector is slowly expanding its operations in the "prison market"—today there are over two dozen for-profit corporations actively seeking and soliciting contracts or actually providing services that also include detention and incarceration (DiIulio, 1988; Chi, 1990).[29] The nation's first private state prison, a minimum-security facility, opened in 1986 in Marion, Kentucky (DiIulio, 1988),[30] and the first maximum-security correctional facility operated by a private firm was opened in Bay County, Florida in the mid-1980s (Bowditch and Everett, 1987).[31]

The history of the involvement of private enterprise in corrections has thoroughly documented the inhuman conditions and brutality attached to such labor-driven prison management:

Black convicts throughout the South were starved, chained to each other at night in over-crowded, dirty stockades, overworked and forced to continue working while sick, and whipped, occasionally to death. (Adamson, 1983: 561)

In many instances, private contractors worked inmates to death, beat or killed them for minor rule infractions, or failed to provide them with the quantity and quality of life's necessities (food, clothing, shelter) specified in often meticulously drafted contracts. (DiIulio, 1988: 3)

Living conditions for the predominantly black convict populations were inhuman. This is demonstrated by the high mortality rates. In 1883 a physician in Alabama estimated that most convicts died within three years. In that year 36 percent of the men working at the Milner coal mine died. The annual death rate at the campus run by the Greenwood and Augusta Railroad reached 53 percent. (Adamson, 1983: 566)

These horror stories documented in the 1880s and 1890s are not that unimaginable for the 1990s. In a recent monograph which addresses contracting with the private sector for the management of corrections facilities, Mullen (1985: 5) asks: "Will the economic motives of business conflict with the objectives of providing decent conditions of confinement?" In light of the conditions under which peoples of color, particularly political prisoners, are currently incarcerated, the answer would have to be resoundingly affirmative. The institutionalized racism prevalent in the corrections system and the nation at large would be as exacerbated by the profit motive as it is in the free world. The stereotypical notion that racial minorities are especially dangerous would undoubtedly be held by the employees, who could conceivably be "ill-trained, under-educated, poorly paid, and unprofessional" in for-profit penal institutions (DiIulio, 1988: 2).

Arguments supporting privatization claim cost-effectiveness, the provision of more prison space, and improved efficiency over the present corrections operations. However, the bottom-line reasoning is that "commercial prisons could save taxpayers money" (Logan and Rausch, 1985: 313). Since these private entrepreneurs do have profits as their primary motivation,

the development of for-profit prisons would create an industry with economic and political interests in prisons and therefore in policies concerning imprisonment. The availability of private prison space might encourage a continued reliance on prison sanctions; in addition, industry lobbies, concerned with maximization of profits, might promote policies that sustain or increase the demand for that space. . . . Because limiting consideration of alternative responses to crime would represent industry interests, research and discussion would focus on the benefits and even on the necessity of an extensive prison system. If this happens, profits—not theoretical justifications for imprisonment—would determine our use of prisons as the primary sanction for criminal behavior. (Bowditch and Everett, 1987: 451)

The consequences of such a possibility are enormous, for, as McShane and Williams (1989: 573) sensitively suggest, "The agenda we obviously do not need is one that promotes the efficient and economical construction of human warehouses."

Notes

Preface

1. For the most part, the focus of this work is on adult male offenders, although where relevant female and juvenile material will be introduced.

2. Terms such as "race," "ethnic," and "minority" will be defined and differentiated in Chapter 2. For the purposes of this book, "minority," or some variation, e.g., "racial minority," includes the racial and ethnic minorities in the United States who have experienced differential treatment because of their skin color—African Americans, Asian Americans, Hispanic Americans, and Native Americans. However, there is objection to the term "minority" because it is believed by some peoples of color to be pejorative and suggestive of inferiority.

3. Obviously, defining "whites" also has its problems. Although "Euro-American" is not a particularly accurate term to describe whites as a subgroup, it was selected as a more comparative term in relation to the African American, Asian American, Hispanic American, and Native American subgroups. "Anglo-American" and "Anglo" are used also, since they reflect the nomenclature used to describe whites in western and southwestern states.

4. Chapter 3, "The Minority 'Crime Problem,' " details the shortcomings of "official" criminal statistics in general, and minority criminal statistics specifically.

5. In its society and criminal justice system, Australia persists in discriminatory treatment of indigenous Aborigines because of color; see, e.g., Eggleston (1976).

6. Although control theory was not developed at the time, a parallel thesis was suggested by Norman S. Hayner in "Social Factors in Oriental Crime," *American Journal of Sociology* (1938): 908-919.

7. See, for example, Philip A. May, "Contemporary Crime and the American Indian: A Survey and Analysis of the Literature," *Plains Anthropologist* 27 (1982): 225-238.

8. In contrast, "crimes in the suites," or the deviance of "white-collar" criminals (e.g., lawyers, doctors, brokers, accountants, corporate businessmen), are most frequently handled by commissions and boards composed in large part of their peers.

1. Defining Race through the Minority Experience

1. While not scientifically acceptable, definitions from the dictionary are included solely because of their common usage by the general public for describing such terms.

2. This is the common nomenclature to describe whites in the West and Southwest.

3. Some Hispanics still do not like the appellation "Chicano" (see Lampe, 1982).

4. These nine states are Arizona, California, Colorado, Florida, Illinois, New Jersey, New Mexico, New York, and Texas.

5. Second-generation Japanese Americans.

2. The Minority "Crime Problem"

1. In 1991 the NCS survey changed its name to the National Crime Victimization Survey (NCVS), so both acronyms are used, depending upon when the data are reported.

2. In this chapter, "white" and "black" are used predominantly in order to coincide with the categorizations in UCRs, victimization reports, and the preponderance of studies of crime and race that use this nomenclature.

3. UCR arrest statistics for 1986 are used because that year was the last in which Hispanics were included as an identifiable offender group.

4. According to U.S. Census population estimates for 1988, whites were 84.4 percent, blacks 12.3 percent, American Indians and Alaska Natives 0.7 percent, Asian and Pacific Islanders 2.7 percent, and persons of Hispanic origin, which could be of any race, 8.1 percent. Without Hispanics, the total estimated minority population would be 15.6 percent (U.S. Census, 1990: 17).

5. Space considerations prohibit tabular listings of the Index, non-Index, and public-order crime arrests, but these tables are available from the author.

6. These categories will not be addressed in depictions of the arrests of the remaining minority groups.

7. For an excellent review of this literature, see Gibbons, 1984.

8. Since the 1980s there has been a proliferation of drug studies related to prostitution.

9. The cities involved were Birmingham, Chicago, Cleveland, Dallas, Detroit, Kansas City, New Orleans, New York, Philadelphia, Phoenix, Portland, St. Louis, San Diego, and Washington, D.C.

10. The figures for female arrestees who tested positive for one or more drugs ranged from 44 to 88 percent.

11. The Drug Use Forecasting Program, begun in 1986 in New York City, first reported on thirteen cities: Cleveland, Dallas, Detroit, Indianapolis, Kansas City, New Orleans, New York, Philadelphia, Portland, St. Louis, San Antonio, San Diego, and Washington, D.C. By the first quarter of 1990 the program involved twenty-three cities, including Birmingham, Chicago, Denver, Fort Lauderdale, Houston, Los Angeles, Phoenix, and San Jose (De Witt, 1990).

12. From an interview with a "crack" user.

13. The states were North and South Dakota, Minnesota, Montana, Oregon, Washington, and Wisconsin.

14. The discrepancy between Native American and white female rates was even more outstanding at 10 times (arrests) and 9.9 times (felonies), respectively.

15. Jeffery (1990: 387) states that Orientals process acetaldehyde differently and are usually unable to drink; thus, they do not have problems with alcoholism.

16. Asian American gambling seems to fit the entertainment theory, or that betting is an enjoyable pastime.

3. Explanations of Minority Crime

1. As indicated in the previous chapter, homicide is largely an intraracial crime; other African Americans are the most frequent victims of African American offenders.

2. We will return to Bernard's theory in the next section when subcultural theory is discussed.

3. This crime measure and its limitations were described in Chapter 2.

4. Interestingly, one facet of Tittle's definition of a subculture of violence clearly does not relate to African Americans: A subculture of violence, in the extreme, is common among super-macho types who thrive on magazines such as *Soldier of Fortune,* patronize army/navy stores, and immerse themselves in techniques of judo or karate as well as the use of guns. Its less extreme forms are often noted as a regional trait (1989: 283).

5. Incidentally, these are "classical" characteristics described in the early works of Park, Wirth, Burgess, et al.

6. This perspective is detailed later in this section.

7. Blau's theory and research of 125 of the largest United States SMSAs will be discussed more fully in the next section. In essence, Blau argues that racial income inequality generates hostility that results in violent crime in metropolitan areas.

8. These ideas are presented in the final section of the chapter, "A Minority View."

9. The Gini index, or Gini coefficient, commonly used in studies of poverty, deprivation, and income inequality, is computed using family incomes as a "function of the relative shares of income received by cumulative proportions of a population" (Loftin and Hill, 1974: 714). Put more simply, the Gini index "expresses the average difference in income between all pairs of individuals in a city relative to the average income of that city" (Liska and Chamlin, 1984: 387).

10. Jacobs points out that size of the community and the definition of robbery might explain this anomaly. Robbery involves confrontation with the victim, which would be hazardous in smaller communities because of the risk of recognition.

11. The Gini coefficient (index) was the measure of economic inequality.

12. Honolulu and New York City were excluded from this analysis.

13. Such a model implies that employment is very complicated and to be properly analyzed must be broken into many components such as quality and meaning of work, job status, etc., rather than being included merely as a dichotomous variable (Davis, 1983).

14. Parker and Horwitz (1986: 755) describe a lagged effect as occurring when "the influence of one variable (unemployment) on another (crime) does not occur immediately, but is delayed in its impact."

15. According to Merton's (1957) strain theory, "criminal involvement should be relatively high whenever legitimate opportunities to achieve success are closed to the individual" (Thornberry and Christenson, 1984: 400).

16. In Chapter 1 this matter of definition was detailed concerning African Americans.

17. These were the extensive heroin-related indictments and imprisonments in the 1950s; the Chicano Movement of the 1960s; and the prison "super-gangs" (e.g., the Mexican Mafia, La Familia) of recent years (see Chapter 6 for details on these prison gangs).

18. Depending on the individual state, these laws, enacted in response to increasing racial and religious terrorism, require separate criminal racial incident statistics and prohibit harassment, intimidation, mask wearing, paramilitary training, and defacement of property (Padgett, 1984: 106).

19. Georges-Abeyie is particularly concerned with widely circulated conclusions such as those drawn by Hindelang (1981), Wilbanks (1987), Petersilia (1985), and Klein, Petersilia, and Turner (1990).

20. As seen in Chapter 1, this same line of reasoning is of course applicable to the other racial/ethnic minorities, whose cultural variables have also been typically ignored.

21. This concept of the black "symbolic assailant" will be discussed more fully in Chapter 4.

4. Law and Its Enforcement against Minorities

1. A large portion of this section is from Coramae Richey Mann and Lance H. Selva, "The Sexualization of Racism: The Black Rapist and White Justice," *The Western Journal of Black Studies* 3 (Fall 1979): 168-177.

2. 106 U.S. 583 (1883).

3. However, Indians did not achieve this right until 1924, when they finally attained full citizenship.

4. *Slaughter-House Cases* 16 (Wallace) U.S. 36 (1873).

5. 92 U.S. 542 (1875).

6. 92 U.S. 214 (1875).

7. 100 U.S. 313 (1879).

8. 163 U.S. 537 (1896).

9. *U.S. v. Kagama,* 118 U.S. 375, 384 (1886), cited in Gubler, 1963: 208.

10. 379 U.S. 184 (1964).

11. 388 U.S. 1 (1967).

12. Murray, 1950: 39, 173-174, 428. The other states legally defining "Negro" were Alabama, Florida, Georgia, Kentucky, Mississippi, Missouri, North Carolina, North Dakota, Oklahoma, South Carolina, South Dakota, and Texas.

13. *Worcester v. Georgia* 31 U.S. 214 (1832), cited in Gubler, 1963: 210.

14. *Native American Church of North America v. U.S.* 272 F.2d 131, 134 (1959).

15. *United States Code, 1976 Edition Vol. Six, Title 25—Indians* (Washington, D.C.: U.S. Government Printing Office, 1977), pp. 1216-1217.

16. According to the U.S. Department of the Interior, *Opinions of the Solicitor, Vol. II* (February 1, 1971): 2024-2026, these states were Alaska, California, Florida, Idaho, Iowa, Kansas, Minnesota, Montana, Nebraska, Nevada, New York, New Mexico, North Carolina, Oklahoma, Oregon, Washington, and Wisconsin.

17. The twenty-nine states are the above (see n. 16) plus Arizona, Louisiana, Maine, Massachusetts, Michigan, Mississippi, North Dakota, South Dakota, Texas, Utah, Virginia, and Wyoming. Source: Carl Waldman, *Atlas of the North American Indian* (New York: Facts on File Publications, 1985), pp. 233-239.

18. Arizona Revised Statutes, Chapter 1, Sec. 13-108 (1985): 11, 27.

19. A recent article published in the *Journal of Research in Crime and Delinquency* by African American criminologists Vernetta Young and Anne Sulton, entitled "Excluded: The Current Status of African-American Scholars in the Field of Criminology and Criminal Justice," accurately pinpoints the problem:

There is an emphasis on funding large-scale data collection efforts, nearly all of which are conducted by White criminologists. As a result, money frequently is not available to fund the advancement of alternative theoretical or policy-oriented perspectives. Smaller, innovative, issue-specific proposals offered by African-American criminologists are not funded, supposedly because no money is available. Consequently, the quest to establish the field as a legitimate academic discipline is stymied. (1991: 112)

20. Police employment and crime rates have been found to be reciprocally related. See, for example, C. Ronald Huff and John M. Stahura, "Police Employment and Suburban Crime," *Criminology* 17, 4 (February 1980): 461-470.

21. This topic is discussed more fully in a later section of the chapter.

22. For a more detailed view of the origins of the police, see, e.g., Jerome H. Skolnick and Thomas C. Gray, *Police in America* (Boston: Little, Brown and Co., 1975).

23. See, e.g., Goldman (1976); McEachern and Bauzer (1964); Piliavin and Briar (1964).

24. This point is detailed in the next section on the police personality.

25. Even Wilbanks (1987: 61) notes that an African American is more than four times as likely to be arrested over a lifetime as is a white.

26. See, e.g., Jack J. Preiss and Howard J. Ehrlich, *An Examination of Role Theory: The Case of the State Police* (Lincoln: U. of Nebraska Press, 1966); Rodney Stark, *Police Riots: Collective Violence and Law Enforcement* (Belmont, CA: Wadsworth, 1972); Jerome H. Skolnick, "Why Police Behave the Way They Do," in Jerome H. Skolnick and Thomas C. Gray, eds., *Police in America* (Boston: Little, Brown and Co., 1975), and "A Sketch of the Policeman's Working Personality," in Jerome H. Skolnick, *Justice without Trial* (New York: Wiley, 1966); Arthur Niederhoffer, "Police Cynicism" and "Authoritarian Police," in *Behind the Shield: The Police in Urban Society* (Garden City, NY: Anchor Press, 1967).

27. See, e.g., Niederhoffer (1967); Preiss and Ehrlich (1966).

28. See, e.g., Goliath J. Davis, "Work Group Cohesion and Job Stress among Police Officers," unpublished Ph.D. dissertation, Florida State University, 1984, p. 29; Donald J. Newman and Patrick R. Anderson, *Introduction to Criminal Justice,* 4th ed. (New York: Random House, 1989), p. 141.

29. See, e.g., William Wilbanks, *The Myth of a Racist Criminal Justice System* (Monterey, CA: Brooks/Cole, 1987), p. 70.

30. See Chapter 1 for the definitions of these terms.

31. The historical implications of the drug/minority issue were detailed in Chapter 2.

32. The notorious Supreme Court case of Edward Lawson, an African American male who wore dreadlocks and was detained or arrested fifteen times simply for walking in white neighborhoods, challenged a California statute that required " 'suspicious' persons to identify themselves to a policeman's satisfaction" (Johnson, 1983: 214). Even this author was pulled over by a member of an urban police force, a flashlight was beamed in my eyes, and a .38 revolver was shoved in my face, simply because I was driving a late model Cadillac convertible. When I asked indignantly why I was receiving such treatment, the officers stated that it was the make of the automobile and the neighborhood that had aroused their suspicions. They apologized when they learned that it was also my neighborhood (which happened to be an integrated community).

33. It is noteworthy that two major Supreme Court cases on this point involved Mexican Americans: *Escobedo v. Illinois* and *Miranda v. Arizona*.

34. According to Morales (1972: 16-17), in 1943, U.S. sailors and Mexican American "zoot-suiters" engaged in a number of minor scrapes in Los Angeles. These skirmishes escalated to summer weekend riots, in one of which two hundred sailors in taxi cabs invaded the barrio and mauled and beat Mexican Americans. The sailors were accompanied by Los Angeles Police Department cars; the police watched the beatings and then jailed the victims. The Mexican government's intervention through protest forced the U.S. government to establish military control and end the riots.

35. According to Fyfe's Table 2, the shooter rates with no injury are: blacks, 84.2 percent; Hispanics, 70 percent; and whites, 45.7 percent.

36. Two comprehensive reviews of these studies are located in articles by Arnold Binder and Lorie Fridell, "Lethal Force as a Police Response," *Criminal Justice Abstracts* 16, 2 (June 1984): 150-180, and by James J. Fyfe, "Police Use of Deadly Force: Research and Reform," *Justice Quarterly* 5, 2 (June 1988): 165-205.

37. U.S. Supreme Court Reports. 85 L Ed 2d., pp. 3-4.

38. Police solidarity appears to increase cynicism and have negative effects on police performance. A recent study (Lester and ten Brink, 1985) indicates that police officers who socialized primarily with other officers when off duty had more tolerance for police misbehavior and were more willing to cover up such behavior. The solidarity extended to officers' being "more likely to take part in the execution of a suspect known to have killed a police officer, both during his apprehension and if he was freed by the courts on a technicality" (ibid.: 326).

39. For a more comprehensive list of the benefits of higher education for law enforcement, see Carter and Sapp (1990: 62-63).

40. For example, the Afro-American Patrolmen's League in Chicago, the Society of Afro-American Policemen with chapters in several cities, and nationwide organizations such as the National Organization of Black Law Enforcement Executives (NOBLE) and the National Black Police Association (NBPA), both based in Washington, D.C.

41. The justification for disapproving views is interwoven throughout the chapter, but is seen most vividly in the sections on police discretion, police prejudice, and police interactions with minorities.

42. The "neutral" category indicates extremely high percentages among African Americans of the middle to upper class (64 percent) and lower class (46 percent), with much lower figures for the other groups studied: white middle to upper class, 22 percent; 1980 Cubans, 16 percent; and 1960 Cubans, 8 percent.

5. Unequal Justice

1. Recently, Zatz (1985: 187) found that speed of felony case processing of African

Americans and Chicanos in California was influenced more by access to economic, political, and social resources than by cultural stereotyping.

2. The proportions for whites were 1.8 percent in 1983 and 18.5 percent in 1985. These figures represent the following increases: whites, +17.7 percent; blacks, +17.4 percent; Hispanics, +30.5 percent; other minorities, +21.7 percent.

3. The states permitting six-member juries are Connecticut, Florida, Louisiana, and Oregon. Nebraska and Utah allow eight-member juries.

4. 304 U.S. 358 (1928).

5. 287 U.S. 45 (1932).

6. 372 U.S. 335 (1963).

7. 407 U.S. 25 (1972).

8. 372 U.S. 353 (1963).

9. The topic of judges, their power and discretion, will be detailed later in the chapter.

10. In order of frequency, the West uses contract indigent defense programs more than any other region (32.9 percent), followed by the Midwest (8.5 percent), the South (6.8 percent), and the Northeast (3.7 percent).

11. See previous discussion of "client control."

12. 404 U.S. 257 (1971).

13. 434 U.S. 357 (1978).

14. Thurgood Marshall, William Brennan, Harry Blackmun, and Lewis Powell were the dissenting judges.

15. More recent data, based on thirty-two jurisdictions, show that an average of 75 percent of felony cases resulted in convictions in 1987 (Dillingham, 1990: 68). Further, that same year police arrested 1.9 million adults for serious crimes (Boland, Conly, Mahanna, Warner, and Sones, 1990: 3).

16. Court clerks, bailiffs, and other ancillary court personnel also exert a terrific amount of influence, but no empirical studies of these court "actors" were located. Court observations by the author confirm their importance in, for example, moving a case up on the docket, obtaining copies of documents, and securing trial transcripts expeditiously.

17. These states are Arkansas, Kentucky, Missouri, Oklahoma, Texas, and Virginia.

18. These incidents were excerpted from unpublished field notes.

19. State sentencing is emphasized, since states process substantially more minorities and are the primary focus of most studies on sentencing. Also, it is generally believed that federal courts are racially fairer than state courts.

20. Because the two reviews discussed (Hagan, 1974; Kleck, 1981) are fairly comprehensive and between them cover the years 1928 to 1979, the individual studies they reviewed will not be detailed. More attention is devoted to the studies on discrimination in sentencing since 1980. Further, only noncapital sentencing is included in this section, since capital punishment is addressed later in the chapter.

21. Following Wilbanks (1987), NDT refers to the nondiscrimination thesis and DT to the discrimination thesis.

22. For details of the research, the interested reader is referred to these reviews, or to the original studies themselves.

23. Zatz (1987: 71) prefers this term to "race" as more reflective of the "overlap between color and culture that may disadvantage minorities." She accurately notes that Latin American minorities are particularly affected and cites the example that a black Puerto Rican could experience racial discrimination a white Puerto Rican would not; however, both could encounter cultural and language obstacles and prejudice.

24. The *Indianapolis Star* studied 1988-1989 drug cases in Marion County (Indianapolis), Indiana. Its review of a random selection of two hundred cocaine-dealing cases revealed "unequal justice": 57 percent of minority defendants received prison sentences, as compared to 45.8 percent of white defendants. Once convicted, minority defendants

received an average 7.5 years in prison; whites' sentences averaged 4.6 years. The racial disparities are particularly shocking for first offenders—whites with average drug possessions of over 600 grams were sentenced to three years, whereas nonwhite first offenders possessed only 27.29 grams of cocaine but averaged over six-year sentences; the white minor criminal who had 553.33 grams was accorded a four-year sentence (McLaren and Niederpruem, 1990).

25. Also, in an earlier, unpublished version of their article, they found that recency of data held no more for studies rejecting the hypothesis of discrimination than for those supporting this hypothesis.

26. Addressing the negative effect of a juvenile record on adult sentencing, Clayton (1983: 19) notes an "element of bias in the sentencing process" by finding that blacks are treated more severely than whites with similar backgrounds and offense charges, and juvenile offenders are treated more harshly than nonjuvenile offenders, regardless of the type of crime.

27. Recall the previous discussion of the influence of social characteristics at stages prior to sentencing (pretrial).

28. While not exhaustive of all studies on race and sentencing, for the most part, both the NDT and DT studies cited include reports in the decade after the Hagan (1974), Kleck (1981), and Hagan and Bumiller (1983) reviews (or from 1980 to 1990). In some instances, references are made to earlier studies on race and sentencing to clarify the study being described. It was not the intention to overselect one view or the other; nonetheless, more DT than NDT reports were found, despite a search through the usual criminal justice and sociological abstract sources.

29. See Chapter 2 for general definitional problems related to race/ethnicity.

30. The authors differentiate between *racial discrimination*—an "ad hoc decision based on an offender's race rather than on clearly defined, legitimate standards"—and *racial disparity*—"when fair standards are applied but the incidence is different for racial groups" (p. 812).

31. Unfortunately, class-based disparities (defendant's income and occupation) and other important variables, such as the race, gender, and social class level of the victim, were omitted from the sample. Since members of other racial/ethnic groups such as Asian and Native Americans and other minorities were included in the "white" category, the results are obviously skewed. More precise definitions are needed, particularly since these groups constituted 10 percent of the white category (for a more detailed criticism of such exclusions, see Zatz, 1987: 82).

32. The states are Arizona (Tucson), Louisiana (New Orleans), Pennsylvania (Delaware County), Texas (El Paso), Virginia (Norfolk), and Washington (Seattle).

33. According to recent evidence from the Bureau of Justice Statistics (Greenfeld, 1989: 5), the minimum execution age in Indiana at the end of 1988 was sixteen. However, in South Dakota a ten-year-old could be tried as an adult and thus be sentenced to death.

34. These figures were calculated from an NAACP-LDF report dated August 23, 1991 and based on the 2,504 death row defendants at that time.

35. The latest report from the LDF (Winter 1991: 4) lists one black victim of a white defendant. However, the September 6, 1991 execution of Donald (Peewee) Gaskins in South Carolina was inappropriately counted by the LDF, since Gaskins had received the death sentence for another slaying of a white and later killed the black inmate in prison. As the head of the South Carolina Office of Appellate Defense stated, Gaskins "killed his black victim before the state could get around to killing him itself" ("Death Penalty Litigation Section," 1991: 5).

36. Streib's research also includes another oppressed group, females on death row; see, e.g., "Death Penalty for Female Offenders," *Cincinnati Law Review* 58, 3 (1990): 845-880.

37. For more comprehensive reviews, see, e.g., Wolfgang and Riedel (1973); Kleck

(1981); Radelet (1981); Baldus, Pulaski, and Woodworth (1983); Hagan and Bumiller (1983); Woodworth (1985); Paternoster (1985); Gross and Mauro (1989); Aguirre and Baker (1990); Keil and Vito (1989).

38. In 1977 the Supreme Court found in *Coker v. Georgia* (433 U.S. 584 [1977]) that the death penalty for the rape of an adult woman constituted cruel and unusual punishment under the Eighth and Fourteenth amendments, but only Justice Marshall raised the issue of racial discrimination (Dillingham, 1990).

39. 408 U.S. 239 (1972).

40. 428 U.S. 1543 (1976).

41. Bowers and Pierce (1980) point out that these four states accounted for about 70 percent of the nation's death sentences in the first five years post-*Furman*.

42. Their study was quite comprehensive and actually followed the stages of the capital process: arrest, charging, indictment, conviction, and sentencing. Bowers and Pierce also looked at arbitrariness by race, place, review process, and the form of the law. Although reference will be made throughout the chapter to these other analyses, the focus in this section is arbitrariness by race.

43. The scale measures deliberateness and heinousness of the killing and whether the victim was a stranger or nonstranger (Keil and Vito, 1989: 514).

44. 107 Sup. Ct. 1756 (1987).

45. Professor David Baldus of the University of Iowa and his colleagues conducted the studies. For more details on this effort see Baldus, Pulaski, and Woodworth (1983) and Baldus, Woodworth, and Pulaski (1990).

46. Gross and Mauro (1989: 12) list the ten statutory aggravating circumstances in Georgia capital offenses: when (1) the murderer has a record of capital felony conviction; (2) the murder was committed during another capital felony, aggravated battery, kidnapping, rape, burglary, or arson; (3) the offender knowingly created a death risk to persons in a public place; (4) the murder was committed for financial gain; (5) a judicial officer or prosecutor was killed for job-related reasons; (6) it was a hired murder; (7) the murder was "outrageously or wantonly vile, horrible or inhuman"; (8) a peace officer was killed in the line of duty; (9) the murderer was a prisoner or escaped prisoner; or (10) the murder was to prevent arrest or incarceration. Under Georgia law, if one or more of these aggravating factors are met, a murderer can receive the death penalty.

47. According to the source used by most psychologists and psychiatrists for the diagnoses, the *Diagnostic and Statistical Manual of Mental Disorders* (American Psychiatric Association, 1980: 318-319), the essential characteristics of an "antisocial personality disorder" tend to diminish after age thirty, "particularly sexual promiscuity, fighting, criminality, and vagrancy." Further, this disorder is found in less than 3 percent of American men, and "is more common in lower-class populations, partly because it is associated with impaired earning capacity and partly because fathers of those with the disorder frequently have the disorder themselves, and consequently their children often grow up in impoverished homes."

48. I recently analyzed data generously shared by the NAACP-LDF on race of offenders on death row on July 27, 1990 and the race of their victims. Of the 3,040 cases in which the race of the victim was known, 920 were minority/nonminority killings and 91 were nonminority/minority murders. These calculations showed that today a minority is ten times more likely to be on death row for killing a nonminority than the reverse.

49. 391 U.S. 510 (1968).

50. 402 U.S. 183 (1971).

51. It should be noted that under the federal system, there is no provision for automatic review of a death sentence (Greenfeld, 1989: 5).

52. 430 U.S. 482 (1977).

53. 364 U.S. 339 (1960).

54. There is more to the problem than the disparity in numbers on the "team." In his discussion of the indigent's right to "effective" counsel, Klein (1986: 663-675) lists several

deficiencies in indigent representation by underfunded defender offices with excessive case loads: inadequate case preparation; insufficient consultation with clients; improper plea bargaining; and insufficient input into the sentencing process. Klein (1986: 675) also points out that "the prosecution receives almost four times the amount of funds spent by state and local governments on indigent defense," and this does not include money spent on case preparation, which is primarily a police expenditure.

55. The more lenient decisions of liberal judges cancel out the severe determinations of racist judges. Another approach to the same problem is described by Miethe and Moore (1984) as "additive models." Such models, for example, combine blacks and whites in examinations of sentence severity based on the assumption that racial differences remain constant across all levels of social and case characteristics.

56. The problem of who is researching whom was addressed more fully in Chapter 2.

6. Warehousing Minorities

1. More recent prison surveys indicate that by the end of 1990, the number of federal and state prisoners was 771,243, a record high that represents a 34 percent increase between 1980 and 1990 (Cohen, 1991).

2. In 1989 there were 1,247,800 adult arrests for drug violations, with almost three-fourths of those confined for drug charges either black or Hispanic (Harlow, 1991: 2).

3. A recalculation removing the Hispanics from the "white" category suggests that only 23,791, or 40.3 percent, of federal prisoners are white.

4. The U.S. Centers for Disease Control on January 16, 1992 reported that among the second 100,000 AIDS cases, which differed from the first 100,000, 31 percent were black and 17 percent were Hispanic ("Spiraling AIDS Count Passes 200,000 Mark," 1992: A3).

5. In Arizona Arkansas, California, Colorado, Connecticut, Florida, Georgia, Hawaii, Indiana, Iowa, Maine, Massachusetts, Michigan, Mississippi, New Jersey, New York, North Carolina, Oregon, Pennsylvania, Utah, Virginia, and Wisconsin.

6. The topics of inmate rape and other violence are addressed later in the chapter.

7. These proportions were calculated from Table 5.6 in *Correctional Populations in the United States, 1989* (Dillingham, 1991: 69). Hispanics were calculated separately for federal (26.6 percent) and state prisons (18 percent), respectively (ibid.: 72). They were 17.4 percent of jail incarcerations (Beck, 1991: 3).

8. A write-up involves the receipt of tickets or incident reports, with records of same placed in administrative files. Infractions vary in seriousness from horseplay to murder (Stephan, 1989: 2).

9. Ironically, at the same time Wilbanks (1987: 132) challenges the validity of prisoner self-report data, he attempts to demonstrate that there is no racial discrimination in work assignments and program participation by drawing upon the inmate self-report findings used by Petersilia (1983) in California, Texas, and Michigan.

10. The status of Hispanic inmates relative to jobs was not given. This is curious in light of the large populations of Hispanics in California and Texas.

11. Although Black Muslims constitute a religious group—the Nation of Islam—because they protect their own and other African Americans and help them achieve pride and respect, they are viewed as a black political organization and seen as "troublesome" by corrections administrations (Morris, 1974).

12. The National Conference on Black Lawyers, the National Alliance against Racist and Political Repression, and the Commission for Racial Justice of the United Church of Christ.

13. The international jurist observers were from India, Sweden, Great Britain, Nigeria, Chile (in exile), Trinidad-Tobago, and Senegal.

14. Under American jurisprudence and common law, a prima facie case exists when the evidence is sufficiently strong in favor of the litigating party such that his opponent is

called upon to answer it, and it can be overthrown only by rebutting evidence by the other side (Hinds, 1979: 3).

15. These Puerto Ricans are among the political prisoners whose plights were investigated by the aforementioned international jurists and found to demonstrate human rights violations.

16. Recall the problems associated with PSRs for minorities delineated in the previous chapter.

17. Explanations of violent behavior were discussed in Chapter 3.

18. For a more detailed review, see Goodstein and MacKenzie (1984). It should also be noted that most of these explanations could apply to other imprisoned minority groups, especially Hispanics.

19. The subculture of violence perspective was detailed in Chapter 3.

20. Stojkovic's (1984) qualitative study of a newly constructed maximum-security prison in a midwestern state identified five basic types of power among inmates: coercive, referent, resource, expert, and legitimate. There was a less developed group or gang system; hence, the minority inmates appeared limited to referent power (black religious groups) and possibly some coercive power (toughness). Older inmates seemed to control legitimate power, while white prisoners commanded resource (drugs) and expert (e.g., jailhouse lawyer) power. Based on the events in older prisons, it would be interesting to see what power configurations are in effect after the "newness" of the facility wears off.

21. See Sabol (1989), who provides in-depth analyses of the caveats involved in these studies.

22. See Chapter 2 for detailed criticisms of UCR statistics and Chapter 5 for the influence of prosecutors' discretion and decisions on minority indictments and sentences and the importance of the presentence investigation report on judicial sentencing.

23. See Chapter 4 for a review of these and other anti-black laws during the post-slavery period.

24. Yet, the "why" according to Hawkins is the result of "historical patterns of racism" which led to more black crime and more labeling of blacks as criminals for a "variety of nonbehavioral reasons" (1985a: 190).

25. Although these laws were described in chapters 2 and 5, the focus here is on the economic subordination of African Americans as a result of these laws and other practices.

26. Wilson (1978: 14) writes of an "ideology of biological racism" that reinforced Jim Crowism. Although Wilson does not address the question of African American crime and the economic ramifications of labor-driven incarceration of African American and other racial minorities, he nonetheless provides a solid grounding for exposure of the racist economic drive behind such practices.

27. These data for 1960 represented nonwhites because of the census classification at the time, but 1970 and 1980 arrest and imprisonment data refer to blacks in Sabol's study.

28. On an investigative tour by women legislators of the Florida women's prison at Lowell, women inmates were observed grinding lenses as a part of this program. They told this author (an observer) that they were paid one dollar per eight-hour day. The lenses were made for eyeglasses sold in the statewide drugstore chain of a private corporation.

29. Some of the most celebrated corporations are the American Corrections Corporation, Behavioral Systems Southwest, Buckingham Security Limited, the Corrections Corporation of America (CCA), the Eckerd Foundation, RCA, and the U.S. Corrections Corporation.

30. U.S. Corrections Corporation.

31. Corrections Corporation of America (CCA).

Bibliography

Abadinsky, Howard. 1987. *Crime and Justice*. Chicago, IL: Nelson-Hall.

Adams, Stuart N. 1976. "The 'Black Shift' Phenomenon in Criminal Justice." *Justice System Journal* 2 (Winter):185-194.

Adamson, Christopher R. 1983. "Punishment after Slavery: Southern State Penal Systems, 1865-1890." *Social Problems* 30 (5):555-569.

Agopian, Michael, Duncan Chappell, and Gilbert Geis. 1974. "Interracial Forcible Rape in a North American City." In I. Drapkin and E. Viano (eds.), *Victimology*. Lexington, MA: Lexington Books.

Agresti, David L., and Richard Dembo. 1984. "A Study of Capital Punishment of Murderers in America since 1800 by Race and Sex of Offender and Victim." Paper presented at annual ASC meeting.

Aguirre, Adalberto, and David V. Baker. 1990. "Racial Discrimination in the Imposition of the Death Penalty." *Criminal Justice Abstracts* 22 (1):135-153.

Aguirre, Lydia R. 1975. *La Causa Chicana: The Movement for Justice*. New York: Family Service Association of America.

Albonetti, Celeste A. 1986. "Criminality, Prosecutorial Screening, and Uncertainty: Toward a Theory of Discretionary Decision Making in Felony Case Processings." *Criminology* 24 (4):623-644.

Allan, Emilie Anderson, and Darrell J. Steffensmeier. 1989. "Youth, Underemployment, and Property Crime: Differential Effects of Job Availability and Job Quality on Juvenile and Young Adult Arrest Rates." *American Sociological Review* 54 (1):107-123.

Allen, Charlotte Lou. 1989. "The Success of Authority in Prison Management." *Insight* (Feb. 13):8-19.

Allen, Donald M. 1980. "Young Male Prostitutes: A Psychosocial Study." *Archives of Sexual Behavior* 9: 399-426.

Allen, Zack W. 1989. *Felony Sentences in State Courts, 1986*. Ann Arbor, MI: CJAIN.

Alpert, Geoffrey P., and Roger G. Dunham. 1988. *Policing Multi-Ethnic Neighborhoods: The Miami Study and Findings for Law Enforcement in the United States*. New York: Greenwood Press.

Alvarez, Rudolfo, and Kenneth G. Lutterman. 1979. *Discrimination in Organizations*. San Francisco, CA: Jossey-Bass.

American Psychiatric Association. 1980. *Diagnostic and Statistical Manual of Mental Disorders*. 3rd ed. Washington, D.C.: American Psychiatric Association.

Amini, Johari M. 1972. *An African Frame of Reference*. Chicago, IL: Institute of Positive Education.

Amir, Menachem. 1971. *Patterns in Forcible Rape*. Chicago, IL: University of Chicago Press.

Apple, Nancy, and David J. O'Brien. 1983. "Neighborhood Racial Composition and Residents' Evaluation of Police Performance." *J. of Police Science and Administration* 11 (1):76-84.

Arizona Advisory Commission. 1977. *Justice in Flagstaff: Are These Rights Inalienable?* Washington, D.C.: U.S. Commission on Civil Rights.

Austin, James, Barry Krisberg, and Paul Litsky. 1985. *Evaluation of the Field Test of Supervised Pretrial Release: Final Report*. Washington, D.C.: U.S. Government Printing Office.

Austin, Roy L. 1983a. "Progress toward Racial Equality and Reduction of Black Criminal Violence." Unpublished paper.

———. 1983b. "The Colonial Model, Subcultural Theory and Intragroup Violence." *J. of Criminal Justice* 11:93-104.

Austin, W. T. 1979. "Portrait of a Courtroom: Social and Ecological Impressions of the Adversary Process." Paper presented at ASC annual meeting.

Avery, Libby. 1989. "Texas Prison Gangs: Committed to Killing." *Corpus Christi (Texas) Caller* (Aug. 13).

Avins, A. 1966. "Anti-Miscegenation Laws and the 14th Amendment: The Original Intent." *Virginia Law Review* 52: 1224-1255.

Avison, William R., and Pamela L. Loring. 1986. "Population Diversity and Cross-National Homicide: The Effects of Inequality and Heterogeneity." *Criminology* 24 (4):733-749.

Bahr, Howard M., Bruce A. Chadwick, and Robert C. Day. 1972. *Native Americans Today*. New York: Harper and Row.

Bailey, William C. 1984. "Poverty, Inequality, and City Homicide Rates." *Criminology* 22 (4):531-550.

Baker, George. 1977. *Indians in the Red*. Washington, D.C.: U.S. Government Printing Office.

Baker, James N., and Linda Wright. 1991. "Los Angeles After Shocks." *Newsweek* (Apr. 1):18-19.

Baker, Timothy, Fredrica Mann, and C. Jack Friedman. 1975. "Selectivity in the Criminal Justice System." *Prison Journal* 55 (1):23-34.

Balch, Robert W. 1972. "The Police Personality: Fact or Fiction?" *J. of Criminology, Criminal Law and Police Science* (Mar.):106-119.

Baldus, David C., Charles Pulaski, and George Woodworth. 1983. "Comparative Review of Death Sentences: An Empirical Study of the Georgia Experience." *J. of Criminal Law and Criminology* 74 (1983):661-753.

Baldus, David C., George Woodworth, and Charles A. Pulaski, Jr. 1990. *Equal Justice and the Death Penalty*. Boston, MA: Northeastern University Press.

Balkan, Shiela, Ronald J. Berger, and Janet Schmidt. 1980. *Crime and Deviance in America: A Critical Approach*. Belmont, CA: Wadsworth Publishing Company.

Ball, John C., and M. P. Lau. 1966. "The Chinese Narcotic Addict in the United States." *Social Forces* 45 (1):68-72.

Ball-Rokeach, Sandra J. 1973. "Values and Violence: A Test of the Subculture of Violence Thesis." *American Sociological Review* 38 (Dec.):736-749.

Banks, Taunya. 1977. "Discretionary Justice and the Black Offender." In Charles E. Owens and Jimmy Bell, *Blacks and Criminal Justice*. Lexington, MA: D. C. Heath and Company.

Bannon, J. D., and G. M. Wilt. 1973. "Black Policemen: A Study of Self-Images." *J. of Police Science Administration* 1:23-29.

Barak, Gregg. 1991. "Cultural Literacy in Criminology and the 'White Wash Effect' in Criminal Justice Pedagogy: On the Emerging Multicultural Discourse." Paper presented at ACJS.

Barlow, Hugh D. 1984. *Introduction to Criminology*. 3rd ed. Boston, MA: Little, Brown and Company.

Bastian, Lisa D. 1990. *Hispanic Victims*. Washington, D.C.: USDJ.

Bastian, Lisa D., and Marshall M. DeBerry, Jr. 1991. *Criminal Victimization, 1990*. Washington, D.C.: USDJ.

Battle, Jackson B. 1971. "In Search of the Adversary System: The Cooperative Practices of Private Criminal Defense Attorneys." *Texas Law Review* 50:60-118.

Baughman, Laurance E. Alan. 1966. *Southern Rape Complex: One Hundred Year Psychosis*. Atlanta, GA: Pendulum Books.

Bayley, David H., and Harold Mendelsohn. 1968. *Minorities and the Police: Confronta-tion in America.* New York: Free Press.

Beah, Jerry L. 1972. "Native Americans and Discrimination in Kansas: Trials from Injus-tice." *Kansas Law Review* 20 (3):468-485.

Beard, Eugene. 1977. "The Black Police in Washington, D.C." *J. of Police Science and Administration* 5 (1):48-52.

Beck, Allen J. 1991. *Profile of Jail Inmates, 1989.* Washington, D.C.: U.S. Department of Justice.

Becker, Howard S. 1963. *Outsiders: Studies in the Sociology of Deviance.* London, Eng-land: Free Press of Glencoe.

Bell, Daniel J. 1983. "Police Attitudes: Based on Beliefs or Race?" *Police Studies* 6 (1):21-26.

Bell, Derrick A. 1973. "Racism in American Courts: Cause for Black Disruption or De-spair?" *California Law Review* 61 (1973):165-204.

Benderoth, Donald. 1983a. "The Effects of the 1980 Cuban Freedom Flotilla, Part One." *Law and Order* 31 (4):32-38.

———. 1983b. "After Shock: The Effects of the 1980 Cuban Freedom Flotilla, Part Two." *Law and Order* 31 (5):44-50.

Bennett, Lerone. 1975. *The Shaping of Black America.* Chicago: Johnson Publishing Company.

Bernard, J. L. 1979. "Interaction between the Race of the Defendant and That of Jurors in Determining Verdicts." *Law and Psychology Review* 5 (Fall):103-111.

Bernard, Thomas J. 1990. "Angry Aggression among the 'Truly Disadvantaged.' " *Crimi-nology* 28 (1):73-96.

Bernstein, Ilene Nagel, William R. Kelly, and Patricia A. Doyle. 1977. "Societal Reaction to Deviants: The Case of Criminal Defendants." *American Sociological Review* 42 (Oct.):743-755.

Bessette, Joseph M. 1989. *BJS Data Report, 1988.* Washington, D.C.: U.S. Government Printing Office.

Best, Joe L. 1982. "Careers in Brothel Prostitution." *J. of Interdisciplinary History* 12:597-619.

Bienen, Leigh. 1987. "Of Race, Crime and Punishment." *The New York Times* (June 21).

Binder, Arnold, and Lorie Fridell. 1984. "Lethal Force as a Police Response." *Criminal Justice Abstracts* 16(2):250-280.

Black, Donald J. 1970. "The Production of Crime Rates." *American Sociological Review* 35:733-748.

Black, Donald J., and Albert J. Reiss. 1970. "Police Control of Juveniles." *American Sociological Review* 35:63-77.

Blau, Peter M., and Judith R. Blau. 1982. "The Cost of Inequality: Metropolitan Struc-ture and Violent Crime." *American Sociological Review* 47 (1):114-129.

Blaut, James. 1977. "Are Puerto Ricans a National Minority?" *Monthly Review* (May):35-55.

Bloch, Herbert A. 1951. "The Sociology of Gambling." *American Journal of Sociology* 57 (3):215-221.

Block, Carolyn Rebecca. 1985. *Lethal Violence in Chicago over Seventeen Years: Homi-cides Known to the Police, 1965-1981.* Chicago, IL: Illinois Criminal Justice Infor-mation Authority.

Block, Richard. 1976. "Homicide in Chicago: A Nine-Year Study (1965-1973)." *J. of Criminal Law and Criminology* 66 (4):496-510.

Blumberg, Abraham S. 1967. "The Practice of Law as Confidence Game." *Law and Society Review* 1 (1967):15-39.

———. 1979. *Criminal Justice: Issues and Ironies.* 2nd ed. New York: New Viewpoints.

Blumberg, Abraham S., and Arthur Niederhoffer. 1985. *The Ambivalent Force: Perspec-tives on the Police.* 3rd ed. New York: Holt, Rinehart and Winston.

Blumstein, Alfred. 1982. "On the Racial Disproportionality of the United States Prison Population." *J. of Criminal Law and Criminology* 73 (3):1259-1281.

――――. 1984. "Sentencing Reforms: Impacts and Implications." *Judicature* 68 (4-5):129-139.

Boggs, Sarah L., and John Galliher. 1975. "Evaluating the Police: A Comparison of Black Street and Household Respondents." *Social Problems* 22:393-406.

Bohm, Robert M. 1987. "American Death Penalty Attitudes: A Critical Examination of Recent Evidence." *Criminal Justice and Behavior* 14 (3):380-396.

Bohm, Robert M., Louise J. Clark, and Adrian F. Aveni. 1990. "The Influence of Knowledge on Reasons for Death Penalty Opinions: An Experimental Test." *Justice Quarterly* 7 (1):175-188.

Boland, Barbara, Catherine H. Conly, Paul Mahanna, Lynn Warner, and Ronald Sones. 1990. *The Prosecution of Felony Arrests, 1987.* Washington, D.C.: U.S. Department of Justice.

Boland, Barbara, and Brian Forst. 1984. *The Prevalence of Guilty Pleas.* Washington, D.C.: U.S. Department of Justice.

Bondavalli, Bonnie J., and Bruno Bondavalli. 1981. "Spanish-Speaking People and the North American Criminal Justice System." In R. L. McNeeley and C. E. Pope (eds.), *Race, Crime and Criminal Justice.* Beverly Hills, CA: Sage Publications.

Booth, Alan, David R. Johnson, and Harvey M. Choldin. 1977. "Correlates of City Crime Rates: Victimization Surveys versus Official Statistics." *Social Problems* 25 (Dec.):187-197.

Bowditch, Christine, and Ronald S. Everett. 1987. "Private Prisons: Problems within the Solution." *Justice Quarterly* 4 (3):441-453.

Bowers, William J., and Glenn L. Pierce. 1980. "Arbitrariness and Discrimination under Post-Furman Capital Statutes." *Crime and Delinquency* 26 (4):563-635.

Bowker, Lee H. 1985. "An Essay on Prison Violence." In M. Braswell, S. Dillingham, and R. Montgomery, Jr. (eds.), *Prison Violence in America.* Cincinnati, OH: Anderson.

Braithwaite, John. 1981. "The Myth of Social Class and Criminality Reconsidered." *American Sociological Review* 46 (1):36-57.

Branson, Reed. 1988. "Parchman Officials Face Rising Gang Participation by Inmates." *(Jackson, Mississippi) Clarion-Ledger* (Sept. 11):1.

Braswell, Michael, Steven Dillingham, and Reid Montgomery, Jr. 1985. *Prison Violence in America.* Cincinnati, OH: Anderson.

Brearley, H. C. 1932. *Homicide in the United States.* Chapel Hill, NC: University of North Carolina Press.

Brenner, Robert N., and Marjorie Kravitz. 1979. *A Community Concern: Police Use of Deadly Force.* Washington, D.C.: U.S. Government Printing Office.

Brosi, Kathleen B. 1979. *A Cross-City Comparison of Felony Case Processing.* Washington, D.C.: U.S. Department of Justice.

Brown, Shirley Vining. 1979. "Race and Parole Hearing Outcomes." In R. Alvarez and K. G. Lutterman (eds.), *Discrimination in Organizations.* San Francisco, CA: Jossey-Bass.

Brown, Stephen, and Thomas W. Woolley. 1983. "Data Analysis and the City Sample of the National Crime Survey Program: A Critique." Unpublished paper presented at ASC meeting, Denver.

Brownfield, David. 1986. "Social Class and Violent Behavior." *Criminology* 24 (3):421-438.

Bryan, James H. 1965. "Apprenticeships in Prostitution." *Social Problems* 12 (Winter):287-297.

Bullington, Bruce. 1977. *Heroin Use in the Barrio.* Lexington, MA: D. C. Heath.

Bullock, Henry Allen. 1961. "Significance of the Racial Factor in the Length of Prison Sentences." *J. of Criminal Law, Criminology and Police Science* 52:411-417.

Burgess, Ernest W. 1926. *The Urban Community*. Chicago, IL: University of Chicago Press.

Burns, Haywood. 1973. "Black People and the Tyranny of American Law." *The Annals of the American Academy of Political and Social Sciences* 407 (May):156-166.

Butts, W. M. 1947. "Prostitutes of the Metropolis." *J. of Clinical Psychopathology* 8 (Apr.).

Buzawa, Eva S. 1981. "The Role of Race in Predicting Job Attitudes of Patrol Officers." *Journal of Criminal Justice* 9 (1):63-77.

Bynum, Tim S. 1981. "Parole Decision Making and Native Americans." In R. L. Mc-Neely and C. E. Pope (eds.), *Race, Crime and Justice*. Beverly Hills, CA: Sage.

———. 1982. "Release on Recognizance: Substantive or Superficial Reform?" *Criminology* 20 (1):67-82.

Bynum, Tim S., Gary W. Cordner, and Jack R. Greene. 1982. "Victim and Offense Characteristics: Impact on Police Investigative Decision-Making." *Criminology* 20 (3-4):301-318.

Campbell, Valencia. 1980. "Double Marginality of Black Policemen: A Reassessment." *Criminology* 17 (4):477-484.

Carey, James T. 1978. *An Introduction to Criminology*. Englewood Cliffs, NJ: Prentice-Hall.

Carney, Louis P. 1974. *Introduction to Correctional Science*. New York: McGraw-Hill.

Carpenter, Bruce N., and Susan M. Raza. 1987. "Personality Characteristics of Police Applicants: Comparisons across Subgroups and with Other Populations." *J. of Police Science and Administration* 15 (1):10-17.

Carriere, Colin C. 1980. "The Dilemma of Individual Violence in Prisons." *New England Journal of Prison Law* 6 (2):195-230.

Carroll, Lee, and Claire P. Cornell. 1985. "Racial Composition, Sentencing Reforms, and Rates of Incarceration, 1970-1980." *Justice Quarterly* 2 (4):473-490.

Carroll, Lee, and Pamela Irving Jackson. 1983. "Inequality, Opportunity, and Crime Rates in Central Cities." *Criminology* 21 (2):178-194.

Carroll, Leo. 1974. *Hacks, Blacks, and Cons: Race Relations in a Maximum Security Prison*. Lexington, MA: D. C. Heath.

———. 1990. "Race, Ethnicity, and the Social Order of the Prison." In Delos H. Kelly (ed.), *Criminal Behavior*. New York: St. Martin's Press.

Carter, Dan T. 1969. *Scottsboro: A Tragedy of the American South*. Baton Rouge, LA: Louisiana State University Press.

Carter, David L. 1986. "Hispanic Police Officers' Perception of Discrimination." *Police Studies* 9 (4):204-210.

Carter, David L., and Allen D. Sapp. 1990. "The Evolution of Higher Education in Law Enforcement: Preliminary Findings from a National Study." *J. of Criminal Justice Education* 1 (1):59-85.

Cash, Wilbur J. 1941. *The Mind of the South*. New York: Alfred A. Knopf.

Casper, Jonathan D. 1972. *American Criminal Justice*. Englewood Cliffs, NJ: Prentice-Hall.

———. 1978. *Criminal Courts: The Defendant's Perspective*. Washington, D.C.: U.S. Department of Justice.

Centers for Disease Control. 1986. *Homicide Surveillance: High-Risk Racial and Ethnic Groups—Blacks and Hispanics, 1979-1983*. Atlanta, GA: Centers for Disease Control.

Chadwick, Bruce A., and Joseph H. Stauss. 1975. "The Assimilation of American Indians into Urban Society: The Seattle Case." *Human Organization* 34 (4):359-369.

Chaiken, Jan, and Douglas McDonald. 1988. *Drug Law Violators, 1980-86*. Washington, D.C.: U.S. Department of Justice.

Chambliss, William J., and Robert B. Seidman. 1971. *Law, Order, and Power*. Reading, MA: Addison-Wesley.

Champion, Dean J. 1990. *Criminal Justice in the United States.* Columbus, OH: Merrill Publishing Company.

Chandras, Kananur V. 1978. *Racial Discrimination against Neither-White-nor Black American Minorities.* San Francisco, CA: R and E Research Associates.

Cheevers, Jack, and Paul Grabowicz. 1988. "Prison Gang Muscles in on Drug Dealers." *(Oakland, CA) Tribune* (Feb. 21).

Chi, Keon S. 1990. "Prison Overcrowding and Privatization: Models and Opportunities." In J. J. Sullivan and J. L. Victor (eds.), *Criminal Justice.* Guilford, CT: Dushkin.

Chin, Ko-Lin. 1990. *Chinese Subculture and Criminology.* Westport, CT: Greenwood Press.

Chiricos, Theodore G. 1987. "Rates of Crime and Unemployment: An Analysis of Aggregate Research Evidence." *Social Problems* 34 (2):187-212.

Chrisman, Robert. 1971. "Black Prisoners, White Law." *The Black Scholar* 2 (8-9):44-46.

Christianson, Scott. 1980. "Racial Discrimination and Prison Confinement: A Follow-Up." *Criminal Law Bulletin* 16 (6):616-621.

————. 1981. "Our Black Prisons." *Crime and Delinquency* 27 (3):364-375.

Clark, Hugh. 1984. "More Contraband Found at Kulani." *(Honolulu, Hawaii) Bulletin and Advertiser* (June 1):1.

Clark, Kenneth B. 1965. *Dark Ghetto.* New York: Harper and Row.

Clayton, Obie Jr. 1983. "A Reconsideration of the Effects of Race in Criminal Sentencing." *Criminal Justice Review* 8 (2):15-20.

Clelland, Donald, and Timothy J. Carter. 1980. "The New Myth of Class and Crime." *Criminology* 18 (3):319-336.

Clinard, Marshall B., and Richard Quinney. 1973. *Criminal Behavior Systems: A Typology.* New York: Holt, Rinehart and Winston.

Cockrell, Tom. 1983. *Sentencing Criminals: Minority vs. White Experience in the Criminal Justice System.* Santa Monica, CA: Rand Checklist.

Cohen, Howard. 1987. "Overstepping Police Authority." *Criminal Justice Ethics* (Summer/Fall):52-60.

Cohen, Lawrence E., and Kenneth C. Land. 1984. "Discrepancies between Crime Reports and Crime Surveys: Urban and Structural Determinants." *Criminology* 22 (4):499-530.

Cohen, Murray L., and Richard J. Boucher. 1972. "Misunderstandings about Sex Criminals." *Sexual Behavior* 2 (3):57-62.

Cohen, Robyn L. 1991. *Prisoners in 1990.* Washington, D.C.: U.S. Department of Justice.

Cole, Johnetta B. 1970. "Culture: Negro, Black and Nigger." *The Black Scholar* 1:40-44.

Collins, James J., Robert L. Hubbard, and J. Valley Rachal. 1985. "Expensive Drug Use and Illegal Income: A Test of Explanatory Hypotheses." *Criminology* 23 (4):743-764.

Combs, Michael W., and John C. Comer. 1981. "Race and Capital Punishment: A Longitudinal Analysis." *Phylon* (Mar.):350-359.

Comer, James P. 1972. *Beyond Black and White.* New York: Quadrangle Books.

"Court: Ruling on Jury Selection Retroactive." 1987. *Tallahassee Democrat* (Jan. 14): 1B, 6A.

Cowley, Geoffrey, Mary Hager, and Ruth Marshall. 1990. "AIDS the Next Ten Years." *Newsweek* (June 25):20-27.

Cox, Verne C., Paul B. Paulus, and Garvin McCain. 1984. "Prison Crowding Research: The Relevance for Prison Housing Standards and a General Approach regarding Crowding Phenomena." *American Psychologist* 39 (10):1148-1160.

Craft, Michael J. 1966. "Boy Prostitutes and Their Fate." *British Journal of Psychiatry* 112 (Nov.):492.

Crank, John P., Robert G. Culbertson, Eric D. Poole, and Robert M. Regoli. 1987. "The Measurement of Cynicism among Police Chiefs." *J. of Criminal Justice* 15:37-48.

Cressey, Donald R. 1980. "Sentencing: Legislative Rule versus Judicial Discretion." In B.

A. Grosman (ed.), *New Directions in Sentencing*. Toronto, Canada: Butterworth and Company.

Criminal Justice Newsletter. 1989. 20 (10):4.

Crockett, G. W. 1972. "Racism in the Law." In L. E. Reasons and J. L. Kuykendall (eds.), *Race, Crime, and Justice*. Pacific Palisades, CA: Goodyear.

Cummings, Harry, and Melzetta Harrison. 1972. "The American Indian: The Poverty of Assimilation." *Antipode* 4 (2):77-87.

Curtis, Lynn A. 1974. "Toward a Cultural Interpretation of Forcible Rape by American Blacks" (mimeo). Washington, D.C.: Bureau of Social Science Research, Inc.

———. 1976. "Rape, Race and Culture: Some Speculations in Search of a Theory." In Maria J. Walker and Stanley L. Brodsky (eds.), *Sexual Assault: The Victim and the Rapist*. Lexington, MA: Lexington Books.

Curwood, Steve. 1986. "Campuses Not Immune to Racism." *Tallahassee (FL) Democrat* (Dec. 26):1A.

Davidson, R. Theodore. 1974. *Chicano Prisoners: The Key to San Quentin*. New York: Holt, Rinehart and Winston.

Davis, Angela. 1991. Public lecture given at Indiana University, Feb. 21.

Davis, Goliath J. III. 1984. "Work Group Cohesion and Job Stress among Police Officers." Unpublished Ph.D. dissertation, Florida State University.

Davis, James R. 1983. "The Relation between Crime and Unemployment—An Econometric Model." Paper presented at annual meeting of ASC.

Davis, Kingsley. 1937. "The Sociology of Prostitution." *American Sociological Review* (Oct.):744-755.

"Death Penalty Litigation Section: National Legal Aid and Defender Association." 1991. *Capital Report* 21 (Oct./Nov.).

Debro, Julius. 1974. "The Black Offender as Victim." *J. of Afro-American Issues* 2:149-165.

Decker, Scott H., and Carol W. Kohfeld. 1985. "Crimes, Crime Rates, Arrests, and Arrest Ratios: Implications for Deterrence Theory." *Criminology* 23 (3):437-450.

DeFleur, Lois B. 1975. "Biasing Influences on Drug Arrest Records: Implications for Deviance Research." *American Sociological Review* 40 (1):88-103.

Dehais, Richard J. 1983. "Racial Disproportionality in Prison and Racial Discrimination in the Criminal Justice Process: Assessing the Empirical Evidence." Paper presented at annual ASC meeting.

Delaney, Anita J. 1979. *Black Task Force Report*. New York: Family Service Association of America.

Deloria, Vine. 1981. "Native American: The American Indian Today." *The Annals* 454 (Mar.):139-149.

Demaris, Ovid. 1970. *America the Violent*. New York: Cowles Book Company.

"Desperately Seeking Oriental DEA Agents." 1988. *Law Enforcement News* 14:1.

Deutsch, Michael E., and Jan Susler. 1991. "Political Prisoners in the United States: The Hidden Reality." *Social Justice* 18 (3):92-106.

De Witt, Charles B. 1990. *Arrestee Drug Use*. Washington, D.C.: U.S. Department of Justice.

DiIulio, John J. Jr. 1988. *Private Prisons*. Washington, D.C.: U.S. Department of Justice.

Dillingham, Steven D. 1990. *BJS Data Report, 1989*. Washington, D.C.: U.S. Department of Justice.

———. 1991. *Correctional Populations in the United States, 1989*. Washington, D.C.: U.S. Department of Justice.

Doerner, William G. 1983. "Why Does Johnny Reb Die When Shot? The Impact of Medical Resources on Lethality." *Sociological Inquiry* 53 (1):1-15.

Dorin, Dennis D. 1981. "Two Different Worlds: Criminologists, Justices and Racial Discrimination in the Imposition of Capital Punishment in Rape Cases." *J. of Criminal Law and Criminology* 72 (4):1667-1698.

Dunn, Marvin. 1987. "In Response: A White System Is Racist." *Miami Review* (Mar. 4):1.

Duster, Troy. 1970. *The Legislation of Morality: Law, Drugs, and Moral Judgment.* New York: Free Press.

――――. 1987. "Crime, Youth Unemployment, and the Black Urban Underclass." *Crime and Delinquency* 33 (2):300-316.

Edwards, G. Franklin. 1968. *E. Franklin Frazier on Race Relations.* Chicago, IL: University of Chicago Press.

Edwards, Thomas. 1988. "Prison Gang Violence Spilling into Streets." *San Antonio (Texas) Express News* (July 7):1.

Eggleston, Elizabeth. 1976. *Fear, Favour or Affection: Aborigines and the Criminal Law in Victoria, South Australia and Western Australia.* Canberra, Australia: Australian National University Press.

Eisenstein, James, and Herbert Jacob. 1977. *Felony Justice: An Organizational Analysis of Criminal Courts.* Boston, MA: Little, Brown and Company.

Erlanger, Howard S. 1979. "Estrangement, Machismo and Gang Violence." *Social Science Quarterly* 60 (2):235-248.

Fairbanks, Robert A. 1973. "The Cheyenne-Arapaho and Alcoholism: Does the Tribe Have a Legal Right to a Medical Remedy?" *American Indian Law Review* 1 (1):55-77.

Fanon, Frantz. 1963. *The Wretched of the Earth.* New York: Grove Press, Inc.

――――. 1967. *Black Skin, White Masks.* New York: Grove Press, Inc.

Farnworth, Margaret, and Patrick M. Horan. 1980. "Separate Justice: An Analysis of Race Differences in Court Processes." *Social Science Research* 9:381-399.

Farrell, Ronald A., and Victoria Lynn Swigert. 1978. "Prior Offense as a Self-Fulfilling Prophecy." *Law and Society Review* 12:437-453.

FBI. 1980. *Crime in the United States—1979.* Washington, D.C.: U.S. Government Printing Office.

――――. 1987. *Crime in the United States—1986.* Washington, D.C.: U.S. Government Printing Office.

――――. 1989. *Crime in the United States—1988.* Washington, D.C.: U.S. Government Printing Office.

Feinman, Clarice. 1986. "Police Problems on the Navajo Reservation." *Police Studies* 9 (4):194-198.

Finckenauer, James O. 1988. "Public Support for the Death Penalty: Retribution as Just Deserts or Retribution as Revenge?" *Justice Quarterly* 5 (1):81-100.

Fishbein, Diana H. 1990. "Biological Perspectives in Criminology." *Criminology* 28 (1):27-72.

Fitzpatrick, Joseph P. 1971. *Puerto Rican Americans.* Englewood Cliffs, NJ: Prentice-Hall.

Fitzpatrick, Joseph P., and Lourdes Travieso Parker. 1981. "Hispanic-Americans in the Eastern U.S." *The Annals* 454 (Mar.):98-110.

Flanagan, Timothy J., and Kathleen Maguire (eds.). 1990. *Sourcebook of Criminal Justice Statistics—1989.* Washington, D.C.: Bureau of Justice Statistics.

Florida Advisory Commission to the U.S. Civil Rights Commission. 1975. *Toward Police/Community Detente in Jacksonville.* Washington, D.C.: U.S. Government Printing Office.

Florida Bureau of Criminal Justice Assistance. 1981. *Citizen Attitudes on Law Enforcement.* Tallahassee, FL: Bureau of Assistance, Division of Public Safety, Planning and Assistance.

Florida Civil Liberties Union. 1964. *Rape: Selective Electrocution Based on Race.* Miami, FL: The Union.

Flowers, Ronald Barri. 1990. *Minorities and Criminality.* New York: Greenwood Press.

Folsom, R. D. 1973. "American Indians Imprisoned in the Oklahoma Penitentiary: 'A

Punishment More Primitive Than Torture.'" *American Indian Law Review* 1 (1):85-109.

Forst, Brian, Judith Lucianovic, and Sarah J. Cox. 1978. *What Happens after Arrest?* Washington, D.C.: U.S. Government Printing Office.

Frazier, Charles E. 1979. "Appearance, Demeanor, and Backstage Negotiations: Bases of Discretion in a First Appearance Court." *International J. of the Sociology of Law* 7 (2):197-209.

Frazier, Charles E., and E. Wilbur Bock. 1982. "Effects of Court Officials on Sentence Severity." *Criminology* 20 (2):257-272.

Frazier, Charles E., E. Wilbur Bock, and John C. Henretta. 1980. "Pretrial Release and Bail Decisions: The Effects of Legal, Community, and Personal Variables." *Criminology* 18 (2):162-181.

Frazier, E. Franklin. 1965. *Black Bourgeoisie.* New York: The Free Press.

Freedman, Jonathan. 1975. *Crowding and Behavior.* New York: Viking Press.

Friedrichs, David O. 1982. "Crime, Deviance and Criminal Justice: In Search of a Radical Humanistic Perspective." *Humanity and Society* 6 (Aug.):200-226.

Fuller, Dan A., and Thomas Orsagh. 1977. "Violence and Victimization within a State Prison System." *Criminal Justice Review* 2 (2):35-55.

Fyfe, James J. 1979. "Race and Extreme Police-Citizen Violence." Paper presented at ASC annual meeting.

————. 1981a. "Observations on Police Deadly Force." *Crime and Delinquency* 27 (3):376-389.

————. 1981b. "Who Shoots? A Look at Officer Race and Police Shooting." *J. of Police Science and Administration* 9 (4):367-382.

————. 1982. *Readings on Police Use of Deadly Force.* Washington, D.C.: Police Foundation.

————. 1983. "Enforcement Workshop: Fleeing Felons and the Fourth Amendment." *Criminal Law Bulletin* 19 (6):525-528.

————. 1986. "Enforcement Workshop: The Supreme Court's New Rules for Police Use of Deadly Force." *Criminal Law Bulletin* 22 (1):62-68.

————. 1988. "Police Use of Deadly Force: Research and Reform." *Justice Quarterly* 5 (2):165-205.

Galey, Margaret E. 1973. *North American Conference on the Protection of Human Rights for Indians and Inuits* (Wingspread Conference).

Gallagher, Mike. 1986a. "Insiders: Prison Drug Rings Thrive." *Lansing (Michigan) State Journal* (July 13):1.

————. 1986b. "Prison Drug Ring Tied to Organized Crime." *Lansing (Michigan) State Journal* (July 20):1.

————. 1986c. "Study: Correction Workers Smuggle in Third of Illegal Drugs." *Lansing (Michigan) State Journal* (July 16):1.

Galvin, Jim. 1983. *Setting Prison Terms.* Washington, D.C.: U.S. Department of Justice.

Garofalo, James, and Michael J. Hindelang. 1977. *An Introduction to the National Crime Survey.* Washington, D.C.: U.S. Government Printing Office.

Gaskins, Carla K. 1984. *Criminal Defense Systems.* Washington, D.C.: U.S. Department of Justice.

————. 1990. *Felony Case Processing in State Courts, 1986.* Washington, D.C.: U.S. Department of Justice.

Geller, William A. 1985. "Officer Restraint in the Use of Deadly Force: The Next Frontier in Police Shooting Research." *J. of Police Science and Administration* 13 (2):153-168.

General Accounting Office (GAO). 1990. *Death Penalty Sentencing.* Washington, D.C.: U.S. Government Accounting Office.

Georges-Abeyie, Daniel E. 1984a. "Definitional Issues: Race, Ethnicity, and Official

Crime/Victimization Statistics." In D. E. Georges-Abeyie (ed.), *The Criminal Justice System and Blacks*. New York: Clark Boardman.

_____ (ed.). 1984b. *The Criminal Justice System and Blacks*. New York: Clark Boardman.

_____. 1989. "Race, Ethnicity, and the Spatial Dynamic: Toward a Realistic Study of Black Crime, Crime Victimization, and Criminal Justice Processing of Blacks." *Social Justice* 16 (4):35-54.

_____. 1990. "The Myth of a Racist Criminal Justice System?" In B. D. MacLean and D. Milovanovic (eds.), *Racism, Empiricism, and Criminal Justice*. Vancouver, Canada: The Collective Press.

Gerard, Jules, and T. R. Terry. 1970. "Discrimination against Negros in the Administration of Criminal Law in Missouri." *Washington University Law Quarterly*:415-437.

Gertz, Marc G. 1980. "The Impact of Prosecutor/Public Defender Interaction on Sentencing: An Exploratory Typology." *Criminal Justice Review* 5 (Spring):43-54.

Gibbons, Donald C. 1976. *Delinquent Behavior*. Englewood Cliffs, NJ: Prentice-Hall.

_____. 1984. "Forcible Rape and Sexual Violence." *Research in Crime and Delinquency* 21 (3):251-269.

Gibson, James L. 1978. "Race as a Determinant of Criminal Sentences: A Methodological Critique and a Case Study." *Law and Society Review* 12:455-478.

Goetting, Ann, and Roy Michael Howsen. 1983. "Blacks in Prison: A Profile." *Criminal Justice Review* 8 (2):21-31.

Gold, Martin, and David J. Reimer. 1975. *Changing Patterns of Delinquent Behavior among Americans 13 to 16 Years Old, 1967-1972*. Ann Arbor, MI: University of Michigan Institute for Social Research.

Goldkamp, John S. 1980. "Philadelphia Revisited: An Examination of Bail and Detention Two Decades after Foote." *Crime and Delinquency* 26 (2):179-192.

_____. 1984. "Bail Discrimination and Control." *Criminal Justice Abstracts* 16 (1):103-127.

Goldman, Nathan. 1976. "The Differential Selection of Juvenile Offenders for Court Appearance." In D. C. Gibbons (ed.), *Delinquent Behavior*. Englewood Cliffs, NJ: Prentice-Hall.

Goldstein, Herman. 1975. "Police Discretion: The Ideal versus the Real." In J. H. Skolnick and T. C. Gray (eds.), *Police in America*. Boston, MA: Little, Brown and Company.

Goodstein, Lynne, and Doris Layton MacKenzie. 1984. "Racial Difference in Adjustment Patterns of Prison Inmates—Prisonization, Conflict, Stress and Control." In D. Georges-Abeyie (ed.), *The Criminal Justice System and Blacks*. New York: Clark Boardman.

Gottfredson, Michael R., and Michael J. Hindelang. 1979. "A Study of the Behavior of the Law." *American Sociological Review* 44:3-17.

Gove, Walter R., Michael Hughes, and Michael Geerken. 1985. "Are Uniform Crime Reports a Valid Indicator of the Index Crimes? An Affirmative Answer with Minor Qualifications." *Criminology* 23 (3):451-501.

Green, Edward. 1970. "Race, Social Status and Criminal Arrest." *American Sociological Review* 35:476-490.

Green, Edward, and Russell P. Wakefield. 1979. "Patterns of Middle and Upper Class Homicide." *J. of Criminal Law* 70:172-179.

Greenberg, Jack. 1959. *Race Relations and American Law*. New York: Columbia University Press.

Greenfeld, Lawrence A. 1989. *Capital Punishment, 1988*. Washington, D.C.: U.S. Department of Justice.

_____. 1990. *Prisoners in 1989*. Washington, D.C.: U.S. Department of Justice.

———. 1992. *Prisons and Prisoners in the United States.* Washington, D.C.: U.S. Department of Justice.

Greenlee, Sam. 1975. *Ammunition! Poetry and Other Raps.* Ealing, London: Bogle-L'Ouverture Publications, Ltd.

Greer, Edward. 1978a. "The Class Nature of the Urban Police during the Period of Black Municipal Power." *Crime and Social Justice* 9 (Spring-Summer):49-61.

———. 1978b. "A Reply to the 'Critique.' " *Crime and Social Justice* 9 (Spring-Summer):70-71.

Grier, William H., and Price M. Cobbs. 1968. *Black Rage.* New York: Basic Books, Inc.

Grieser, Robert C. 1988. *Wardens and State Corrections Commissioners Offer Their Views in National Assessment.* Washington, D.C.: U.S. Department of Justice.

Gross, Samuel R., and Robert Mauro. 1989. *Death and Discrimination: Racial Disparities in Capital Sentencing.* Boston, MA: Northeastern University Press.

Grossman, Joel B. 1967. "Social Backgrounds and Judicial Decisions: Notes for a Theory." *J. of Politics* 29 (1967):334-351.

Gubler, Brenda H. 1963. "A Constitutional Analysis of the Criminal Jurisdiction and Procedural Guarantees of the American Indian." Unpublished Ph.D. dissertation, Syracuse University.

Guterman, Stanley S. (ed.). 1972. *Black Psyche.* Berkeley, CA: Glendessary Press.

Guynes, Randall. 1988. *Nation's Jail Managers Assess Their Problems.* Washington, D.C.: U.S. Department of Justice.

Hacker, Andrew. 1988. "Black Crime, White Racism." *New York Review* (Mar. 3):36-41.

Haft, Marilyn G. 1976. "Hustling for Rights." In Laura Crites (ed.), *The Female Offender.* Lexington, MA: D. C. Heath.

Haft-Picker, Cheryl L. 1980. "Beyond the Subculture of Violence: An Evolutionary and Historical Approach to Social Control." In G. R. Newman (ed.), *Crime and Deviance: A Comparative Perspective.* Beverly Hills, CA: Sage.

Hagan, John. 1974. "Extra-legal Attributes and Criminal Sentencing: An Assessment of a Sociological Viewpoint." *Law and Society Review* 8 (3):357-383.

Hagan, John, and Ilene Nagel Bernstein. 1979. "Conflict in Context: The Sanctioning of Draft Resisters, 1963-76." *Social Problems* 27:109-122.

Hagan, John, and Kristin Bumiller. 1983. "Making Sense of Sentencing: A Review and Critique of Sentencing Research." In A. Blumstein et al. (eds.), *Research on Sentencing: The Search for Reform.* Washington, D.C.: National Academy Press.

Hall, Edwin L., and Albert A. Simkus. 1975. "Inequality in the Types of Sentences Received by Native Americans and Whites." *Criminology* 13 (2):199-222.

Hall, Gilbert H. 1979. *Duty of Protection: The Federal-Indian Trust Relationship.* Washington, D.C.: Institute for the Development of Indian Law.

Hamm, Mark S. 1989. "Legislator Ideology and Capital Punishment: The Special Case for Indiana Juveniles." *Justice Quarterly* 6 (2):219-232.

Hammett, Theodore M. 1986. *AIDS in Prisons and Jails: Issues and Options.* Washington, D.C.: U.S. Department of Justice.

———. 1987. *AIDS in Correctional Facilities: Issues and Options.* Washington, D.C.: U.S. Department of Justice.

Hammett, Theodore M., and Saira Moini. 1990. *Update on AIDS in Prisons and Jails.* Washington, D.C.: U.S. Department of Justice.

Haney, Craig. 1980. "Juries and the Death Penalty: Readdressing the Witherspoon Question." *Crime and Delinquency* 26 (4):512-527.

Hannerz, Ulf. 1969. *Soulside: Inquiries into Ghetto Culture and Community.* New York: Columbia University Press.

Harlow, Caroline Wolf. 1987. *Robbery Victims.* Washington, D.C.: U.S. Bureau of Justice Statistics.

———. 1991. *Drugs and Jail Inmates, 1989.* Washington, D.C.: U.S. Department of Justice.

Harries, Keith D. 1980. *Crime and the Environment.* Springfield, IL: Charles C. Thomas.

––––––. 1984. "Black Crime and Criminal Victimization." In D. Georges-Abeyie (ed.), *The Criminal Justice System and Blacks.* New York: Clark Boardman.

Harris, Philip W. 1986. "Over-simplification and Error in Public Opinion Surveys on Capital Punishment." *Justice Quarterly* 3 (4):429-455.

Haskell, Martin R., and Lewis Yablonsky. 1974. *Crime and Delinquency.* Chicago, IL: Rand McNally.

Hatchett, David. 1990. "Equal Justice under the Law." *Crisis* 98 (4):12-17, 46.

Hawkins, Darnell F. 1983. "Black and White Homicide Differentials: Alternatives to an Inadequate Theory." *Criminal Justice and Behavior* 10 (4):407-440.

––––––. 1985a. "Trends in Black-White Imprisonment: Changing Conceptions of Race or Changing Patterns of Social Control?" *Crime and Social Justice* 24:187-209.

––––––. 1985b. "Black Homicide: The Adequacy of Existing Research for Devising Prevention Strategies." *Crime and Delinquency* 31 (1):83-103.

––––––. 1986a. "Trends and Patterns of Homicide." In D. F. Hawkins (ed.), *Homicide among Black Americans.* Lanham, MD: University Press of America.

––––––. 1986b. "Race, Crime Type and Imprisonment." *Justice Quarterly* 3 (3):251-269.

–––––– (ed.). 1986c. *Homicide among Black Americans.* Lanham, MD: University Press of America.

––––––. 1987. "Devalued Lives and Racial Stereotypes: Ideological Barriers to the Prevention of Family Violence among Blacks." In R. L. Hampton (ed.), *Violence in the Black Family.* Lexington, MA: D. C. Heath.

Hayner, Norman S. 1938. "Social Factors in Oriental Crime." *American Journal of Sociology* 43:908-919.

––––––. 1942. "Variability in the Criminal Behavior of American Indians." *American Journal of Sociology* 47:602-613.

Headley, Bernard D. 1982-83. " 'Black on Black' Crime: The Myth and the Reality." *Crime and Social Justice* 20:50-61.

Heard, Chinita A. 1990. "Forecasting Models for Managing a Changing Inmate Population: Implications for Public Policy." Paper presented at ACJS annual meeting.

Heckler, Margaret M. 1985. *Black and Minority Health.* Washington, D.C.: U.S. Government Printing Office.

Heilbrun, Alfred B., Allison Foster, and Jill Golden. 1989. "The Death Sentence in Georgia, 1974-1987: Criminal Justice or Racial Injustice?" *Criminal Justice Behavior* 16 (2):139-154.

Heilbrun, Alfred B., and Kirk S. Heilbrun. 1977. "The Black Minority Criminal and Violent Crime: The Role of Self-Control." *Criminal Justice Behavior* 17 (4):370-377.

Helmer, John. 1975. *Drugs and Minority Oppression.* New York: Seabury Press.

Hester, Tom. 1989. *Correctional Populations in the United States, 1987.* Washington, D.C.: U.S. Department of Justice.

Heyl, Barbara. 1979. "Prostitution: An Extreme Case of Sex Stratification." In F. Adler and R. Simon (eds.), *The Criminology of Deviant Women.* Boston, MA: Houghton Mifflin.

Hill, Herbert. 1965. "State Laws and the Negro: Social Change and the Impact of Law." *African Forum* 1 (Fall):92-105.

Hilliard, Thomas O., Harold Dent, William Hayes, William Pierce, and Ann Ashmore Poussaint. 1974. "The Angela Davis Trial: Role of Black Psychologists in Jury Selection and Court Consultations." *J. of Black Psychology* 1 (1):56-60.

Hindelang, Michael J. 1969. "Equality under the Law." *J. of Criminal Law, Criminology, and Police Science* 60:306-313.

––––––. 1974. "The Uniform Crime Reports Revisited." *J. of Criminal Justice* 2:17.

––––––. 1978. "Race and Involvement in Common Law Personal Crimes." *American Sociological Review* 43 (1):93-109.

———. 1981. "Variations in Sex-Race-Age-Specific Incidence Rates of Offending." *American Sociological Review* 46 (4):461-474.

Hinds, Lennox S. 1979. "Report of International Jurists' Visit with Human Rights Petitioners in the United States, August 3-20, 1979." Unpublished paper, mimeo.

Hirschi, Travis. 1969. *Causes of Delinquency.* Berkeley, CA: University of California Press.

Hodges, Harold M. Jr. 1974. *Conflict and Consensus: An Introduction to Sociology.* 2nd ed. New York: Harper and Row.

Hoffman, Martin. 1972. "The Male Prostitute." *Sexual Behavior* 2:19-21.

Hoffman, Vincent J. 1981. "Asian-Americans in Law Enforcement: The Right to Be Policed by 'One's Own.' " *Police Chief* 48 (5):31-33.

Hollinger, Richard C. 1984. "Race, Occupational Status, and Pro-Active Police Arrest for Drinking and Driving." *Journal of Criminal Justice* 12 (2):173-183.

Holmes, Malcolm D., and Howard C. Daudistel. 1984. "Ethnicity and Justice in the Southwest: The Sentencing of Anglo, Black and Mexican Origin Defendants." *Social Science Quarterly* 65:265-277.

"Hour by Hour: Crack." 1988. *Newsweek* (Nov. 28):64-75.

Huff, C. Ronald, and John M. Stahura. 1980. "Police Employment and Suburban Crime." *Criminology* 17 (4):461-470.

Hughes, Langston. 1969. *Black Misery.* New York: Eriksson, Inc.

Humphrey, John A., and Timothy J. Fogarty. 1987. "Race and Plea Bargained Outcomes: A Research Note." *Social Forces* 66 (1):176-182.

Humphrey, John A., and Stuart Palmer. 1986. "Race, Sex, and Criminal Homicide Offender-Victim Relationships." In D. F. Hawkins (ed.), *Homicide among Black Americans.* Lanham, MD: University Press of America.

Hyer, Marjorie. 1988. "Church Council Calls Hate-Related Violence a 'National Epidemic.' " *The Washington Post* (Jan. 14):1.

Inciardi, James A. 1974. "Drugs, Drug-Taking and Drug-Seeking: Notations on the Dynamics of Myth, Change, and Reality." In J. Inciardi and C. Chambers (eds.), *Drugs and the Criminal Justice System.* Beverly Hills, CA: Sage Publications.

———. 1975. *Careers in Crime.* Chicago, IL: Rand McNally.

———. 1984. *Criminal Justice.* Orlando, FL: Academic Press.

———. 1986. *The War on Drugs.* Palo Alto, CA: Mayfield Publishing Company.

Inciardi, James A., and Carl D. Chambers. 1974. *Drugs and the Criminal Justice System.* Beverly Hills, CA: Sage Publications.

Innes, Cristopher A. 1987. *The Effects of Prison Density on Prisoners.* Ann Arbor, MI: CJAIN.

———. 1988. Profile of State Prison Inmates, 1986. Washington, D.C.: U.S. Department of Justice.

"J. Edgar Hoover Speaks Out with Vigor." 1970. *Time* (Dec. 14):16-17.

Jackson, Pamela Irving. 1985. "Ethnicity, Region, and Public Fiscal Commitment to Policing." *Justice Quarterly* 2 (2):167-195.

Jackson, Pamela Irving, and Leo Carroll. 1981. "Race and the War on Crime: The Sociopolitical Determinants of Municipal Police Expenditures in 90 Non-Southern U.S. Cities." *American Sociological Review* 46 (3):290-305.

Jacobs, David. 1981. "Inequality and Economic Crime." *Sociology and Social Research* 66 (Oct.):12-28.

Jacobs, James B. 1976. "Stratification and Conflict among Prison Inmates." *Criminology* 66 (4):476-482.

James, Jenifer. 1976. "Motivations for Entrance into Prostitution." In Laura Crites (ed.), *The Female Offender.* Lexington, MA: D. C. Heath.

James, Jenifer, and Peter P. Vitaliano. 1979. "The Transition from Primary to Secondary Deviance in Females." Unpublished paper.

Jamieson, Katherine M., and Timothy J. Flanagan. 1989. *Sourcebook of Criminal Justice Statistics—1988*. Washington, D.C.: U.S. Government Printing Office.

Jeffery, C. Ray. 1977. *Crime Prevention through Environmental Design*. Beverly Hills, CA: Sage.

———— (ed.). 1979. *Biology and Crime*. Beverly Hills, CA: Sage.

————. 1990. *Criminology: An Interdisciplinary Approach*. Englewood Cliffs, NJ: Prentice-Hall.

Jendrek, Margaret Platt. 1984. "Sentence Length: Interactions with Race and Court." *Journal of Criminal Justice* 12 (6):567-578.

Jersild, J. 1956. *Boy Prostitution*. Copenhagen, Denmark: G. E. C. Gad.

Johns, Christina Jacqueline. 1992. *Power, Ideology, and the War on Drugs*. New York: Praeger.

Johnson, Joan M., and Marshall M. DeBerry. 1989. *Criminal Victimization, 1988*. Washington, D.C.: U.S. Department of Justice.

Johnson, Sheri Lynn. 1983. "Race and the Decision to Detain a Suspect." *Yale Law Journal* 93 (2):214-258.

————. 1985. "Black Innocence and the White Jury." *Michigan Law Review* 83 (7):1611-1708.

Johnson, Weldon T., Robert E. Petersen, and L. Edward Wells. 1977. "Arrest Probabilities for Marijuana Users as Indicators of Selective Law Enforcement." *American Journal of Sociology* 83 (3):681-699.

Johnston, J. H. 1970. *Race Relations in Virginia and Miscegenation in the South, 1776-1860*. Amherst, MA: University of Massachusetts Press.

Jones, Terry. 1978. "The Court System and Black America: A Critical Analysis." *Western J. of Black Studies* 2 (4):259-267.

Jordon, W. D. 1974. *The White Man's Burden*. New York: Oxford University Press.

Joyner, Irving. 1982. "Legal Theories for Attacking Racial Disparity in Sentencing." *Criminal Law Bulletin* 18 (2):101-116.

"Justice Thurgood Marshall's Dissenting Opinion: Bakke Decision." 1979. *Dollars and Sense* (June-July):56-61.

Kamiya, Gary. 1989. "The Crack Epidemic: The Season of Hard Choices." *The Crisis* (Mar.):11-15, 32.

Kania, Richard R. E., and Wasle C. Mackey. 1977. "Police Violence as a Function of Community Characteristics." *Criminology* 15 (1):27-48.

Kaplan, Carol. 1987. *Sentencing and Time Served*. Washington, D.C.: U.S. Department of Justice.

Kasirika, Kaidi (Kenneth Divans), and Maharibi Muntu (Larry M. West). 1971. "Prison or Slavery?" *The Black Scholar* (Oct.):6-12.

Keil, Thomas J., and Gennaro F. Vito. 1989. "Race, Homicide Severity, and Application of the Death Penalty: A Consideration of the Barnett Scale." *Criminology* 27 (3):511-535.

Kelly, Henry E. 1976. "A Comparison of Defense Strategy and Race as Influences in Differential Sentencing." *Criminology* 14 (2):241-249.

Kempf, Kimberly L., and Roy L. Austin. 1983. "Older and More Recent Evidence on Racial Discrimination in Sentencing." Unpublished paper, Pennsylvania Commission on Sentencing.

————. 1986. "Older and More Recent Evidence on Racial Discrimination in Sentencing." *J. of Quantitative Criminology* 2 (1):29-48.

Kennedy, Leslie W., and Robert A. Silverman. 1988. *Homicide from East to West: A Test of the Impact of Culture and Economic Inequality in Regional Trends of Violent Crime in Canada*. Edmonton, Alberta, Canada: Centre for Criminological Research.

Kennedy, Steven, and Kenneth Carlson. 1988. *Pretrial Release and Detention: The Bail Reform Act of 1984*. Washington, D.C.: U.S. Department of Justice.

Kim, Hyung-Chan. 1977. "Education of the Korean Immigrant Child." *Integrated Education* 15 (1):15-18.

Kirkham, George L., and Laurin A. Wollan. 1980. *Introduction to Law Enforcement.* New York: Harper and Row.

Kitano, Harry H. L. 1981. "Asian-Americans: The Chinese, Japanese, Koreans, Pilipinos, and Southeast Asians." *The Annals* 454 (Mar.):125-138.

Kleck, Gary. 1981. "Racial Discrimination in Criminal Sentencing: A Critical Evaluation of the Evidence with Additional Evidence on the Death Penalty." *American Sociological Review* 46 (6):783-805.

————. 1985. "Life Support for Ailing Hypotheses: Modes of Summarizing the Evidence in Racial Discrimination in Sentencing." *Law and Human Behavior* 9:271-285.

Klein, Richard. 1986. "The Emperor Gideon Has No Clothes: The Empty Promise of the Constitutional Right to Effective Assistance of Counsel." *Hastings Constitutional Law Quarterly* 13 (4):625-693.

Klein, Stephen, Joan Petersilia, and Susan Turner. 1990. "Race and Imprisonment Decisions in California." *Science* 247 (4944):812-816.

Klein, Stephen P., Susan Turner, and Joan Petersilia. 1988. *Racial Equity in Sentencing.* Santa Monica, CA: Rand Corporation.

Kline, Susan. 1990. *Jail Inmates, 1989.* Washington, D.C.: U.S. Department of Justice.

Klockars, Carl B. 1986. "Street Justice: Some Micro-Moral Reservations—Comment on Sykes." *Justice Quarterly* 3 (4):513-516.

Kluegel, James R. 1990. Trends in Whites' Explanations of the Black-White Gap in Socioeconomic Status, 1977-1989." *American Sociological Review* 55 (4):512-525.

Koiwai, E. Karl. 1987. "Deaths Allegedly Caused by the Use of 'Choke Holds' (Shime-Waza)." *J. of Forensic Sciences* 32 (2):419-432.

Kovel, Joel. 1970. *White Racism: A Psychohistory.* New York: Pantheon Books.

Krahn, Harvey, Timothy F. Hartnagel, and John W. Gartrell. 1986. "Income Inequality and Homicide Rates: Cross-National Data and Criminological Theories." *Criminology* 24 (2):269-295.

Krulitz, Leo M. 1979. "Criminal Jurisdiction: PL 280." *Indian Law Reporter* (Jan. 12):1-3.

Kuykendall, Jack L. 1970. "Police and Minority Groups: Toward a Theory of Negative Contacts." *Police* 15 (Sept.-Oct.):47-56.

————. 1981. "Trends in the Use of Deadly Force by Police." *J. of Criminal Justice* 9:359-366.

Kvålseth, Tarald O. 1977. "A Note on the Effects of Population Density and Unemployment on Urban Crime." *Criminology* 15 (1):105-110.

LaFree, Gary D. 1982. "Male Power and Female Victimization: Toward a Theory of Interracial Rape." *American J. of Sociology* 88 (2):311-328.

————. 1985. "Official Reactions to Hispanic Defendants in the Southwest." *J. of Research in Crime and Delinquency* 22 (3):213-237.

Lampe, Philip E. 1982. "Ethnic Labels: Naming or Name Calling?" *Ethnic and Racial Studies* 5 (4):542-548.

Langan, Patrick A. 1985. "Racism on Trial: New Evidence to Explain the Racial Composition of Prisons in the U.S." *J. of Criminal Law and Criminology* 76 (3):666-683.

Langan, Patrick A., and John M. Dawson. 1990. *Profile of Felons Convicted in State Courts, 1986.* Washington, D.C.: U.S. Department of Justice.

Laub, John H. 1983. "Urbanism, Race, and Crime." *J. of Research in Crime and Delinquency* 20 (2):183-198.

Leerhsen, Charles, and Lynda Wright. 1991. "L.A.'s Violent New Video." *Newsweek* (Mar. 18):53.

Lefkowitz, Joel. 1975. "Psychological Attributes of Policemen: A Review of Research and Opinion." *J. of Social Issues* 31:3-26.

Lehnen, Robert G., and Wesley G. Skogan. 1981. *The National Crime Survey: Working Papers, Vol. I.* Washington, D.C.: U.S. Government Printing Office.

Lemert, Edwin M. 1951. *Social Pathology.* New York: McGraw-Hill.

Lesieur, Henry R., and Robert Klein. 1985. "Prisoners, Gambling and Crime." Paper presented at the annual meeting of the Academy of Criminal Justice Sciences.

Lester, David, and William ten Brink. 1985. "Police Solidarity and Tolerance for Police Misbehavior." *Psychological Reports* 57:326.

Letkemann, Peter. 1973. *Crime as Work.* Englewood Cliffs, NJ: Prentice-Hall.

Levine, James P., Michael C. Musheno, and Dennis J. Palumbo. 1986. *Criminal Justice in America.* New York: Wiley and Sons.

Levinson, Arlene. 1989. "Study Says Racist Crimes More Violent Than Thought" (AP, Boston). (*Bloomington*) *Indiana Daily Student* (Mar. 28):1.

Levy, Jerrold E., and Steven J. Kunitz. 1971. "Indian Reservations, Anomie, and Social Pathologies." *Southwestern J. of Anthropology* 27 (2):97-126.

———. 1974. *Indian Drinking: Navajo Practices and Anglo-American Theories.* New York: John Wiley and Sons.

Levy, Jerrold E., Steven J. Kunitz, and Michael Everett. 1969. "Navajo Criminal Homicide." *Southwestern J. of Anthropology* 25 (1969):124-152.

Light, Ivan H. 1974. "From Vice District to Tourist Attraction: The Moral Career of American Chinatowns, 1880-1940." *Pacific Historical Review*:367-394.

———. 1977a. "The Ethnic Vice Industry." *American Sociological Review* 42 (June):464-479.

———. 1977b. "Numbers Gambling among Blacks: A Financial Institution." *American Sociological Review* 42 (Dec.):892-904.

Liska, Allen E., and Mitchell B. Chamlin. 1984. "Social Structure and Crime Control among Macrosocial Units." *American Journal of Sociology* 90 (2):383-395.

Lizotte, Alan J. 1978. "Extra-Legal Factors in Chicago's Criminal Courts: Testing the Conflict Model of Criminal Justice." *Social Problems* 25:564-580.

Lockwood, Daniel. 1980. *Prison Sexual Violence.* New York: Elsevier N. Holland.

Loftin, Colin, and Robert H. Hill. 1974. "Regional Subculture and Homicide: An Examination of the Gastil-Hackney Theses." *American Sociological Review* 39 (Oct.):714-724.

Logan, Charles H., and Sharla P. Rausch. 1985. "Punish and Profit: The Emergence of Private Enterprise Prisons." *Justice Quarterly* 2 (3):303-318.

Long, Elton, James Long, Wilmer Leon, and Paul B. Weston. 1975. *American Minorities: The Justice Issue.* Englewood Cliffs, NJ: Prentice-Hall.

López-Rivera, Oscar. 1989. "Political Prisoners in the U.S." *Critical Criminologist* 2 (Spring):10-11.

Loya, Fred, and James A. Mercy. 1985. *The Epidemiology of Homicide in Los Angeles, 1970-79.* Washington, D.C.: U.S. Government Printing Office.

Loye, David. 1971. *The Healing of a Nation.* New York: Dell Publishing Company.

Luckenbill, David F. 1986. "Deviant Career Mobility: The Case of Male Prostitutes." *Social Problems* 33 (4):283-296.

Luckenbill, David F., and Daniel P. Doyle. 1989. "Structural Position and Violence: Developing a Cultural Explanation." *Criminology* 27 (3):419-436.

Lundy, George F. 1985. "Death as Punishment." *Blueprint for Social Justice* 39 (1):1-6.

McDougall, Ellis. 1985. Foreword to *Prison Violence in America,* ed. M. Braswell, S. Dillingham, and R. Montgomery. Cincinnati, OH: Anderson.

McEachern, Alexander W., and Riva Bauzer. 1964. "Factors Related to Disposition in Juvenile Police Contacts." In Malcolm W. Klein (ed.), *Juvenile Gangs in Context: Theory, Research and Action.* Englewood Cliffs, NJ: Prentice-Hall, Inc.

McGarrell, Edmund F. 1992. "Institutional Theory and the Stability of a Conflict Model of the Incarceration Rate." Unpublished paper.

McGarrell, Edmund F., and Timothy J. Flanagan. 1987. "Measuring and Explaining Legislator Crime Control Ideology." *J. of Research in Crime and Delinquency* 24 (2):102-118.

McKanna, Clare V. 1985. "Ethnics and San Quentin Prison Registers: A Comment on Methodology." *Journal of Social History* 18 (Spring):477-482.

McLaren, George, and Kyle Niederpruem. 1990. "Minorities Do More Time for Cocaine Dealing." *The Indianapolis Star* (Apr. 30):A-1, A-6.

MacLean, Brian D., and Dragan Milovanovic (eds.). 1990. *Racism, Empiricism and Criminal Justice.* Vancouver, Canada: The Collective Press.

McNeely, R. L., and Carl E. Pope. 1978. "Race and Involvement in Common Law Personal Crime: A Response to Hindelang." *The Review of Black Political Economy* 8:405-410.

———. 1980. "Racial Issues in the Measurement of Criminal Involvement." *J. of African-Afro-America Affairs* 4:9-26.

———. 1981a. *Race, Crime, and Criminal Justice.* Beverly Hills, CA: Sage Publications.

———. 1981b. "Socioeconomic and Racial Issues in the Measurement of Criminal Involvement." In R. L. McNeely and C. E. Pope (eds.), *Race, Crime, and Criminal Justice.* Beverly Hills, CA: Sage Publications.

McShane, Marilyn D., and Frank P. Williams III. 1989. "Running on Empty: Creativity and the Correctional Agenda." *Crime and Delinquency* 35 (4):562-576.

Mahan, Sue. 1985. "An 'Orgy of Brutality' at Attica and the 'Killing Ground' at Santa Fe: A Comparison of Prison Riots." In M. Braswell, S. Dillingham, and R. Montgomery, Jr. (eds.), *Prison Violence in America.* Cincinnati, OH: Anderson.

Malcolm X with Alex Haley. 1966. *The Autobiography of Malcolm X.* New York: Grove Press.

Mancini, Norma. 1988. *Our Crowded Jails: A National Plight.* Washington, D.C.: U.S. Department of Justice.

Mann, Coramae Richey. 1984. "Race and Sentencing of Women Felons: A Field Study." *International J. of Women's Studies* 7 (2):160-172.

———. 1987. "Black Women Who Kill." In R. L. Hampton (ed.), *Violence in the Black Family.* Lexington, MA: D. C. Heath.

———. 1990. "Black Female Homicide in the U.S." *J. of Interpersonal Violence* 5 (2):176-201.

Mann, Coramae Richey, and Lance H. Selva. 1979. "The Sexualization of Racism: The Black Rapist and White Justice." *Western J. of Black Studies* 3 (3):168-177.

Manual of Indian Law. 1977. American Indian Lawyer Training Program.

Marquart, James W. 1990. "Prison Guards and the Use of Physical Coercion as a Mechanism of Prisoner Control." In D. H. Kelly (ed.), *Criminal Behavior.* New York: St. Martin's.

Marquart, James W., and Ben M. Crouch. 1984. "Coopting the Kept: Using Inmates for Social Control in a Southern Prison." *Justice Quarterly* 1 (4):491-509.

Martin, Mark D. 1988. "A Look at Indian Jails." *American Jails* (Spring):19-21.

Martínez, Elizabeth. 1989. "Histories of the 'Sixties': A Certain Absence of Color." *Social Justice* 16 (4):175-185.

Massey, Douglas S. 1986. "The Settlement Process among Mexican Migrants to the United States." *American Sociological Review* 51 (5):670-684.

Mauer, Marc. 1990. *Young Black Men and the Criminal Justice System: A Growing National Problem.* Washington, D.C.: The Sentencing Project.

Maxfield, Michael G., Dan A. Lewis, and R. Szoc. 1980. "Producing Official Crimes: Verified Crime Reports as Measures of Police Output." *Social Science Quarterly* 61:221-236.

May, Philip A. 1977. "Explanations of Native American Drinking: A Literature Review." *Plains Anthropologist* 22:223-232.

———. 1982a. "Contemporary Crime and the American Indian: A Survey and Analysis of the Literature." *Plains Anthropologist* 27 (97):225-238.

_____. 1982b. "Susceptibility to Substance Abuse among American Indians: Variation across Sociocultural Settings." In *Problems of Drug Dependence, 1981.* Washington, D.C.: Department of Health and Human Services.

Meier, Matt S., and Feliciano Rivera. 1972. *The Chicanos: A History of Mexican Americans.* New York: Hill and Wang.

Merton, Robert K. 1957. *Social Theory and Social Structure.* Glencoe, IL: Free Press.

Messner, Steven F. 1982. "Poverty, Inequality, and the Urban Homicide Rate." *Criminology* 20 (1):103-114.

_____. 1983. "Regional Differences in the Economic Correlates of the Urban Homicide Rate: Some Evidence on the Importance of Cultural Context." *Criminology* 21 (4):477-488.

_____. 1989. "Economic Discrimination and Societal Homicide Rates: Further Evidence of the Cost of Inequality." *American Sociological Review* 54 (4):597-611.

Messner, Steven, and Kenneth Tardiff. 1986. "Economic Inequality and Levels of Homicide: An Analysis of Urban Neighborhoods." *Criminology* 24 (2):297-317.

Miethe, Terance D., and Charles A. Moore. 1984. "Racial Difference in Criminal Court Sentencing Decisions: A Comparison of Aggregate and Race-Specific Models of Criminal Processing." Paper presented at annual meeting of the American Society of Criminology.

Miller, Kent S. 1966. "Race, Poverty and the Law." In J. tenBroek (ed.), *The Law of the Poor.* San Francisco, CA: Chandler Publishing Company.

Minnis, Mhyra S. 1972. "The Relationship of the Social Structure of an Indian Community to Adult and Juvenile Delinquency." In H. Bahr, B. Chadwick, and R. Day (eds.), *Native Americans Today.* New York: Harper and Row.

"Minorities Continue to Be Underrepresented in College." 1984. *Tallahassee Democrat* (Nov. 10):1-2A.

Mintz, Betty. 1973. "Patterns in Forcible Rape: A Review-Essay." *Criminal Law Bulletin* 9 (8):703-710.

Mirande, Alfredo. 1980. "Fear of Crime and Fear of the Police in a Chicano Community." *Sociology and Social Research* 64 (4):528-541.

Mizio, Emelicia. 1979. *Puerto Rican Task Force Report.* New York: Family Service Association of America.

Moore, Howard Jr., and Jane Bond Moore. 1973. "Some Reflections: On the Criminal Justice System, Prisons and Repressions." *Howard Law Journal* 17 (4):833-843.

Moore, Joan W. 1970. "Colonialism: The Case of the Mexican Americans." *Social Problems* 171:463-472.

_____. 1976. *Mexican Americans.* Englewood Cliffs, NJ: Prentice-Hall.

_____. 1985. "Isolation and Stigmatization in the Development of an Underclass: The Case of Chicano Gangs in East Los Angeles." *Social Problems* 33:1-12.

Morales, Armando. 1972. *Ando Sangrando (I Am Bleeding): A Study of Mexican American Police Conflict.* La Puente, CA: Perspective Publications.

Morganthau, Tom, and Mark Miller. 1988. "Getting Tough on Cocaine." *Newsweek* (Nov. 28):76-79.

Morris, Frank L. 1974. "Black Political Consciousness in Northern State Prisons." In Herbert Jacob (ed.), *The Potential for Reform of Criminal Justice.* Beverly Hills, CA: Sage Publications.

Moss, James A. (ed.). 1971. *The Black Man in America: Integration and Separation.* New York: Dell Publishing Company.

Moss, Larry E. 1977. *Black Political Ascendancy in Urban Centers and Black Control of the Local Police Function: An Exploratory Analysis.* San Francisco, CA: R and E Research Associates, Inc.

Mullen, Joan. 1985. *Corrections and the Private Sector.* Washington, D.C.: U.S. Department of Justice.

Murphy, Clyde E. 1988. "Racial Discrimination in the Criminal Justice System, North Carolina." *Central Law Journal* 17 (2):171-190.

Murphy, Linda, and Richard W. Dodge. 1981. "The Baltimore Recall Study." In R. G. Lehnen and W. G. Skogan (eds.), *The National Crime Survey: Working Papers,* Vol. 1. Washington, D.C.: U.S. Government Printing Office.

Murray, Pauli. 1950. *States' Laws on Race and Color.* Cincinnati, OH: Woman's Division of Christian Service.

Musto, David F. 1973. *The American Disease: Origins of Narcotic Control.* New Haven, CT: Yale Press.

———. 1987. *The American Disease: Origins of Narcotic Control, Expanded Edition.* New York: Oxford University Press.

Myers, Martha. 1988. "Social Background and the Sentencing Behavior of Judges." *Criminology* 26 (4):649-675.

Myers, Martha A. 1987. "Economic Inequality and Discrimination in Sentencing." *Social Forces* 65 (3):746-766.

Myrdal, Gunnar. 1944. *An American Dilemma.* New York: Harper Brothers.

Nacci, Peter, and Thomas R. Kane. 1983. "The Incidence of Sex and Sexual Aggression in Federal Prisons." *Federal Probation* 47 (4):31-36.

Nagel, Ilene. 1983. "The Legal/Extra-legal Controversy: Judicial Decisions in Pretrial Release." *Law and Society Review* 17 (3):481-515.

Nagel, Stuart S. 1973. "Effects of Alternative Types of Counsel on Criminal Procedure Treatment." *Indiana Law Journal* 48:404-426.

National Advisory Commission on Civil Disorders. 1968. *Report of the National Advisory Commission on Civil Disorders.* New York: Bantam Books.

National Association for the Advancement of Colored People—Legal Defense Fund (NAACP-LDF). 1991. *August 23 Death Row U.S.A.* New York: NAACP Legal Defense and Educational Fund, Inc.

———. 1992. *Death Row U.S.A.* (Spring). New York: NAACP Legal Defense and Educational Fund, Inc.

National Institute of Justice Reports (NIJ). 1989. No. 215 (July-Aug.). Washington, D.C.: U.S. Department of Justice.

National Minority Advisory Council on Criminal Justice (NMAC). 1980. *The Inequality of Justice.* Washington, D.C.: U.S. Department of Justice.

Neely, David. 1978. "Capital Punishment: An Indicator of Institutionalized Discrimination." *Western Journal of Black Studies* 2 (4):268-274.

Nettler, Gwynn. 1978. *Explaining Crime.* New York: McGraw-Hill.

Newman, Donald J., and Patrick R. Anderson. 1989. *Introduction to Criminal Justice.* 4th ed. New York: Random House.

Niederhoffer, Arthur. 1967a. "Police Cynicism." In A. Niederhoffer (ed.), *Behind the Shield: The Police in Urban Society.* Garden City, NY: Doubleday.

———. 1967b. *Behind the Shield: The Police in Urban Society.* Garden City, NY: Doubleday.

"1990 Census: Black Population Growth Soaring." 1990. *The Crisis* 98 (3):29.

Nislow, Jennifer. 1988. "How to Find Psychologically Sound Recruits." *Law Enforcement News* 14 (268):1.

"A Not So Simple Game: Forget Taxes and the Gulf; Congress's Secret Obsession Is Redistricting." 1991. *Newsweek* (Jan. 14):21.

Nugent, Hugh, and J. Thomas McEwen. 1988. *Judges and Trial Court Administrators Assess Nation's Criminal Justice Needs.* Washington, D.C.: U.S. Department of Justice.

Oaks, Dallin H., and Warren Lehman. 1970. "Lawyers for the Poor." In A. S. Blumberg (ed.), *The Scales of Justice.* Chicago, IL: Aldine.

O'Brien, Robert. 1987. "The Interracial Nature of Violent Crimes: A Reexamination." *American J. Sociology* 92 (6):817-835.

O'Carroll, Patrick W., and James A. Mercy. 1986. "Patterns and Recent Trends in Black Homicide." In D. F. Hawkins (ed.), *Homicide among Black Americans*. Lanham, MD: University Press of America.

O'Connell, Brian J., Herbert Holzman, and Barry R. Armandi. 1986. "Police Cynicism and the Modes of Adaptation." *J. of Police Science and Administration* 14 (4):307-313.

O'Hare, William P., and Judy C. Felt. 1991. *Asian Americans: America's Fastest Growing Minority Group*. Washington, D.C.: Population Reference Bureau.

Oldroyd, Richard J., and Robert J. Howell. 1977. "Personality, Intellectual, and Behavioral Differences between Black, Chicano, and White Prison Inmates in the Utah State Prison." *Psychological Reports* 41:187-191.

Olivero, Michael. 1990. "The Treatment of AIDS behind the Walls of Correctional Facilities." *Social Justice* 17 (1):113-125.

Ong, Vickie. 1984. "Arms, Pot Lode Crop Up in Search at Kulani Prison." *(Honolulu, Hawaii) Bulletin and Advertiser* (Mar. 15):1.

Ost, Laura. 1987. "Innocent Have Died in Chair, Study Finds." *Tallahassee (Florida) Democrat* (Dec. 27):1E, 7E.

Owens, Charles E., and Jimmy Bell. 1977. *Blacks and Criminal Justice*. Lexington, MA: D. C. Heath and Company.

Ozanne, Marq R., Robert A. Wilson, and Dewaine L. Gedney, Jr. 1980. "Toward a Theory of Bail Risk." *Criminology* 18 (2):147-161.

Pachon, Harry P., and Joan W. Moore. 1981. "Mexican Americans." *The Annals* 454 (Mar.):111-124.

Padgett, Gregory L. 1984. "Racially-Motivated Violence and Intimidation: Inadequate State Enforcement and Federal Civil Rights Remedies." *J. of Criminal Law and Criminology* 75 (1):103-138.

Pao-Min, Chang. 1981. "Health and Crime among Chinese-Americans: Recent Trends." *Phylon* 42 (4):356-368.

Parisi, Nicolette. 1982. "Exploring Female Crime Patterns." In N. H. Rafter and E. A. Stanko (eds.), *Judge Lawyer Victim Thief*. Boston, MA: Northeastern University Press.

Park, Robert E. 1926. "The Urban Community as a Spatial Pattern and a Moral Order." In E. W. Burgess (ed.), *The Urban Community*. Chicago, IL: University of Chicago Press.

———. 1936. "Succession: An Ecological Concept." *American Sociological Review* 1 (Apr.):171-179.

Park, Robert E., and Ernest W. Burgess. 1925. *The City*. Chicago, IL: University of Chicago Press.

Parker, Robert Nash, and Allan V. Horwitz. 1986. "Unemployment, Crime, and Imprisonment: A Panel Approach." *Criminology* 24 (4):751-773.

Parrillo, Vincent N. 1985. *Strangers to These Shores: Race and Ethnic Relations in the U.S.* New York: John Wiley.

Partington, D. H. 1965. "The Incidence of the Death Penalty for Rape in Virginia." *Washington and Lee Law Review* 22:43.

Paternoster, Raymond. 1985. "Racial Discrimination and Arbitrariness in Capital Punishment: A Review of the Evidence." In G. W. Woodworth (ed.), *Proceedings of the Third Workshop on Law and Justice Statistics*. Washington, D.C.: U.S. Department of Justice.

Peak, Ken. 1989. "Criminal Justice, Law, and Policy in Indian Country: A Historical Perspective." *J. of Criminal Justice* 17 (5):393-407.

Peek, Charles W., George D. Lowe, and Jon P. Alston. 1981. "Race and Attitudes toward Local Police." *Journal of Black Studies* 11 (3): 361-374.

Pepinsky, Harold E. 1975. "Police Decision-Making." In D. M. Gottfredson (ed.), *Deci-

sion-Making in the Criminal Justice System. Washington, D.C.: U.S. Government Printing Office.

———. 1982. "Humanizing Social Control." *Humanity and Society* 6 (3):227-242.

———. 1991. *The Geometry of Violence and Democracy.* Bloomington: Indiana University Press.

Petersilia, Joan. 1983. *Racial Disparities in the Criminal Justice System.* Santa Monica, CA: Rand.

———. 1985. "Racial Disparities in the Criminal Justice System: A Summary." *Crime and Delinquency* 31 (1):15-34.

Petersilia, Joan, Peter W. Greenwood, and Marvin Lavin. 1977. *Criminal Careers of Habitual Felons.* Santa Monica, CA: Rand.

Petersilia, Joan, and Susan Turner. 1985. *Guideline-Based Justice: The Implications for Racial Minorities.* Santa Monica, CA: Rand Corporation.

Peterson, Ruth D., and John Hagan. 1984. "Changing Conceptions of Race: Towards an Account of Anomalous Findings of Sentencing Research." *American Sociological Review* 49 (1):56-70.

Petroski, William. 1989. "Iowa Inmates Claim Racism, Mistreatment." *Des Moines (Iowa) Register* (Aug. 15):1.

———. 1990. "Prisons See Surge in Gang Membership." *Des Moines (Iowa) Register* (Feb. 14):1.

Pettigrew, Thomas F., and Rosalind Barclay Spier. 1962. "The Ecological Structure of Negro Homicide." *American J. of Sociology* 67 (6):621-629.

Phillips, Charles David, and Sheldon Ekland-Olson. 1982. " 'Repeat Players' in a Criminal Court." *Criminology* 19 (4):530-545.

Piliavin, Irving, and Scott Briar. 1964. "Police Encounters with Juveniles." *American Journal of Sociology* 70 (Sept.):206-214.

Pilla, Thomas V. 1980. *Police-Community Relations in San Jose.* Washington, D.C.: U.S. Government Printing Office.

Pitler, Barry. 1977. "Chicago's Korean American Community." *Integrated Education* 15 (4):44-47.

Platt, Tony. 1978. " 'Street' Crime—A View from the Left." *Crime and Social Justice* 9 (Spring/Summer):26-34.

Plumpp, Sterling. 1972. *Black Rituals.* Chicago, IL: Third World Press.

Pokorny, Alex D. 1965. "A Comparison of Homicides in Two Cities." *J. of Criminal Law, Criminology, and Police Science* 56 (Dec.):479-487.

"Police Discretion and the Judgment That a Crime Has Been Committed: Rape in Philadelphia." 1968. *U. of Pennsylvania Law Review* 117:277-322.

"Police Kill Fewer Blacks." 1986. *Crime Control Digest* (Oct. 27):3-4. Washington, D.C.: The Crime Control Institute.

Poole, Eric D., and Robert M. Regoli. 1980. "Role Stress, Custody Orientation, and Disciplinary Actions." *Criminology* 18 (2):215-226.

Pope, Carl E. 1977. *Crime-Specific Analysis: The Characteristics of Burglary Incidents.* Washington, D.C.: U.S. Government Printing Office.

Popenoe, David. 1974. *Sociology.* New York: Appleton-Century-Crofts.

Portes, Alejandro, and Alex Stepick. 1985. "Unwelcome Immigrants: The Labor Market Experiences of 1980 (Mariel) Cubans and Haitian Refugees in South Florida." *American Sociological Review* 50 (4):493-514.

Poussaint, Alvin F. 1972. *Why Blacks Kill Blacks.* New York: Emerson Hall.

———. 1983. "Black-on-Black Homicide: A Psychological-Political Perspective." *Victimology* 8:161-169.

Powell, Dennis D. 1981. "Race, Rank, and Police Discretion." *J. of Police Science and Administration* 9 (4):383-389.

Preiss, Jack J., and Howard J. Ehrlich. 1966. *An Examination of Role Theory: The Case of the State Police.* Lincoln, NE: University of Nebraska Press.

Pruitt, Charles R., and James O. Wilson. 1983. "A Longitudinal Study of the Effect of Race on Sentencing." *Law and Society Review* 17 (4):613-635.

Quinney, Richard. 1974. *Critique of Legal Order.* Boston, MA: Little, Brown and Company.

_____ . 1977. *Class, State and Crime.* New York: David McKay Company.

Radelet, Michael L. 1981. "Racial Characteristics and the Imposition of the Death Penalty." *American Sociological Review* 46 (6):918-927.

Rand, Michael R. 1985. *Household Burglary.* Washington, D.C.: U.S. Government Printing Office.

_____ . 1991. *Crime and the Nation's Households, 1990.* Washington, D.C.: U.S. Government Printing Office.

"Raw Racism Shocks Jurists." 1980. *Tallahassee Democrat* (June 22):1B, 8B.

Rayfield, Susan. 1988. "Drug Use Plagues Prisons." *(Lewiston-Auburn, Maine) Sun-Journal* (July 10):1.

Reasons, Charles. 1972. "Crime and the American Indian." In H. M. Bahr, B. A. Chadwick, and R. C. Day (eds.), *Native Americans Today: Sociological Perspectives.* New York: Harper and Row.

_____ . 1974. "The Politics of Drugs: An Inquiry in the Sociology of Social Problems." *Sociological Quarterly* 15:381-404.

Reasons, Charles E., and Jack L. Kuykendall. 1972. *Race, Crime and Justice.* Pacific Palisades, CA: Goodyear.

Reaves, Brian. 1989. *Profile of State and Local Law Enforcement Agencies, 1987.* Washington, D.C.: U.S. Government Printing Office.

Reaves, Brian A. 1992. *State and Local Police Departments, 1990.* Washington, D.C.: U.S. Government Printing Office.

Reay, Donald T., and Richard L. Mathers. 1983. "Physiological Effects Resulting from Use of Neck Holds." *FBI Law Enforcement Bulletin* (July 12-15).

Reich, Charles. 1973. "The Law and the Corporate State." In W. J. Chambliss (ed.), *Sociological Readings in the Conflict Perspective.* Reading, MA: Addison-Wesley.

Reid, Sue Titus. 1979. *Crime and Criminology.* New York: Holt, Rinehart and Winston.

Reiman, Jeffrey. 1990. *The Rich Get Richer and the Poor Get Prison.* 3rd ed. New York: Macmillan.

Reiss, Albert J. 1968. "Police Brutality—Answers to Key Questions." *Transaction* 5 (Aug.):10-19.

Reuben, William A., and Carlos Norman. 1987. "The Women of Lexington Prison." *The Nation* (June 27):881-883.

Rhodes, William. 1984. *Bank Robbery.* Washington, D.C.: U.S. Department of Justice.

_____ . 1985. *Pretrial Release and Misconduct.* Washington, D.C.: U.S. Department of Justice.

Rice, Robert. 1989. "Indian Inmates Won't Accept Offer for Quasi–Sweat Lodge." *(Salt Lake City, Utah) Desert News* (Feb. 3):1.

Riedel, Marc. 1976. "Discrimination in the Imposition of the Death Penalty: A Comparison of the Characteristics of Offenders Sentenced Pre-Furman and Post-Furman." *Temple Law Quarterly* 49 (2):261-287.

_____ . 1984. "Blacks and Homicide." In D. Georges-Abeyie (ed.), *The Criminal Justice System and Blacks.* New York: Clark Boardman.

Riedel, Marc, and Margaret A. Zahn. 1985. *The Nature and Pattern of American Homicide.* Washington, D.C.: U.S. Government Printing Office.

Riffenburgh, Arthur S. 1964. "Cultural Influences and Crime among Indian-Americans of the Southwest." *Federal Probation* 23 (1):38-46.

Roberts, David J. 1984. "Effects of Court Officials on Sentence Severity: Do Judges Make a Difference? A Comment." *Criminology* 22 (1):135-138.

Rogan, Arlene. 1985. "Alcohol and Ethnic Minorities: Hispanics—An Update." *Alcohol Health and Research World* 10 (1):81-82.

Rollins [Jabali], Clifford. 1971. "Fascism at Soledad." *The Black Scholar* (Apr.-May):24-27.

Rose, Harold M. 1981. *Black Homicide and the Urban Environment.* Washington, D.C.: U.S. Government Printing Office.

Rose, Peter I. 1974. *They and We: Racial and Ethnic Relations in the United States.* New York: Random House.

Rosecrance, John. 1985. "The Probation Officers' Search for Credibility: Ball Park Recommendations." *Crime and Delinquency* 31 (4):539-554.

Rosen, Lawrence. 1976. *American Indians and the Law.* New Brunswick, NJ: Transaction Books.

Rothman, David J. 1983. "Sentencing Reforms in Historical Perspective." *Crime and Delinquency* 29 (4):631-647.

Rubio-Festa, Gilda S. 1979. "Crimen y Justicia: Crime and Justice for Hispanics." Mimeo. Racine, WI: Wingspread Symposium.

Sabol, William J. 1989. "Racially Disproportionate Prison Populations in the United States." *Contemporary Crises* 13:405-432.

Sackrey, Charles. 1973. *The Political Economy of Urban Poverty.* New York: Norton Publishing.

Safire, William. 1990. "Attorney General Employing a Double Standard." *The Herald Times (Bloomington, IN)* (May 30):A8.

Salvato, Al. 1990. "Prison 'Ready to Blow': Racial Hatred Plagues Lucasville." *Cincinnati (Ohio) Post* (Feb. 19):1.

Sample, Barry C., and Michael Philip. 1984. "Perspectives on Race and Crime in Research and Planning." In D. E. Georges-Abeyie (ed.), *The Criminal Justice System and Blacks.* New York: Clark Boardman.

Sampson, Robert J. 1985a. "Race and Criminal Violence: A Demographically Disaggregated Analysis of Urban Homicide." *Crime and Delinquency* 31 (1):47-82.

————. 1985b. "Structural Sources of Variation in Race–Age-Specific Rates of Offending across Major U.S. Cities." *Criminology* 23 (4):647-673.

————. 1987. "Urban Black Violence: The Effect of Male Joblessness and Family Disruption." *American J. of Sociology* 93 (2):348-382.

Sanborn, Joseph B. Jr. 1986. "A Historical Sketch of Plea Bargaining." *Justice Quarterly* 3 (2):111-138.

sánchez, ricardo. 1978. *Milhaus Blues and Gritos Norteños.* Milwaukee, WI: University of Wisconsin College of Letters and Science.

Savitz, Leonard D. 1973. "Black Crime." In K. Miller and R. Dreger (eds.), *Comparative Studies of Blacks and Whites in the United States.* New York: Seminar Press.

Scaglion, Richard, and Richard Condon. 1980. "Determinants of Attitudes toward City Police." *Criminology* 17 (4):485-494.

Schneider, Anne L. 1981. "Differences between Survey and Police Information about Crime." In R. G. Lehnen and W. G. Skogan (eds.), *The National Crime Survey: Working Papers, Vol. 1.* Washington, D.C.: U.S. Government Printing Office.

Schultz, Donald O., and J. Gregory Service. 1981. *The Police Use of Force.* Springfield, IL: Charles C. Thomas.

Schwendinger, Herman, and Julia Schwendinger. 1974. "Rape Myths: In Legal, Theoretical, and Everyday Practice." *Crime and Social Justice* 13 (Summer):18-26.

————. 1977. "Social Class and the Definition of Crime." *Crime and Social Justice* 7 (Spring/Summer):4-13.

Selva, Lance H. 1985. "Toward a Critical Legal Theory: Development of an Oppositional Legal Discourse under Late Capitalism." Unpublished Ph.D. dissertation, Florida State University.

Sexton, George E., Franklin C. Farrow, and Barbara J. Auerbach. 1985. *The Private Sector and Prisons.* Washington, D.C.: U.S. Department of Justice.

Shade, Oscar D. 1982. "Determinate Sentencing: A Racist Reform?" *Corrections Today* 44:62-65.

Shaw, Clifford R., and Henry D. McKay. 1942. *Juvenile Delinquency and Urban Areas.* Chicago, IL: University of Chicago Press.

Sheehan, Bernard W. 1972. "Indian-White Relations in Early America: A Review Essay." In H. M. Bahr, B. A. Chadwick, and R. C. Day (eds.), *Native Americans Today.* New York: Harper and Row.

Sheley, Joseph F. 1985. *America's "Crime Problem."* Belmont, CA: Wadsworth Publishing Company.

Sherman, Lawrence W. 1980. "Causes of Police Behavior: The Current State of Quantitative Research." *J. of Research in Crime and Delinquency* 17:69-100.

————. 1986. *Citizens Killed by Big City Police, 1970-1984.* Washington, D.C.: Crime Control Institute.

Silberman, Charles E. 1978. *Criminal Violence, Criminal Justice.* New York: Random House.

Simpson, Janice C. 1988. "White Justice, Black Defendants." *Time* (Aug. 8):17.

Sissons, Peter L. 1979. *The Hispanic Experience of Criminal Justice.* Bronx, NY: Hispanic Research Center (Fordham University).

Skinner, Curtis. 1990. "Overcrowded Prisons: A Nation in Crisis." *Crisis* 98 (4):18-21, 45-46.

Skogan, Wesley G. 1974. "The Validity of Official Crime Statistics: An Empirical Investigation." *Social Science Quarterly* 55:25-38.

————. 1975. "Measurement Problems in Official and Survey Crime Rates." *J. of Criminal Justice* 3:17-32.

————. 1977. "Patterns of Weapon Use in Robbery." Paper presented at annual meeting of American Society of Criminology.

————. 1981. *Issues in the Measurement of Victimization.* Washington, D.C.: U.S. Government Printing Office.

Skolnick, Jerome H. 1966. "A Sketch of the Policeman's Working Personality." In J. H. Skolnick, *Justice without Trial: Law Enforcement in a Democratic Society.* New York: Wiley.

————. 1967. "Social Control and the Adversary System." *J. of Conflict Resolution* 11:53-70.

————. 1975. "Why Police Behave the Way They Do." In J. H. Skolnick and T. C. Gray (eds.), *Police in America.* Boston, MA: Little, Brown and Company.

Skolnick, Jerome H., and Thomas C. Gray. 1975. *Police in America.* Boston, MA: Little, Brown and Company.

Smart, Carol. 1976. *Crime and Criminology: A Feminist Critique.* Boston, MA: Routledge and Kegan Paul.

Smith, Douglas A., and Christy A. Visher. 1981. "Street-level Justice: Situational Determinants of Police Arrest Decisions." *Social Problems* 29 (2):167-177.

Smith, Douglas A., Christy A. Visher, and Laura A. Davidson. 1984. "Equity and Discretionary Justice: The Influence of Race on Police Arrest Decisions." *J. of Criminal Law and Criminology* 75 (1):234-249.

Smith, Jack C., James A. Mercy, and Mark L. Rosenberg. 1984. *Comparison of Homicides among Anglos and Hispanics in Five Southwestern States.* Atlanta, GA: Centers for Disease Control.

Smith, M. Dwayne. 1987. "Patterns of Discrimination in Assessments of the Death Penalty: The Case of Louisiana." *J. of Criminal Justice* 15 (4):279-286.

Smith, Ronald W., and Frederick W. Preston. 1977. *Sociology: An Introduction.* New York: St. Martin's Press.

Smith, Wes. 1987. "Pontiac Prison Gangs' Ultimate Weapon Is Fear." *Chicago Tribune* (Sept. 20):1.

Smith, Wes, and Ray Gibson. 1988. "Drugs Are Lifeblood of Pontiac Gangs." *Chicago Tribune* (July 19):1.

Sorensen, George A. 1986. "Probe Uncovers Bizarre World of Drugs in Prison." *Salt Lake City (Utah) Tribune* (Nov. 30):1.

Sorin, Martin D. 1985. *Out on Bail.* Washington, D.C.: U.S. Department of Justice.

Sowell, Thomas. 1981. *Ethnic America: A History.* New York: Basic Books, Inc.

Spangenberg, Robert L., Judy Kapuscinski, and Patrick A. Smith. 1988. *Criminal Defense for the Poor, 1986.* Washington, D.C.: U.S. Department of Justice.

"Spiraling AIDS Count Passes 200,000 Mark." 1992. *The Herald-Times (Bloomington, IN)* (Jan. 17):A3.

Spohn, Cassia, John Gruhl, and Susan Welch. 1981-82. "The Effect of Race on Sentencing: A Re-examination of an Unsettled Question." *Law and Society Review* 16 (1):71-88.

Spohn, Cassia, and Susan Welch. 1987. "The Effect of Prior Record in Sentencing Research: An Examination of the Assumption That Any Measure Is Adequate." *Justice Quarterly* 4 (2):287-302.

Stampp, Kenneth M. 1970. *The Civil Rights Record: Black Americans and the Law, 1849-1970.* New York: Crowell.

Staples, Robert. 1975. "White Racism, Black Crime and American Justice: An Application of the Colonial Model to Explain Crime and Race." *Phylon* (Mar.):14-22.

Stark, Rodney. 1972. *Police Riots: Collective Violence and Law Enforcement.* Belmont, CA: Wadsworth.

———. 1987. "Deviant Places: A Theory of the Ecology of Crime." *Criminology* 25 (4):893-909.

Steinberg, Allen. 1984. "From Private Prosecution to Plea Bargaining: Criminal Prosecution, the District Attorney, and American Legal History." *Crime and Delinquency* 30 (4):568-592.

Stengel, Richard. 1985. "When Brother Kills Brother." *Time* (Sept. 16):32-36.

Stephan, Cookie, and Judy Corder Tully. 1977. "The Influence of Physical Attractiveness of a Plaintiff on the Decisions of Simulated Jurors." *J. of Social Psychology* 101:149-150.

Stephan, James. 1989. *Prison Rule Violators.* Washington, D.C.: U.S. Department of Justice.

———. 1990. *Census of Local Jails, 1988.* Washington, D.C.: U.S. Department of Justice.

Stephan, James J., and Louis W. Jankowski. 1991. *Jail Inmates, 1990.* Washington, D.C.: U.S. Department of Justice.

Stewart, Omer C. 1964. "Questions regarding American Indian Criminality." *Human Organization* 23 (Spring):61-66.

Stoddard, Ellwyn R. 1973. *Mexican Americans.* New York: University Press of America.

Stojkovic, Stan. 1984. "Social Bases of Power and Control Mechanisms among Prisoners in a Prison Organization." *Justice Quarterly* 1 (4):511-528.

Streib, Victor L. 1989. "Persons on Death Row as of July 15, 1989, for Crimes Committed While under Age Eighteen" (32nd ed.). Unpublished paper, July 19.

———. 1991. "The Juvenile Death Penalty Today: Present Death Row Inmates under Juvenile Death Sentences and Death Sentences and Executions for Juvenile Crimes, January 1, 1973, to September 30, 1991." Unpublished paper.

Sulton, Cynthia G., and Phillip Cooper. 1979. "Summary of Research on the Police Use of Deadly Force." In R. N. Brenner and M. Kravitz, *A Community Concern: Police Use of Deadly Force.* Washington, D.C.: U.S. Government Printing Office.

Sutherland, Edwin. 1937. *The Professional Thief.* Chicago, IL: University of Chicago Press.

Sutherland, Edwin H., and Donald L. Cressey. 1978. *Criminology.* Philadelphia, PA: J. B. Lippincott.

Swett, Daniel H. 1969. "Cultural Bias in the American Legal System." *Law and Society Review* 4 (Aug.):79-109.

Sykes, Gary W. 1986. "Street Justice: A Moral Defense of Order Maintenance Policing." *Justice Quarterly* 3 (4):497-512.

Taft, Philip B. 1981a. "Behind Prison Walls, Indians Reclaim Their Heritage." *Corrections Magazine* 7 (3):6-14.

———. 1981b. "Indian Offender Program: And Then There Was One." *Corrections Magazine* 7 (3):15-18.

Takagi, Paul. 1981. "Race, Crime, and Social Policy: A Minority Perspective." *Crime and Delinquency* 27 (1):48-63.

Takagi, Paul, and Tony Platt. 1978. "Behind the Gilded Ghetto: An Analysis of Race, Class and Crime in Chinatown." *Crime and Social Justice* 9 (Spring/Summer):2-25.

Tallahassee Democrat. 1988. (Aug. 8).

Taylor, Bruce M. 1989. *New Directions for the National Crime Survey.* Washington, D.C.: U.S. Department of Justice.

Taylor, Stuart Jr. 1986. "The Day They Discarded All the Labels." *New York Times* (May 26):A20.

Teahan, John E. 1975a. "Role Playing and Group Experiences to Facilitate Attitude and Value Changes among Black and White Police Officers." *J. of Social Issues* 31 (1):35-45.

———. 1975b. "A Longitudinal Study of Attitude Shifts among Black and White Police Officers." *J. of Social Issues* 31 (1):47-56.

tenBroek, J. (ed.). 1966. *The Law of the Poor.* San Francisco, CA: Chandler Publishing Company.

Thio, Alex. 1978. *Deviant Behavior.* Boston, MA: Houghton Mifflin.

Thornberry, Terence P. 1973. "Race, Socioeconomic Status and Sentencing in the Juvenile Justice System." *J. of Criminal Law and Criminology* 64 (1):90-98.

Thornberry, Terence P., and R. L. Christenson. 1984. "Unemployment and Criminal Involvement: An Investigation of Reciprocal Causal Structures." *American Sociological Review* 49 (3):398-411.

Timrots, Anita, Candi Byme, and Christine Finn. 1991. *Fact Sheet: Drug Data Summary.* Washington, D.C.: U.S. Department of Justice.

Timrots, Anita D., and Michael R. Rand. 1987. *Violent Crime by Strangers and Non-strangers.* Washington, D.C.: U.S. Department of Justice.

Tittle, Charles R. 1989. "Urbanness and Unconventional Behavior." *Criminology* 27 (2):273-306.

Tittle, Charles R., Wayne J. Villemez, and Douglas A. Smith. 1978. "The Myth of Social Class and Criminality: An Empirical Assessment of the Empirical Evidence." *American Sociological Review* 43 (5):643-656.

"To Shoot or Not to Shoot." 1980. *Time* (Aug. 18):44.

Todd, Thomas N. 1979. "From Dred Scott to Bakke and Beyond: The Evolution of a Circle." *Dollars and Sense* (June-July):64-74.

Tracy, Charles A. 1980. "Race, Crime and Social Policy: The Chinese in Oregon, 1871-1885." *Crime and Social Justice* (Winter):11-25.

Turner, Ralph H. (ed.). 1967. *Robert E. Park on Social Control and Collective Behavior.* Chicago, IL: University of Chicago Press.

Turque, Bill, Linda Buckley, and Lynda Wright. 1991. "Brutality on the Beat." *Newsweek* (Mar. 25):32-34.

Uhlman, Thomas M. 1979. *Racial Justice.* Lexington, MA: Lexington Books.

Uhlman, Thomas M., and N. Darlene Walker. 1979. "A Plea Is No Bargain: The Impact of Case Disposition on Sentencing." *Social Science Quarterly* 60 (2):218-234.

"Under the Thumb of What They Call the Justice System." 1983. *Jericho: Newsletter of the National Moratorium on Prison Construction* 32 (Summer):6-7.

Unnever, James D., Charles E. Frazier, and John C. Henretta. 1980. "Race Differences in Criminal Sentencing." *Sociological Quarterly* 21 (Spring):197-205.

U.S. Census. 1980. *Statistical Abstracts of the United States, 1980.* Washington, D.C.: U.S. Government Printing Office.

———. 1986. *U.S. Summary: General Population Characteristics, 1980.* Washington, D.C.: U.S. Department of Commerce, Bureau of the Census.

———. 1990. *Statistical Abstracts of the United States, 1990.* Washington, D.C.: U.S. Government Printing Office.

U.S. Commission on Civil Rights. 1981. *Who Is Guarding the Guardians? A Report on Police Practices.* Washington, D.C.: U.S. Government Printing Office.

U.S. Department of Commerce. 1990. *Statistical Abstract of the United States, 1990.* Washington, D.C.: U.S. Government Printing Office.

U.S. Department of Health and Human Services. 1983. *Morbidity and Mortality Weekly Report,* Vol. 32, No. 35. Atlanta, GA: Centers for Disease Control.

———. 1986. *Black and Minority Health, Vol. V: Homicide, Suicide, and Unintentional Injuries.* Washington, D.C.: U.S. Government Printing Office.

U.S. Department of Health, Education, and Welfare. 1978. *Indian Health Trends and Services.* Washington, D.C.: U.S. Government Printing Office.

U.S. Department of Justice. 1980. *The Hispanic Victim.* Washington, D.C.: Bureau of Justice Statistics.

———. 1984. *Sourcebook of Criminal Justice Statistics.* Washington, D.C.: U.S. Department of Justice.

———. 1985. *Crime and Justice Facts, 1985.* Washington, D.C.: Bureau of Justice Statistics.

———. 1986. *Police Employment and Expenditure Trends.* Washington, D.C.: Bureau of Justice Statistics.

———. 1987. *Criminal Victimization in the United States, 1985.* Washington, D.C.: Bureau of Justice Statistics.

———. 1988. *Profile of State and Local Law Enforcement Agencies.* Washington, D.C.: Bureau of Justice Statistics.

———. 1990a. *Criminal Victimization in the United States, 1988.* Washington, D.C.: U.S. Government Printing Office.

———. 1990b. *Drugs and Crime Facts, 1989.* Washington, D.C.: Bureau of Justice Statistics.

Useem, Bert. 1985. "Disorganization and the New Mexico Prison Riot of 1980." *American Sociological Review* 50 (5):677-688.

Valdivieso, Rafael, and Cary Davis. 1988. *U.S. Hispanics: Challenging Issues for the 1990s.* Washington, D.C.: Population Reference Bureau.

Vetter, Harold J., and Ira J. Silverman. 1986. *Criminology and Crime.* New York: Harper and Row.

Vilar, Juan. 1990. "Union for Puerto Rican Students Commemorates the 10th Anniversary of the Capture of the Puerto Rican Prisoners of War." *Critical Criminologist* 2 (1):13.

Vlasak, Theresa. 1989. "A Bad Problem Just Gets Worse." *The Compiler* (Summer):11-13.

von Hentig, Hans. 1945. "The Delinquency of the American Indian." *J. of Criminal Law* 36:75-84.

Walker, Maria J., and Stanley L. Brodsky. 1976. *Sexual Assault: The Victim and the Rapist.* Lexington, MA: Lexington Books.

Walker, Samuel A. 1985a. *Sense and Nonsense about Crime.* Monterey, CA: Brooks/Cole Publishing Company.

———. 1985b. "The Limits of Segregation in Prisons: A Reply to Jacobs." *Criminal Law Bulletin* 21 (6):485-494.

Walsh, Anthony. 1985. "The Role of the Probation Officer in the Sentencing Process:

Independent Professional or Judicial Hack?" *Criminal Justice and Behavior* 12 (3):289-303.

Walters, Glenn D., and Thomas W. White. 1989. "Heredity and Crime: Bad Genes or Bad Research?" *Criminology* 27 (3):455-485.

Washburn, Wilcomb E. 1976. "The Historical Context of American Indian Legal Problems." In L. Rosen (ed.), *American Indians and the Law*. New Brunswick, NJ: Transaction Books.

Webster's New Collegiate Dictionary. 1976. Springfield, MA: G. and C. Merriam Company.

Weiss, Kurt, and Sandra S. Borges. 1973. "Victimology and Rape: The Case of the Legitimate Victim." *Issues in Criminology* 8 (2):71-115.

Welch, Susan, Michael Combs, and John Gruhl. 1988. "Do Black Judges Make a Difference?" *American J. of Political Science* 32 (1):126-136.

Welch, Susan, John Gruhl, and Cassia Spohn. 1984. "Sentencing: The Influence of Alternative Measures of Prior Record." *Criminology* 22 (2):215-227.

Welch, Susan, and Cassia Spohn. 1986. "Evaluating the Impact of Prior Record on Judges' Sentencing Decisions: A Seven-City Comparison." *Justice Quarterly* 3 (4):389-407.

Welch, Susan, Cassia Spohn, and John Gruhl. 1985. "Convicting and Sentencing: Differences among Black, Hispanic and White Males in Six Localities." *Justice Quarterly* 2 (1):67-77.

Westermeyer, J., and J. Brantner. 1972. "Violent Death and Alcohol Use among the Chippewa in Minnesota." *Minnesota Medicine* 55 (8):749-752.

Wheeler, Gerald R., and Carol L. Wheeler. 1980. "Reflections on Legal Representation of the Economically Disadvantaged: Beyond Assembly Line Justice." *Crime and Delinquency* 26 (3):319-332.

Whitaker, Catherine J. 1990. *Black Victims*. Washington, D.C.: U.S. Department of Justice.

Widom, Cathy Spatz. 1983. "A Multidimensional Model of Prostitution." Paper presented at annual meeting of American Society of Criminology.

Wilbanks, William. 1985. "Is Violent Crime Intraracial?" *Crime and Delinquency* 31 (1):117-128.

———. 1986. "Criminal Homicide Offenders in the U.S.: Black vs. White." In D. F. Hawkins (ed.), *Homicide among Black Americans*. Lanham, MD: University Press of America.

———. 1987. *The Myth of a Racist Criminal Justice System*. Monterey, CA: Brooks/ Cole Publishing Company.

———. 1988. "Reactions to McClesky vs. Georgia." *The Prosecutor* 21 (4):21-26.

———. 1990. "Response to the Critics of the Myth of a Racist Criminal Justice System." In B. MacLean and D. Milovanovic (eds.), *Racism, Empiricism and Criminal Justice*. Vancouver, Canada: The Collective Press.

Wildeman, John, and Jorge Sanchez. 1990. "Struggle at the Bar: African Americans in the Profession of Law." Unpublished paper.

Wiley, Mary Glennard, and Terry L. Hudik. 1974. "Police-Citizen Encounters: A Field Test of Exchange Theory." *Social Problems* 22 (1):119-126.

Wilkins, Roy. 1985. "Stop and Frisk." In A. Niederhoffer and A. S. Blumberg (eds.), *The Ambivalent Force: Perspectives on the Police*. New York: Holt, Rinehart and Winston.

Williams, Hubert, and Patrick V. Murphy. 1990. *The Evolving Strategy of Police: A Minority View*. Washington, D.C.: U.S. Department of Justice.

Williams, Millree. 1982. "Blacks and Alcoholism: Issues in the 1980s." *Alcohol Health and Research World* 6 (4):31-40.

———. 1985. "Alcohol and Ethnic Minorities: Black Americans—An Update." *Alcohol Health and Research World* 9 (3):52-54.

Wilson, Basil, and John L. Cooper. 1979. "Ghetto Reflections and the Role of the Police Officer." *J. of Police Science and Administration* 7 (1):28-35.

Wilson, James Q. 1974. *Varieties of Police Behavior: The Management of Law and Order in Eight Communities.* New York: Atheneum.

Wilson, James Q., and Richard J. Herrnstein. 1985. *Crime and Human Nature.* New York: Simon and Schuster, Inc.

Wilson, William J. 1978. *The Declining Significance of Race: Blacks and Changing American Institutions.* Chicago, IL: University of Chicago Press.

———. 1987. *The Truly Disadvantaged.* Chicago, IL: University of Chicago Press.

Wiltz, C. J. 1985. "Poverty, Family Structure and Black Homicides." Paper presented at annual meeting of the Academy of Criminal Justice Sciences.

Winfree, L. Thomas, and Curt T. Griffiths. 1983. "Youth at Risk: Marijuana Use among Native American and Caucasian Youths." *International J. of the Addictions* 18 (1):53-70.

Winfree, L. Thomas, Curt T. Griffiths, and Christine S. Sellers. 1989. "Social Learning Theory, Drug Use, and American Indian Youths: A Cross-Cultural Test." *Justice Quarterly* 6 (3):395-417.

Winfree, L. Thomas, Harold E. Theis, and Curt T. Griffiths. 1981. "Drug Use in Rural America: A Cross-Cultural Examination of Complementary Social Deviance Theories." *Youth and Society* 12 (4):465-489.

Wingspread Conference. 1973. *North American Conference on the Protection of Human Rights for Indians and Inuits.* Racine, WI: Johnson Foundation.

Winick, Charles, and Paul M. Kinsie. 1971. *The Lively Commerce.* Chicago, IL: Quadrangle Books.

Wirth, Louis. 1938. "Urbanism as a Way of Life." *American J. of Sociology* (July):1-24.

Wise, Eric D., and Joyce Ann O'Neil. 1989. *Drug Use Forecasting (DUF) Research Update.* Washington, D.C.: National Institute of Justice.

Wolfgang, Marvin E. 1958. *Patterns in Criminal Homicide.* Philadelphia: University of Pennsylvania Press.

Wolfgang, Marvin E., and Franco Ferracuti. 1967. *The Subculture of Violence.* London, England: Social Science Paperbacks.

Wolfgang, Marvin E., and Marc Riedel. 1973. "Race, Judicial Discretion, and the Death Penalty." *The Annals* 407 (May):119-133.

Woodworth, George G. 1985. "Recent Studies of Race and Victim Effects in Capital Sentencing." In G. C. Woodworth (ed.), *Proceedings of the Third Workshop on Law and Justice Statistics.* Washington, D.C.: U.S. Department of Justice.

Wright, Bruce McM. 1984. "A View from the Bench." In D. Georges-Abeyie (ed.), *The Criminal Justice System and Blacks.* New York: Clark Boardman.

Young, Thomas J. 1990. "Native American Crime and Criminal Justice Require Criminologists' Attention." *J. of Criminal Justice Education* 1 (1):111-116.

Young, Vernetta, and Anne Thomas Sulton. 1991. "Excluded: The Current Status of African-American Scholars in the Field of Criminology and Criminal Justice." *J. of Research in Crime and Delinquency* 28 (1):101-116.

Zatz, Marjorie S. 1984. "Race, Ethnicity, and Determinate Sentencing: A New Dimension to an Old Controversy." *Criminology* 22 (2):147-171.

———. 1985. "Pleas, Priors, and Prison: Racial/Ethnic Differences in Sentencing." *Social Science Research* 14:169-193.

———. 1987. "The Changing Forms of Racial/Ethnic Biases in Sentencing." *J. of Research in Crime and Delinquency* 24 (1):69-92.

———. 1990. "A Question of Assumptions." In B. MacLean and D. Milovanovic (eds.), *Racism, Empiricism, and Criminal Justice.* Vancouver, Canada: The Collective Press.

Zavitz, Marianne W. 1988. *Report to the Nation on Crime and Justice.* Washington, D.C.: U.S. Department of Justice.

Zavitz, Marianne W., Thimi R. Mina, C. Mae Kuykendall, Lawrence A. Greenfeld, and Joseph L. White. 1983. "The Response to Crime." In *Report to the Nation on Crime and Justice*. Washington, D.C.: U.S. Government Printing Office.

Index

CORAMAE RICHEY MANN, Professor of Criminal Justice at Indiana University, is the author of scholarly articles on the juvenile and criminal justice systems and the author of *Female Crime and Delinquency*.